# THE ENGLISH HIS
## CONSTITUT

The fundamental legal and institutional changes of recent decades – the development of European Community law, the devolution of government, the passing of human rights legislation, and the modification of the Lord Chancellor's office, *inter alia* – have brought the constitution itself into question. Accompanying issues have been the extent to which its traditional character and main features have been changed, lost their former appeal and retained their distinctness amidst the developing legal and political structures of the European Union. They are not readily addressed in everyday thinking about a constitution simply conceived as unwritten or in constitutional accounts variously preoccupied with analysing changing legal doctrines at fleeting moments of analysis, with emphasising the primacy of politics or with identifying principles applicable to Western liberal democracies in general. The English Historical Constitution addresses these issues by developing a historical constitutional approach and thus elaborating on continuity and change in the constitution's main doctrines and institutions. From an English legal perspective, it offers a complement or corrective to analytical, political and normative approaches by reforming an old conception of the historical constitution and of its history, partly obscured and long neglected through the modern analytical preoccupation with its law as an abstract scheme of rules, principles and practices.

J.W.F. ALLISON is a Senior Lecturer in the Faculty of Law, University of Cambridge, and a Fellow of Queens' College.

# THE ENGLISH HISTORICAL CONSTITUTION

## CONSTITUTION

Continuity, Change and European Effects

J.W.F. ALLISON

CAMBRIDGE
UNIVERSITY PRESS

CAMBRIDGE UNIVERSITY PRESS
Cambridge, New York, Melbourne, Madrid, Cape Town, Singapore, São Paulo, Delhi

Cambridge University Press
The Edinburgh Building, Cambridge CB2 8RU, UK

Published in the United States of America by Cambridge University Press, New York

www.cambridge.org
Information on this title: www.cambridge.org/9780521702362

First published 2007

Printed in the United Kingdom at the University Press, Cambridge

A catalogue record for this publication is available from the British Library

ISBN 978-0-521-87814-2 hardback
ISBN 978-0-521-70236-2 paperback

# CONTENTS

# TABLE OF CASES

# PREFACE

In my first book *A Continental Distinction in the Common Law* (Oxford: Oxford University Press, rev. edn, 2000), I advocated a historical-comparative jurisprudence to reconsider the development in recent decades of an English public law distinct from private law. I sought to explain related problems by elaborating upon systemic interconnections between an autonomous public law and other features of its legal and political context. Completion of that book and responses to it left me with two abiding concerns. One is the extent to which English public law is sufficiently understood as itself systemic and operating within a larger legal and political system. Another is the theoretical detachment or limited engagement pursuant to adopting a historical comparative method. Both of these concerns are reflected in the chapters below.

This, my second book, attempts to put forward a historical constitutional understanding of basic doctrines and institutions of English constitutional law, not preoccupied with their supposedly systemic character. One feature of its historical constitutional approach is recognition of the constitutional significance of both internal and external points of view. Voltaire's doubt about the effect of detachment may be compared with De Lolme's confidence. '[H]ow was it possible for a Foreigner to pierce thro' their Politicks, that gloomy Labyrinth, in which such of the *English* themselves as are best acquainted with it, confess daily that they are bewilder'd and lost?' was the rhetorical question posed in the preface to Voltaire's *Letters Concerning the English Nation* (London: C. Davis and A. Lyon, 1733). In contrast, De Lolme, coming to England from Geneva, confidently laid claim to 'a degree of advantage' over the English themselves, who 'having their eyes open ... upon their liberty, from their first entrance into life, are perhaps too much familiarised with its enjoyment, to inquire, with real concern, into its causes' (*The Constitution of England* (Dublin: W. Wilson, 1775), pp. 2–3). For De Lolme, the English were 'like a Man who, having always had a beautiful and extensive scene before his eyes, continues for ever to view it with indifference' or 'like the recluse inhabitant of a Palace, who is perhaps in the worst situation for attaining a complete idea of the whole, and

never experienced the striking effect of its external structure and elevation' (*ibid.* p. 3). Although De Lolme's glowing approbation has long
been anachronistic, his claim to the insight of an outsider remains
relevant. I hope that the following chapters will help dispel doubts
about the significance of detachment and interaction between internal
and external points of view, both in the past and in present political
communities formed from what have become highly mobile constituents. They are written in recognition of the many who, from varying
points of view, contribute to constitutional formation and, in particular,
for someone who has done what she could in adverse circumstances.

Chapters Four and Five on the separation of powers and parliamentary sovereignty were developed from chapters that have already been
published but are not readily accessible. I originally wrote them with this
book in mind, and they have been updated and related to the other
chapters in an attempt not to detract unduly from their original content
and overall character. For comments on early drafts of these or of other
chapters, I would like to thank Trevor Allan, John Bell, Roger Cotterrell,
David Dyzenhaus, Christopher Forsyth, Jeffrey Goldsworthy, Carol
Harlow, Richard Helmholz, Jeffrey Jowell, Matthew Kramer, Martin
Loughlin, Rose Melikan, Dawn Oliver, Amanda Perreau-Saussine,
Mike Taggart, Colin Turpin and Reinhard Zimmermann as well as the
late Geoffrey Marshall and Sir William Wade.

In the years I have been working on this book, I have benefited greatly
from numerous discussions with my friends and colleagues Murray Milgate
and, in the field of public law, Trevor Allan, whose leading liberal theory of
constitutionalism has stimulated a number of the critical responses in the
pages below. For their general advice and that of John Bell, Paul Craig, David
Feldman, Jeffrey Goldsworthy, David Ibbetson, Martin Loughlin, Dawn
Oliver and Bob Summers, I am particularly grateful. I am indebted to the
Law School of the University of California at Berkeley for a Senior Robbins
Fellowship, which facilitated my early research towards this book, and to the
Arts and Humanities Research Council for an award under their Research
Leave Scheme. I am also indebted to Quertin Stafford-Fraser for facilitating
the production of tables on my computer and to Finola O'Sullivan, Richard
Woodham, Paula Devine, Wendy Gater and others at CUP for their effi-
ciency and friendly assistance. Finally, I would like to thank my family and
other friends for all their support.

J. W. F. Allison
Queens' College, Cambridge
December 2006

# 1

# Introduction

Change, not continuity, attracts attention. Constitutional rules that remain unchanged and practices that continue become familiar, are readily taken for granted and easily pass unnoticed. Legislative constitutional changes, in comparison, are easily noticed, and their scope and frequency are ready causes of controversy.

The constitutional changes of recent decades have been frequent, far-reaching and ongoing. The European Communities Act 1972 provides for the domestic application of Community law, and the courts have accepted the implications of its primacy for statutes of the Westminster Parliament.[1] Further domestic, legal and political responses to the continuing process of constitution-building in the European Union[2] are to be expected. The government's constitutional modernisation programme since the Labour Party came to power in 1997 has resulted in devolution legislation, the Human Rights Act 1998, statutory provision for a Supreme Court and substantial modifications to the office of Lord Chancellor, *inter alia*.[3] Legislative and other official initiatives, further, in response to the security fears following the attacks of 11 September 2001 and later atrocities have constitutional implications for the exercise and interpretation of human rights,[4] the scope of which will become clearer in years to come.

---

[1] *R v. Secretary of State for Transport ex parte Factortame Ltd (No. 2)* [1991] 1 AC 603.

[2] See generally J. Shaw, 'Europe's constitutional future' [2005] *PL* 132; I. Pernice and M. P. Maduro (eds.), *A Constitution for the European Union: First Comments on the 2003 Draft of the European Convention* (Baden-Baden: Nomos Verlagsgesellschaft, 2004).

[3] Scotland Act 1998; Government of Wales Act 1998; Northern Ireland Act 1998; Constitutional Reform Act 2005.

[4] See, e.g., Anti-terrorism, Crime and Security Act 2001; Prevention of Terrorism Act 2005; *A v. Secretary of State for the Home Department* [2005] 2 AC 68; [2004] UKHL 56; *A v. Secretary of State for the Home Department (No. 2)* [2006] 2 AC 221; [2005] UKHL 71. See generally Dame Mary Arden, 'Human rights in the age of terrorism' (2005) 121 *LQR* 604.

The extent, form and frequency of the many changes have called into question the common and longstanding assumption[5] that the constitution is characterised by gradual or evolutionary change and, further, that it remains unwritten. Certain statutes, such as the European Communities Act 1972 and the Human Rights Act 1998, have, arguably, acquired or are acquiring special constitutional status[6] and are sufficiently comprehensive in important areas to afford some basis for Vernon Bogdanor's recent conclusion that the constitution is 'half way' to codification by 'piecemeal means'.[7] Such a conclusion would certainly be significant and might be tempting were it not for implicit doubts and overt reactions.

The doubts are implicit in the conclusion that the process is only piecemeal and half-complete – 'a unique constitutional experiment'[8] – thus quite unlike introducing a written or codified constitution, both in process and outcome. The doubts would seem to arise from the continuing lack of the necessary consensus within government and the real governing political will actually to bring about a written constitution as well as from caution about what may be a typical preoccupation with recent legislative change to the exclusion of earlier change[9] and barely-noticed continuity. A few years ago, Bogdanor himself rightly recognised the lack of the required political will or consensus to go further and that it 'is of course far too early even to speculate with any degree of

---

[5] See, e.g., A. W. Bradley and K. D. Ewing, *Constitutional and Administrative Law* (Harlow, England: Pearson Education, 14th edn, 2007), pp. 31–2; N. Bamforth and P. Leyland (eds.), *Public Law in a Multi-Layered Constitution* (Oxford: Hart Publishing, 2003), p. v.

[6] Through judicial recognition, *inter alia*, that they cannot be impliedly repealed: *Thoburn v. Sunderland City Council* [2003] QB 151 at [60]–[64]; [2002] 1 CMLR 50; [2002] EWHC 195. But see G. Marshall, 'Metric measures and martyrdom by Henry VIII clause' (2002) 118 *LQR* 493 at 495f.

[7] V. Bogdanor, 'Conclusion' in V. Bogdanor (ed.), *The British Constitution in the Twentieth Century* (Oxford: Oxford University Press, 2003), pp. 689–720, especially at p. 719. See also V. Bogdanor, 'Our new constitution' (2004) 120 *LQR* 242, especially at 246, 259. For Bogdanor, the increased reliance upon referenda that relate to certain statutes is also the beginning of a process by which they are accorded a distinct constitutional status, *ibid*. 246. No referendum, however, has been held in relation to the Human Rights Act 1998, presented by Bogdanor as the potential 'cornerstone of the new constitution', *ibid*. Cf. generally Anthony King's account of what he suggests are fundamental changes in *Does the United Kingdom Still Have a Constitution?* (London: Sweet & Maxwell, 2001). See ch. 2 below, especially pp. 41f.

[8] Bogdanor, 'Conclusion' in Bogdanor (ed.), *British Constitution in the Twentieth Century*, n. 7 above, p. 719.

[9] See generally K. D. Ewing, 'The politics of the British constitution' [2000] *PL* 405, especially at 405.

detachment upon the likely consequences of the extensive programme of constitutional reform which began in 1997'.[10] A change in the political priorities of government might occur,[11] but the change would need to be substantial and enduring for the massive task of introducing a written constitution to be undertaken and successfully completed.

The overt reactions to many of the reforms that have occurred have been to their substance and particularly to the manner in which they have been brought about. Although, in substance, many have been successfully promoted in the cause of modernisation,[12] Eurosceptic reactions have been longstanding and the most apparent. Reactions to the reform process itself have been more recent but, for present purposes, are of similar constitutional significance, suggesting constitutional impropriety and going well beyond criticism[13] of governmental failures to deliberate and consult. One early reaction took the form of scathing criticism of the manner in which a 'constitutional revolution' was being brought about: 'It is the muddled, messy work of practical men and women, unintellectual when not positively anti-intellectual, apparently oblivious of the long tradition of political and constitutional reflection of which they are the heirs, responding piecemeal and ad hoc to conflicting pressures – a revolution of sleepwalkers who don't know quite where they are going or quite why.'[14] In particular, the measures of the government first to establish a new Department for Constitutional Affairs, abolish the Lord Chancellor's office and create a Supreme Court, announced by press release as 'far reaching reforms' – 'a substantial package of . . . reform measures' – and in relation to a cabinet reshuffle,

---

[10] 'Conclusion' in Bogdanor (ed.), *British Constitution in the Twentieth Century*, n. 7 above, pp. 718–19, especially at p. 718. See also, Bogdanor, 'Our new constitution', n. 7 above, 246.

[11] Chancellor Gordon Brown, who is widely expected to succeed Tony Blair as Prime Minister before the next General Election, recently made a veiled reference to a written constitution: 'And while we do not today have a written constitution it comes back to being sure about and secure in the values that matter: freedom, democracy and fairness. The shared values we were brought up with and must not lose: fair play, respect, a decent chance in life'. Speech to the Labour Party Conference, Manchester, 25 September 2006.

[12] See generally Lord Irvine, *Human Rights, Constitutional Law and the Development of the English Legal System: Selected Essays* (Oxford: Hart Publishing, 2003); Ewing, 'Politics of the British constitution', n. 9 above, especially at 428ff.

[13] Cf. generally the wide-ranging criticisms of Lord Butler in an interview reported by Boris Johnson, 'How not to run a country', *Spectator*, 11 December 2004, p. 12.

[14] D. Marquand, 'Pluralism v populism', *Prospect*, June 1999, p. 27. For a response comparable in substance but not expressed as scathing criticism, see King, *Does the United Kingdom Still Have a Constitution?*, n. 7 above, especially pp. 99–101.

and then to concede that the office should be retained although substantially modified,[15] were events in quick succession that have provoked charges of 'constitutional vandalism' and of reforms drafted 'on the back of an envelope'.[16] These charges from within the legal profession have followed others of 'constitutional change under anaesthetic' and of a checklist approach[17] to reform, coming from at least a few working within the media, none the less significant for the metaphoric language in which they have been couched. The 'Just do it!' approach of earlier programmes of privatisation appears to have been adopted for the reform of long-established institutions of government.

That the reform process itself has somehow been going seriously wrong has been clear from the overt reactions and perhaps a more general unease, but what exactly has been going wrong and whether wrong for purely political and/or constitutional reasons remain questions without clear answers. In contrast to onerous amendment provisions of a written constitution, we have the legacy of Dicey's assertion

---

[15] 'Modernising government' – Lord Falconer appointed Secretary of State for Constitutional Affairs', Downing Street press release, 12 June 2003. For the outcome of the measures, see the Constitutional Reform Act 2005. See generally Lord Windlesham, 'The Constitutional Reform Act 2005: ministers, judges and constitutional change' [2005] *PL* 806; Lord Windlesham, 'The Constitutional Reform Act 2005: the politics of constitutional reform' [2006] *PL* 35; R. Stevens, 'Reform in haste and repent at leisure: Iolanthe, the Lord High Executioner and *Brave New World*' (2004) 24 *Legal Studies* 1; ch. 4 below, pp. 94ff.

[16] 'On the back of an envelope . . .: constitutional reform or constitutional vandalism?', Seminar on the British Constitution, Lincoln's Inn, London, 15 September 2004. To Lord Chief Justice Woolf, the announcement of 12 June 2003, preceded by what had already been 'a torrent of constitutional changes' . . . 'clearly indicated an extraordinary lack of appreciation of the significance of what was being proposed.' 'The rule of law and a change in the constitution', The Squire Centenary Lecture, Faculty of Law, University of Cambridge, 2 March 2004, published in [2004] *CLJ* 317, especially at 319, 323. To Sir John Baker, '[t]he very idea of a Minister for Constitutional Affairs is an affront to the true concept of a constitution – as something above government, limiting what it may do. The creation of the new ministry on 12 June – without any prior warning or consultation – was effectively an announcement that we no longer have a constitution in that sense, that the constitution is now subject to the same kind of incessant tinkering and experiment as the management of hospitals or railways.' 'The constitutional revolution', Lecture, St Catharine's College, Cambridge, 20 April 2004, pp. 4–5.

[17] Mary Riddell, a columnist for the *Observer*, speaking from the floor in the Panel Discussion, 'The British constitution – can we learn from history?', British Academy, London, 18 June 2003. See also William Rees-Mogg's exclamation in response to the constitutional reform measures announced on 12 June 2003: 'No deliberation, no forethought, no debate, no consultation.' 'The Supreme Court: isn't there some law against it?', *The Times*, 4 August 2003.

that, in the exercise of Parliament's legal sovereignty 'one law, whatever its importance, can be passed and changed by exactly the same method as every other law'.[18] It is still commonly echoed today,[19] indeed amplified by the critical recognition[20] that the parameters of government activity can be changed even without recourse to Parliament where it takes place, not under statute, but under common law, as is often the case. The reforms accord with the orthodox Diceyan emphasis on the legal changeability of constitutional law through the exercise of Parliament's sovereignty. The negative reactions they have provoked, however, are reasons to question the sufficiency of that orthodoxy, and, to the extent they suggest constitutional impropriety, the implicit understanding of the constitution by which the reform process has been improper. In a context where the constitution is still commonly assumed to be, or characterised as, evolutionary, many of these reactions are plausibly interpreted as normative expressions of sentiment still derived from traditional understandings of the constitution and to which they still owe much of their appeal.

The chapters below are written in recognition of the doubts about the many constitutional changes of recent decades and the reactions to them. Through a reformation of traditional understandings, their primary purpose is to elaborate upon a conception of a historical constitution to which change, continuity and their relative significance are central. Their secondary purpose is to respond to the Eurosceptic reaction by duly recognising both domestic peculiarities and past and present effects of European legal developments – national and supranational – upon this historical constitution.

This book is about change and also about continuity over a long period. Although various recent statutes and cases have each been heralded as the most important since the Reform Acts of the nineteenth century or since *Entick* v. *Carrington* of the eighteenth,[21] it provides an overview that does not focus on each of them. It is necessarily limited in scope. It does not, for example, deal with the important legal changes that are

---

[18] A. V. Dicey, *An Introduction to the Study of the Law of the Constitution* (London: Macmillan, 10th edn, 1958), p. 90.

[19] Bradley and Ewing, *Constitutional and Administrative Law*, n. 5 above, p. 7; E. Barendt, *An Introduction to Constitutional Law* (Oxford: Oxford University Press, 1998), pp. 27–8, 34.

[20] D. Oliver, *Constitutional Reform in the UK* (Oxford: Oxford University Press, 2003), p. 7.

[21] (1765) 19 St. Tr. 1029.

occurring in response to the recent and continuing threats to security. It also does not deal with devolution but reflects the implications[22] of devolution for what an author of a work on the constitution can reasonably claim. Because of the constitutional significance of the devolution legislation of 1998[23] and, to Scotland in particular, of the Treaty of Union of 1706 and consequent Acts of Union of the English Parliament of 1706 and of the Scottish Parliament of 1707, I only suggest an understanding of the constitution from an English perspective. The historical constitution in this book's title is English in perspective and, as such, will vary in relevance or applicability elsewhere in the United Kingdom.

The approach I will take is explained in Chapter Two. In subsequent chapters, I will use it to consider the Crown as the constitution's long-standing institutional centrepiece, the increasingly-invoked separation of powers and Dicey's twin pillars of the constitution – parliamentary sovereignty and the rule of law. I have been necessarily selective of subject and focus, and, in so far as I have been selective, the approach to the selections I have made is significant and itself in special need of justification.

---

[22] See generally D. Feldman, 'None, one or several? Perspectives on the UK's constitution(s)' [2005] *CLJ* 329, especially at 346ff.
[23] See the references at n. 3 above.

# 2

# A historical constitutional approach

Amidst competing notions of the constitution and various approaches to understanding it or addressing related concerns, any notion or approach requires justification. For much of the twentieth century, Dicey's analytical approach, if not necessarily the content of his analysis, predominated but, I will suggest, proved significantly problematic. In this chapter, I advocate a historical constitutional approach through a reorientation of Dicey and in relation to other approaches that are prominent in current constitutional debates.

## Dicey's analytical approach

In *Law of the Constitution*, Dicey described his approach to the subject of constitutional law in considerable detail. He famously presented his professorial duty as that of an expounder:

> At the present day students of the constitution wish neither to criticise, nor to venerate, but to understand; and a professor whose duty it is to lecture on constitutional law, must feel that he is called upon to perform the part neither of a critic nor of an apologist, nor of an eulogist, but simply of an expounder; his duty is neither to attack nor to defend the constitution, but simply to explain its laws.[1]

He expressly distinguished the legal from the historical view of the constitution. He relegated the historical view in legal study so that lawyers might properly study 'the law as it now stands' and not 'think so much of the way in which an institution has come to be what it is, that they cease to consider with sufficient care what it is that an institution has become'.[2] Dicey's approach was not simply intended for the study

---

[1] A. V. Dicey, *An Introduction to the Study of the Law of the Constitution* (London: Macmillan, 10th edn, 1959), pp. 3–4.
[2] *Ibid.* pp. 15ff, especially at pp. 15, vii.

and teaching of law. He suggested the significance of his analytical method in his *Law and Opinion in England*:

> A Court, when called upon to decide cases which present some difficulty, is often engaged – unconsciously it may be – in the search for principles. If an author of ingenuity has reduced some branch of the law to a consistent scheme of logically coherent rules, he supplies exactly the principles of which a Court is in need. Hence the development of English law has depended, more than many students perceive, on the writings of the authors who have produced the best text-books.[3]

Dicey's approach was intended to benefit the student, the lawyer and the judge.

Influenced by the scientific rationalism of the nineteenth century, Dicey aspired to a scientific approach in pursuit of a consistent and logically coherent scheme of legal rules and principles. His method[4] was that of observation and objective description through the composition of sets or categories and the division or subdivision of their components. He presented his law of the constitution as a formal scheme of sets and distinctions: between one set of laws 'in the strictest sense' and a second set of rules consisting mainly of conventions; between parliamentary sovereignty and the rule of law as the constitution's two fundamental features; between the positive and negative dimensions of parliamentary sovereignty; between the rule of law's three meanings, and so on.[5]

Dicey's analytical method was confounded by three problems – fidelity, ossification and insularity. First, a method that pretended only objectively to describe a scheme of rules and principles could not prescribe or maintain fidelity to that scheme. The constitution's appeal or its source or sources of fidelity were left analytically obscure or indistinct, as was the normative force of a judicial or other claim that official conduct be constitutional or unconstitutional. The problem of their obscurity was to increase as the constitutional complacency that Dicey could still presuppose[6] was variously undermined during the twentieth century.[7]

---

[3] A. V. Dicey, *Lectures on the Relation between Law and Public Opinion in England during the Nineteenth Century* (London: Macmillan, 2nd edn, 1914), p. 365. See generally R. W. Blackburn, 'Dicey and the teaching of public law' [1985] PL 679, especially at 681ff.

[4] See generally M. Loughlin, *Public Law and Political Theory* (Oxford: Oxford University Press, 1992), pp. 13–17; C. Harlow, 'Disposing of Dicey: from legal autonomy to constitutional discourse' (2000) 48 *Political Studies* 356.

[5] *Law of the Constitution*, n. 1 above, especially at p. 23. See, e.g., *ibid.* pp. 23–5, 40–1, 183–4, 202–3.

[6] See *ibid.* pp. 3–4.     [7] See ch. 8 below, pp. 186ff.

Secondly, Dicey's analytical scheme of sets and distinctions was rendered static by his relegation of the historical view and consequent focus on constitutional form, not formation. It was imposed upon an evolving constitution at a relatively arbitrary and fleeting moment – the moment of analysis. In proportion to the considerable extent Dicey's analysis remained constant in necessarily multiple editions of the same analytical textbook, enjoyed influence or acceptance and continued to be applied, it ossified or encapsulated a changing constitution.

Thirdly, focusing on constitutional form, not formation, Dicey's analytical method neglected the dynamic interaction of political communities and their respective constitutional forms. Dicey knew much of other jurisdictions, and frequently referred to them, but his references were principally illustrative and served an insular purpose. He expressly used federalism in the USA, for example, as an opposite with which to illustrate and emphasise English unitarianism through the exercise of Parliament's central and supreme legislative power.[8] He similarly used French *droit administratif* to demonstrate how it is different from, indeed incompatible with, the English rule of law.[9] In these and numerous other examples, he presented other jurisdictions, not as actual or potential sources of influence, but as anti-models with which to demonstrate the peculiarity of the sets of rules and principles and accompanying distinctions that made up his analytical scheme of the English law of the constitution.

## A descriptive analytical legacy

The many constitutional changes[10] since the publication of the tenth edition of Dicey's *Law of the Constitution* – changes in government and governance, the impact of European Community law, devolution, the passing of the Human Rights Act 1998, doctrinal shifts in the meaning and significance of parliamentary sovereignty and the rule of law etc – have all aggravated the problems of fidelity, ossification[11] and insularity,

---

[8] *Law of the Constitution*, n. 1 above, ch. 3.

[9] *Ibid.* chs. 4, 12. See J. W. F. Allison, *A Continental Distinction in the Common Law: A Historical and Comparative Perspective on English Public Law* (Oxford: Oxford University Press, rev. pbk. edn, 2000), pp. 18–23.

[10] For a sense of the scope of these changes since the mid-1980s, compare the various editions of J. Jowell and D. Oliver, *The Changing Constitution* (Oxford: Oxford University Press, 1985, 1989, 1994, 2000, 2004).

[11] An analytical scheme is imposed or designed at the fleeting and relatively arbitrary moment of analysis but, if it is to retain relevance, must itself include practices or conventions that change and rules or principles that formally allow for legal change. One obvious

described above. They raise two related questions. First, what remains of the sets of rules and principles and accompanying distinctions encapsulated in Dicey's analytical scheme to serve as a distinctly legal and/or political object of fidelity? Secondly, how do remnants of Dicey's analytical scheme remain both relevant and still peculiarly English in a constitution subject to increasing European legal influence?

Many explicit and implicit current references to the constitution, betraying the loss of much of its appeal and normative force, are Dicey's descriptive analytical legacy. The 'unwritten constitution' is a simple negative and strictly inaccurate descriptive term in common discussion. The constitution is variously described in constitutional law texts, often in unflattering terms. In one, it is depicted as 'a jumble of diffuse statutes and court rulings, supplemented by extra-legal conventions and practices'.[12] In another, it is a spider's web – 'a more subtle and varied network of relationships [than previously understood] between laws or rules of different kinds and from different sources' – in the process of being spun with Parliament at its centre.[13] It is understandably said to be an unclear and unreliable basis for public debate on constitutionality or a judicial ruling that official conduct is 'unconstitutional',[14] a term described elsewhere as having 'no defined content'.[15]

example is parliamentary sovereignty through respect for which law can be changed by Parliament. A second related example is the developed doctrine of *ultra vires*. It is analytically significant as a flexible and formalistic device by which judges can develop the grounds of judicial review and thus the rule of law, supposedly as authorised or intended by Parliament, in determining what is beyond an authority's powers. An analytical scheme, however, that incorporates the doctrine of *ultra vires* provides for change in the rule of law by presupposing a rigid judicial conception of parliamentary sovereignty, clearly evident in Sir William Wade's identification of a judicial revolution when that conception changes, ch. 5 below, pp. 110ff. Flexibility in the rule of law's future development is secured by ossifying parliamentary sovereignty, both as conceived at the moment of analysis and as presupposed thereafter. See generally C. F. Forsyth (ed.), *Judicial Review and the Constitution* (Oxford: Hart Publishing, 2000); M. Elliott, *The Constitutional Foundations of Judicial Review* (Oxford: Hart Publishing, 2001); P. P. Craig and N. Bamforth, Review article of *The Constitutional Foundations of Judicial Review* by M. Elliott, 'Constitutional analysis, constitutional principle and judicial review' [2001] *PL* 763; T. R. S. Allan, 'The constitutional foundations of judicial review: conceptual conundrum or interpretive enquiry?' [2002] *CLJ* 87.

12  E. Barendt, *An Introduction to Constitutional Law* (Oxford: Oxford University Press, 1998), p. 33.

13  D. Oliver, *Constitutional Reform in the United Kingdom* (Oxford: Oxford University Press, 2003), p. 357. For Dawn Oliver's comprehensive and non-metaphoric descriptive definition, see *ibid.* p. 6.

14  Barendt, *Introduction to Constitutional Law*, n. 12 above, pp. 30ff.

15  A. W. Bradley and K. D. Ewing, *Constitutional and Administrative Law* (Harlow, England: Pearson Education, 14th edn, 2007), p. 26.

In their innovative edited volume, *Public Law in a Multi-Layered Constitution*, Nicholas Bamforth and Peter Leyland respond to the changes – principally devolution and the impact of both European Community law and the jurisprudence of the European Court of Human Rights – with their model of a multi-layered constitution in place of the traditional unitary model.[16] They use it to stimulate and structure the various contributions to their volume. On the 'analytical foundation' of the claim that 'any understanding of the dimensions of public law presupposes a coherent account of the constitutional terrain', they present the constitution as having 'taken on the appearance of a structure with multiple, but inter-connected and sometimes overlapping layers'.[17] They repeatedly describe that structure with metaphors – terrain, architecture and landscape – that connote essentially static constitutional arrangements. In their Preface, they nonetheless recognise that the constitution 'has been – and still is – characterised by evolutionary change'.[18] Their characterisation calls into question the significance of their analytical contribution and metaphors other than in the immediately contemporary or current constitution. At one point, in response to Martin Loughlin's contribution, they rightly question 'whether it is meaningful to analyse a constitution using any particular analytical framework, if constitutions are of the provisional character identified by Loughlin'.[19] Certainly their own analytical claim is at odds with the constitution they still characterise as evolutionary and is in tension with the many changes to which their leading work is an illuminating and revealing response.

## Dicey's methodological predicament

Dicey's descriptive analytical legacy is reason for seeking a methodological reorientation by considering Dicey's methodological choices and their justification. Dicey's reasons for distinguishing and relegating the historical view of the constitution are not entirely clear. One possibility is institutional.

---

[16] N. Bamforth and P. Leyland, 'Public law in a multi-layered constitution' in N. Bamforth and P. Leyland (eds.), *Public Law in a Multi-Layered Constitution* (Oxford: Hart Publishing, 2003), pp. 1–25, especially at p. 12.

[17] *Ibid.* pp. 1, 3.    [18] *Ibid.* p. v.

[19] *Ibid.* p. 12. At one point, they suggest fragmented judicial approaches to proportionality, *ibid.* p. 21, which call into question the extent to which even their limited analytical claim to constitutional layers can generally illuminate or long be sustained in a potentially fragmented or convergent case law.

He distinguished the legal from the historical view to consolidate the study of constitutional law in its own right as distinct from the study of history under which it had previously been subsumed, shortly after the Oxford Law School had been detached from the old School of Law and Modern History.[20] Another possibility, or rather, a probability, is polemical. In his Preface to the first edition of *The Growth of the English Constitution*, published in 1872, Edward Freeman had claimed that 'constitutional history has been perverted at the hands of lawyers' through their complete inattention to original sources.[21] In reply, Dicey acknowledged both his considerable indebtedness to Freeman and that Freeman's 'vigorous statements' forced upon his attention 'the essential difference between the historical and the legal way of regarding our institutions, and compelled [him] to consider whether the habit of looking too exclusively at the steps by which the constitution has been developed does not prevent students from paying sufficient attention to the law of the constitution as it now actually exists'.[22] He then used Freeman's 'first-rate specimen of the mode in which an historian looks at the constitution' to illustrate the antiquarianism of the historical view.[23] Dicey's possible educational institutional concerns and probable defensive polemical motive perhaps facilitate our understanding[24] of his analytical method, but afford us little with which to justify it.

Others who wrote on the constitution shortly before Dicey's *Law of the Constitution* first appeared in print sensed that the relationship between historical and current legal or political views of the constitution was problematic. They devoted attention to it accordingly but differed in their responses. As a whig historian, Freeman claimed that '[o]ur ancient history' is 'the possession of the Liberal' and sought principally 'to show that the earliest institutions of England ... are not mere matters of curious speculation, but matters closely connected with our present political being'.[25] A different response from Dicey's was not confined to whig historians. The following methods of Hearn and Cox were also available.

---

[20] F. H. Lawson, *The Oxford Law School, 1850–1965* (Oxford: Oxford University Press, 1968), chs. 1–3, especially at pp. 40, 66; Blackburn, 'Dicey and the teaching of public law', n. 3 above, 681–2; Lord Bingham, 'Dicey revisited' [2002] *PL* 39 at 41–2.

[21] E. A. Freeman, *The Growth of the English Constitution from the Earliest Times* (London: Macmillan, 3rd edn, 1876), pp. x–xii, especially at p. x.

[22] *Law of the Constitution*, n. 1 above, p. vii.    [23] *Ibid.* pp. 12ff, especially at pp. 12–13.

[24] For Lord Bingham, Dicey's attitude was 'to some extent', 'perhaps understandable', 'Dicey revisited', n. 20 above, 41.

[25] *Growth of the English Constitution*, n. 21 above, pp. x, ix.

William Hearn, identified as a political theorist by Dicey and to whom he expressed great indebtedness,[26] sought 'to describe the Constitution of England as it is now understood, *and* to trace the steps by which it has attained its present form'.[27] His analytical object was not 'to advocate any particular political views' or to inquire 'whether or how it [the Constitution] should be changed'.[28] It was 'to obtain not fruit but light': 'I seek only to ascertain what the Constitution of England now is, *and* how it became what it is'.[29] The historical was juxtaposed, not reconciled, with the analytical, but they were at least presented as being of equal significance.

Homersham Cox attempted an analytical approach in the sense of a systematic and impartial elucidation of the actual institutions and principles of government.[30] From his book *The Institutions of the English Government*, he did partially exclude 'historical and theoretical researches' but only for the practical purpose of confining his work 'within the limits of a compendium' and not where germane to 'the purpose of illustrating the use and operation of established principles and institutions of Government' according to Coke's dictum '*Scire autem propriè est rem ratione et per causam cognoscere*'.[31] Recited in Cox's statement on method, Coke's conception of *causa* as instrinsic to proper understanding was available to Dicey, and a historical *causa* for an established principle or institution of government would have made proper understanding of it necessarily historical.

Dicey's *Law of the Constitution* was itself not as methodologically consistent or coherent as his own exposition of his analytical method would seem to have required. Despite his relegation of the historical

---

[26] Dicey's identification of Hearn as a political theorist was for the reason that Hearn was, according to Dicey, preoccupied 'with political understandings and conventions and not with rules of law', *Law of the Constitution*, n. 1 above, p. 20. See also *ibid*. pp. vi, 7.

[27] W. E. Hearn, *The Government of England: Its Structure and Its Development* (London: Longman, Green, Reader, and Dyer, 1st edn, 1867), p. 9 (emphasis added).

[28] *Ibid*. p. 14.     [29] *Ibid*. (emphasis added).

[30] H. Cox, *The British Commonwealth* or *A Commentary on the Institutions and Principles of British Government* (London: Longman, Brown, Green, and Longman, 1854), especially at pp. xxf.

[31] H. Cox, *The Institutions of English Government; Being an Account of the Constitution, Powers, and Procedure, of its Legislative, Judicial, and Administrative Departments with Copious References to Ancient and Modern Authorities* (London: H. Sweet, 1863), p. ix. The dictum is translated literally as 'yet to know is properly to understand a thing with reason and through its cause' and is derived from Co. Inst. I, 183b, where it is attributed to Arist. 1 *Metaphys.*

view, he relied heavily on the whig historians Hallam, Gardiner and Freeman and acknowledged that 'without constant reference' to them, not 'a page of [his] lectures could have been written'.[32] Indeed, historical (and comparative) references – particularly to legal triumphs in the constitutional struggles of the seventeenth century but also to earlier and later legal landmarks – are everywhere in *Law of the Constitution*.[33] They were, however, strictly extraneous to his legal analysis, described by him elsewhere in the abstract as the reduction of a 'branch of the law to a consistent scheme of logically coherent rules'[34] and has been perhaps best exemplified in a branch of the law without an evolving constitution as its principal concern. In the conflict of laws, his famous textbook remains distinctive in its 'formulaic, canonical style of presentation, reducing the law to a series of carefully devised rules'.[35] In constitutional law, Dicey recognised that whatever 'may be the advantages of a so-called "unwritten" constitution, its existence imposes special difficulties on teachers bound to expound its provisions'.[36] In *Law of the Constitution*, Dicey thus referred to the 'unwritten constitution' but, for comparative purposes in unpublished lectures that he long refrained from finalising,[37] he recognised that it was a historical constitution in the main sense of being ancient and also in the sense of having grown spontaneously, not in accordance with a deliberate plan or design. How the history of this constitution might be subsumed or recognised in legal analysis so as to explain the constitutional significance of the innumerable historical references Dicey felt compelled to make is the methodological predicament or challenge dating back to Dicey and his contemporaries.

---

[32] *Law of the Constitution*, n. 1 above, especially at p. vi. See also *ibid.* pp. 1ff, 12ff, 15ff; ch. 7 below, pp. 167ff.

[33] See ch. 7 below, pp. 165ff.

[34] *Law and Public Opinion in England*, n. 3 above, p. 365.

[35] R. Fentiman, 'Legal reasoning in the conflict of laws: an essay in law and practice' in W. Krawietz, N. MacCormick and G. H. von Wright (eds.), *Prescriptive Formality and Normative Rationality in Modern Legal Systems*, Festschrift for Robert S. Summers (Berlin: Duncker & Humblot, 1994), pp. 443–61, especially at p. 459.

[36] *Law of the Constitution*, n. 1 above, p. 4. See also *ibid.* pp. 89–90.

[37] G. J. Hand, 'A. V. Dicey's unpublished materials on the comparative study of constitutions' in G. J. Hand and J. McBride (eds.), *Droit Sans Frontieres: Essays in Honour of L. Neville Brown* (Birmingham: Holdsworth Club, 1991), pp. 77–93, especially at pp. 77–81, 86. The lectures, with the title 'Comparative study of constitutions' probably preferred by Dicey, are in the Codrington Library, All Souls College, Oxford, MS 323. Ch. 1 is entitled 'Historical constitutions and non-historical constitutions', *ibid.* p. 79.

## The historical constitution

Concepts of the constitution or perspectives on it are abundant[38] in constitutional debate, as they have been in the past. Three historical conceptions, varying in their emphasis on change and/or continuity, have been prominent at different times. The first is the conception of the ancient constitution characterised by antiquity and continuity and embedded in the ancient common law,[39] the vast antiquity of which is invoked to suggest its venerability, inevitability, obvious necessity, transcendent quality etc. Such a conception,[40] however, is rare today and unconvincing in modern thinking, which is disinclined to venerate what is (or made to appear) ancient because it is ancient.

The second historical conception of the constitution or of constitutionalism invokes, or is inspired by, an exemplary period in the past – perhaps, in bygone centuries, a real or romanticised golden age – or, what is now more usual, from the immense complexity of that period's legal and political fabric, strands of legal or political thought, as evident, for example, in Coke's championing of the common law[41] or a kind of

---

[38] See, e.g., D. Feldman, 'None, one or several? Perspectives on the UK's constitutions(s)' [2005] *CLJ* 329; G. Marshall, 'The constitution: its theory and interpretation' in V. Bogdanor (ed.), The *British Constitution in the Twentieth Century* (Oxford: Oxford University Press, 2003), pp. 29–68; N. Walker, 'The idea of constitutional pluralism' (2002) 65 *MLR* 317; T. Daintith and A. C. Page, The *Executive in the Constitution: Structure, Autonomy, and Internal Control* (Oxford: Oxford University Press, 1999), especially ch. 1; J. Raz, 'On the authority and interpretation of constitutions: some preliminaries' in L. Alexander (ed.), *Constitutionalism: Philosophical Foundations* (Cambridge: Cambridge University Press, 1998), pp. 152–93.

[39] See, e.g., J. G. A. Pocock, *The Ancient Constitution and the Feudal Law, A Study of English Historical Thought in the Seventeenth Century: A Reissue with a Retrospect* (Cambridge: Cambridge University Press, 1987), especially Pt. 1, chs. 2 & 3, Pt. 2, ch. 1; J. P. Sommerville, *Politics and Ideology in England, 1603–1640* (London: Longman, 1986), ch. 3. In his unpublished lectures, 'Comparative study of constitutions', n. 37 above, Dicey emphasised the historical constitution's 'antiquity' and 'continuity' but characterised it also by its 'spontaneity' and 'originality'.

[40] For both this conception and a modern view of its insufficiency, see Lord Hailsham, The *Dilemma of Democracy: Diagnosis and Prescription* (London: Collins, 1978), ch. 21, especially at pp. 133f. See also *ibid.* chs. 26, 36.

[41] See, e.g., the epigraph in T. R. S. Allan, *Constitutional Justice: A Liberal Theory of the Rule of Law* (Oxford: Oxford University Press, 2001), p. v, which is taken from Coke in *Bonham's Case* (1609) 8 Co. Rep. 107 at 118a. See also T. R. S. Allan, *Law, Liberty, and Justice: The Legal Foundations of British Constitutionalism* (Oxford: Oxford University Press, 1993), pp. 267ff; T. R. S. Allan, 'The rule of law as the rule of reason: consent and constitutionalism' (1999) 115 *LQR* 221 at 241–2. See ch. 8 below, pp. 208f.

parliamentary Republicanism selected from later writings.[42] This second conception, in its complete form, is revolutionary in an old sense of the word.[43] Explicit or implicit in the conception is a form of temporal discontinuity in some degree – a turning back to the past period for inspiration, guidance or support. It is, however, not very historical. Apart from that discontinuity between past and present, selection of period, or the usual strands of thought within a period, is historically arbitrary in its dependence upon the politics of the present or its legal and political values by which the constitution is principally understood. Its invocations of history are therefore readily regarded by those with a different politics or normative legal approach as manipulative or simply unpersuasive.

The third conception, and the concern of this book, is of constitutional arrangements that have continued from the recent or distant past into the present with change or reform intrinsic to those arrangements. It differs from the first conception in its focus upon change; and from the second in its focus upon continuity. It was commonplace amongst conservatives and liberals alike before the publication of Dicey's *Law of the Constitution* but became increasingly indistinct during the twentieth century. Focussed on both continuity and change within the constitution, this conception was, for example, expressed in the following observation by George Custance: 'Not that perfection attaches to our Constitution, or that it is free from abuse; but there is *a constant tendency in it* to correct the latter and promote the former'.[44] In the political constitutional debates culminating in the Reform Acts of the nineteenth century, it was similarly evident in the evolutionary gradualism of Earl John Russell – his support for correcting 'the abuses of our Constitution' by 'amendments strictly conformable to its spirit', his opposition to devising a constitution *à priori*, his repeated warnings against being 'deceived by the cry of "New lamps for old" ' in the story of Aladdin and his refusal 'to deviate from *the track of the Constitution* into

---

[42] See, e.g., A. Tomkins, *Our Republican Constitution* (Oxford: Hart Publishing, 2005), especially at pp. 46ff, 67ff, and his heavy reliance on Quentin Skinner's recent work, including 'Classical liberty, Renaissance translation and the English civil war' in Q. Skinner, *Visions of Politics*, 3 vols., *Volume II, Renaissance Virtues* (Cambridge: Cambridge University Press, 2002), pp. 308–43. See below, pp. 35f.

[43] See generally H. Arendt, *On Revolution* (London: Faber & Faber, 1963), ch. 1.

[44] *A Concise View of the Constitution of England* (London: the Author, 1808), p. 11 (emphasis added).

the maze of fancy, or the wilderness of abstract rights'.[45] This historical conception was implicit and the ultimate transformative effect explicit in Walter Bagehot's famous claim that in England a 'Republic has insinuated itself beneath the folds of a Monarchy'.[46]

Dicey contributed to a decline of this third historical conception in two ways. On the one hand, his analytical approach brought to the forefront of constitutional debate an analytical legal scheme – sets of rules and principles and accompanying distinctions – not the formation of that scheme or the modes by which it was formed and acquired legitimacy. On the other hand, in demonstrating the theoretically limitless legal character of parliamentary sovereignty – one of the two fundamental features in his analytical scheme – and the difference between written and unwritten constitutions, he emphatically asserted 'that one law, whatever its [constitutional] importance, can be passed and changed by exactly the same method as every other law'.[47] Dicey's assertion of the constitution's ready changeability is still echoed today[48] and amplified by Dawn Oliver with the critical observation that because 'of the fact that the UK does not have a [written] Constitution and that much of governmental activity is conducted under common law rather than statutory or Constitutional powers, . . . the system can be changed or reformed in many respects without the need even to secure the passage of legislation through Parliament'.[49] In the appreciation of the constitution's changeability, the general lack of focus on the modes by which the legitimacy of any change is achieved or enhanced is part of Dicey's analytical legacy.

The historical conception of the constitution characterised by continuity with the past and inherent change, when not invisible behind the

---

[45] *An Essay on the History of the English Government and Constitution from the Reign of Henry VII to the Present Time* (London: Longman, Green, Longman, Roberts, & Green, new edn, 1865), especially at pp. xiii, xxviii–xxix, xxx (emphasis added). In 1790, Edmund Burke had made similar warnings and also emphasised the need for change: 'A state without the means of some change is without the means of its conservation. Without such means it might even risque the loss of that part of the constitution which it wished the most religiously to preserve', *Reflections on the Revolution in France and on the Proceedings in Certain Societies in London Relative to that Event*, C. C. O'Brien (ed.) (London: Penguin, 1968), p. 152, especially at p. 106.

[46] *The English Constitution*, M. Taylor (ed.) (Oxford: Oxford University Press, 2001), p. 48.

[47] *Law of the Constitution*, n. 1 above, p. 90.

[48] See, e.g., Bradley and Ewing, *Constitutional and Administrative Law*, n. 15 above, p. 7. See also *ibid.* pp. 31–2.

[49] *Constitutional Reform in the UK*, n. 13 above, p. 7.

common and strictly inaccurate alternative – the unwritten constitution –
is still occasionally evident in emphasis upon the constitution's flexibility and its evolutionary character.[50] It would seem to underlie Lord
Bingham's assertion that Dicey's separation of legal and historical
enquiries, '[i]n the field of constitutional law', 'seems to me not only
anti-intellectual, but plainly misguided'.[51] In view of concerns about
Dicey's method and the many far-reaching legal changes in recent
decades, how this third historical conception of constitutional continuity and inherent change might be developed so as to reintegrate legal and
historical views of the constitution requires careful reconsideration.

The plausibility of conceptions of the historical constitution is
affected by the history of the concept of constitution itself – the meanings attributed to it and the connotations it has carried. In brief outline,
*constitutio* was possibly coined by Cicero[52] probably as an approximate
Latin translation of the Greek *politeia* referring to a political community.
In translation, 'the Latin connotation of "establishment"' was added 'to
the *polis*-ness of *politeia*' and 'to gather up past experience' has been
described as its 'chief function'.[53] In context, the outcome of that
experience was the *res publica* – the balanced form of limited government in the Roman Republic known to Cicero.[54] *Constitutio* acquired
the authoritarian connotation of an imperial edict in the Empire but, in
the sixteenth and seventeenth centuries, a notion similar to Cicero's was
assimilated in the English concept of constitution and adapted to refer
both to the establishment and 'something more like "the composition of
the political community"'.[55]

The historical constitution may be understood as an elaboration
upon certain connotations of the concept of constitution, suggested in
the skeletal conceptual history above. It is plausibly conceived to

---

[50] See, e.g., Bradley and Ewing, *Constitutional and Administrative Law*, n. 15 above, pp. 31–2;
Bamforth and Leyland, *Public Law in a Multi-Layered Constitution*, n. 16 above, p. v.

[51] 'Dicey revisited', n. 20 above, 42 (emphasis added).     [52] *De re publica* 1.69.

[53] G. Maddox, 'Constitution' in T. Ball, J. Farr and R.L. Hanson (eds.), *Political
Innovation and Conceptual Change* (Cambridge: Cambridge University Press, 1989),
pp. 50–67, especially at p. 51.

[54] Cicero, *De Legibus* III. v. 12: 'res cum sapientissime moderatissimeque constituta esset a
maioribus nostris' ('the wisest and most evenly balanced state has been established by
our own ancestors').

[55] Maddox, 'Constitution', n. 53 above, especially at p. 59. See also H.A. Lloyd,
'Constitutionalism' in J.H. Burns (ed.), *The Cambridge History of Political Thought
1450–1700* (Cambridge: Cambridge University Press, 1991), pp. 254–97, especially at
pp. 254–5.

embrace the forms of government that are established, in the connotation of Cicero's *constitutio*, to accumulate past experience in such a way as to compose the *politeia*, the body politic or the political community. Qualifying the constitution as historical emphasises, in addition, the dynamic – the process of establishing forms and the modes of formation integral to it in the accumulation of past experience and the composition of the political community. Emphasising a dynamic process, this historical conception does not, in the abstract, prescribe a substantive outcome. It lacks a necessarily Republican or any other definitive content. As such, it de-reifies the *res publica*. The historical constitution is, according to this conception, the varying and variable forms of government – the legal and political rules, principles, and practices relating to government – that are established through being given constitutional significance by a political community in view of their historical formation – the modes by which they were attained and the normative historical accounts of their attainment. Its general appeal or legitimacy may be compared with that of a codified or written constitution. A codified constitution's appeal would seem to depend significantly upon appreciation of the singularity of its original formation,[56] whether by popular convention or a superior legislature's enactment and whether, for example, in the conferment of independence or reconstruction after war or revolutionary struggle. In contrast, the appeal of the historical constitution is to be explained below in relation to the role of history and normative historiography in what is a continuing process of formation.

The history in service of the historical constitution is not the document-based best-evidence English legal or general history inaugurated or influenced by Maitland.[57] In his inaugural lecture, Maitland

---

[56] This singularity can be confirmed, renewed or replaced in constitutional amendment or overhaul.

[57] F. W. Maitland, 'Why the history of English law is not written', Inaugural Lecture, 13 October 1888, published in H. A. L. Fisher (ed.), *The Collected Papers of Frederic William Maitland, Downing Professor of the Laws of England*, 3 vols. (Cambridge: Cambridge University Press, 1911), Vol. I, pp. 480–97. See J. H. Baker, 'Why the history of English law has not been finished', Inaugural Lecture, 14 October 1998, published in [2000] *CLJ* 62, especially at 63f. For Maitland's wider influence, see G. R. Elton, *F. W. Maitland* (London: Weidenfeld and Nicolson, 1985). For an extensive overview of various forms of history of varying serviceability, see K. J. M. Smith and J. P. S. McLaren, 'History's living legacy: an outline of "modern" historiography of the common law' (2001) 21 *Legal Studies* 251.

famously called for the separation of the historian's 'logic of evidence' from the lawyer's 'logic of authority'.[58] Sir John Baker presents Maitland's approach as pervasive today amongst English legal historians: 'Maitland's approach to legal history, which we all now take for granted, was to uncover as far as possible the original records and writings that constitute the body of contemporary evidence, and then to interpret them according to the social and intellectual setting in which they were produced.'[59] That history, however, is too preoccupied with plea rolls and manuscript law reports, with evidence of the past rather than with the needs of the present, too complex and nuanced, too vast and abundant in detail, to serve constitutional purposes. That history is about change and continuity,[60] as is the history in the historical constitution, and, when not neglectful of public law, provides essential sustenance.[61] Disavowing authority, however, and norma-tivity, in its preoccupation with contemporary evidence, and lacking in abridgement and ready or simple intelligibility, it cannot serve the constitutional purposes of accessibility, appeal and fidelity. A legal history that is either unable, or, of necessity, slow to be written through the absence of reliable, or the inaccessibility of the best, evidence is not readily or perhaps ever to be understood even by the scholarly legal historian, let alone the wider political community. It is ill-suited to a constitution by which such a community is to be composed, which appeals to it and to which that community has reason to be faithful.

More relevant to the historical constitution than Maitland's docu-ment-based best-evidence history is William Holdsworth's effective legal history as elaborated upon in his book with the revealing title *Some Lessons from Our Legal History*. Holdsworth distinguished 'effec-tive legal history' from 'mere antiquarianism' by orientating it explicitly to the present: 'The legal historian must have his eye on the end of the story, and be able to pick out the beginnings of those principles and rules

---

[58] 'Why the history of English law is not written', n. 57 above, pp. 491–2.

[59] 'Why the history of English law has not been finished', n. 57 above, 64.

[60] Smith and McLaren, 'History's living legacy', n. 57 above, especially at 312–15. See generally D. J. Ibbetson, 'What is legal history a history of?' in A. Lewis and M. Lobban (eds.), *Law and History* (Oxford: Oxford University Press, 2004), pp. 33–40, especially at p. 40; Baker, 'Why the history of English law has not been finished', n. 57 above, 64.

[61] Baker, 'Why the history of English law has not been finished', n. 57 above, especially at 78, 84.

and institutions which have survived and are operative today.'[62] For Holdsworth, legal history was 'necessary to the understanding and intelligent working of all long established legal systems':

> [A]ll long established legal systems must possess a background of old institutions, and of old technical principles and rules, sufficiently stable to give security to the ordering of society, and yet sufficiently elastic to allow the changes needed by altered social needs, and an altered public opinion. It is because the legal systems of Rome and England solved this difficult problem of combining stability with elasticity that they have become two of the greatest legal systems that the world has ever seen.[63]

In short, Holdsworth advocated legal history as a means to an understanding of the stability and elasticity necessary to secure legal progress and the 'intelligent working' of a legal system.[64] Holdsworth's advocacy of an effective historical view of the common-law system was pre-eminently applicable to constitutional law. In relation to the writ of *habeas corpus*, he observed that 'there can be no real understanding of some of the most salient characteristics of our constitutional law without a study of our legal history'.[65] With disparaging comparative reference to Continental theories of both absolute, and fictitious legal, sovereignty, he expressed an English historical pragmatism:

> Looking at theories of this kind from the standpoint of our legal history, I think it is obvious that they ignore the fact that the acceptance of the doctrine of sovereignty does not involve its absolute and logical application to all the facts of state life ... In the past, when continental states stretched the rights of sovereignty so far that the rights of individuals were in danger of being forgotten, English law was unique in the extent of the protection which it afforded to those rights.[66]

---

[62] W. S. Holdsworth, *Some Lessons from Our Legal History* (New York: Macmillan, 1928), Lecture I, 'The importance of our legal history', especially at p. 6. Cf. generally Holdsworth's critical description of the lawyers as 'the first offenders' to be followed by the historians in 'an extensive reading back into medieval constitutional history of the ideas of later centuries', 'The influence of the legal profession on the growth of the English constitution', Creighton History Lecture, University College, London, 1 December 1924, W. S. Holdsworth, *Essays in Law and History*, A. L. Goodhart and H. G. Hanbury (eds.) (Oxford: Oxford University Press, 1946), pp. 71–99, at p. 74.

[63] Lecture I, n. 62 above, pp. 8–9.     [64] *Ibid.*

[65] *Ibid.* Lecture II, 'The common law's contribution to political practice and theory', especially at p. 60.

[66] *Ibid.* Lecture III, 'The rule of law', pp. 133ff, especially at pp. 135, 140.

For Holdsworth, effective legal history was a teaching from the experience of the balanced course invariably followed by English lawyers and statesmen who admitted the doctrine of sovereignty but also 'all sorts of imperfections in practice'.[67] In what he saw as a world diminishing in size because of the inventions of modern science, he perceived the danger 'that students who have specialized in these continental theories [of sovereignty], and who know little of the spirit of our historic system of law, may mislead those who know less'.[68] The danger of being 'blown hither and thither by every wind of doctrine', he relied upon the study of legal history to help avert.[69]

Holdsworth's effective legal history – comparative, orientated to the present and educative of progress to the present – resembles methodologically the whig history of the constitutional historians, such as Hallam, Freeman and Gardiner, who preceded Holdsworth and upon whom Dicey relied heavily. These historians, Dicey's reliance upon them and their effect upon the appeal of his analysis of the rule of law are discussed at length in Chapter Seven.[70] In brief, Henry Hallam's history[71] is illustrative. It was a history of progress to the present with reference to key developments, such as the creation of Magna Carta or Bracton's assertion that the King is subject to God and the law. As in the case of Holdsworth's effective legal history, it served an educative (liberal) purpose and was significantly comparative, expressive of reactions to various Continental legal or constitutional developments and appreciative of contrasting English achievements. Hallam's history was also openly abridged, the anticipated imperfections and superficiality of which he regarded as justified by his educative liberal purpose.

Herbert Butterfield famously exposed the deficiencies of whig history in historical study. His most important criticism was of whig history's orientation to the present – its story of progress to the present, of its origins, of how the past anticipates or turns into the present – and its frequent expression of fervour through 'the transference into the past of an enthusiasm for something in the present, an enthusiasm for democracy or freedom of thought or the liberal tradition'.[72] He criticised its story of progress to the present for 'assuming a false continuity in events', for endorsing or promulgating judgments of value and, in the

---

[67] *Ibid.* especially at p. 137.    [68] *Ibid.* especially at p. 156.
[69] *Ibid.* especially at p. 157.    [70] See pp. 165ff.
[71] See, e.g., H. Hallam, *View of the State of Europe during the Middle Ages*, 3 vols. (London: John Murray, 2nd edn, 1819), Vol. I, pp. xii–xiii, Vol. II, pp. 374ff, 459ff, 476ff.
[72] *The Whig Interpretation of History* (London: W. W. Norton & Company, 1965), especially at p. 96.

face of apparent discontinuity, dividing history into 'great watersheds', such as the Reformation (or the seventeenth-century conflict between Crown and Parliament), beyond which the whig historian would not enquire.[73] He criticised whig history's explicit abridgment for an over-simplification that detracts from the concrete study of the past in all its detailed and nuanced complexity. The 'total result', he suggested, was 'to impose a certain form upon the whole historical story'.[74]

For Butterfield, whig history was poor history, but the very deficiencies he identified are significant in the historical constitution. Abridgment and oversimplification are sources of ready intelligibility and constitutional accessibility. The imposition of form upon the historical story integrates constitutional forms with their formation. A past understood as progress to the present is implicitly normative, is or can be related to present needs and can serve as a vehicle of fervour for the present and as a source of constitutional fidelity. In the absence of some sort of break with the past and consequent written constitution understood as 'the legally uncaused cause of all legal effects',[75] a story of constitutional progress to the present understood in terms of the past approximates to an alternative constitutional foundation. Looking in the past for what has already been found in the present may be a circular historical enquiry,[76] but, for constitutional purposes, the history produced is intelligible, accessible, foundational, a possible focus of fervour and a potential source of fidelity. That history is what, despite his analytical pretensions, appealed to Dicey[77] and, it will be argued in a later chapter,[78] contributed to the undoubted appeal of his analytical account to generation upon generation of students and lawyers.

Butterfield's criticisms are in need of a complement and a corrective. The complement is whig history's comparative or reactive dimension neglected by Butterfield in his Whig Interpretation of History but clearly evident in Dicey's Law of the Constitution and the whig histories upon which Dicey relied.[79] The corrective is to avoid presupposing the liberal

---

[73] Ibid. especially at pp. 87, 51–2.   [74] Ibid. p. 12.
[75] N. MacCormick, H.L.A. Hart (London: Edward Arnold, 1981), p. 4. Cf. generally Raz, 'Authority and interpretation of constitutions' in Alexander (ed.), Constitutionalism, n. 38 above, pp. 160ff.
[76] Butterfield, Whig Interpretation of History, n. 72 above, pp. 62–3.
[77] See pp. 13f above.   [78] Ch. 7 below, pp. 165ff.
[79] See, e.g., Dicey, Law of the Constitution, n. 1 above, pp. 202–5, ch. 12; Hallam, State of Europe during the Middle Ages, n. 71 above, Vol. II, pp. 476ff. For further examples, see ch. 7 below, pp. 172ff. Cf. the greater comparative dimension in Butterfield's later work, published towards the end of the Second World War, The Englishman and His History (Cambridge: Cambridge University Press, 1944), especially at pp. v–vii, 1–11, 103–17,

substantive content of what Butterfield called 'whig history' but criticised for essentially methodological reasons of abridgment, orientation to the present and so forth, applicable to any history whatever be the present or understandings of the present to which it be orientated. As complemented and corrected, what becomes a kind of formal normative comparative history is of further relevance to the historical constitution. Formalising a relationship of contrast with other political communities and the respective development of their institutions, it is a source of identity for the political community composed by the historical constitution. Dispensing, further, with a necessarily whig substance, the history in the historical constitution is open to wide-ranging debate and legal and political interpretations. The constitutional significance of whig history, as complemented and corrected, is indicative of the potential role of history in the historical constitution. The methodological challenge is still to realise that potential with more modern approaches to history, of which those of Maitland, Butterfield and Baker are illustrative, in full view.

## Towards a methodological reformation

The features of what Butterfield called whig history – constitutionally significant but deficient as history – are clues to reforming the relationship between the historical constitution and constitutional history. An unacceptable alternative is not to treat them as clues and to avoid enquiring into that relationship either by simply separating the historical from the legal and relegating its role in constitutional legal analysis, as did Dicey, or by conflating the legal and the historical. The role of history in the historical constitution is then either underestimated or overestimated: underestimated, as if of little or no constitutional legal

and his emphasis on the influence of the nineteenth-century German historical school in England, *Man on His Past: The Study of the History of Historical Scholarship* (Cambridge: Cambridge University Press, 1955), especially at p. 22. Cf. generally Pocock's emphasis on comparison in his work on the seventeenth century, as well as upon the relevance of a basis for comparison and French humanist influences upon modern historiography, *Ancient Constitution*, n. 39 above, especially at pp. viii–ix, Pt. I, chs. 1, 3, 4, Pt. II, ch. 1. See also J. P. Sommerville, 'The ancient constitution reassessed: the common law, the court and the languages of politics in early modern England' in R. M. Smuts (ed.), *The Stuart Court and Europe: Essays in Politics and Political Culture* (Cambridge: Cambridge University Press, 1996), pp. 39–64; J. P. Sommerville, 'English and European political ideas in the early seventeenth century: revisionism and the case of absolutism' (1996) 35 *Journal of British Studies* 168.

significance; overestimated, as if whig history or its modern constitutional equivalent[80] is real history, approximating or aspiring to Maitland's document-based best-evidence history. Rather, so as to facilitate assessment of historical plausibility and public debate about what is constitutionally significant in a political community, the whig-like features of the history in the historical constitution are explicitly recognised and their various manifestations justified or explained.

One feature of whig-like history is the abridged historical story of constitutional progress to the present, each aspect of which requires recognition and explanation. The historical story's abridgment, which serves constitutional accessibility, necessitates a conscious and justified selection of historical period. Its orientation to the present, furthermore, necessitates a similar treatment of, for example, doctrinal or institutional focus, and its implicit or explicit suggestions of progress warrant normative consideration of constitutional achievement.

A second feature is the imposition of form on the historical story, which renders it formulaic and schematic, but, for the purposes of the historical constitution, also readily intelligible in its integration of constitutional forms with their formation. So as not to pretend that the formulaic story in the historical constitution is real history and, as such, vulnerable to Butterfield's criticism, constitutional sources are explicitly treated differently. In the historical constitution, the lawyer's usual analytical distinction between legal and historical sources[81] of the constitution is rendered doubly indistinct. It is obscured partially though the usual working of the common law's doctrine of precedent by which what is historic is attributed legal authority. Additionally, it is obscured through the intelligibility and legitimacy afforded to constitutional legal forms by an appreciation of their historic formation. The historian's distinction between secondary and primary or original sources is similarly indistinct. Both secondary and primary sources are constitutionally significant according to their effect or influence. In the historical constitution, the common report of the landmark case, for example, may well be more constitutionally significant than an original manuscript. The first and widely-used editions of a leading text, such as Blackstone's

---

[80] For a few recent examples in the work of Jeffrey Goldsworthy, Trevor Allan and Mark Walters, see M. D. Walters, 'Common law, reason, and sovereign will' (2003) 53 *University of Toronto Law Journal* 65, especially at 73–6, 82–6; M. D. Walters, 'St German on reason and parliamentary sovereignty' [2003] *CLJ* 335, especially at 335–6, 368–9.

[81] See Bradley & Ewing, *Constitutional and Administrative Law*, n. 15 above, p. 12.

*Commentaries*, may well differ similarly in significance. Maitland's distinction between the historian's logic of evidence and the lawyer's logic of authority,[82] is, for constitutional purposes, expressly blurred. In variable degrees, both primary and secondary sources are evidential, authoritative and sources of appeal and fidelity.

A third and final feature in special need of reformation is the comparative treatment – disparaging or approving – of the historical comparative formation of other political communities, whether neighbouring or overarching. This too is expressly recognised and, by being recognised, can be openly addressed where necessary, for example, to correct insularity or lack of identity, hostility or over-admiration. The corrective is a reformed historical constitutional account that duly recognises outside influence or domestic peculiarity, comparative institutional success elsewhere or relative institutional failure at home.

## Aims and method

The historical constitutional approach taken in this book was developed in view of contemporary concerns about recent constitutional changes, the deficiencies and constitutional significance of whig history and the problems of fidelity, ossification and insularity[83] confounding a Diceyan analytical legal method in modern constitutional law doctrine. The chapters below are thematically bifocal. Responding to Dicey's relegation of a historical view and the many constitutional changes in recent years, their one point of focus is constitutional formation – the relationship between change and continuity, the 'problem of combining[84] elasticity with stability' – in different periods and modes of change as sources of constitutional legitimacy or partial consensus in the absence of affirmation or articulation in a codified constitutional text. Their other point of focus is interaction between English constitutional formation and European or Continental European developments in political communities proximate to, or overlapping with, the English. Their purpose is to correct Dicey's insularity, to avoid the disparaging comparative references of whig history and to help illuminate the many recent changes in the constitutional relationship to Europe. The chapters below are therefore an attempt to give proper recognition to European or Continental European influences or effects in

---

[82] 'Why the history of English law is not written', n. 57 above, pp. 491–2.
[83] See pp. 8ff above.
[84] Holdsworth, *Some Lesson from Our Legal History*, n. 62 above, p. 9. See p. 21 above.

the past without negating the constitution's peculiarity. In short, they are written in the hope of remedying legal doctrinal neglect of basic historical and geopolitical dimensions to the English constitution.

The chapters below are expressly selective of subject, perspective and historical period. The features of the constitution, they elaborate upon – the Crown, the separation of powers, parliamentary sovereignty and the rule of law – have been selected because of their centrality or prominence from a legal or legal doctrinal perspective. At least since Dicey, parliamentary sovereignty and the rule of law have usually been regarded in legal doctrine as the constitution's twin pillars. The Crown has been its longstanding institutional centrepiece in law. A separation of powers, although not rigid in the past and frequently disparaged in doctrine,[85] has long been implicit in the constitution, at least in the form of judicial independence, and has recently been invoked expressly to justify judicial deference, the statutory modification of the Lord Chancellor's office and the introduction of a Supreme Court to replace the House of Lords in its judicial capacity. In their treatment of features of the constitution, the chapters below, taken together, deal mainly with three periods: first, the early-modern period culminating in the seventeenth-century constitutional settlement; secondly, the late nineteenth century from which Dicey's analysis in *Law of the Constitution* came to prevail; and, thirdly, the last few decades of far-reaching constitutional modernisation and increased legal interaction with Continental Europe. These periods have been selected because of their general formative significance. Where legal landmarks in the formation of the constitution's features occurred at other times, they may be noted but only occasionally elaborated upon in recognition of the significance they were attributed in these periods.

The risk of a historical constitutional approach is that, by distinguishing the history in the historical constitution from what really happened in all its detailed complexity, in other words, from real history exemplified in the document-based best-evidence legal history inaugurated in England by Maitland, it expressly contributes to a contortion of history, much as Butterfield feared, but arguably more problematic for its express character and purpose. The ultimate danger is that the history of the historical constitution degenerates, at best, into the theatre[86] of its

---

[85] See ch. 4 below, pp. 83ff.

[86] Butterfield emphasised whig history's 'over-dramatisation of the historical story', *Whig Interpretation of History*, n. 72 above, especially at p. 34 (see ch. 7 below, p. 185).

'*theatrical* elements' exciting 'the most easy reverence'[87] and, at worst, into a kind of constitutional propaganda, propagating a noble neo-conservative, neo-socialist or neo-liberal lie. The danger is averted by attending to the reformation of the features of whig-like history described above. Central to the reformation of these features is express recognition of viewpoint – whether legal, political, normative, institutional, comparative etc – and, most importantly, not pretending to be historical in any modern orthodox sense. That viewpoint is not simply internal[88] but is expressed precisely in recognition of the role of other external viewpoints as complementary, even if competing,[89] and as constitutive of the historical constitution through which an entire political community in all its complexity is composed. In relation to the English rule of law, I will argue that even viewpoints external to the English political community, such as those of De Lolme, Montesquieu, Voltaire and De Tocqueville, have also profoundly affected English constitutional formation.[90] One has reason to hope that from a range of disparate viewpoints – internal and external both to the individual and to the political community – any noble lie will be exposed and ignored, or perhaps often used to illustrate its contortion of history, provided the viewpoint from which it is told is explicit.

In recognition of multiple viewpoints and their constitutional significance, a historical constitutional approach would not seem necessarily incompatible with an analytical legal method. It is available to the exponent of analytical legal doctrine and deserves reconsideration as a means with which to confront the methodological problems of fidelity, ossification and insularity,[91] inherited from Dicey and arising from or exacerbated by his distinction between legal and historical views of the constitution. To the analytical legal focus on constitutional forms, it adds a historical constitutional focus on their formation by which the analytical exponent might explain or assess their appeal and historic legitimacy – how or whether rules really are, in the words of Sir William Wade, 'legitimated by history'.[92] A historical constitutional approach

---

[87] Bagehot, *English Constitution*, n. 46 above, p. 9.

[88] Cf. generally Allan's dichotomy between the external viewpoint of 'a detached observer' and the necessarily internal viewpoint of the judge, politician and *constitutional theorist* from which a rule or convention, if it is asserted to exist, is necessarily said to be justified and binding, *Law, Liberty, and Justice*, n. 41 above, pp. 243–6, expecially at p. 244.

[89] See pp. 39f below.    [90] See ch. 7 below, pp. 176ff.    [91] See pp. 8ff above.

[92] H. W. R. Wade, 'The Crown, ministers and officials: legal status and liability' in M. Sunkin and S. Payne (eds.), *The Nature of the Crown: A Legal and Political Analysis*

readily embraces varying points of view provided they are express and ready to recognise their own limitations as a result.

## The liberal normativist alternative

A prominent alternative to the analytical legal approach inherited from Dicey is that of liberal normativism, also called legal or common law constitutionalism.[93] Whereas Dicey's analytical approach was in pursuit of a logically coherent formal scheme of constitutional legal rules and principles, the liberal normativist approach is preoccupied with liberal principles of legal and political morality in constitutional interpretation. These principles include individual autonomy and dignity and various civil liberties through respect for which they are secured. Although not entrenched in a written constitution, they are partially or substantially subsumed in constitutional interpretation of the rule of law and in the articulation of the common law which 'embodies (or is intended to embody) the experience and more enduring values of the community' and of which the judges are the 'authoritative exponents'.[94]

The approach of the liberal normativist partially remedies the three problems – fidelity, ossification and insularity – that confound a Diceyan analytical method.[95] Constitutional fidelity is secured through the appeal of the legal and political principles that the common law or its rule of law is interpreted to embrace. Ossification and insularity are avoided through the way principles are conceived. Most clearly in Trevor Allan's constitutional theory under the influence of Dworkin's conception,[96] principles have the attribute of weight:

> It is not possible for *principles* to be enacted, rather than rules, because a principle has no real existence apart from its weight. (A principle which had

(Oxford: Oxford University Press, 1999), pp. 23–32, especially at pp. 31–2. See generally ch. 3 below, especially pp. 71ff.

[93] See, e.g., Allan, *Law, Liberty, and Justice*, n. 41 above; Allan, 'Rule of law as the rule of reason', n. 41 above; Allan, *Constitutional Justice*, n. 41 above. See generally, Loughlin, *Public Law and Political Theory*, n. 4 above, especially at pp. 206ff; T. Poole, 'Back to the future? Unearthing the theory of common law constitutionalism' (2003) 23 *OJLS* 435; T. Poole, 'Questioning common law constitutionalism' (2005) 25 *Legal Studies* 142; Tomkins, *Our Republican Constitution*, n. 42 above, pp. 10ff.

[94] Allan, 'Rule of law as the rule of reason', n. 41 above, especially at 240, 239. Cf. Allan, *Law, Liberty, and Justice*, n. 41 above, especially at p. 4, with J. Jowell, 'Beyond the rule of law: towards constitutional judicial review' [2000] PL 671. See ch. 8 below, pp. 191ff.

[95] See pp. 8ff above.

[96] R. Dworkin, *Taking Rights Seriously* (London: Duckworth, 1977), pp. 22ff, 71ff.

no weight would not, in any intelligible sense, be a principle at all.) And weight or force cannot be enacted: it clearly cannot be determined in advance of any particular case arising for decision. A principle's weight will vary infinitely within an infinite range of facts and circumstances: it is precisely this elastic quality which eludes the straitjacket-nature of rules. A principle is applied to particular facts because – and only to the extent that – it is *understood* to be appropriate; and such understanding (or according of weight) cannot be enacted. It is precisely the character of a principle, as opposed to a rule, that its weight is a function of its intrinsic appeal to reason.[97]

Ossification is avoided because the constitutional significance of principles necessarily varies with their weight[98] as the common law evolves. Furthermore, insularity is absent because the weight of principles cannot be enacted and are therefore not confined to the legal text or texts of any particular political community. Whenever they affect interpretation elsewhere, jurisdictional boundaries are transcended. In *Constitutional Justice*, Trevor Allan therefore draws freely and 'heavily on the constitutional law of several common law jurisdictions' and describes his endeavour as seeking 'to identify and illustrate the basic principles of liberal constitutionalism, broadly applicable to every liberal democracy of the familiar Western type'.[99]

The liberal normativist approach, however, remedies the problems of constitutional fidelity, ossification and insularity at a high cost. Fidelity is secured through the appeal of principles, only attributed a dimension of weight, with the potential to transcend jurisdictional boundaries and to vary in constitutional significance as the common law evolves. Elaboration upon their centrality begs various questions: first, what is the constitution or what does it constitute; secondly, can that which is constituted serve as a distinct object of fidelity; and, thirdly, how does it relate to any particular political community? The usual talk of constitutionalism, rather than of a constitution, accentuates the first of these questions – respect for the principles of what exactly does

---

[97] *Law, Liberty, and Justice*, n. 41 above, p. 93.

[98] Jeffrey Jowell made the polemical observation that 'parliamentary sovereignty is not worth the stone in which it was not set', 'Exclusion of judicial review – can it be justified?', Meeting of the Constitutional Law Group, British Institute of International and Comparative Law, Institute for Advanced Legal Studies, London, 26 April 2004. Indeed, in the historical constitution, nothing is set in stone, and the rule of law can simply be interpreted or reinterpreted under the weight of changing values. Cf. generally Jowell, 'Beyond the rule of law', n. 94 above.

[99] Note 41 above, p. vii.

constitutionalism prescribe? Mention had already been made of the loose and unflattering descriptive definitions of Eric Barendt and Dawn Oliver.[100] As descriptive definitions, they cannot be used to address Stephen Sedley's critical observation that 'we have a constitutional law without having a constitution' in the sense of 'governing principles' from which the governing arrangements that are described derive legitimacy: 'if we ask what the governing principles are ... we find ourselves listening to the sound of silence'.[101]

Allan's theory is not one of constitutionalism without a constitution. For him, a constitution is evident – 'a common law constitution' – in the sense that 'the rule of law serves in Britain as a form of constitution' in the absence of the higher constitutional law of a written constitution: 'It is in this fundamental sense that Britain has a *common law constitution*: the ideas and values of which the rule of law consists are reflected and embedded in the ordinary common law'.[102] Allan has reason to be circumspect in suggesting only what serves as a form of constitution in a certain, albeit fundamental, sense. Whether a rule of law shifting from formality or changing in substance with the weight of the principles according to which its requirements are determined is sufficiently distinct itself to serve as a constitution is open to doubt and is considered in Chapter Eight below. Furthermore, offering the rule of law as a common law form of constitution, Allan makes historical claims interwoven in his theoretical arguments about the content of the common good articulated by the common law 'according to the society's shared values and traditions' through the particularity of the judicial interpretation of precedent in concrete cases.[103] These historical claims are about 'the

---

[100] Barendt, *Introduction to Constitutional Law*, n. 12 above, p. 33; Oliver, *Constitutional Reform in the UK*, n. 13 above, pp. 6, 357.

[101] 'The sound of silence: constitutional law without a constitution' (1994) 110 LQR 270 at 270.

[102] *Law, Liberty, and Justice*, n. 41 above, p. 4. The rule of law's constitutional centrality is similarly apparent in *Constitutional Justice* subtitled *A Liberal Theory of the Rule of Law*, n. 41 above. The conception of a common law constitution is perhaps prevalent at least amongst English lawyers: 'It is conventional wisdom, at least among lawyers, that the constitution of the United Kingdom is in its essentials the creation of the common law – an accretion of legal principles derived from judicial decisions which determine for the most part how the country is to be run from day to day', Sir Stephen Sedley, 'The common law and the constitution' in Lord Nolan and Sir Stephen Sedley, *The Making and Remaking of the British Constitution* (London: Blackstone Press Limited, 1997), pp. 15–31, especially at p. 15. Sedley's 'metaphor of the constitution', albeit suggested before 1998, is 'a scattering of statutory islands in a sea of common law', *ibid.* p. 18.

[103] See, e.g., 'Rule of law as the rule of reason', n. 41 above, especially at 239.

historical and practical wisdom of the common law', about its historical evolution 'by reflection on experience' and, most contentiously, about its real or intended embodiment of 'the experience and more enduring values of the community'.[104] These historical claims in what is, *inter alia*, an 'argument from history'[105] are crucial in establishing a relationship with a political community, as befits a constitution, but their plausibility is seriously affected by the legal and political principles by reference to which the history of the common law is interpreted.[106] If these historical claims are essentially normative, they compete with contrary historical claims, from interpretations of history affected by the weight of different principles or different allocations of weight to the same principles or different regard for what is the best institution to which their authoritative interpretation or articulation is to be entrusted. They do, for example,[107] compete with the claim that, if the product of any centralised institution embodies (or is intended to embody) the enduring values of the community so as to be central to the constitution, it is parliamentary legislation or practice, or long-standing governmental promotion of the common good under the control of parliament, not the common law, of which the judges are the authoritative exponents. These historical claims are also contradicted by the rival claim that, in their preoccupation with principles of legal and political morality, they neglect a longstanding judicial pragmatism – an economy of principle – in the history of the common law.[108] Allan does not elaborate on the justifiability of his normative use of history as such. His liberal normativist conception of a common law constitution nonetheless hinges upon his conception of the role of history in relating the common law to a particular political community, rendered all the more difficult by the weight of its principles that readily transcend a community's jurisdictional boundaries.

---

[104] *Constitutional Justice*, n. 41 above, p. 20; 'Rule of law as the rule of reason', n. 41 above, 241, 240. Cf. generally R. Cotterrell, 'Judicial review and legal theory' in G. Richardson and H. Genn (eds.), *Administrative Law and Government Action: The Courts and Alternative Mechanisms of Review* (Oxford: Oxford University Press, 1994), pp. 13–34.

[105] Poole, 'Questioning common law constitutionalism', n. 93 above, 151. See also Poole, 'Back to the future', n. 93 above, 444ff.

[106] See, e.g., Allan's invocations of Coke and Dicey, described in ch. 8 below, pp. 208ff.

[107] See J. Goldsworthy, *The Sovereignty of Parliament: History and Philosophy* (Oxford: Oxford University Press, 1999); J. Goldsworthy, 'The myth of the common law constitution' in D. Edlin (ed.), *Common Law Theory* (Cambridge: Cambridge University Press, forthcoming).

[108] See ch. 5 below.

The liberal normativist is invited to reconsider the historical constitution to end the sound of silence or expressly, and substantially, to historicise the common law constitution in the interpretation of the rule of law. In taking a historical constitutional approach, the rules and practices of the constitution are readily viewed from an explicitly normative perspective in terms of constitutional progress or achievement and, from that perspective, interpreted expressly with reference to liberal legal and political principles. Furthermore, under a constitution centred on history, the normative weight of principles can vary and transcend jurisdictional boundaries without calling into question the constitution itself – what exactly is or can conceivably be constituted – its relationship to any particular political community and the distinctness of that community. By taking a historical constitutional approach, the liberal normativist would expressly address the role of history in the common law constitution – its historical relationship with a political community and rival accounts of that relationship. The liberal normativist would, furthermore, explain the relationship between the constitution's legal and political principles and what is presented in Chapter Five below as an overarching pragmatism – a judicial sense that, particularly when highly contentious, principles are often best served, not by being trumpeted, but by being left largely unsaid – in the evolution of the common law. In short, a historical constitutional approach affords the liberal normativist the opportunity fully to explain the history in any historical claims and invocations, how it is pertinent and why it is to be believed.

## The political constitution

In a famous lecture, John Griffith elaborated upon his notion of the political constitution expressly as a response to the liberal legal or constitutional proposals of Lord Hailsham and Lord Scarman and to Ronald Dworkin's *Taking Rights Seriously*.[109] His objections to

---

[109] Seventh Chorley Lecture, London School of Economics, London, 14 June 1978, published as 'The political constitution' (1979) 42 *MLR* 1; Lord Hailsham, *Dilemma of Democracy*, n. 40 above; Lord Scarman, *English Law – The New Dimension* (London: Stevens & Sons, 1974); Dworkin, n. 96 above. For his later responses to the writings of Sir John Laws and Sir Stephen Sedley, see J. A. G. Griffith, 'The brave new world of Sir John Laws' (2000) 63 *MLR* 159; J. A. G. Griffith, 'The common law and the political constitution' (2001) 117 *LQR* 42. See also Sir Stephen Sedley, 'The common law and the political constitution: a reply' (2001) 117 *LQR* 68.

enhancing constitutional legal restrictions on government power by relying on legal devices and human rights in particular were, and seem to have remained, twofold – philosophical and political. His philosophical objection has been 'that so-called individual or human rights are no more and no less than political claims made by individuals on those in authority' within a society 'endemically in a state of conflict between warring interest groups, having no consensus or unifying principles sufficiently precise to be the basis of a theory of legislation'.[110] His 'fundamental political objection' has been 'that law is not and cannot be a substitute for politics', and that, in any event, as later described, 'law is politics carried on by other means, that law is the creature of politics, that law expresses the ways the hegemon seeks to manage society'.[111] Griffith has conceived of society as characterised by conflicts and of politics as 'what happens in the continuance or resolution of those conflicts'.[112] The outcome of his understanding and of his philosophical and political objections has been his political constitution:

> The constitution of the United Kingdom lives on, changing from day to day for the constitution is no more and no less than what happens. Everything that happens is constitutional. And if nothing happened that would be constitutional also.[113]

His notion of the constitution is purely descriptive – neither legally prescriptive nor morally normative. His stated approach has been to oppose making the constitution prescriptive or restrictive with 'formal or written statements':

> Indeed it [the constitution] must go in the opposite direction. For the best we can do is to enlarge the areas for argument and discussion, to liberate the processes of government, to do nothing to restrict them, to seek to deal with the conflicts which govern our society as they arise.[114]

His approach has been political and averse, in particular, to constitutional legal restrictions upon the working of politics.

Griffith's approach is not confounded by two of the problems – insularity and ossification – that confound the Diceyan analytical method in constitutional law. Any analytical constitutional legal

---

[110] 'Political constitution', n. 109 above, 19.

[111] *Ibid.* 16; Griffith, 'Common law and the political constitution', n. 109 above, 59. See generally J. A. G. Griffith, *The Politics of the Judiciary* (London: Fontana Press, 4th edn, 1991).

[112] 'Political constitution', n. 109 above, 20.    [113] *Ibid.* 19.    [114] *Ibid.* 20.

scheme, indeed the constitution itself, is political and, as such, is as insular as its politics may or may not be, changes 'from day to day'[115] and, politically, is not to be allowed to restrict politics. On the issue of fidelity to the politics of the political constitution, however, Griffith's famous lecture, is, at best, paradoxical, and, at worst, contradictory. His notion of the political constitution is purely descriptive but his political approach is, as such, prescriptive – 'to liberate the processes of government'.[116] A descriptive political constitution and a prescriptive politics is the paradox or contradiction that Griffith's lecture has left for those it has influenced. In response to the paradox or contradiction, one option is to make his descriptive political constitution prescriptive;[117] a second option is to make it purely theoretical.[118]

The first option, however, elevates to a prescriptive level both Griffith's descriptive constitution and its conflation of law and politics. Griffith's political argument and reductive descriptive assertion tantamount to 'Well, it's all just politics'[119] made with the polemical purpose of confronting liberal constitutional legal proposals are transformed into articles of faith. The outcome is to replace Griffith's polemical argument against those proposals with a dichotomy[120] of competing political and legal constitutions. The provocative recent book *Our Republican Constitution* by Adam Tomkins is illustrative. Tomkins advocates his Republican constitution centred on political accountability through Parliament by constructing legal constitutionalism as a model, or rather an anti-model, to be rejected along with the various liberal legal views he readily subsumes under it or certain of its tenets.[121] In constructing his Republican alternative, he neglects the legal

---

[115] *Ibid.* 19.    [116] *Ibid.* 20.

[117] See, e.g., Tomkins, *Our Republican Constitution*, n. 42 above.

[118] See, e.g., M. Loughlin, *The Idea of Public Law* (Oxford: Oxford University Press, 2003).

[119] See generally M. Loughlin, 'Constitutional law: third order of the political' in Bamforth and Leyland (eds.), *Public Law in a Multi-Layered Constitution*, n. 16 above, pp. 27–51, especially at pp. 29ff.

[120] Trevor Allan refers to the presentation of the political constitution as an alternative to the legal one as 'a false antithesis', Review of *Our Republican Constitution* by A. Tomkins [2006] *PL* 172 at 174.

[121] *Our Republican Constitution*, n. 42 above, pp. 10ff. See also his rejection of the Republicanism of Frank Michelman and Cass Sunstein in the United States for its liberalism and legalism, *ibid.* pp. 42–6. Cf. generally his limited initial claim that it 'is not a novel argument to suggest that the British constitution is *primarily* political rather than legal in character', *ibid.* p. vii (emphasis added). Cf. generally the approach of I. Ward, *The English Constitution: Myths and Realities* (Oxford: Hart Publishing, 2004), pp. 190ff.

constitutionalist dimension to the work of Philip Pettit upon which he principally relies.[122] In his invocation of history he is highly selective of a Republican parliamentary strand of political thought from the multiple legal and political strands in the seventeenth-century revolutionary struggles.[123] For example, he relies heavily upon recent work of Quentin Skinner, presented by Skinner himself as a corrective to modern historical accounts in which the constitutional debates about the royal prerogative culminating in the English Civil War of 1642 'have too readily been treated as if they were couched *entirely* in the language of common law'.[124] In short, by way of a dichotomous treatment of history, authorities, and a range of views, Tomkins transforms Griffith's descriptive political constitution into a dubious and one-sided prescriptive Republican constitutional exclusion, or expurgation, of legal constitutionalism. Dichotomies artificially narrow rather than enlarge 'the areas for argument and discussion'[125] of which Griffith spoke.

The second option in response to Griffith's paradoxical or contradictory descriptive political constitution and prescriptive political method is to elaborate upon Griffith's political constitution in the purely theoretical terms of the 'scholar' as distinct from the political prescriptions of the ideologically-motivated 'actor'.[126] Martin Loughlin's recent book *The Idea of Public Law* illustrates this option. In what is expressly presented as a pure theory of public law in 'being stripped of political ideology', he endorses or describes the 'primacy of the political' in the management or mediation of

---

[122] *Our Republican Constitution*, n. 42 above, pp. 46ff. See, e.g., P. Pettit, *Republicanism: A Theory of Freedom and Government* (Oxford: Oxford University Press, 1997), ch. 6. He relies heavily upon Pettit although, for 'Pettit, as a true defender of liberty, the free polity is an empire of laws', Allan, Review of *Our Republican Constitution* by A. Tomkins, n. 120 above, 173.

[123] *Our Republican Constitution*, n. 42 above, pp. 52ff, 67ff. Cf. generally the complex historical accounts of, e.g., Pocock, *Ancient Constitution*, n. 39 above, pp. 306ff; A. Cromartie, *The Constitutionalist Revolution: An Essay on the History of England, 1450–1642* (Cambridge: Cambridge University Press, 2006), ch. 8; Sommerville, *Politics and Ideology in England, 1603–1640*, n. 39 above. In legal writings on the constitution, cf. generally Ward's use of historical sources, *English Constitution*, n. 121 above, pp. 182ff.

[124] Skinner, 'Classical liberty' in Skinner, *Visions of Politics, Volume II, Renaissance Virtues*, n. 42 above, especially at p. 312 (emphasis added). See also Q. Skinner, 'John Milton and the politics of slavery' in Skinner, *Visions of Politics*, 3 vols., *Volume II, Renaissance Virtues*, n. 42 above, pp. 286–307, also relied upon by Tomkins, *Our Republican Constitution*, n. 42 above, pp. 52ff, 76.

[125] 'Political constitution', n. 109 above, 20.

[126] M. Loughlin, 'Theory and values in public law' [2005] *PL* 48, especially at 65–6.

conflict.[127] Politics, alongside governing, representation, sovereignty and constituent power, is one of the foundational concepts upon which Loughlin constructs an intricate conceptual architecture for public law, ultimately presented as abstract propositions in the numbered paragraphs of his final chapter. Within that conceptual architecture, constitutional law is said to be 'best understood as a set of practices embedded within, and acquiring its identity from, a wider body of political practices'.[128] He addresses the reductive inference 'Well, it's all just politics' by elaborating upon constitutional law as the 'third order of the political' – as a body of law 'that is not handed down from above but which exists as part of the self-regulatory processes of an autonomous political realm, and which may therefore be conceptualized as principles or maxims of political prudence'.[129] Loughlin describes what he suggests is the prudential method of public law – expressly offered as 'a juristic interpretation of Machiavelli's thought' – in bleak terms:

> In public law, we make use of a variety of devices – rhetorical tricks, silences, accommodations, self-imposed jurisdictional limitations and the like – that enable us to pay lip-service to universal ideals of justice while according due recognition to the interests of the state.[130]

Loughlin thus avoids[131] one dichotomy – between political and legal constitutions – by introducing or entrenching another – between theory and practice. His dichotomy leaves a chasm – between a Machiavellian prudence in the practice of public law and a pure theory by which constitutional law is theorised as 'the third order of the political'.[132]

---

[127] *Idea of Public Law*, n. 118 above, especially at pp. 4, 51. See *ibid.* pp. 155–6. See generally J. W. F. Allison, Review of *The Idea of Public Law* by M. Loughlin (2005) 68 *MLR* 344. See also Loughlin, 'Constitutional law: third order of the political' in Bamforth and Leyland (eds.), *Public Law in a Multi-Layered Constitution*, n. 16 above, pp. 27–51.

[128] *Idea of Public Law*, n. 118 above, p. 43.

[129] 'Constitutional law: third order of the political' in Bamforth and Leyland (eds.), *Public Law in a Multi-Layered Constitution*, n. 16 above, especially at pp. 29f; *Idea of Public Law*, n. 118 above, pp. 42ff, especially at p. 44.

[130] *Idea of Public Law*, n. 118 above, pp. 149, 157.

[131] Loughlin's pure theory is also illuminating and innovative, at least in the English context, in contributing a concept of constituent power as a generative principle through recognition of which constitutional arrangements are viewed dynamically rather than crystallised in analytical legal doctrine, *Idea of Public Law*, n. 118 above, ch. 6. The problem of ossification, as described above, pp. 8ff, is avoided.

[132] *Idea of Public Law*, n. 118 above, pp. 42ff; 'Constitutional law: third order of the political' in Bamforth and Leyland (eds.), *Public Law in a Multi-Layered Constitution*, n. 16 above, pp. 27–51. Cf. generally Loughlin's dichotomy in *Idea of*

Loughlin's theory, however impressive as an abstraction, is complex and rarefied. Abstract in being theorised and pure in 'being stripped of political ideology',[133] his pure theory is doubly detached from its historical (and sociological) context. By implication, the pure theorist is somehow able to stand aloof, high above politics and history,[134] as if occupying quarters in a celestial palace of concepts. Why Loughlin's pure theory of public law or of a political constitution should persuade, to what end and in what context are left unclear.

Descriptive, prescriptive and pure theorists of the political constitution are invited to reconsider the potential of a historical constitutional approach so as to transcend the dichotomy between political and legal constitutions or between constitutional theory and the practice of public law. It affords an opportunity to view the management of conflict through the changing forms of government or modes of governance in the historical constitution from an expressly political and/or legal point of view. A historical constitutional approach can be used expressly to emphasise political accountability through parliamentary practice and/ or legal accountability through judicial interpretation of the implications of constitutional rules and principles in concrete cases. It provides an opportunity to justify a selective historical account of constitutional formation, indeed requires that selections be carefully explained and justified. Preoccupied with both existing constitutional forms and their historic formation, its theory, whether legal and/or political, is not pure but significantly contextual. It is also prudential in its attempt to elaborate upon the pragmatic modes of change, of formation and reformation, that, it will be suggested in the chapters below, have contributed

---

*Public Law* with his more moderate and qualified distinction between the roles of 'actor' and 'scholar' in 'Theory and values in public law', n. 126 above, 65–6.

[133] *Idea of Public Law*, n. 118 above, p. 4.

[134] Ironically, Loughlin initially undertook what was 'largely a historical investigation' to 'uncover the foundations of public law' in Britain, *Idea of Public Law*, n. 118 above, p. vii. Though dissatisfaction with 'much of what passes for received wisdom in the field', he tried to sketch 'the conceptual foundations of public law as part of a larger, more historically orientated study', *ibid*. When 'this proved unwieldy', he effected what he describes as 'a partial separation between the conceptual and the historical', about which he expresses unease, *ibid.*, and which significantly understates the effect of his pure theory that he decided to present as highly abstract propositions in the numbered paragraphs of his final chapter. See generally Allison, Review of *Idea of Public Law* by M. Loughlin, n. 127 above. Cf. generally Loughlin's innovative and influential earlier contextual contribution to the theoretical understanding of public law and the development of public law thought in twentieth-century Britain in his book *Public Law and Political Theory*, n. 4 above.

and still contribute to constitutional appeal and legitimacy or, when disregarded, to their diminution or loss. To the extent that the historical constitution still provides for its own reformation through these general modes[135] and to the extent that its history, as orientated to the present and the management of conflict in the present, is amenable to varying interpretations from varying expressed viewpoints, Griffith's call 'to enlarge the areas for argument and discussion, ... to do nothing to restrict them', may be answered.[136]

## Complementary and competing points of view

A historical constitutional approach can be taken by both court-centred legalists and adherents to the political constitution because the historical constitution itself, as the outcome of a multiplicity of expressed points of view,[137] transcends the distinction between legal and political constitutions. The history within the historical constitution is not given but is interpreted, and interpretations are scrutinised, from multiple points of view. Viewpoints vary, for example, with institutional affiliation, personal background, individual interest and sense of purpose or value. They are crucial to constitutional debate and whatever consensus is attainable on the formative moments in the historical constitution's history – whether, for example, the judicial development of the writ of *habeas corpus* or the passing of the Habeas Corpus Acts, whether Coke's confrontation with the Crown or a Republican response to his failure, whether the judicial refusal to recognise slavery or parliamentary enactments in the process of decolonisation. The historical constitution serves to compose a political community and is not that to which any individual or group can effectively lay claim. In composing a political

---

[135] If constituent power be conceived as the generative principle of constituted power, Loughlin, *Idea of Public Law*, n. 118 above, ch. 6, in the English context these may approximate to its historical modes of generation or mediation. Cf. generally the potential of conceiving their effect as a partial historical realisation or illustration of Unger's proposal for a constitution as a 'structure-denying structure': R. M. Unger, *Politics, A Work in Constructive Social Theory*, 3 vols., Part I, *False Necessity: Anti-Necessitarian Social Theory in the Service of Radical Democracy* (Cambridge: Cambridge University Press, 1987), especially at p. 572.

[136] 'Political constitution', n. 109 above, 20.

[137] For various responses to divergence in approach, vision or perspective, cf. generally Feldman, 'None, one or several?', n. 38 above; Daintith and Page, *Executive in the Constitution*, n. 38 above, ch. 1; Loughlin, 'Theory and values in public law', n. 126 above; P. P. Craig, 'Theory, "pure theory" and values in public law' [2005] *PL* 440.

community of varying interests that is limited in resources and rich in diversity, and in which consensus is partial and precarious and conflict unavoidable or endemic, it is necessarily the outcome of complementary and competing points of view.

In elaborating upon the historical constitution in this book by taking the approach suggested in this chapter, an attempt is made to transcend a dichotomy of internal and external viewpoints[138] in three related ways. One way is to recognise the constitutional role and significance of multiple points of view within a political community. A second way is to try to relate, as a methodological priority, the historical constitution to constitutional history, or, more particularly, the history of what seems constitutionally important from an internal point of view to constitutional history as interpreted from the historian's external viewpoint. A third way is to elaborate upon the role of various outsiders to the English political community – such as De Lolme, De Tocqueville, Montesquieu – in affecting the formation of the English constitution by clarifying (or clouding) for insiders what they, as insiders, may have been inclined to take for granted or not to notice.[139] The European effects with which this book is concerned are attributed, *inter alia*, to reaction, imitation and the role of outsiders, already evident well before the increase in global interactions of the last 100 years.

If recognition of multiple points of view is a virtue or aspiration in theoretical work generally,[140] it is a historical constitutional necessity. Central to the historical constitution is a versatile history in service of a political community for which it is a source of unity – real but not necessarily apparent – direct and indirect: direct, when agreed or assumed; indirect, when controversial or contested. A versatile history will not readily reassure those accustomed to or attracted by the certainty – real and/or apparent – of a written constitution as an expression of agreement and a symbol of unity. In the historical constitution, however, when not contested, that history is a source of continuity and, when contested, it is a focus for constitutional debate from complementary and competing points of view and thus a means to a developing consensus and consequent change.

---

[138] Cf. Allan, *Law, Liberty, and Justice*, n. 41 above, pp. 243–6, especially at p. 244. See p. 28, n. 88 above.

[139] See, e.g., ch. 7 below, pp. 176ff. F. A. Hayek's claim to special insight from his once being an outsider is comparable, *The Road to Serfdom* (London: Routledge, 1944), p. 1 (see ch. 8 below, pp. 201ff).

[140] See Allison, *Continental Distinction in the Common Law*, n. 9 above, pp. 39–41.

## The historical constitution's relevance

In view of the far-reaching constitutional reforms of recent decades, a sceptical reader may doubt the current relevance of the notion of a historical constitution. As mentioned in Chapter One, a few years ago, in his concluding observations on the British constitution at the end of the twentieth century, Vernon Bogdanor claimed that the constitution is coming to lose its 'historic' character, in the specified sense of being 'original and spontaneous, the product not of deliberate design but of a long process of evolution'.[141] On the basis of the major legislative reforms effected by the passing of the European Communities Act 1972, the devolution legislation and the Human Rights Act 1998, he concluded that Britain has moved 'by piecemeal means' towards a codified written constitution and is now in 'a half-way house'.[142] He did, however, see 'little political will to complete the process, and little consensus on what the final goal should be'.[143] Another leading constitutionalist noted that the issue of a written constitution 'is not high on the realistic political agenda' but that 'a resurgence of interest ... could take place if it were felt that only a written Constitution could protect the UK from unwelcome encroachment by the European Union' or if relations between the Westminster Parliament and the devolved bodies 'became strained' as a result of devolution.[144]

Disparate statements about a written constitution have recently been made by leading figures within government,[145] but, thus far, a

---

[141] 'Conclusion' in V. Bogdanor (ed.), *British Constitution in the Twentieth Century*, n. 38 above, pp. 689–720, especially at p. 719. See also V. Bogdanor, 'Our new constitution' (2004) 120 *LQR* 242 at 259. For a comparable sense of change and for emphasis upon a 'new constitution' that 'lacks not only a planner but a plan', see A. King, *Does the United Kingdom Still Have a Constitution?* (London: Sweet & Maxwell, 2001), especially at p. 100.

[142] Bogdanor, 'Conclusion' in Bogdanor (ed.), *British Constitution in the Twentieth Century*, n. 38 above, p. 719. Bogdanor also claims that fundamental law is beginning to be recognised as an effect of a referendum on a statutory reform, 'Our new constitution', n. 141 above, 245–6. No referendum, however, has been held to validate or enhance the legitimacy of the Human Rights Act 1998 presented by Bogdanor as the potential 'cornerstone of the new constitution', *ibid.* 246.

[143] 'Conclusion' in Bogdanor (ed.), *British Constitution in the Twentieth Century*, n. 38 above, p. 719. See also Bogdanor, 'Our new constitution', n. 141 above, 246.

[144] Oliver, *Constitutional Reform in the UK*, n. 13 above, p. 387.

[145] Whereas Chancellor Gordon Brown has referred to a written constitution in veiled terms, speech to the Labour Party Conference, Manchester, 25 September 2006 (see ch. 1 above, n. 11), Lord Chancellor Falconer has argued against a written constitution, fringe meeting, Labour Party Conference, 26 September 2006.

widespread resurgence of interest has not occurred in response to devolution or a sense of the need for legal protection against encroachment by the European Union or by government generally. In promoting relatively flexible constitutional arrangements, the bulk of which were enacted by the Constitutional Reform Act 2005, and in urging the government to withdraw the infamous or highly controversial ouster 'clause 11' in the Bill that became the Asylum and Immigration (Treatment of Claimants, etc.) Act 2004, Lord Woolf raised the spectre of a written constitution:

> [I]f this clause were to become law, it would be so inconsistent with the spirit of mutual respect between the different arms of government that it could be the catalyst for a campaign for a written constitution ... The response of the government and the House of Lords to the chorus of criticism of clause 11 will produce the answer to the question of whether our freedoms can be left in their hands under an unwritten constitution.[146]

Shortly after the Lord Chief Justice made these observations, the government withdrew the clause at the second reading of the Bill in the House of Lords.[147] For the spectre of a written constitution to become a reality in the near future, only a severe and continuing conflict between governing institutions or the arms of government could be expected to occasion the kind of substantial and lasting change that would probably be needed in legal and governmental appreciation of political needs and priorities. A less substantial change – perhaps through recognition of the symbolic value of a written constitution promoted as eye-catching innovation or as a further or final stage in constitutional modernisation – may well be more likely. Less likely would seem its sufficiency for the massive task of introducing a written constitution to be undertaken and successfully completed.

---

[146] 'The rule of law and a change in the constitution', The Squire Centenary Lecture, Faculty of Law, University of Cambridge, 3 March 2004, published in [2004] *CLJ* 317, especially at 329. See also Sir John Baker, 'The constitutional revolution', Lecture, St Catharine's College, Cambridge, 20 April 2004, pp. 15–16; Lord Windlesham, 'The Constitutional Reform Act 2005: ministers, judges and constitutional change' [2005] *PL* 806, especially at 819. On the ouster clause and its withdrawal, see generally A. Le Sueur, 'Three strikes and it's out? The UK government's strategy to oust judicial review from immigration and asylum decision-making' [2004] *PL* 225; R. Rawlings, 'Review, revenge and retreat' (2005) 68 *MLR* 378; Lord Windlesham, 'The Constitutional Reform Act 2005: the politics of constitutional reform' [2006] *PL* 35 at 40–2.

[147] *Hansard*, HC col. 49, 15 March 2004.

In assessing the existing situation and the impact upon the constitution's character of the extensive recent programme of reforms that have occurred, a certain temporal parochialism should be avoided. The recent reforms were preceded by numerous other major constitutional reforms. Apart from the various reforms constituting the seventeenth-century revolutionary settlement, they include the extensions of the franchise in the nineteenth and early-twentieth centuries, parliamentary reforms before the First World War and the many changes in government and governance, particularly just after the Second World War and then again through privatisation from 1979. Keith Ewing rightly emphasises that 'the current spate of reform is simply the latest stage in the modernisation of a dynamic constitution, a modernisation which started in 1832 and will extend well beyond 2032.'[148] Many changes over a long period can constitute a form of continuity and can, as such, readily be neglected in the usual preoccupation with recent change.

Furthermore, even if a shift to a written constitution were already evident or complete,[149] I would suggest that the historical constitution – its forms and their modes of formation as sources of appeal and legitimacy – deserves consideration for relevance in various possible ways, which might become important at some point in the future but are not the subject of this book. First, it might be pertinent to developments now widely recognised to take place beyond the constitutional text,[150] whether because, when in force, its amendment procedures prove too politically onerous to be followed or whether because, at the outset, when agreed, matters are too controversial to be incorporated or too commonplace to be noticed or to seem to require written confirmation. Secondly, the historical constitution might be relevant to changes in the interpretation of the constitutional text in circumstances not considered or differently considered by its founders. Thirdly, the historical constitution – its forms and modes of formation – might be relevant to

---

[148] 'The politics of the British constitution' [2000] PL 405 at 431. See also *ibid*. 405, 437.

[149] For possible implications, see ch. 9 below, pp. 238ff.

[150] See generally, e.g., M. Foley, *The Silence of Constitutions: Gaps, 'Abeyances' and Political Temperament in the Maintenance of Government* (London: Routledge, 1989); King, *Does the United Kingdom Still Have a Constitution?*, n. 141 above, especially pp. 2–6; H. van Goethem (ed.), *Gewoonte en Recht* (Brussel; VWK, 2002), Iuris Scripta Historica XVI; E. Smith, 'Introduction' in E. Smith (ed.), *Constitutional Justice under Old Constitutions* (The Hague: Kluwer Law International, 1995), pp. xi–xix, especially at pp. xvii–xviii.

changes in the written constitution itself, its amendment or substitution. In view of a history of many such changes in European jurisdictions, Raoul van Caenegem asks whether 'the history of public law [is] no more than a graveyard of deceased Constitutions, where we can only wander aimlessly and shake our heads over so much misguided effort'.[151] A partial answer may lie in a historical constitutional relationship between change and continuity from one constitution to the next. The historical constitution's relevance may well match the futility of expecting a written constitution to be somehow ahistorical, to stand outside history in a certain sense – to be comprehensive and continuing but nonetheless fixed or settled in ever-changing circumstances.

Although implications for European constitutional developments[152] are also not the subject of this book, the English historical constitution might be of interest to European constitutional lawyers, whether or not a written or codified European constitution is introduced. If one is introduced, the historical constitution might be relevant as it would or might be to other written constitutions, discussed above, but with a history[153] more difficult and challenging in scope and complexity. If and while a codified European constitution cannot be introduced, whether for want of the required confidence in the fine detail of its substantive provisions on competence,[154] for example, or whether as a symbol of European encroachment upon national identity serving as a focal point of resistance to ratification, something akin to a historical constitution

---

[151] R. C. van Caenegem, *An Historical Introduction to Western Constitutional Law* (Cambridge: Cambridge University Press, 1995), p. 32. See *ibid.* pp. 292ff.

[152] See generally J. Shaw, 'Europe's Constitutional Future' [2005] *PL* 132; I. Pernice and M. P. Maduro (eds.), *A Constitution for the European Union: First Comments on the 2003 Draft of the European Convention* (Baden-Baden: Nomos Verlagsgesselschaft, 2004); P. Allott, *The Health of Nations: Society and Law beyond the State* (Cambridge: Cambridge University Press, 2002), especially ch. 7; N. MacCormick, 'The health of nations and the health of Europe', Mackenzie-Stuart Lecture, Faculty of Law, University of Cambridge, 11 November 2004, published in (2004–2005) 7 *Cambridge Yearbook of European Legal Studies* 1; J. H. H. Weiler, 'A constitution for Europe? Some hard choices' (2002) 40 *Journal of Common Market Studies* 563; J. H. H. Weiler, *The Constitution of Europe: "Do the New Clothes Have an Emperor?" and Other Essays on European Integration*' (Cambridge: Cambridge University Press, 1999).

[153] See generally P. Gowan and P. Anderson (eds.), *The Question of Europe* (London: Verso, 1997), chs. 1–3.

[154] See generally P. P. Craig, 'Competence: clarity, containment and consideration' in Pernice and Maduro (eds.), *Constitution for the European Union*, n. 152 above, pp. 75–93.

might be desirable or inevitable and is arguably[155] already evident. Its desirability might be affected by the extent to which the English example or model is itself significantly European, as elaborated upon in the coming chapters.

The scope of European effects in the formation of the English constitution is one main theme of the chapters below. The other is its modes of formation securing continuity and change in varying degrees and serving as sources of constitutional appeal and legitimacy. These chapters, I hope, will help dispel doubts about the historical constitution's continuing relevance, at least in its English context.

---

[155] See Weiler, 'Constitution for Europe', n. 152 above, especially at 566f; N. Walker, 'After the constitutional moment' in Pernice and Maduro (eds.), *Constitution for the European Union*, n. 152 above, pp. 23–43, especially at pp. 27f; MacCormick, 'Health of nations', n. 152 above, especially at 10–11, 16.

# 3

# The Crown: evolution through institutional change and conservation

The Crown's central significance and its continuing conceptual obscurity or incoherence are commonplace in English literature on the constitution. In *Law of the Constitution*, Dicey used the vast powers ascribed to the Crown, but not actually exercised by it, to illustrate the 'unreality' of the lawyer's view of the constitution and 'the hopeless confusion, both of language and of thought' that resulted and to which his own analytical approach was, in part, a response.[1] In their reassessment, Sunkin and Payne rightly emphasise that while 'the Crown may be at the heart of the constitution, the nature of the Crown and its powers remain shrouded in uncertainty and continue to generate controversy'.[2] The result is a paradox. The institutional centrepiece of the constitution remains poorly understood and inadequately analysed. If this central paradox is inexplicable, English constitutional analysis or theory may well be dismissed as an oxymoron, or the constitution itself, as a puzzle, mystery or mere muddle. Explaining the Crown is confounded further by another paradox. The traditional conception of the Crown as a corporation sole has been attributed simultaneously to the Romans

---

[1] A. V. Dicey, *An Introduction to the Study of the Law of the Constitution* (London: Macmillan, 10th edn, 1959), pp. 7ff, especially at p. 7. Cf. *ibid.* pp. 325ff.

[2] M. Sunkin and S. Payne, 'The nature of the Crown: an overview' in M. Sunkin and S. Payne (eds.), *The Nature of the Crown: A Legal and Political Analysis* (Oxford: Oxford University Press, 1999), pp. 1–21 at p. 1. See, in particular, F. W. Maitland, 'The Crown as corporation' (1901) 17 LQR 131, also published in H. A. L. Fisher (ed.), *The Collected Papers of Frederic William Maitland, Downing Professor of the Laws of England*, 3 vols. (Cambridge: Cambridge University Press, 1911), Vol. III, pp. 244–70; D. Runciman and M. Ryan (eds.), *State, Trust and Corporation* (Cambridge: Cambridge University Press, 2003), pp. 32–51. See also, e.g., P. Allott, 'The theory of the British constitution' in H. Gross and R. Harrison (eds.), *Jurisprudence: Cambridge Essays* (Oxford: Oxford University Press, 1992), pp. 173–205, pp. 187, 191–2; H. Woolf and J. Jowell, *de Smith, Woolf & Jowell, Judicial Review of Administrative Action* (London: Sweet & Maxwell, 5th edn, 1995), 4-004, especially at n. 15.

and 'the … genius of the English nation'.[3] At least in its origins, the conception of the Crown would seem both peculiarly English and Continental European.

In this chapter, I will seek to explain the Crown's central significance and reduce its paradoxical obscurity and peculiarity by taking the historical constitutional approach described in the last chapter. I elaborated upon that approach in response to Dicey's express relegation of the historical view of the constitution so that the lawyer might properly study 'the law as it now stands'.[4] My approach in this chapter, as in later chapters, is designed to correct the consequent analytical legal preoccupation with the constitution as a static and insular system of institutions, rules and principles, rational in the degree to which it conforms to a formal scheme of sets and distinctions, between, for example, kinds[5] of constitutional rules or kinds[6] of corporation, sole and aggregate. My focus is upon rationality, not of legal system or substantive outcome, but of constitutional process or evolution.

Here, as in later chapters, I will attempt to do justice to both European influence and the peculiarity of the common law. I will elaborate on three prominent interactions: the domestication of medieval ideas of the corporation, the effect of Continental thinking on Maitland's devastating criticism of the English conception of the Crown and the impact of Community law. In describing the evolution of the Crown, I will invite the reader to view the constitution as not, at heart, some central institution, rule or principle, abstracted and ossified at the arbitrary and fleeting moment of analysis. Rather, centrally constituted in the English historical constitution, I will suggest, are modes or methods of change that both assure continuity of governmental institutions, rules and practices and allow openness, whether to internal innovation or external influence.

## The medieval European matrix

In England, the early medieval uses of the Crown as an abstraction were various and not closely or clearly related to the later uses. In the decades after the Norman conquest, *corona* did, on occasion, serve as more than

---

[3] W. Blackstone, *Commentaries on the Laws of England*, 4 vols. (Chicago: The University of Chicago Press, Facsimile of 1st edn of 1765–1769, 1979), Vol. I, pp. 456–7.

[4] Dicey, *Law of the Constitution*, n. 1 above, p. 15. See ch. 2 above, pp. 7ff.

[5] See, e.g., Dicey, *Law of the Constitution*, n. 1 above, pp. 23–5.

[6] See, e.g., Blackstone, *Commentaries*, n. 3 above, Vol. I, p. 457. See p. 53 below.

a mere symbol for regality. Evoking the ceremonies developed by the Norman Kings to assert and reassert their status, it was notably used as a metonym for royal tenurial powers by Eadmer in his *Historia Novorum*.[7] At a time, however, when the King's undifferentiated *regnum* was the nexus in a framework of personalised legal relations, it did not distinguish an official from a personal capacity of the King. It appears to bear little relation to the developed medieval conception.[8]

In the first half of the twelfth century, the Crown in an abstract sense served a different purpose. It was used to refer to the lasting rights and immunities, abstracted from or reflecting those of the King, that were conferred upon Crown churches in perpetuity whether or not they were, or remained, actual repositories of a physical Crown.[9] This abstract concept, however, responded to the needs and emphasised the rights and immunities of churches and only indirectly reflected those identified with the King.

The developed English conception of the Crown owes much to theological thought, Roman law and, in particular, canonist doctrine. In grappling with practical problems, such as the effect of the Pope's death on papal appointments, how legally to protect the church's assets[10] and how to conceive of the church or an *ecclesia* as a continuing institution, canonists drew upon various interrelating theological and legal notions that made up the medieval European matrix. Three of these notions or sets of notions were to contribute significantly to the developed notion of the Crown as a continuing corporate entity both identified with the King and separate from his physical body. The first, common to Christian thinking and what Kantorowicz calls medieval political theology, was of a duality identified in one person or body – Christ

---

[7] See, e.g., *Historia Novorum in Anglia*, M. Rule (ed.), in Rolls Series (London, 1884), pp. 53ff.

[8] G. Garnett, 'The origins of the Crown' in J. Hudson (ed.), *The History of English Law: Centenary Essays on 'Pollock and Maitland'* (Oxford: Oxford University Press, 1996), pp. 171–214, especially at pp. 171ff.

[9] *Ibid.* pp. 199ff.

[10] For the medieval development of institutions that facilitated the consolidation of the church's patrimony, see generally S. Herman, '*Utilitas ecclesiae*: the canonical conception of the trust' (1996) 70 *Tulane Law Review* 2239; S. Herman, 'Trusts sacred and profane: clerical, secular, and commercial uses of the medieval *commendatio*' (1997) 71 *Tulane Law Review* 869; S. Herman, '*Utilitas ecclesiae* versus *radix malorum*: the moral paradox of ecclesiastical patrimony' (1999) 73 *Tulane Law Review* 1231; R. Zimmermann, *Roman Law, Contemporary Law, European Law: The Civilian Tradition Today* (Oxford: Oxford University Press, 2001), pp. 165f.

both human and divine, his representative, the King, human by nature and divine by grace, and his body, his *corpus verum* on the cross, and his *corpus mysticum* in the Church.[11]

The second notion was the Roman *universitas* or corporation. It was evident but undeveloped in Roman law,[12] little known by early medieval English lawyers and not elaborated upon by Bracton to establish a general or coherent theory.[13] By studying the Digest, the medieval European jurists did, however, begin to distinguish the *universitas* from *societas* and *communio*, to relate it to the eternal *genera* of Aristotelian thought and to use it to meet the practical need for institutional continuity.[14] The canonists applied and further developed the *universitas*. In the mid-thirteenth century, Pope Innocent IV proclaimed that the church or *ecclesia* is a *universitas* and the *universitas* is a person, a *persona ficta*.[15] This conception of church as *universitas* was not merely of theoretical interest when canonists were facing the problems of institutional continuity occasioned by the death of a bishop or solitary parish priest.

The third notion was of the Pope's *dignitas*, his Holy office or authority, distinguished from his human body, undying and Phoenix-like in its singularity and perpetuity.[16] Pope Boniface VIII authoritatively endorsed the maxim *Dignitas non moritur* by including it in a decretal of his *Liber Sextus* to clarify the continuity, on the Pope's death, of appointments made with papal authority.[17]

[11] E. H. Kantorowicz, *The King's Two Bodies: A Study in Medieval Political Theology* (Princeton: Princeton University Press, 1957), chs. 4, 5.

[12] See, e.g., D. 3. 4. 7; D. 4. 3. 15. 1; D. 46. 1. 22; I. 2. 1. 6. See generally P. W. Duff, *Personality in Roman Private Law* (Cambridge: Cambridge University Press, 1938), especially ch. 9.

[13] See the various references in Bracton, *De Legibus et Consuetudinibus Angliae*, G. E. Woodbine (ed.) (New Haven: Yale University Press, 1915–1942), f.8, f.56b, f.102, f.171b, f.180b, f.207b, f.228b; *Select Passages from the Works of Bracton and Azo*, F. W. Maitland (ed.) (London: Selden Society, Vol. 8, 1895), pp. 87, 90, 95; F. Pollock and F. W. Maitland, *The History of English Law before the Time of Edward I* (Cambridge: Cambridge University Press, 2nd edn, 1898), pp. 494ff.

[14] Kantorowicz, *King's Two Bodies*, n. 11 above, ch. 6.

[15] O. von Gierke, *Das Deutsche Genossenschaftsrecht*, 3 vols. (Berlin: Weidmann, 1868–1881), Vol. III, pp. 279f.; F. W. Maitland, 'Introduction' in O. Gierke, *Political Theories of the Middle Ages*, F. W. Maitland (tr.)(Cambridge: Cambridge University Press, 1900), pp. vii–xlv, especially at xviii–xix.

[16] Kantorowicz, *King's Two Bodies*, n. 11 above, pp. 383–401.

[17] 'Tunc enim, quia sedes ipsa non moritur, durabit perpetuo, nisi a successore fuerit revocata': *Corpus Iuris Canonici*, E. Friedberg (ed.) (Lipsiae: Bernhard Tauchnitz, 1879–1881), Pt. 2, p. 939: 'Then for the reason that the [Holy] See itself does not die, will last forever, unless revoked by a successor'.

These three notions were not confined to a distinct ecclesiastical realm: 'Under 'the *pontificalis maiestas* of the pope, who was styled also "Prince" and "true emperor," the hierarchical apparatus of the Roman Church tended to become the perfect prototype of an absolute and rational monarchy on a mystical basis, while at the same time the State showed increasingly a tendency to become a quasi-Church or a mystical corporation on a rational basis'.[18] At a time when the transference of ideas back and forth between the ecclesiastical and the secular was commonplace, these notions were circulating in the European matrix for juristic thought on the powers of the English King.

### The Crown as a corporation sole

The medieval English jurists grappled with the problem of dynastic continuity on the death of the King, as had the canonists with problems occasioned by the death of the Pope. Their arguments in all their complexity are beyond the scope of this chapter. The three notions above, prevalent in medieval European thought, were, however, crucial to their tangled arguments and eventual answer, described at length by Kantorowicz in his influential book *The King's Two Bodies*.[19]

First, at an early stage, the English jurists began to conceive a certain duality in the King and his Crown. By the end of the twelfth century, they were beginning to use the Crown, mainly in the legal and fiscal context, as not quite conterminous with the King, but as a concept identified with him, somehow separate from his natural body and suggestive of a more general public, governmental or administrative sphere. Such use of the Crown is evident in Glanvill's treatment of pleas *ad coronam*[20] and in the King's promise to preserve the rights of

---

[18] *King's Two Bodies*, n. 11 above, pp. 193–4. On the relationship between spirituality and temporality in the early modern period, see generally P. Prodi, *The Papal Prince, One Body and Two Souls: The Papal Monarchy in Early Modern Europe* (Cambridge: Cambridge University Press, 1987).

[19] Note 11 above. For a brief account, see M. Loughlin, 'The state, the Crown and the law' in Sunkin and Payne (eds.), *Nature of the Crown*, n. 2 above, pp. 33–76 at pp. 51ff.

[20] See, e.g., *De Legibus et Consuetudinibus Regni Angliae*, G. E. Woodbine (ed.) (New Haven: Yale University Press, 1932), lib. 1. c. 1, lib. 10. c. 5; Kantorowicz, *King's Two Bodies*, n. 11 above, pp. 342–5. See also, e.g., Bracton, *De Legibus*, n. 13 above, f.55b: 'Est enim corona facere iustitiam et iudicium, et tenere pacem, et sine quibus corona consistere non poterit, nec tenere' ('It is for the Crown to judge and dispense justice, and to keep the peace, and in their absence the Crown will not be able to stand firm, nor maintain its hold').

the Crown that, at least by the time of the coronation of Edward I in 1274, was included in the coronation oath.[21]

Secondly, English jurists began to see in the Crown the Romanist *universitas* or corporation. In effect, they embodied or incorporated the Crown in the late Middle Ages to include more than the King – the King in Council, the King in Parliament, the King, Lords and Commons – a corporation somehow separate from his natural body.[22]

Thirdly, they embodied or incorporated not merely the organic unity, including King, Lords and Commons, identified with the Crown. They also embodied the 'successional entity'[23] symbolised in a further elaboration of the duality above, what came to be regarded as the King's two bodies – his natural body and his immortal body politic – graphically represented in funerary ceremonies and sepulchral monuments.[24] In so doing, they echoed the canonist maxim *dignitas non moritur* but understood as *dignitas* the King's body politic, the corporate body of the Crown. Through the notion of the King's two bodies, in a development apparently peculiar to England, they fused the dignity or office of the King with his body politic or corporate Crown. So, from one perspective, they incorporated only the King, as they did only the parish parson through a comparable English development in church property law.[25] Kantorowicz concludes that 'it would appear that a fusion, and an indeed pardonable confusion, of Crown and Dignity was at the bottom of the legal fiction of the "King as Corporation" or as "corporation sole" ', a corporation of only one.[26]

The later stages in the interplay of the notions above and their confused outcome are evident in a series of late Tudor and early Stuart cases in the Reports of Edmund Plowden and those of Sir Edward Coke.

---

[21] H. G. Richardson, 'The English coronation oath' (1941) 23 *Transactions of the Royal Historical Society* 129 at 131f. See Kantorowicz's description of the influence of the earlier oaths of Popes and bishops, a further illustration of canonist influence on the English conception of the Crown: *King's Two Bodies*, n. 11 above, pp. 347–58.

[22] Kantorowicz, *King's Two Bodies*, n. 11 above, pp. 358–64. See generally *ibid.* pp. 364–83.

[23] Loughlin, 'State, Crown and law' in Sunkin and Payne (eds.), *Nature of the Crown*, n. 2 above, pp. 33–76 at p. 56.

[24] See generally Kantorowicz, *King's Two Bodies*, n. 11 above, pp. 419–37. A good example can be seen in Canterbury Cathedral.

[25] See F. W. Maitland, 'The corporation sole', *Collected Papers*, n. 2 above, Vol. III, pp. 210–43 at pp. 219–25; Maitland, 'Crown as corporation', *Collected Papers*, n. 2 above, Vol. III. Maitland's 'The corporation sole' is also published in (1900) 16 *LQR* 335; Runciman and Ryan (eds.), *Maitland: State, Trust and Corporation*, n. 2 above, pp. 9–31.

[26] *King's Two Bodies*, n. 11 above, pp. 383–450, especially at p. 448.

The leading cases of *Hill* v. *Grange* and the *Duchy of Lancaster Case* are exemplary. In *Hill* v. *Grange*, the Court of Common Pleas held that statutes which referred to the King bound his heirs and successors. The following reasoning prevailed: 'the King is a Body politic, and when an Act says, *the King*, or says, *we*, it is always spoken in the Person of him as King; and in his Dignity Royal, and therefore it includes all those who enjoy his Function'.[27] The King, as King, was regarded as a body politic separate from his body natural and with an everlasting *dignitas*:

> And King is a Name of Continuance, which shall always endure as the Head and Governor of the People (as the Law presumes) as long as the People continue, *quia ubi non est gubernator, ibi dissipabitur populus*, and in this Name the King never dies. And therefore the Death of him who is the King is in Law called the Demise of the King, and not the Death of the King, because thereby he demises the Kingdom to another, and lets another enjoy the Function, so that the Dignity always continues.[28]

The embodiment or incorporation of the King as body politic is apparent, as is the fusion of that body with an immortal *dignitas*.

A few years later, in the *Duchy of Lancaster Case*, the Crown lawyers gathered at Serjeant's Inn clarified that the King as King was unaffected, not only by the death of his natural body, but also by its other infirmities. In relation to the lease of the Duchy of Lancaster by Edward VI before he became of age, they agreed 'that by the common Law no Act which the King does as King, shall be defeated by his nonage'.[29] In their argument, though they recognised that both the King's body natural and his body politic were 'incorporated in one person', they suggested an extensive and inclusive body politic: 'his Body politic is a Body that cannot be seen or handled, consisting of Policy and Government, and constituted for the Direction of the People, and the Management of the public-weal, and this Body is utterly void of Infancy, and old Age, and other natural Defects and Imbecilities, which the Body natural is subject to'.[30] The Tudor lawyers incorporated in the King's body politic an

---

[27] (1556–1557) Plowden 163 at 176.
[28] *Ibid*. 177–177a, especially at 177a. See also the implications of the King's two bodies for the effect of King Edward VI's accession upon the service rendered to the Prince Edward by Sir Thomas Wroth: *Thomas Wroth's Case* (1573) Plowden 452, especially at 455a–456.
[29] (1561) Plowden 212 at 213.    [30] *Ibid*.

undying 'successional entity'[31] as well as an extensive and inclusive governing unity.

By the time Sir Edward Coke had become Lord Chief Justice, the outcome of the earlier cases was clear and authoritatively stated: 'And it is to be known, that every corporation or incorporation, or body politic or incorporate, which are all one, either stands upon one sole person, as the King, bishop, parson, etc. or aggregate of many, as mayor, commonalty, dean and chapter, etc. and these are in the civil law called *universitas sive collegium*'.[32] In his *Commentary upon Littleton* in his *Institutes of the Laws of England*, Coke reiterated the categorisation of bodies politic or corporate as either sole or aggregate and re-emphasised an equivalence with the *universitates* of the civil law.[33]

In his *Commentaries on the Laws of England*, Blackstone eloquently confirmed the development culminating in Coke's exposition:

> The first division of corporations is into *aggregate* and *sole* ... Corporations sole consist of one person only and his successors, in some particular station, who are incorporated by law, in order to give them some legal capacities and advantages, particularly that of perpetuity, which in their natural persons they could not have had. In this sense the King is a sole corporation: so is a bishop.[34]

Blackstone's eloquent and influential summary entrenched, in the modern period, the late-medieval English conception of the Crown as a corporation sole. It perpetuated a tradition which Lord Cranworth would later assume when he simply stated that the 'Crown is a Corporation sole, and has perpetual continuance'.[35] In a manner comparable to that of Coke, Blackstone did not present the English conception in isolation:

> The honour of originally inventing these political Constitutions [i.e., corporations] entirely belongs to the Romans ... They were afterwards

---

[31] Loughlin, 'State, Crown and law' in Sunkin and Payne (eds.), *Nature of the Crown*, n. 2 above, pp. 33–76 at p. 56.

[32] *Sutton's Hospital Case* (1614) 10 Co. Rep. 1a at 29b. See also *Calvin's Case* (1609) 7 Co. Rep. 1.

[33] Co. Inst. I, 250a. See also *ibid*. 15b.

[34] Note 3 above, Vol. I, p. 457. See also *ibid*. p. 242. For implications of the King's two bodies for the treason trials of the 1790s, see generally J. Barrell, *Imagining the King's Death: Figurative Treason, Fantasies of Regicide, 1793–1796* (Oxford: Oxford University Press, 2000), especially at p. 40.

[35] *Obiter dictum* in *AG v. Köhler* (1861) 9 HLC 654 at 671.

much considered by the civil law ... [T]hey were adopted also by the canon law, for the maintenance of ecclesiastical discipline; and from them our spiritual corporations are derived. But our laws have considerably refined and improved upon the invention, according to the usual genius of the English nation: particularly with regard to sole corporations, consisting of one person only, of which the Roman lawyers had no notion.[36]

Blackstone thus explained and elaborated upon the equivalence with the *universitas* that Coke had emphasised. In categoric terms he recognised the extensive indebtedness to the civil law of the peculiarly English conception of the King or Crown as corporation sole.

## English constitutional adaptation

The conceptual development culminating in Coke's exposition confirmed by Blackstone was not purely in the realm of ideas. It involved the domestication of notions common to European thought in the evolving English political context. It corresponded with actual political conditions and developments, with institutions both old and new, with both the enduring and changing English political reality.

On the one hand, the developed conception of the Crown must have appealed to the late-medieval English monarchs. The grandiose legal phrases used to describe the King and his bodies, the inherence of a commonwealth of lands and other entitlements in the Crown and hence also in the King and an inclusive and extensive incorporation in the King's body politic were, no doubt, aspects of a doctrine 'apt to flatter the vanity' and appeal to the interests of the Tudor monarchs.[37]

On the other hand, the conception of the Crown did not merely respond to monarchical interests and sensibilities. The English conception developed in view of, and accommodated, the concrete reality of parliamentary institutions in England. Whereas Continental jurists, unfamiliar with comparable institutions in the late Middle Ages, developed an abstract notion of the state identified initially with the Prince

---

[36] *Commentaries*, n. 3 above, Vol. I, pp. 456–7.

[37] Pollock and Maitland, *History of English Law*, n. 13 above, pp. 525–6 and especially at p. 511; Maitland, 'Crown as corporation', *Collected Papers*, n. 2 above, Vol. III, pp. 248–9.

and separate from its members, the English jurists adapted their conception of the Crown to the reality of the King in Parliament.[38]

The Crown's inclusive character and democratic potential were evident at an early stage in the application to the Crown of the Romano-Canonical maxim *Quod omnes tangit ab omnibus comprobetur* interpreted, as it had come to be interpreted, to require community representation.[39] For example, in 1275, Edward I wrote to Pope Gregory X on the subject of England's tribute to Rome. He claimed that by his coronation oath he was not only required to maintain unimpaired the rights of the Crown but also to do '*nec aliquid quod diadema tangat regni eiusdem absque ipsorum [prelatorum et procerum] requisito consilio*'.[40] In other words, what affected the Crown had to be approved by all through the highest representatives of the body politic.

By the late Middle Ages, the Crown and the King's body politic were capacious terms. The Crown was a 'hieroglyphic of the laws, where justice, etc. is administered' and which signified, *inter alia*, the doing of justice and the distinguishing of right from wrong.[41] The King's body politic connoted 'Government' and the 'Management of the publicweal'.[42] It included not only the King in Parliament, the King, Lords and Commons, but also the people, the King's subjects who with the King 'together compose the Corporation' in which 'he is incorporated with them, and they with him, and he is the Head, and they are the

[38] Kantorowicz, *King's Two Bodies*, n. 11 above, especially at pp. 223–31, 382–3, 446ff. Cf. the development of the concept of the state in France: J. W. F. Allison, *A Continental Distinction in the Common Law: A Historical and Comparative Perspective on English Public Law* (Oxford: Oxford University Press, rev. pbk edn, 2000), ch. 4.

[39] 'That which affects all must be approved by all', from C. 5. 59. 5. 2. See generally G. Post, 'A Romano-canonical maxim, "quod omnes tangit", in Bracton' (1946) 4 *Traditio* 197; G. Post, *Studies in Medieval Legal Thought: Public Law and the State, 1100–1322* (Princeton: Princeton University Press, 1964), pp. 163–238; B. Tierney, *Religion, Law, and the Growth of Constitutional Thought, 1150–1650* (Cambridge; Cambridge University Press, 1982), pp. 19–25; J. Martínez-Torrón, *Anglo-American Law and Canon Law: Canonical Roots of the Common Law Tradition* (Berlin: Duncker & Humblot, 1998), pp. 151ff.

[40] To do 'nothing that affects the Diadem of this realm without having sought the counsel of prelates and magnates': F. Palgrave (ed.), *Parliamentary Writs*, 4 vols. (London, 1827–1834), Vol. I, pp. 381f. See generally Richardson 'English coronation oath', n. 21 above, 132ff.

[41] *Calvin's Case*, n. 32 above, 11b.

[42] *Duchy of Lancaster Case*, n. 29 above, 213. See generally Sir John Baker, *The Oxford History of the Laws of England, Volume VI, 1483–1558* (Oxford: Oxford University Press, 2003), pp. 55ff.

Members, and he has the sole Government of them'.[43] Although the King was clearly conceived as the head, both he and his subjects were recognised as interdependent constituents and participating members of the body politic. Their collective incorporation would permit changes in the relationship of interdependence and in the scope, forms and significance of their participation.

Because of the Crown's inclusive character, Maitland had good reason later to suggest that the King was not, in reality, a corporation sole but 'the head of a complex and highly organised "corporation aggregate of many" – of very many'.[44] Although contradictory and, as such, incongruous in legal analysis,[45] the English Crown evolved into a corporation both sole and aggregate. From a historical constitutional rather than an orthodox analytical point of view, the Crown became, in one sense, a corporation sole consisting of or standing upon the King alone, in another, a corporation aggregate that connoted the innumerable members of his body politic. Whereas the one sense reflected the Crown's origins in a medieval monarchy, the other, its potential in a modern democracy. The ambivalence of the developed conception of the Crown assured continuity with a monarchical past and an opportunity for a democratic future. In England, the Crown had become a monarchical means to impersonal representative government.

The accommodation in the Crown of the reality of representative institutions exemplified at least three related features of development in the English historical constitution. First, it exemplified a predilection or propensity for using legal fiction. By fiction, the Crown became more than a 'piece of jewelled headgear under guard at the Tower of London'.[46] By fiction, the Crown became a corporation or body politic; and by further fiction, only the King was deemed to be incorporated. If Continental Europe conceived states within states, the English Crown exemplified

---

[43] *Willion* v. *Berkley* (1561) Plowden 223 at 234. See also *Hill* v. *Grange*, n. 27 above, 177a.

[44] 'Crown as corporation', *Collected Papers*, n. 2 above, Vol. III, p. 259. See also *ibid.* p. 258.

[45] See Judge Romer's comments, *Re Mason* [1928] Ch. 385 at 401, those of Lord Woolf, *M* v. *Home Office* [1993] 3 WLR 433 at 465CD, and those of Woolf and Jowell, *Judicial Review*, n. 2 above, 4-004, n. 15. Cf. H. W. R. Wade and C. F. Forsyth, *Administrative Law* (Oxford, Oxford University Press, 9th edn, 2004), pp. 814–15. For Sir Stephen Sedley, the question of whether the Crown is a corporation sole or aggregate is 'arid', 'The sound of silence: constitutional law without a constitution' (1994) 110 *LQR* 270 at 289.

[46] Lord Simon in *Town Investments* v. *Department of the Environment* [1978] AC 359 at 397F.

fictions[47] within fictions. Their prevalence in legal thinking illustrated a certain economy of the common law, upon which Chapter Five below elaborates further. What was novel, unknown or unclear was accommodated, not through open innovation, but through minimal revision, through a limited equation – in particular respects and for particular purposes – with what was established, known or at least a little clearer.

Secondly, the conceptual development exemplified an attempt[48] to avoid abstraction through[49] the use and elaboration of familiar or common terms such as person, body or Crown. The English medieval jurists did embrace the Romanist *universitas* but incorporated in it the person or body of the King, in part, because 'English law has liked its persons to be real',[50] as Maitland pointed out.

Thirdly, the Crown's accommodation of representative political institutions exemplified the incremental adaptation of forms to a changing political context. The adaptation secured both continuity and change: the retention of old, and the accommodation of new, or changing, institutions so as 'to harmonise modern with ancient law'.[51] The monarchical form – the Crown – signified the King but, as the King in Parliament, or the King in his courts, accommodated the evolution of parliamentary sovereignty, as it did refinements to the rule of law. Viewed sympathetically, in a positive pragmatic light, the old institution, formally enshrined, was retained[52] until the representative

---

[47] The phrase, although not the comparison, is that of Kantorowicz, *King's Two Bodies*, n. 11 above, p. 5.

[48] But the use of even simple anthropomorphic or organicist metaphors, confirmed in legal fiction, easily descends into abstraction and difficulty: see, e.g., Pollock and Maitland, *History of English Law*, n. 13 above, pp. 491f.

[49] By way of what Pollock and Maitland call 'inadequate analogies supplied to us by the objects which we see and handle', *ibid.* p. 489.

[50] 'Corporation sole', *Collected Papers*, n. 2 above, Vol. III, p. 242.

[51] Pollock and Maitland, *History of English Law*, n. 13 above, pp. 511–12. See generally Loughlin, 'State, Crown and law' in Sunkin and Payne (eds.), *Nature of the Crown*, n. 2 above, pp. 33–76 at pp. 43ff.

[52] Burke warned in 1790 that 'it is with infinite caution that any man ought to venture upon pulling down an edifice which has answered in any tolerable degree for ages the common purposes of society, or on building it up again, without having models and patterns of approved utility before his eyes', E. Burke, *Reflections on the Revolution in France and on the Proceedings in Certain Societies in London Relative to that Event*, C. C. O'Brien (ed.) (London: Penguin Books, 1968), p. 152. A few decades later, Lord John Russell voiced or appealed to similar caution in his famous refusal to substitute 'new lamps for old', to embrace radical parliamentary reform 'for the chance of obtaining a prize in the lottery of constitutions', speech of 14 December 1819, *Selections from Speeches of Earl Russell 1817 to 1841 and from Despatches 1859 to 1865,*

institutional innovations were seen or assumed to be working and thereafter at the cost of a widening gap between form and substance, between apparent and real political power.

Common to all these features of development in the English historical constitution was a conservation or economy of existing forms. It involved their pragmatic extension through fiction, their attempted elaboration in familiar terms and their incremental adaptation to changing circumstances. The developed English conception of the Crown was the ambivalent institutional outcome – a corporation arguably both aggregate and sole, both progressive and retrospective, open to the evolution of representative government and attractive to royal interests and sensibilities. It was thus a means to democratisation and a cover for continuing immunities,[53] the object of Burke's respect and Paine's ridicule,[54] in short, the early manifestation of an English republic's insinuating itself 'beneath the folds of a Monarchy'.[55]

### Later European influences: Maitland and modernisation

The conception of the Crown as a corporation sole was famously ridiculed by Maitland. His comments on cases, such as *Willion* v. *Berkley* in Plowden's Reports, was damning: 'I do not know where to look in the whole series of our law books for so marvellous a display of metaphysical – or we might say metaphysiological – nonsense'.[56] At one point, he denied that the corporation sole, in its ecclesiastical form, was a juristic person: 'he

---

2 vols. (London: Longmans, Green, 1870), Vol. I, pp. 182–201, especially at pp. 198–9. Almost half a century later, Russell quoted his own speech as indicative of his general approach to reform of the franchise, Earl John Russell, *An Essay on the History of the English Government and Constitution from the Reign of Henry VII to the Present Time* (London: Longman, Green, Longman, Roberts, & Green, new edn, 1865), pp. xxviii–xxx. Cf. generally Roman constitutional evolution, in particular, the gradual demise of the Republican institutions of the praetor and the senate in the Principate, and the changing significance of the resulting legal strata. See W. Kunkel, *An Introduction to Roman Legal and Constitutional History*, J. M. Kelly (tr.) (Oxford: Oxford University Press, 2nd edn, 1973), pp. 81–3, 125–7.

[53] See, e.g., Blackstone, *Commentaries*, n. 3 above, Vol. I, pp. 238f.

[54] See, e.g., Burke, *Reflections on the Revolution in France*, n. 52 above, pp. 97ff., 111ff; T. Paine, *Rights of Man, Common Sense, and Other Political Writings*, M. Philp (ed.) (Oxford: Oxford University Press, 1995), pp. 175ff.

[55] W. Bagehot, *The English Constitution*, M. Taylor (ed.) (Oxford: Oxford University Press, 2001), p. 48. Pollock and Maitland similarly recognised that under 'the cover of the Crown . . . our slow Revolution is accomplishing itself', *History of English Law*, n. 13 above, p. 525.

[56] 'Crown as corporation', *Collected Papers*, n. 2 above, Vol. III, p. 249; *Willion* v. *Berkeley*, n. 43 above.

or it is either natural man or juristic abortion'.[57] Maitland's ridicule of what he presented as a profound confusion or contortion of analysis, despite the brilliance of his general exposition, is vulnerable to the charge of anachronism from an orthodox historical perspective. It lacked a certain sensitivity to the medieval environment of thought and sentiment[58] in which the conceptions he criticised arose and made some sense. From a historical constitutional perspective, however, it reflects the contemporary influences upon him and reveals his modern concerns.

Maitland was strongly influenced by rationalist Continental theory and, in particular, by Gierke's realist theory of corporations. He acknowledged that his work on the Crown 'was suggested by Dr Gierke's *Genossenschaftsrecht*',[59] a substantial section of which he had translated into English. In the introduction to his translation, Maitland expressly presented the criticism he imagined the German realist would make of English law,[60] criticism reflected in his later articles on the corporation sole. The extent of Gierke's influence upon Maitland can be appreciated by comparing the first and second editions of Pollock and Maitland's *History of English Law*, published in 1895 and 1898 respectively. Although Gierke was already frequently cited in the first edition, Pollock and Maitland attributed the changes in the section on corporations of the second edition to a 'repeated perusal of Dr Gierke's great book'.[61] They changed the heading 'Fictitious Persons', with its implicit endorsement of the fiction, to 'Corporations and Churches', as they did related subheadings.[62] They excluded their earlier description of the

---

[57] 'Corporation sole', *Collected Papers*, n. 2 above, Vol. III, p. 243.

[58] See generally Kantorowicz, *King's Two Bodies*, n. 11 above, pp. 3–6. Maitland's treatment of the Crown, under the influence of the realist theory of corporations, would seem to exemplify what he himself described, from what became an orthodox legal historical point of view, as the 'unsatisfactory compound' of legal dogma and legal history, 'Why the history of English law is not written', Inaugural Lecture, 13 October 1888, published in *Collected Papers*, n. 2 above, Vol. I, pp. 480–97, especially at p. 491. See generally J. H. Baker, 'Why the history of English law has not been finished', Inaugural Lecture, 14 October 1998, published in [2000] *CLJ* 62; ch. 2 above, pp. 19ff.

[59] 'Crown as corporation', *Collected Papers*, n. 2 above, Vol. III, p. 246, n. 1; Gierke, *Genossenschaftsrecht*, n. 15 above.

[60] Note 15 above, pp. xxxiiff.

[61] *History of English Law* (2nd edn), n. 13 above, p. 486, n. 1. Gierke's extensive influence is also evident in Pollock's treatment of artificial persons in his book on contract: P. H. Winfield, *Pollock's Principles of Contract* (London: Stevens, 13th edn, 1950), pp. 90–4.

[62] *The History of English Law before the Time of Edward I* (Cambridge: Cambridge University Press, 1st edn, 1895), pp. 469–71; *History of English Law*, 2nd edn, n. 13 above, pp. 486–9.

juristic person as an 'artifice of science', a rare 'discovery comparable to the discoveries made by other sciences or other arts'.[63] They mentioned the contemporary questioning of the fiction theory on the Continent and presented the anthropological view of the corporation as one of the 'difficulties that beset us'.[64] They added, further, the observation that 'the theory which speaks of the corporation's personality as fictitious, a theory which English lawyers borrowed from medieval canonists, has never suited our English law very well'.[65] Maitland's famous articles on the Crown and the corporation sole were published shortly after the second edition of *Pollock and Maitland* and his translation of *Gierke*. By then, he had thoroughly absorbed the rationalist scepticism of fictitious personality in Continental realist theory. It was manifest in his scathing criticism of the English conception of the Crown as a corporation sole, of its multiple fictions, their obscurity and their lack of utility.

Maitland was less than clear in his exposition of an alternative. At one point, while explicitly adopting the position of the realist historian, he described an English struggle 'to find some expression, however clumsy, for the continuous life of the State'.[66] In a flirtation with the Continental concept, he suggested that 'possibly there is not much difference now-a-days between the Public, the State, and the Crown'.[67] Elsewhere, he observed that we 'cannot get on without the State, or the Nation, or the Commonwealth, or the Public, or some similar entity'.[68] In the end, however, he seemed to settle on the conception of the Crown, not as a corporation sole, but as the more realistic and less fictitious 'corporation aggregate of many', 'complex and highly organized', headed by the monarch and preferably called the Commonwealth.[69] The influence of the Continental concept of the state was evident but ultimately superficial. In both editions of the *History of English Law* Book II, Pollock and Maitland nonetheless treated King and Crown, not independently as they would the state, but alongside 'aliens', 'lepers' and 'lunatics' under the heading 'The Sorts and Conditions of Men', as did earlier and contemporaneous English arrangements of the law of persons.[70]

---

[63] 1st edn, n. 62 above, p. 469.    [64] 2nd edn, n. 13 above, p. 489.    [65] *Ibid.*

[66] 'Introduction' in Gierke, *Political Theories of the Middle Ages*, n. 15 above, p. xxxvii.

[67] *Ibid.* p. xxxvi.

[68] 'Crown as corporation', *Collected Papers*, n. 2 above, Vol. III, p. 253.

[69] *Ibid.* p. 259.

[70] Cf., e.g., Sir Matthew Hale, *An Analysis of the Civil Part of the Law* (4th edn, 1779), secs. 2ff.; Blackstone, *Commentaries*, n. 3 above, Vol. I, Bk. 1.

The Continental concept of the state did not take hold in England[71] but judicial treatment of the Crown did, on occasion, show signs of modernisation. In suggesting that '"the Crown" is very often a suppressed or partially recognized corporation aggregate', Maitland cited *Mersey Docks Trustees* v. *Gibbs* as evidence of language 'used by judges when they are freely reasoning about modern matters and are not feeling the pressure of old theories'.[72] The Mersey Docks Trustees had argued that, as public servants, they were not liable in negligence for the acts of their fellow public servants. In reply, Mr. Justice Blackburn held that the Trustees were not public servants and, so, distinguished the authorities 'that where a person is a public officer in the sense that he is a servant of the Government, and as such has the management of some branch of the Government business, he is not responsible for any negligence or default of those in the same employment as himself': 'these cases were decided upon the ground that the Government was the principal and the Defendant merely the servant . . . And all that is decided by this class of cases is, that the liability of a servant of the public is no greater than that of the servant of any other principal, though the recourse against the principal (the public) cannot be by an action.'[73] In short, Mr Justice Blackburn viewed servants of the Crown as public servants or agents of government, as one would representatives of any corporation aggregate. Similarly, in *Dyson*, where the power in issue was exercised by and held in the name of the Commissioners of Inland Revenue, the Court of Appeal affirmed the Court's jurisdiction 'to maintain an action against the Attorney-General as representing the Crown'.[74] Maitland's view of the Crown as a corporation aggregate was acknowledged in *Re Mason*. Judge Romer cited Maitland's view as well as the general view of the Crown as a corporation sole but held that the corporation, however viewed, would be required to refund money paid to it in error during the reign of a preceding monarch.[75]

Maitland's realist exposition, the conception of government and its servants in *Mersey Docks Trustees* and the identification of the Crown

---

[71] See Allison, *Continental Distinction in the Common Law*, n. 38 above, pp. 72–82. J. W. F. Allison, 'Theoretical and institutional underpinnings of a separate administrative law' in M. Taggart (ed.), *The Province of Administrative Law* (Oxford: Hart Publishing, 1997), pp. 71–89 at pp. 74–83.

[72] 'Crown as corporation', *Collected Papers*, n. 2 above, Vol III, p. 258.

[73] *Mersey Docks Trustees* v. *Gibbs* (1866) 11 HLC 686 at 712. Cf. the granting of injunctions against Crown officers in *Rankin* v. *Huskisson* (1830) 4 Sim. 13, especially at 15, and against the Prime Minister in *Ellis* v. *Earl Grey* (1833) 6 Sim. 214.

[74] *Dyson* v. *Attorney-General* [1911] KB 410 at 416.

[75] *Re Mason*, n. 45 above, 401. See also *ibid*. 398.

with its officers, also evident in *Dyson*,[76] contributed to a process of modernisation that culminated in the decision of the House of Lords in *Town Investments* v. *Department of the Environment*. In his concurring minority judgment, Lord Simon cited Pollock and Maitland's *History of English Law*, emphasised that the language used to symbolise the powers of government 'cannot be understood without regard to constitutional history' and explicitly adopted the conception of the Crown as a corporation aggregate.[77] In his majority judgment, Lord Diplock suggested that the concept of government replace that of the Crown. Preoccupied with the modern constitutional reality, he presented the concept of the Crown as anachronistic:

> These relationships [between Her Majesty, ministers of the Crown and civil servants] have in the course of centuries been transformed with the continuous evolution of the constitution of this country from that of personal rule by a feudal landowning monarch to the constitutional monarchy of today; but the vocabulary used by lawyers in the field of public law has not kept pace with this evolution and remains more apt to the constitutional realities of the Tudor or even the Norman monarchy than to the constitutional realities of the 20th century ... [N]owadays to speak of 'the Crown' as doing legislative or executive acts of government, which, in reality as distinct from legal fiction, are decided on and done by human beings other than the Queen herself, involves risk of confusion ... Where, as in the instant case, we are concerned with the legal nature of the exercise of executive powers of government, I believe that some of the more Athanasian-like features of the debate in your Lordships' House could have been eliminated if instead of speaking of 'the Crown' we were to speak of 'the government'.[78]

Lord Diplock understood 'the Crown' or, rather, 'the government' to 'embrace both collectively and individually all of the ministers of the Crown and parliamentary secretaries under whose direction the administrative work of government is carried on'.[79] His Lordship therefore held that the Crown was the tenant where a lease was granted to a minister. *Town Investments* reflected significant modernisation, both in the way Lord Diplock embraced public law as separate from private

---

[76] See also *Merricks* v. *Heathcoat-Amory* [1955] 1 Ch. 567.

[77] *Town Investments*, n. 46 above, 397EF, 400C.     [78] *Ibid*. 380F–381B.

[79] *Ibid*. 381B. His passing description of the Crown as 'in law a corporation sole' elsewhere in his judgment is at odds with his definition and with his equation of the Crown with the government, *ibid*. 384D. Cf. the view of Lord Morris in his dissenting judgment, *ibid*. 393E–G.

law, the outcome of Continental influence described elsewhere,[80] and in his conception of the Crown as the government.

The modernisation to which Maitland, under the influence of Continental European theory, contributed was slow to occur. More than seventy years separate Maitland's exposition and Lord Diplock's speech in *Town Investments*. The slowness of the modernisation and the continuing avoidance of the Continental concept of the state were the outcome of various influences. A Diceyan aversion to alien institutions, the absence of the state from his elaboration of the English rule of law,[81] a lasting distrust of abstraction, difficult to avoid in discussion of the state,[82] the repeated use of the Crown in proliferating post-War statutes and, in short, the continuing conservation of constitutional forms, described above, limited the pace and scope of modernisation.

The enactment of the Crown Proceedings Act 1947[83] reflected the limited modernisation. It curtailed Crown immunities expressed in the maxim *The King can do no wrong* but retained and confirmed the concept of the Crown with the help of a further fiction. Section 2(1) of the Act introduced the liability of the Crown in tort by providing that 'the Crown shall be subject to all the liabilities in tort to which, if it were a private person of full age and capacity, it would be subject'. In other words, it established Crown liability in tort by fictitiously attributing private legal personality to the Crown.

The 1947 Act also preserved various Crown immunities. Significantly for later remedial developments in Community and English law, s 21 excluded injunctive relief against the Crown in subsection 1 and, in subsection 2, 'against an officer of the Crown if the effect of granting the injunction ... would be to give any relief against the Crown which could not have been obtained in proceedings against the Crown'. In *Merricks* v. *Heathcoat-Amory*, the court interpreted s 21 to preclude an injunction against either the Crown or an officer of the Crown.[84] As in

---

[80] See Allison, *Continental Distinction in the Common Law*, n. 38 above, especially at pp. 4–12, 23–7.

[81] See, e.g., *Law of the Constitution*, n. 1 above, chs. 4, 12.

[82] See, e.g., J. A. G. Griffith's dismissive attitude in 'The political constitution' (1979) 42 *MLR* 1, especially at 16, and the struggle of the House of Lords to define the state in *Chandler* v. *Director of Public Prosecutions* [1964] AC 763, especially at 790, 804, 806–7.

[83] For a contemporaneous presentation of the principal changes, see generally Sir Thomas Barnes, 'The Crown Proceedings Act 1947' (1948) 26 *Canadian Bar Review* 387.

[84] *Merricks*, n. 76 above. See generally T. Cornford, 'Legal remedies against the Crown and its officers before and after *M*' in Sunkin and Payne (eds.), *Nature of the Crown*, n. 2 above, pp. 233–65 at pp. 245ff.

the cases of *Mersey Docks Trustees*, *Dyson* and *Town Investments*, discussed above, Judge Upjohn identified the Crown with its officers, simply conceived as representatives of the Crown, with no official capacity other than a representative capacity. For decades, *Merricks* remained the leading authority on the interpretation of s 21 – a modern memorial to a measure of common sense in service of Crown immunity.

## The impact of Community law

An early phase of the *Factortame* litigation raised the issue of the availability of interim relief against the Crown and its officers. The facts are well-known and may be briefly stated. Pending a preliminary ruling by the European Court of Justice (ECJ) on the substantive contravention of Community law by the Merchant Shipping Act 1988, the applicants sought interim relief in the form of disapplication of the Act by the Transport Secretary. In the first *Factortame* case, the House of Lords ruled that, as a matter of English law, such relief would not be available. Lord Bridge gave two main reasons for its unavailability. His first reason, discussed in Chapter Five below, was that 'the effect of the interim relief granted would be to have conferred upon them [the applicants] rights directly contrary to Parliament's sovereign will'.[85] His second reason, the concern of this chapter, was that s 21 of the Crown Proceedings Act 1947 excluded the Court's jurisdiction to grant an injunction against the Crown.[86]

A few years earlier, the Divisional Court in *Herbage* had noted the former authority of *Merricks* but had held that the reforms to Order 53 of the then Rules of the Supreme Court, confirmed in s 31 of the Supreme Court Act 1981, had extended the availability of an injunction such that it had become available against officers of the Crown in the same circumstances in which the prerogative writs had been available.[87] In the first *Factortame* case, the House of Lords overruled *Herbage* on the effect of the Order 53 reforms and affirmed that, in purely English law, the injunction remained available as had been established in *Merricks*. The House of Lords therefore sought a preliminary ruling from the ECJ

---

[85] *R. v. Secretary of State for Transport ex parte Factortame Ltd* [1990] 2 AC 85 at 143AB.
[86] *Ibid.* 150H.
[87] *R. v. Secretary of State for the Home Department ex parte Herbage* [1987] QB 872, especially at 882G–883A, 885E–886C; *Merricks*, n. 76 above. See also *R. v. Licensing Authority ex parte Smith Kline (No. 2)* [1990] QB 574, especially at 598H, 599E and 604F.

on the question whether the overriding principle of Community law that national remedies provide effective protection of directly-enforceable rights required, nonetheless, interim relief in the form requested.[88] The ECJ affirmed that the House of Lords 'had jurisdiction, in the circumstances postulated, to grant interim relief for the protection of directly enforceable rights under Community law and that no limitation on ... [that] jurisdiction imposed by any rule of national law could stand as the sole obstacle to preclude the grant of such relief'.[89] In the second *Factortame* case,[90] to give effect to the ECJ's ruling, the House of Lords disregarded the rule in s 21 of the Crown Proceedings Act 1947 and, after considering whether a proper case had been made out on the facts, concluded that interim relief be granted in the form requested. The outcome of the early *Factortame* litigation was a clear disparity between the remedial protection afforded to rights under purely English law (as in the first *Factortame* case) and that afforded to rights under Community law (as in the second *Factortame* case). Only under Community law would an injunction be available against the Crown and its officers.

The English courts regarded the remedial disparity between Community law and purely English law as anomalous and undesirable. In *M* v. *Home Office*, described by distinguished commentators as the most important constitutional case for 200 years or more, Lord Woolf stressed that it 'would be most regrettable if an approach which is inconsistent with that which exists in Community law should be allowed to persist if this is not strictly necessary'.[91] Lord Goff made a similar statement in a different context,[92] as did Lord Donaldson in the Court of Appeal in *M* v. *Home Office*: 'It is anomalous and wrong in principle that the powers of the courts to "hold the ring" pending the resolution of a dispute should be limited where central government is a party to the dispute, particularly when these limitations have been removed by European Community law if the dispute concerns rights under that

---

[88] First *Factortame* case, n. 85 above, especially at 143EF, 147E–148C, 150H.

[89] As described by Lord Bridge in *R.* v. *Secretary of State for Transport ex parte Factortame Ltd (No. 2)* [1991] 1 AC 603 at 658D.

[90] Note 89 above.

[91] *M* v. *Home Office*, n. 45 above, 463E; H. W. R. Wade, 'The Crown – old platitudes and new heresies' (1992) 142 *NLJ* 1275, 1315 at 1275; M. Beloff QC as reported in *The Times*, 28 July 1993, p. 20.

[92] *Woolwich Equitable Building Society* v. *Inland Revenue Commissioners* [1993] AC 70 at 177E.

law.'[93] The judicial sense of anomaly, together with the implications of immunity for the rule of law, prompted a reinterpretation.

In *M v. Home Office*, the House of Lords reinterpreted s 21 of the Crown Proceedings Act 1947 only to protect the Crown's own immunity and therefore, in sub-section 2, only to bar an injunction against officers of the Crown in the very rare situation where they represent the Crown by exercising statutory powers conferred, not upon them in their own official capacities, but upon the Crown or the Queen. Lord Woolf disapproved or distinguished the various authorities, discussed above, in which the Crown was simply identified with its officers, agents or representatives. His Lordship disagreed with the reasoning in *Merricks*, restricted *Town Investments* to its very different facts, and dismissed the relevant discussion in the first *Factortame* case as a 'side-show' to the position in Community law.[94]

Central to Lord Woolf's reinterpretation of s 21 was the distinction between the Crown and its officers, between powers conferred upon the Crown (or the Queen) and powers conferred upon its officers in their independent official capacities. Lord Woolf regarded the distinction as fundamental:

> Although in reality the distinction between the Crown and an officer of the Crown is of no practical significance in judicial review proceedings, in the theory which clouds this subject the distinction is of the greatest importance.[95]

A pressing reason for his reliance on this distinction, despite the acknowledged obscurity[96] of its theory and significant authority to the

---

[93] [1992] 2 WLR 73 at 101C–D. See also *ibid.* 99H–100B.

[94] *M v. Home Office*, n. 45 above, 453G–454E, 455E–456E and especially at 448C.

[95] *Ibid.* 448G.

[96] For further analytical obscurity, see the Quark litigation, recently before the House of Lords, *R v. Secretary of State for Foreign and Commonwealth Affairs ex parte Quark Fishing Limited* [2005] UKHL 57. The Crown is distinct from its officers, but one of those officers may be acting on behalf of the Crown in the right of the government of the UK or on behalf of the Crown in the right of the government of a British Overseas Territory (BOT). Lord Bingham's starting point was that, 'whatever may once have been thought', the Crown itself is now clearly 'not one and indivisible', at [9]. See also Lord Hope's speech at [71]–[72]; Lord Justice Pill's judgment in the Court of Appeal, [2004] EWCA Civ. 527 at [45]–[46]; Woolf and Jowell, *Judicial Review*, n. 2 above, 4-006. But, where the Secretary of State has been acting in the interests of the UK and is accountable to Parliament in the UK, to hold that the Secretary is acting on behalf of the Crown in the right of the government of the BOT, or strictly to separate the Crown as Queen of the UK and the Crown as Queen of the BOT, would seem 'an abject surrender of substance

contrary, appears in the preceding paragraph of his judgment – that, since the second *Factortame* decision, the 'unhappy situation' had existed that the citizen was entitled to obtain injunctive relief against the Crown or an officer of the Crown to protect his interests under Community law but could not do so in respect of his other interests which might be equally important.[97] Restricting the emergent disparity between English and Community law was an end[98] to which the distinction was the technical means. With a view to harmonising purely English law with a development in Community law, Lord Woolf revived and entrenched an English distinction between the Crown and its officers, a distinction incompatible with *Town Investments* and its modern conception in which they were united under the rubric of 'the government'.[99]

## Domestic English resources

Before *M* v. *Home Office*, Sir William Wade had long criticised the identification of the Crown with its officers as contrary to constitutional principle. Concerned with implications of Crown immunity for the rule of law, he had criticised[100] *Merricks* and the first *Factortame* case, discussed above, and argued for the interpretation of s 21 of the Crown Proceedings Act 1947 that was quoted with approval in *Herbage*[101] and eventually adopted by the House of Lords. After *M* v. *Home Office* had been considered by the Court of Appeal but not yet by the House of Lords, Wade repeated his argument and criticism: 'Of course it is convenient to speak of 'the Government' as carrying out the services

to form', as Pill LJ asserted in the Court of Appeal, at [50], and with which, in the House of Lords, Baroness Hale agreed, at [94]–[95], and Lord Bingham did not, at [19]. The analytical alternative – an indivisible Crown – would negate the historical development of formally distinct governments of BOTs (under their own constitutions) in relation to the government of the UK. Understandably, Lord Nicholls, Lord Hoffmann and Baroness Hale avoided deciding on the basis of the Crown's divisibility.

[97]  *M* v. *Home Office*, n. 45 above.
[98]  Lord Irvine later applauded this outcome as illustrative of the 'greatness of the common law' lying in its 'flexibility and ability to adapt' and as indicative of the likely spillover effect of incorporating the European Convention on Human Rights beyond its sphere of guaranteed application, 'The development of human rights in Britain under an incorporated Convention on Human Rights' [1998] *PL* 221 at 229–32, especially at 232.
[99]  *Town Investments*, n. 46 above, 381B.
[100]  H. W. R. Wade, *Administrative Law* (Oxford: Oxford University Press, 5th edn, 1982), p. 519; H. W. R. Wade, 'Injunctive relief against the Crown and ministers' (1991) 107 *LQR* 4.
[101]  n. 87 above, 883C.

of the Crown, but that does not mean that 'the Government' has any meaning in law, or that we ought to say goodbye to the vital legal distinction between the Crown and its servants upon which so much constitutional law is based.'[102] He emphasised that, according to long-standing authorities, the Crown remains a corporation sole. His traditional conception was, arguably, implicit in the distinction, a resource with which to explain how the Crown, as a corporation of only one, is apart from its officers. Although Lord Woolf still described the Crown as a corporation either sole or aggregate,[103] Wade and Forsyth modified Wade's textbook after *M* v. *Home Office* to clarify the traditional status of the Crown as a corporation sole.[104] They thus confirmed or reinstated the 'unreality' to which Dicey's analytical method was, in part, a response.[105]

In the English historical constitution, the traditional conception of the Crown continues to serve as a domestic resource with which to explain and try to analyse the distinction between the Crown and its officers, the related constitutional resource used in *M* v. *Home Office* to curtail[106] Crown immunity and help harmonise purely English law with a development in Community law. That longstanding Anglicised civilian or canonist conception survived Maitland's devastating criticism, under the influence of Continental realist theory, and remained available for recovery and service in the cause of European legal harmonisation.

---

[102] 'The Crown', n. 91 above, 1275–6.

[103] *M* v. *Home Office*, n. 45 above, 465CD. See also Woolf and Jowell, *Judicial Review*, n. 2 above, 4-004, n. 15.

[104] H. W. R. Wade and C. F. Forsyth, *Administrative Law* (Oxford: Oxford University Press, 7th edn, 1994), pp. 819–20. Their position is maintained in the ninth and most recent edition of their textbook, n. 45 above, pp. 814–15. See also H. W. R. Wade, 'The Crown, ministers and officials: legal status and liability' in Sunkin and Payne (eds.), *Nature of the Crown*, n. 2 above, pp. 23–32, especially at p. 24; Sedley, 'Sound of silence', n. 45 above, 288–9; Sir Stephen Sedley, 'The Crown in its own courts' in C. F. Forsyth and I. Hare (eds.), *The Golden Metwand and the Crooked Cord: Essays on Public Law in Honour of Sir William Wade QC* (Oxford: Oxford University Press, 1998), pp. 253–66, especially at pp. 264ff.

[105] *Law of the Constitution*, n. 1 above, pp. 7ff, especially at p. 7.

[106] On the Crown's immunity from criminal liability, see generally M. Sunkin, 'Crown immunity from criminal liability in English law' [2003] *PL* 716; M. Andenas and D. Fairgrieve, 'Reforming Crown immunity – a comparative law perspective' [2003] *PL* 730.

## English peculiarities and European influences

English and European developments have been intertwined in the evolution of the Crown. In the medieval period, English lawyers made use of the civilian or canonist notion of the corporation, *inter alia*. In our modern period, with a view to the injunction's availability in Community law, English lawyers have, in effect, extended its availability in purely English law by invoking the traditional distinction between the Crown and its officers. Even at the turn of the nineteenth century, in a period of assertive nation states and high nationalist sentiment, Continental European influence was manifest in Maitland's criticism of the traditional conception of the Crown. The extensive European influences, however, have not precluded, but have significantly coincided with, English peculiarities – with the uniqueness of the corporation sole, its gradual adaptation to English representative institutions and its revival under the impact of Community law.

In the Crown's evolution, the interactions between English and European developments have varied significantly from period to period. Medieval English jurists drew on common European resources – notions circulating in the medieval European matrix – to help answer the practical and dogmatic problems of their particular locality. They were not so much borrowing from elsewhere, or transplanting from one context to another, as drawing on common or general resources. In contrast, the House of Lords in *M* v. *Home Office* was drawing on a national domestic resource – the distinction between the Crown and its officers – to help harmonise purely English law with a development in Community law. The earlier interaction was the converse of the later: in the first, a drawing on the general to fit the particular; in the second, a drawing on the particular to fit the general. The difference in approach and in preoccupation with national domestic resources was an outcome of the long period of nationalism between the two interactions. The nationalism of that period was manifest in Blackstone's perception of the corporation's refinement 'according to the usual genius of the English nation',[107] in Dicey's insular view of alien institutions and even in Maitland's treatment of the Crown. Despite Maitland's general interest in Continental developments and the Continental source of his inspiration, his treatment repeatedly expressed, not a sense of European unity, but a preoccupation with national difference – between the

[107] *Commentaries*, n. 3 above, Vol. I, p. 457.

Continent and England impoverished or '[f]ortunate in littleness and insularity', between the perspective of a German realist and that of 'an Englishman' or common lawyer, between 'Roman invention' or canonist doctrine and 'traditional English materials' to which they were applied or, rather, upon which they were imposed.[108] Maitland's comparative references in his treatment of the Crown were consistent with his view of legal history in general:

> History involves comparison and the English lawyer who knew nothing and cared nothing for any system but his own hardly came in sight of the idea of legal history ... [B]ut ... there is nothing that sets a man thinking and writing to such good effect about a system of law and its history as an acquaintance however slight with other systems and their history.[109]

His strong sense of national difference was implicit in his description of legal history as comparative.

The fundamental shift from a more European to a more nationalist point of view, evident in Blackstone, Dicey and Maitland, and its lasting residue in our modern preoccupation with national domestic legal resources obstruct the return or restoration of the old medieval *ius commune* in the new *ius commune* of Community law.[110] But whatever the changes in viewpoint, the history of the English Crown has been strikingly open rather than insular. Its history's lack of insularity calls into question the historical comparability of the separation of powers and parliamentary sovereignty, elaborated upon in the next two chapters. If the history of the Crown is paradigmatic, the English historical constitution will always have been open to European influence even in the formation of its peculiar institutions.

## Sources of rationality and legitimacy

Sensitivity to internal change and external influence is one advantage of properly appreciating the evolutionary character of the English

---

[108] 'Introduction' in Gierke, *Political Theories of the Middle Ages*, n. 15 above, pp. x, xxff; Maitland, 'Corporation sole', *Collected Papers*, n. 2 above, Vol. III, pp. 211, 212. See also, e.g., Pollock and Maitland, *History of English Law*, n. 13 above, pp. 489, 502–3. But cf. *ibid.* p. 486.

[109] 'Why the history of English law is not written', *Collected Papers*, n. 2 above, Vol. I, pp. 488, 489.

[110] Cf. generally R. H. Helmholz, 'Continental law and common law: historical strangers or companions?' [1990] *Duke Law Journal* 1207.

constitution. Another is avoiding the constitutional implications of the Diceyan analytical alternative, particularly when illuminated in its application to the Crown. That alternative is to distinguish the historical from the legal, relegate the historical and accordingly try to analyse the constitution principally as a static and formal scheme of institutions, rules and principles, as did Dicey.[111] If so analysed, the Crown and its vast powers do illustrate 'unreality' and 'hopeless confusion'.[112] The constitution's institutional centre is then a confused notion of the Crown, an 'unpersoned person',[113] a corporation sole from one perspective, perhaps aggregate from another, somehow separate from its officers, a King who can do no wrong. That notion is reason to suspect, at best, a constitution significantly incoherent in form and content and, at worst, an 'anaesthetizing fantasy constitution',[114] or a form of government from which a real constitution is absent and in which reason has been corrupted.[115] The Diceyan analytical alternative, ahistorical in its preoccupation does, however, neglect a significant source of common sense and rationality – a common appreciation of sensible development and a rationality of historical process rather than substantive outcome or supposed system. If the constitution is to reflect whatever rationality or common sense be evident, historical modes of adapting to a changing political and administrative context should again be viewed as central to it in constitutional analysis or theory.

A historical or dynamic view of the constitution and of the Crown within it has a long history in the common law, and traces[116] survived even in the work of the late Sir William Wade, who inherited[117] Dicey's analytical approach. In response to contemporary criticism of the Crown, Wade appealed to history:

> I agree with his [Loughlin's] broad theme, that our law has failed to produce a coherent theory of the State, and that the situation has been made more tolerable only by a highly artificial distinction between the Crown and its servants. But I do not think that the House of Lords [in M

---

[111] *Law of the Constitution*, n. 1 above, pp. vii, 15ff. See ch. 2 above, pp. 7ff.

[112] Dicey, *Law of the Constitution*, n. 1 above, p. 7.

[113] Allott, 'Theory of the British constitution', n. 2 above, pp. 191–2.

[114] *Ibid.* especially at pp. 187, 198.

[115] Paine, *Rights of Man*, n. 54 above, especially at pp. 175, 182, 191.

[116] See also, e.g., the speeches of Lord Diplock and Lord Simon in *Town Investments*, n. 46 above, 380F–381A, 397E–398F.

[117] See generally M. Loughlin, *Public Law and Political Theory* (Oxford: Oxford University Press, 1992), pp. 184ff.

v. *Home Office*] ought to have produced some new theory based on the *dicta* in the *Town Investments* case. Those maverick remarks are irreconcilable with fundamental constitutional law, and to unsettle that might well be disastrous. Personally *I prefer to uphold the rules legitimated by history*, unsatisfying as they may be to political theorists. The immunity of the Crown and the non-immunity of its servants represent a compromise, which is well suited to a state, which is both a monarchy and a democracy.[118]

Wade did not, however, and could not by way of a Diceyan analytical approach, which distinguishes the legal and relegates the historical, have explained why the incoherence and the compromise are tolerable or how they can be legitimated by history.

Only from a historical view of the constitution focused on its modes or mechanisms of change or formation can the issue of its legitimation by history be addressed. The history of the Crown has illustrated a gradual, evolutionary, mode of formation *par excellence*. The incremental and minimal adaptation of the familiar monarchical form through fiction to representative political institutions has illustrated a mode of formation that accommodates change or innovation but is reassuring in the formal continuity it entails. Its justification is pragmatic. It involves a conservation of forms for the sake of appearance and gradual progress, a partial and apparent retention of the old while the new is established, tested and refined or further developed.

The Crown's evolutionary mode of formation shares features with the customary and economical modes elaborated upon in the next two chapters. Its assimilation of representative political institutions and its formal conservation as a corporation sole have illustrated the gradualism and respect for continuity, which, it will be suggested in Chapter Four, have been evident in the customary practices through which the separation of powers has generally evolved. Its minimising of change or the appearance of change has also illustrated a certain economy, as have recent adaptations to the doctrine of parliamentary sovereignty, discussed in Chapter Five.

Viewed historically, the Crown is not a central constitutional anomaly – a confusing fiction within a fiction – but a lasting, unmistakeable, outcome and striking institutional illustration of constitutional change and continuity, a modern manifestation of a constitution that has

---

[118] Wade, 'Crown, ministers and officials' in Sunkin and Payne (eds.), *Nature of the Crown*, n. 2 above, pp. 23–32 at pp. 31–2 (my emphasis).

provided for its own reformation according to changing circumstances, however they have varied in the intensity of conflict or the attainment of partial consensus. A view of a historical constitution, with change and continuity once more at its centre, allows us to resolve the paradox of the Crown's analytical centrality and obscurity. In its incoherence or ambivalence and its institutional compromise – an insinuation[119] of 'a Republic . . . beneath the folds of a Monarchy' – the Crown derives what legitimacy it retains from the constitutional means by which it has been formed and its formation has come to be viewed historically.

The Crown's incoherence and the compromise it reflects continue to invite disagreement and controversy.[120] The Crown remains today the ambivalent outcome of institutional change and conservation – a historical means to democracy and a limited but lasting realm of immunity, an English equivalent of the state and its incomplete alternative. It remains both a source – real and symbolic – for the unity and loyalty of an independent civil service and a guise for executive plurality and increasing fragmentation, in short, deserving of due recognition but vulnerable to devastating Republican and other criticism. Its current resilience and level of stability despite the contrasting ways in which it is viewed demonstrate the constitutional significance – a continuing power to legitimate – of the historical constitution's evolutionary mode of institutional development.

[119] Bagehot, *English Constitution*, n. 55 above, p. 48.

[120] For a variety of contemporary viewpoints, see F. Mount, *The British Constitution Now* (London: Mandarin, 1993), pp. 102–7; C. Vincenzi, *Crown Powers, Subjects and Citizens* (London: Pinter, 1998), especially at p. 316; T. Daintith and A. C. Page, *The Executive in the Constitution: Structure, Autonomy, and Internal Control* (Oxford: Oxford University Press, 1999), pp. 12–13, 26–8; Loughlin, 'State, Crown and law' in Sunkin and Payne (eds.), *Nature of the Crown*, n. 2 above, pp. 33–76; P. P. Craig, 'The European Community, the Crown and the state' in Sunkin and Payne (eds.), *Nature of the Crown*, n. 2 above, pp. 315–36; A. Tomkins, *Our Republican Constitution* (Oxford: Hart Publishing, 2005), pp. 139–40. See also related debates about retaining or adapting the institution of monarchy: R. Brazier, 'A British republic' [2002] *CLJ* 351; R. Brazier, 'The Monarchy' in V. Bogdanor (ed.), *The British Constitution in the Twentieth Century* (Oxford: Oxford University Press, 2003), pp. 69–95; V. Bogdanor, 'Conclusion' *ibid.* pp. 689–720 at pp. 703–5; I. Ward, *The English Constitution: Myths and Realities* (Oxford: Hart Publishing, 2004), especially at pp. 176ff.

# 4

## The separation of powers as a customary practice

In Chapter Three, I suggested that the Crown, however confused from an analytical perspective, proved capacious and accommodated the reality of representative institutions as they evolved in the English historical constitution. The Crown's singularity and the unity it symbolised did not preclude the development of various democratic institutions and powers and even talk of their separation on both sides of the Channel. In this chapter, I will elaborate on the doctrine of the separation of powers to illustrate both further interactions between the English common law and Continental European law and the peculiar significance of the English historical constitution's customary mode of formation or development.

Historians have had reason to describe a unity in European constitutional development absent from the history of European private law. For example, in *An Historical Introduction to Western Constitutional Law*, Raoul van Caenegem emphasises the lack of a difference between constitutional evolution in England and that on the Continent comparable to the difference he describes in his earlier work on the history of private law:

> The English constitutional evolution was not essentially distinct from that of the Continent. There were differences in timing and accent, but the main ingredients such as monarchy, feudalism, absolutism, parliaments, constitutions, bureaucratization and the welfare state were common. The absence from the English common law of the *Corpus Iuris Civilis*, which was so vital a factor in the private field, was unimportant for constitutional development.[1]

This chapter was developed from 'The separation of powers: constitutional principle or customary practice?' For 'Constitutions and Customs', Colloquium, Koninklijke Vlaamse Academie van België voor Wetenschappen en Kunsten, Brussels, Belgium, 4 December 1998, H. van Goethem (ed.), *Gewoonte en Recht* (Brussels: VWK, 2002), Iuris Scripta Historica XVI, pp. 89–106.
[1] Cambridge: Cambridge University Press, 1995, p. 7. See R. C. van Caenegem, *The Birth of the English Common Law* (Cambridge: Cambridge University Press, 2nd edn, 1988), ch. 4; R. C. van Caenegem, *Judges, Legislators and Professors* (Cambridge: Cambridge

With reference to fundamental rights and the separation of powers *inter alia*, other historians, such as Helmut Coing and Franz Wieacker, have made similar observations.[2] A certain unity is also evident in the development of the doctrine of the separation of powers and is well illustrated even in its contrasting manifestations in England and France. The development of the separation of powers in the proximate French and English jurisdictions is a history of clear and significant constitutional interaction across the divide between Continental European law and the English common law. On the one hand, Montesquieu's theory of separate powers in *Spirit of the Laws*,[3] if not derived from, was certainly developed in view of, the English constitution.[4] On the other hand, Blackstone in England 'domesticated' Montesquieu's theory by emphasising the centrality of judicial independence in his elaboration of separate powers.[5]

The separation of powers common to Continental and English constitutional history is also a manifestation of various differences that, I will suggest, call into question the extent of what is common and what is really different. First, it evolved in England to bear a meaning quite different from that of the radical separation of powers initiated on the Continent in France. Secondly, it did not culminate in English judicial institutions comparable to the separate Continental administrative jurisdictions. Thirdly, it evolved into a kind of standard in England different from that of the French equivalent. The first two differences are dealt

---

University Press, 1987), ch. 3; R. C. van Caenegem, *An Historical Introduction to Private Law* (Cambridge: Cambridge University Press, 1992), pp. 159–65.

[2] H. Coing, 'European common law: historical foundations' in M. Cappelletti (ed.), *New Perspectives for a Common Law of Europe* (Leyden: Sijthoff, 1978), pp. 31–44 at pp. 34–5; F. Wieacker, 'Foundations of European legal culture' (1990) 38 *American Journal of Comparative Law* 1, especially at 5–7, 20–7. See also C. O. Lenz, 'Gemeinsame Grundlagen und Grundwerte des Rechts der Europäischen Gemeinschaften' (1988) 21 *Zeitschrift für Rechtspolitik* 449 at 450–1.

[3] Montesquieu, *The Spirit of the Laws*, A. M. Cohler, B. C. Miller and H. S. Stone (ed. and tr.) (Cambridge: Cambridge University Press, 1989), Bk. 11, ch. 6.

[4] See R. Shackleton, *Montesquieu: A Critical Biography* (Oxford: Oxford University Press, 1961), pp. 298–301; M. J. C. Vile, *Constitutionalism and the Separation of Powers* (Indianapolis: Liberty Fund, 2nd edn, 1998), pp. 91–3; J. W. F. Allison, *A Continental Distinction in the Common Law: A Historical and Comparative Perspective on English Public Law* (Oxford: Oxford University Press, rev. pbk edn, 2000), pp. 16–18.

[5] Vile, *Separation of Powers*, n. 4 above, pp. 111–15; W. Blackstone, *Commentaries on the Laws of England*, 4 vols. (Chicago: The University of Chicago Press, Facsimile of 1st edn of 1765–1769, 1979), Vol. I, pp. 257–60. For a further recent interaction, see the effect of the incorporation of the right to a determination by an independent and impartial tribunal under Art. 6 of the European Convention on Human Rights on the judicial reform initiatives that culminated in the Constitutional Reform Act 2005, pp. 94ff below.

with elsewhere.[6] The third I will attempt to clarify by arguing that the modern English separation of powers evolved as a customary historical constitutional practice and was not established through legislation, doctrine and case law as a declared constitutional principle remotely similar to the French. By *declared constitutional principle*, I mean a standard that is to be observed consistently as a requirement of justice or general political morality that has been authoritatively declared to establish, organise or rule governmental bodies. In contrast, by *customary historical constitutional practice*, I mean a course of conduct relating to government that is followed in variable degrees of consistency, not because it conforms to a standard that has been declared authoritatively, but because it has long been commonly followed, presumably for good reason, and, in being followed, is adapted and continues to evolve.

In this chapter, I will first briefly recall, for the purpose of comparison, the kind of standard established after the Revolution as the French separation of powers. I will then suggest that the statements of constitutional principle by Locke and Blackstone did not identify in English constitutional legislation or themselves establish a standard that approximated to it. I will argue that, while the separation of powers did not survive in England, as a declared constitutional principle, the barrage of doctrinal criticism directed at Montesquieu, Locke and Blackstone, it did endure as a customary practice to be confirmed in case law, still open to adaptation and recently brought to the fore in the developing judicial doctrine of deference and in the Constitutional Reform Act 2005. At issue is the extent to which the separation of powers has both crossed European constitutional boundaries and continues to illustrate the peculiar significance of a customary mode of formation in the English historical constitution.

## The French standard

After the Revolution, Montesquieu's famous declaration that there is no 'liberty if the power of judging is not separate from legislative power and from executive power'[7] was the theoretical inspiration for a range of constitutional enactments. Article 16 of the Declaration of the Rights of

---

[6] See Allison, *Continental Distinction in the Common Law*, n. 4 above, ch. 7; J. W. F. Allison, 'Cultural divergence, the separation of powers and the public-private divide' (1997) 9 *European Review of Public Law* 305.

[7] *Spirit of the Laws*, n. 3 above, Bk. 11, ch. 6, p. 157.

Man 1789 declared that a separation of powers is indispensable for constitutional government. Decisively in 1790, the Constituent Assembly proclaimed the sweeping prohibition that was repeated in the Constitutions of 1791 and 1799 and reinforced with provisions in the Penal Code:

> Judicial functions are distinct and will always remain separate from administrative functions. It shall be a criminal offence for judges of the ordinary courts to interfere in any manner whatsoever with the operation of the administration, nor shall they call administrators to account before them in respect of the exercise of their official functions.[8]

A constitutional principle declared in more authoritative and general terms is difficult to imagine.

In the nineteenth century, the *Conseil d'Etat's* developing administrative jurisdiction confirmed, rather than undermined, the principle's status. It was required precisely because the principle, as authoritatively declared, prohibited interference by the ordinary courts. The range of legislative measures that judicialised the *Conseil d'Etat's* administrative jurisdiction then institutionalised through authoritative enactment a principle implied by or related to Montesquieu's theory of separate powers – the principle of judicial independence. A decree of 1806 created the judicial section (the *Commission du Contentieux*, called the *Section du Contentieux* after 1849) to stand alongside the advisory sections of the *Conseil*.[9] Then, in 1831, an ordinance excluded members associated with the active administration from judicial deliberations, and established the office of *Commissaire du Gouvernement*, an office that was to acquire the role of representing the public interest independent of hierarchical governmental control.[10] In 1849, another ordinance further detached the judicial section from the rest of the *Conseil* by dispensing with the requirement that decisions of the judicial section be formally approved by the *Conseil's* General Assembly.[11] Finally, a law of 24 May 1872 formally enacted a principle of judicial independence by dispensing with decisions in the form of advice to the Head of State and

---

[8] Law of 16–24 August 1790, Title II, Art. 13 (tr. L. N. Brown and J. S. Bell) *French Administrative Law* (Oxford: Oxford University Press, 4th edn, 1993), p. 123. See also *ibid.* Art. 10; Constitution of 1791, Art. 203; Constitution of 1799, Art. 75; Penal Code of 1810, Art. 127.

[9] Decree of 11 June 1806, Art. 24.    [10] Ordinance of 12 March 1831.

[11] Ordinance of 26 May 1849.

by empowering the *Conseil* to pronounce judgments in the name of the French people.[12]

The many legislative provisions, although underpinning principles of judicial independence and the separation of powers, did not preclude the significance of customary practice, whether to their enactment, interpretation or implementation.[13] Three examples should suffice. First, the office of *Commissaire du Gouvernement* acquired an independent role in practice, but seems to have been created by ordinance originally to limit the independence of the *Conseil d'Etat's* judicial section by representing the government's interest in its judicial proceedings. Secondly, the law of 24 May 1872 enacted and confirmed symbolically an independent power of judgment that the *Conseil* had already assumed in general practice but had not been formally institutionalised in principle. Thirdly, it was the *Conseil's* 1889 judicial decision in *Cadot*,[14] not legislation, that dispensed with the requirement that the individual aggrieved by administrative action must first complain to the appropriate minister, who, in appearance at least, had been a judge in his own cause. But, although customary practice was clearly significant in these examples, the separation of powers and judicial independence, formally enacted and repeatedly buttressed by legislation, were unquestionably established as constitutional principles principally through authoritative declaration.[15]

## Early English advocacy

In English doctrine, the principal advocates of separate powers were John Locke and William Blackstone: Locke, towards the end of the seventeenth-century revolutionary struggles between King and Parliament; Blackstone, when the revolutionary settlement was already established. In his *Two Treatises of Government*, Locke distinguished a 'Legislative Power' (the power of making laws and the supreme power) from an 'Executive Power' (the power of executing laws) and from a 'Federative Power' (concerned with security and foreign relations). In a famous passage, he reasoned that:

---

[12] Law of 24 May 1872, Art. 9. See generally R. Drago, 'La Loi du 24 Mai 1872' (1972) 25 EDCE 13; V. Wright, 'La réorganisation du Conseil d'Etat en 1872' (1972) 25 EDCE 21.

[13] See generally M. Krygier, 'The traditionality of statutes' (1988) 1 *Ratio Juris* 20.

[14] CE, 13 December 1889.

[15] See generally Allison, *Continental Distinction in the Common Law*, n. 4 above, pp. 142–6.

[I]t may be too great a temptation to human frailty apt to grasp at Power, for the same Persons who have the Power of making Laws, to have also in their hands the power to execute them, whereby they may exempt themselves from Obedience to the Laws they make, and suit the Law, both in its making and execution, to their own private advantage, and thereby come to have a distinct interest from the rest of the Community, contrary to the end of Society and Government.[16]

A separation of powers was thus a prominent feature of the 'well order'd Commonwealths' described by Locke.[17]

In England, Locke was not the first to advocate some sort of separation of powers.[18] Writers had long been concerned with the old theory of mixed government with its focus on the respective roles of King, Lords and Commons. Under its enduring influence, Locke, like other English writers of the seventeenth century, did not identify an independent judicial power in his analytical discussion of separate powers. But, elsewhere in his *Two Treatises of Government*, he repeatedly stressed the importance of 'indifferent judges'. Their absence, he described as a principal defect of the 'State of Nature'; their presence, as an object or 'End of Political Society and Government':

In the State of Nature there wants *a known and indifferent Judge*, with Authority to determine all differences according to the established Law. For every one in that state being both Judge and Executioner of the Law of Nature, Men being partial to themselves, Passion and Revenge is very apt to carry them too far, and with too much heat, in their own Cases.[19]

At about the time of the Glorious Revolution, Locke thus commended to the emerging settlement between Crown and Parliament[20] both a separation of powers and judicial independence as principles of good government.

After Montesquieu's *Spirit of the Laws* and constitutional changes to judicial tenure in particular, Blackstone went further than could Locke

---

[16] J. Locke, *Two Treatises of Government*, P. Laslett (ed.) (Cambridge: Cambridge University Press, 1988), Second Treatise, chs. 12 and 13, paras. 143–8, especially at para. 143.

[17] *Ibid.* See generally Vile, *Separation of Powers*, n. 4 above, 63–74.

[18] See, e.g., J. Harrington, *Oceana*, J. Toland (ed.) (Dublin: R. Reilly, J. Smith and W. Bruce, 1737). See generally Vile, *Separation of Powers*, n. 4 above, pp. 31–63.

[19] *Two Treatises of Government*, n. 16 above, Second Treatise, para. 125. See also *ibid.* paras. 13, 90, 91, 131.

[20] See generally P. Laslett, '"Two Treatises of Government" and the Revolution of 1688' in his 'Introduction', Locke, *Two Treatises of Government*, n. 16 above, pp. 45–66.

to describe judicial independence and a separate judicial power as established features of the English constitution:

> In this distinct and separate existence of the judicial power, in a peculiar body of men, nominated indeed, but not removeable at pleasure, by the crown, consists one main preservative of the public liberty; which cannot subsist long in any state, unless the administration of common justice be in some degree separated both from the legislative and also from the executive power.[21]

In support, Blackstone cited three statutes that may usefully be compared with the various French enactments of constitutional principle.

### Historic legislation on judicial power and judicial tenure

The earliest statute invoked by Blackstone was that which abolished the Court of the Star Chamber in 1641.[22] Blackstone claimed that by this statute 'effectual care is taken to remove all judicial power out of the hands of the king's privy council; who, as then was evident from recent instances, might soon be inclined to pronounce that for law, which was most agreeable to the prince or his officers'.[23] As an enactment of constitutional principle this statute is open to question. It did abolish a prerogative court but the common law courts and the Court of Chancery were also prerogative in the sense that they too were originally derived from the *Curia Regis* through the exercise of the royal prerogative of justice confirmed in the coronation oath. Blackstone himself stressed that a 'consequence of this prerogative is the legal *ubiquity* of the king. His Majesty, in the eye of the law, is always present in all his courts, though he cannot personally distribute justice'.[24] Furthermore, insofar as is known from the surviving records, the Star Chamber had long been a useful and successful court, which the Long Parliament seems initially to have intended to reform rather than abolish.[25] In its final years, it was used for the trial of high-profile political cases, often

---

[21] *Commentaries*, n. 5 above, Vol. I, pp. 257–60, especially at p. 259.
[22] Stat. 16 Car. I, c. 10.    [23] *Commentaries*, n. 5 above, Vol. I, p. 260.    [24] *Ibid.*
[25] S. B. Chrimes, 'Introductory essay' in W. S. Holdsworth, *A History of English Law*, Vol. I, A. L. Goodhart and H. G. Hanbury (eds.) (London: Methuen, 7th edn, 1956), pp. 1–77, especially at pp. 57–60; T. G. Barnes, 'Star Chamber mythology' (1961) 5 *American Journal of Comparative Law* 1; T. G. Barnes, 'Star Chamber litigants and their counsel 1596–1641' in J. H. Baker (ed.), *Legal Records and the Historian* (London: Royal Historical Society, 1978), pp. 7–28.

involving ecclesiastical officials, but the King's Bench was also used by the Stuart monarchs for their own purposes and Chancery too was the object of criticism.[26]

The reasons for abolition stated in the statute are the existence of 'proper Remedy and Redress' in the common law courts, the Star Chamber's burdensome procedures which had been found to be 'the Means to introduce an arbitrary Power and Government', its interference in civil cases and the resulting uncertainty 'concerning Men's Rights and Estates'.[27] A statement of general principle is lacking. Indeed, abolition was motivated by the professional rivalry of common lawyers, exasperation with procedural problems and antagonism towards the church hierarchy rather than by some notion of judicial independence or separate powers.[28] The statute, no doubt, later acquired a symbolic quality, reflected in Blackstone, but through subsequent practice, not its own import or intended effect.

Blackstone cited two further statutes. The first was the Act of Settlement 1701, which required that judges in the superior courts hold judicial commissions *quamdiu se bene gesserint*, rather than at the King's pleasure, that they be removed only upon an address of both Houses of Parliament to the King and that their salaries be 'ascertained and established'.[29] Judicial tenure, however, still ended with the King's death, which served as an opportunity for effective dismissal through a refusal to renew existing commissions.[30] The second statute was therefore enacted in 1760, shortly before Blackstone wrote his *Commentaries*, to render the first statute more effective. It provided for the continuance of commissions and salaries notwithstanding the demise of the King. Whereas the first statute took the form of a technical provision without

---

[26] See, e.g., H. E. Bell, *An Introduction to the History and Records of the Court of Wards and Liveries* (Cambridge: Cambridge University Press, 1953), pp. 135, 136. See J. H. Baker, *An Introduction to English Legal History* (London: Butterworths LexisNexis, 4th edn, 2002), pp. 117ff, 167f, 213f.

[27] Stat. 16 Car. I, c. 10.

[28] Chrimes, 'Introductory essay', n. 25 above, pp. 59–60; Barnes, 'Star Chamber litigants', n. 25 above, especially at 28; J. H. Baker, 'The conciliar courts' in 'Introduction', *The Reports of Sir John Spelman, Vol. II*, J. H. Baker (ed.) (London: Selden Society, Vol. 94, 1978), pp. 70–4, especially at p. 74. See generally Bell, *History of the Court of Wards*, n. 26 above, pp. 133ff; L. M. Hill, 'Introduction' in J. Caesar, *The Ancient State Authoritie, and Proceedings of the Court of Requests*, L. M. Hill (ed.) (Cambridge: Cambridge University Press, 1975), pp. xli–xliii.

[29] Stat. 12 & 13 Gul. III, c. 2.

[30] See D. A. Rubini, 'The precarious independence of the judiciary, 1688–1701' (1967) 83 LQR 343.

statement of principle, the second was accompanied by a declaration attributed to the King and quoted by Blackstone:

> Your Majesty has been graciously pleased to declare from the Throne to both Houses of Parliament that You look upon the Independency and Uprightness of Judges as essential to the impartial Administration of Justice, as one of the best Securities to the Rights and Liberties of Your loving Subjects, and as most conducive to the Honour of your Crown.[31]

The passing and implementation of the Act of Settlement was a considerable achievement, a landmark in a continuing struggle. Together with the second statute, it provided for dismissal only through the formal collaboration of both Lords and Commons, which were not anticipated easily to concur. Nonetheless, dismissal was still a possibility for whatever might be adjudged to be misbehaviour in an address by both Houses. In 1830, Sir Jonah Barrington, a judge of the High Court of Admiralty in Ireland, was dismissed after he had been found guilty of embezzlement. That he is the only judge to have been dismissed under the procedure provided by the Act of Settlement must be attributed, in part, to the sufficiency of lesser extra-statutory measures,[32] such as private or public rebuke, and, in part, to customary practice, to an evolving tradition of respect for judicial independence, rather than simply to statutory provisions. More revealing than what the statutes did provide was what they did not.[33] They did not deal with those lesser measures, which could also endanger judicial independence. They did not apply to the majority of judges, who were not in the senior courts, and they did not alter the crucial process of initial appointment or promotion by the Crown. They did not preclude the possibility of Crown patronage in that process. Although their provisions have, in substance, remained on the statute-book to this day[34] and have only recently been substantially complemented,[35] these statutes,

---

[31] Stat. 1 Geo. III, c. 23.

[32] See, e.g., D. Woodhouse, *The Office of Lord Chancellor* (Oxford: Hart Publishing, 2001), pp. 29ff.

[33] See generally D. Lemmings, 'The independence of the judiciary in eighteenth-century England' in P. Birks (ed.), *The Life of the Law: Proceedings of the Tenth British Legal History Conference Oxford 1991* (London: Hambledon Press, 1993), pp. 125–49; Baker, *Introduction to English Legal History*, n. 26 above, pp. 166–9.

[34] Supreme Court Act 1981 (amended to become the Senior Courts Act 1981 when the amending provisions of the Constitutional Reform 2005 have come into force), ss 11, 12; Constitutional Reform Act 2005, ss 33, 34, 109.

[35] On the scope and exercise of disciplinary powers over senior and other judges, see Constitutional Reform Act 2005, ss 108ff, Schedule 14.

of limited scope and justified only by reference to the King's declaration, did not approximate to the French enactments of constitutional principle, such as the Law of 16–24 August 1790. What symbolic significance they did acquire was not effected by their own provisions, but must have emerged in doctrine or evolved in practice.

## Doctrinal scepticism

In England, constitutional doctrine did not produce the principle lacking in legislation. The doctrinal claims to a constitutional principle by Locke, Montesquieu and Blackstone did not go unchallenged. In fact, few doctrines have been subject to more damning and repeated criticism than that to which the separation of powers has been subject, usually for analytical reasons.

In the early nineteenth century, Jeremy Bentham began the onslaught. Although not quite prepared 'absolutely to exclude' the terms 'legislative power', 'executive power' and 'judicial power', he stressed their vagueness, obscurity and inaccuracy in 'representing the true elements of political powers'.[36] A few decades later, Walter Bagehot went further in *The English Constitution*. He explicitly contradicted the doctrine of Montesquieu 'domesticated'[37] by Blackstone. He described 'the efficient secret of the English Constitution' as 'the nearly complete fusion of the executive and legislative powers', a union effected through the Cabinet as the '(greatest) committee of the legislative body selected to be the executive body'.[38]

Dicey, pre-eminent amongst the lawyers who came to dominate discussion of the English constitution towards the end of the nineteenth century, was generally content to ignore the separation of powers in his analysis of the law of the constitution. His chapter on French administrative law referred to their 'so-called "separation of powers"' as a 'dogma' based on a 'double misconception' – Montesquieu's misunderstanding of the English constitution and the French revolutionaries' misunderstanding or misapplication of Montesquieu's doctrine.[39] In his unpublished lectures on the comparative study of constitutions, he

---

[36] J. Bentham, *Works*, J. Bowring (ed.), 11 vols. (London: Simpkin, Marshall, & Co., 1843), Vol. III, ch. 21. See generally Vile, *Separation of Powers*, n. 4 above, pp. 123ff.

[37] Vile, *Separation of Powers*, n. 4 above, pp. 111–15.

[38] W. Bagehot, *The English Constitution*, M. Taylor (ed.) (Oxford: Oxford University Press, 2001), chs. 1 and 6, especially at p. 11.

[39] A. V. Dicey, *An Introduction to the Study of the Law of the Constitution* (London: Macmillan, 10th edn, 1959), ch. 12, especially at pp. 337–8. See also *ibid.* p. 227.

noted that the separation of powers was 'not really carried out under the English constitution, though more nearly in Montesquieu's time than in any other'.[40]

Doctrinal criticism continued into the twentieth century and was sustained. In his *History of English Law*, William Holdsworth explained Montesquieu's doctrine as a misunderstanding of the English constitution. He showed comprehensively how the separation between Crown, Parliament and the courts was not complete or clear-cut in Montesquieu's day.[41] Holdsworth drew attention, *inter alia*, to the Crown's legislative role, the legislative and judicial functions of the House of Lords, the nature of the Lord Chancellor as judge and government minister and the enormous influence exercised by the Cabinet over Parliament. He described Montesquieu's doctrine as an exaggeration and attributed it to neglect of 'the historical causes which had led to the division of the powers of the English state'.[42] He argued that Montesquieu had consequently failed to notice that, because the English institutions originated in the Middle Ages and developed gradually along their own lines to meet changing needs, the separation between them was not likely to be clear-cut and logical. In short, he described the rough separation that did exist as an outcome of historical evolution pre-dating the statements or misstatements of principle. From a historical constitutional perspective, a strict analytical doctrine of the separation of powers clearly did not correlate with history in the historical constitution.

In his study of the British constitution, first published in 1928, William Robson reached a more damning conclusion than did Holdsworth, who had recognised some validity to Montesquieu's doctrine. With reference to other institutions such as the coroner's inquest into death and the justice of the peace, fulfilling both administrative and judicial functions, Robson stressed the traditional mixing of functions as a matter of convenience and practicability. He exposed what he called the 'legendary separation of powers', 'that antique and rickety

---

[40] G. J. Hand, 'A. V. Dicey's unpublished materials on the comparative study of constitutions' in G. J. Hand and J. McBride (eds.), *Droit sans Frontieres: Essays in Honour of L. Neville Brown* (Birmingham: Holdsworth Club, 1993), pp. 77–93 at p. 89. The lectures, with the title 'Comparative study of constitutions' probably preferred by Dicey, are in the Codrington Library, All Souls College, Oxford, MS 323.

[41] W. S. Holdsworth, *A History of English Law*, Vol. X (London: Methuen, 1938), pp. 713–24, especially at p. 718.

[42] *Ibid.* p. 718.

chariot . . ., so long the favourite vehicle of writers on political science and constitutional law for the conveyance of fallacious ideas'.[43]

The most sustained analytical attack on the separation of powers was that of Geoffrey Marshall in 1971. He described the phrase 'separation of powers' as 'one of the most confusing in the vocabulary of political and constitutional thought'.[44] He identified within it a 'cluster of overlapping ideas', principally the *'legal incompatibility'* of holding certain offices simultaneously, *'isolation, immunity, or independence'* from external interference and the *'checking or balancing* of one branch of government by the action of another'.[45] Marshall described how this equivocal doctrine could therefore be used for diverse purposes, for example, to support or oppose judicial review of legislation – to support it as a check and to oppose it as an interference. He concluded that 'the principle [of the separation of powers] is infected with so much imprecision and inconsistency that it may be counted little more than a jumbled portmanteau of arguments for policies which ought to be supported or rejected on other grounds'.[46]

Furthermore, the institutions combining state functions, such as the Cabinet and the office of Lord Chancellor, continued to compromise, or appear to compromise, the principle. In the late 1980s, Anthony Bradley had reason to claim that 'all well-catechised lawyers know [the office of Lord Chancellor as both government minister and head of the judiciary] to be living proof that the separation of powers does not exist in Britain and that we are better off without it'.[47] The doctrinal scepticism that began with Bentham in the nineteenth century cannot be dismissed as that of a radical minority. It expressed recognition of the incompatibility between what had previously and elsewhere been offered as a key feature in constitutional analysis and the pragmatic evolution of governing institutions in the English historical constitution. Until the separation of powers was invoked by the government to justify the initiatives that

---

[43] W. A. Robson, *Justice and Administrative Law: A Study of the British Constitution* (London, Greenwood Press, 3rd edn, 1951), pp. 4–22, especially at p. 16. See also the reservations of W. I. Jennings, *The Law and the Constitution* (London: University of London Press, 5th edn, 1959), pp. 7–28, 280–304.

[44] G. Marshall, *Constitutional Theory* (Oxford: Oxford University Press, 1971), ch. 5, especially at p. 97.

[45] *Ibid.* p. 100.    [46] *Ibid.* p. 124.

[47] 'Constitutional change and the Lord Chancellor' [1988] *PL* 165 at 165.

culminated in the Constitutional Reform Act 2005, only occasionally was the separation of powers as such advocated with vigour.[48]

## Doctrinal inconsistency

Prevailing doctrinal scepticism did not preclude recognition of judicial independence or a limited, implicit or begrudging acceptance of some sort of separation of powers, even by its severest critics, such as Bentham, Dicey and Robson. Bentham was scornful of the separation of powers as understood by Locke and Blackstone but did distinguish the judicial from the legislative power by reference to the adversarial nature of the procedures for its exercise:

> Before a judge can issue his orders as a judge, a concurrence of circum-stances is requisite, which is not requisite for legalizing the acts of the legislature: –
>
> 1. It is necessary that an interested party should come and require the judge to issue the order in question. Here there is an individual to whom belongs the initiative, the right of putting into activity the judicial power.
> 2. It is necessary that the parties to whom the orders of the judge may prove prejudicial should have the power of opposing them. Here there are other individuals who have a species of negative power – power of stopping the acts of the judicial power.
> 3. It is necessary that it should have proof produced of some particular fact upon which the complaint is founded and that the adverse party be permitted to furnish proof to the contrary.[49]

In this way, Bentham emphasised a procedural manifestation of judicial independence – the judge's acting only as an umpire for a contest primarily between adversaries.

Dicey was disparaging about the French separation of powers, but, implicit in his analysis of the rule of law and his rejection of *droit*

---

[48] See C. R. Munro, 'The separation of powers: not such a myth' [1981] *PL* 19; T. R. S. Allan, *Law, Liberty, and Justice: The Legal Foundations of British Constitutionalism* (Oxford: Oxford University Press, 1993), ch. 3; T. R. S. Allan, *Constitutional Justice: A Liberal Theory of the Rule of Law* (Oxford: Oxford University Press, 2001), chs. 1, 2, pp. 244ff; E. Barendt, 'Separation of powers and constitutional government' [1995] *PL* 599; E. Barendt, *An Introduction to Constitutional Law* (Oxford: Oxford University Press, 1998), pp. 7, 14ff, 34ff.

[49] *Works*, n. 36 above, Vol. III, ch. 21.

*administratif* was a separation of powers involving judicial independence. In chapter Four of *Law of the Constitution*, Dicey again and
again stressed the role of the 'ordinary courts' in all disputes whether
they involve individuals or officials.[50] There and in chapter 12, Dicey
rejected *droit administratif* for England precisely because of the asso-
ciation of the *tribunaux administratifs* with the administration. To
emphasise, further, his overall argument with seventeenth-century
revolutionary fervour, Dicey drew an analogy between the abuse of the
Stuart prerogative courts and the way in which he supposed the French
administrative courts favoured or protected the administration with
which they were associated.[51] Dicey nonetheless defended the Lord
Chancellor's judicial and ministerial roles.[52]

Two other famous critics of the separation of powers, Robson and
Jennings, did not entirely abandon it. Robson doubted whether a distinguishing criterion could be found that was workable in modern
society but nonetheless appreciated the value of judicial independence
and accepted for 'practical purposes' the 'three powers . . . as designating
somewhat imperfectly the chief functions of government'.[53] Jennings
was similarly critical of the separation of powers but only as a material
concept with which to distinguish the functions of government according to their characteristics as opposed to a formal concept distinguishing
authorities according to their composition and methods.[54] He still
rejected placing functions 'under any unified control' and regarded the
need for independent judges as obvious.[55]

## Evolving judicial practice

What the critics of the separation of powers could not ignore was
judicial independence originating in 'a general independence of spirit'
that began to be assumed by judges in practice centuries before[56] Dicey

---

[50] Dicey, n. 39 above, pp. 183–205.
[51] *Ibid.* pp. 369–73, 379–81. See also, e.g., *ibid.* pp. 227f. According to Dicey, 'the action . . .
of Parliament [in England] has tended as naturally to protect the independence of the
judges, as that of other sovereigns to protect the conduct of officials', *ibid.* pp. 409–10.
[52] *Ibid.* pp. 352–3, 380–1.
[53] *Justice and Administrative Law*, n. 43 above, pp. 4–24, 383–8, especially at pp. 15, 16.
[54] *Law and the Constitution*, n. 43 above, pp. 7–28, especially at pp. 24–5.
[55] *Ibid.* p. 303. See also Marshall, *Constitutional Theory*, n. 44 above, pp. 117–23.
[56] Baker, *Introduction to English Legal History*, n. 26 above, pp. 165ff, especially at p. 166.
See also Sir John Baker, *The Oxford History of the Laws of England, Volume VI,
1483–1558* (Oxford: Oxford University Press, 2003), pp. 63–9.

wrote his *Law of the Constitution*. By way of an appeal to judicial practices since the Conquest, that independence was championed by Lord Chief Justice Coke in his confrontation with the Crown.[57] It was emphasised by Locke and was reinforced by the statutes on judicial tenure and by Blackstone. Notwithstanding the doctrinal rejection of the principle of the separation of powers in the nineteenth and twentieth centuries, at least judicial independence remained paramount, a professional priority, in judicial attitudes and practice.

The continuing centrality of judicial independence was evident in Lord Chief Justice Hewart's influential book published between the wars. In *The New Despotism*, he argued in favour of abolishing the administrative tribunals that were proliferating in the early decades of this century. He rejected an English administrative law associated with them by invoking judicial independence:

> [T]he phrase ['the separation of powers'] … is often misused. In a country like our own, where the notion of 'droit administratif' serves only by way of comparison and contrast, for the reason that the thing itself is completely opposed to the first principles of our Constitution, the 'separation of powers' refers, and can refer only, to the principle that the Judges are independent of the Executive.[58]

In short, he condemned the administrative tribunals, *inter alia*, for their lack of independent judges protected by the provisions on dismissal in the Act of Settlement 1701.

In various cases this century, the English courts recognised judicial independence and confirmed or assumed a separation of powers relating to it. The Privy Council in particular found a separation of powers to be implicit in the written Commonwealth constitutions that it was required to interpret. In the *Bribery Commissioner* v. *Ranasinghe*, it found that the framers of the 1946 Constitution of Ceylon had the implicit intention to secure 'the independence of judges' and to maintain 'the dividing line between the judiciary and the executive'.[59] In *Liyanage* v. *The Queen*, it confirmed the existence of such an intention 'to secure in the judiciary a freedom from political, legislative and executive control'.[60] As in *Ranasinghe*,[61] it inferred the intention from the Constitution's provisions for security of judicial tenure and for the appointment of judges by

---

[57] See, e.g., *Prohibitions del Roy* (1608) 12 Co. Rep. 63.
[58] London: Ernest Benn Ltd., 1929, pp. 37–45, especially at p. 41. See also *ibid.* ch. 7.
[59] [1965] AC 172 at 190D.     [60] [1967] AC 259 at 287FG.
[61] *Ranasinghe*, n. 59 above, 190E–G.

a Judicial Service Commission. The Privy Council held that parliamentary legislation designed specifically to deal with the perpetrators of a *coup d'etat* was *ultra vires* – a usurpation of judicial power by the legislature.

The written Commonwealth constitutions were distinguishable from an unwritten constitution. In *Liyanage*, Lord Pearce therefore doubted the usefulness of any analogy with the British constitution,[62] but, a decade later, in *Hinds* v. *The Queen*, Lord Diplock assumed just such an analogy in his survey of what he regarded as constitutions which follow the Westminster or English model.[63] In his majority judgment, Lord Diplock argued that all of the written Commonwealth constitutions 'were negotiated as well as drafted by persons nurtured in the tradition of that branch of the common law of England that is concerned with public law and familiar in particular with the basic concept of separation of legislative, executive and judicial power as it has been developed in the unwritten constitution of the United Kingdom'.[64] He identified them as constitutions on the Westminster model with reference to their 'provisions dealing with the method of appointment and security of tenure of the members of the judiciary'.[65] He then applied the 'basic principle of separation of legislative, executive and judicial powers that is implicit in a constitution on the Westminster model'[66] to the facts of the case. The Privy Council found provisions of the Jamaican Parliament's Gun Court Act 1974 that transferred certain judicial powers over sentences to a mainly executive Review Board to be unconstitutional. Judicial recognition of an English separation of powers was here a byproduct of a Commonwealth case.

Subsequent cases dealt explicitly with the constitution in the United Kingdom. In *Duport Steels Ltd* v. *Sirs*, the House of Lords invoked the separation of powers to rebuke the English Court of Appeal for exceeding its constitutional role by effectively making law in the context of a trade union dispute. Lord Diplock emphasised that it 'endangers continued public confidence in the political impartiality of the judiciary, which is essential to the continuance of the rule of law, if judges, under the guise of interpretation, provide their own preferred amendments to statutes'.[67] He held that 'at a time when more and more cases involve the application of legislation which gives effect to policies that are the subject of bitter public and parliamentary controversy, it cannot be

---

[62] *Liyanage*, n. 60 above, 288AB.    [63] [1977] AC 195 at 211D–213H.    [64] *Ibid.* 212AB.
[65] *Ibid.* 213AB.    [66] *Ibid.* 225G.    [67] [1980] 1 WLR 142 at 157H.

too strongly emphasised that the British constitution, though largely unwritten, is firmly based upon the separation of powers; Parliament makes the laws, the judiciary interpret them'.[68] Similarly, Lord Scarman, although recognising a creative role for judges like Lord Denning, warned that 'the constitution's separation of powers, or more accurately functions, must be observed if judicial independence is not to be put at risk'.[69] A few years earlier, Lord Reid had argued extrajudicially that 'impartiality is the first essential in any judge' and endangering it is the 'real difficulty about judges making law'.[70] In *Duport Steels*, the House of Lords expressed similar concerns.

Well before the recent constitutional reform initiatives that culminated in the Constitutional Reform Act 2005, the separation of powers had undeniably evolved into a standard, evident in the case law and clearly normative in its emphasis on judicial independence. For at least three reasons, however, it did not begin to approximate to a declared constitutional principle as in France. First, it was long regarded, at least in analytical doctrine, as precluded or compromised by the historical fusing of functions principally in the role of the Cabinet and the office of Lord Chancellor.[71] Even if a purely functional separation of powers was nonetheless tenable, where actual institutional manifestations were absent, the separation's significance and adherence to the principle of separation[72] were open to question.

Secondly, the separation of powers evolved in practice and was only subsequently recognised in specific cases. In *Hinds* and *Duport Steels*, the English courts simply identified, or assumed the existence of, the separation of powers in the constitution without reference to legislation or any judicial precedent.[73] The prominent, more recent, cases of the *Fire Brigades Union*, *Venables* and the *ProLife Alliance*, decided in the years just before or soon after the passing of the Human Rights Act 1998, are

---

[68] *Ibid.* 157B.    [69] *Ibid.* 169C.

[70] Lord Reid, 'The judge as law maker' (1972) 12 *Journal of the Society of Public Teachers of Law* 22 at 23.

[71] See the doctrinal scepticism described above, pp. 83ff.

[72] Questions were, e.g., raised in February 2001 about the independence of the Lord Chancellor's role as head of the judiciary after Lord Irvine invited lawyers to a Labour fundraising dinner. See generally Lord Woolf, 'Judicial review: the tensions between the executive and the judiciary' (1998) 114 *LQR* 579 at 582–5.

[73] *Hinds*, n. 63 above; *Duport Steels*, n. 67 above. See also *DPP* v. *Humphreys* [1977] AC 1, especially at 26D; *Attorney General* v. *BBC* [1980] 3 All ER 161, especially at 181J–182B; *R* v. *HM Treasury ex parte Smedley* [1985] 1 All ER 589, especially at 593BC.

comparable.[74] In the *Fire Brigades Union* case, the various speeches of their Lordships simply asserted or assumed the relevance of some sort of separation of powers to judicial determination of the lawfulness of executive failure to implement a statutory compensation scheme.[75] Only the dissenting speech of Lord Mustill confirmed the separation of powers with reference to the 'boundaries of the distinction between court and Parliament established in, and recognised ever since, the Bill of Rights 1689 (1 Will. & Mary, sess. 2, c. 2)'.[76] But the Bill of Rights did not enact as a principle the separation of powers implicit in its various specific provisions prohibiting, *inter alia*, the suspending of laws or the levying of money by the Crown without parliamentary authorisation. It is not cited elsewhere as authority. In *Venables*, Lord Steyn asserted that, in fixing a tariff or minimal period before the elapse of which an offender could not be released, the Home Secretary was 'carrying out, contrary to the constitutional principle of separation of powers, a classic judicial function', which should be exercised as such by the Home Secretary.[77] He referred the House to *Hinds* and *Duport Steels* for Lord Diplock's explanation of the importance of the separation of powers between the executive and the judiciary but, nonetheless, did not hold the exercise of a classic judicial function by the Home Secretary to be *per se* unlawful in principle. In the *ProLife Alliance* case, Lord Hoffmann also simply presented the separation of powers as fundamental so as to explain the substance of the judicial doctrine of deference that has rapidly developed in the wake of the margin of appreciation doctrine of European human rights jurisprudence:

> My Lords, although the word 'deference' is now very popular in describing the relationship between the judicial and the other branches of

---

[74] *R v. Secretary of State for the Home Department ex parte Fire Brigades Union* [1995] 2 WLR 464; *R v. Secretary of State for the Home Department ex parte Venables* [1998] AC 407; *R (ProLife Alliance) v. British Broadcasting Corporation* [2004] 1 AC 185; [2003] UKHL 23.

[75] Note 74 above. See the speeches of Lord Browne-Wilkinson at 472E and 474B, Lord Lloyd at 492H, Lord Nicholls at 495D, Lord Keith at 466H–467A and 468B–E and Lord Mustill at 487H–488F. See generally E. Barendt, 'Constitutional law and the criminal injuries compensation scheme' [1995] *PL* 357; T. R. S. Allan, 'Parliament, ministers, courts and prerogative: criminal injuries compensation and the dormant statute' [1995] *CLJ* 481.

[76] Note 74 above, at 488E.

[77] Note 74 above, at 526C–G. The House of Lords held on other grounds that the Home Secretary had acted unlawfully. Cf. the ruling of the European Court of Human Rights in *V and T v. United Kingdom* (2000) 30 EHRR 121 at 185–7.

government, I do not think that its overtones of servility, or perhaps gracious concession, are appropriate to describe what is happening. *In a society based upon the rule of law and the separation of powers*, it is necessary to decide which branch of government has in any particular instance the decision-making power and what the legal limits of that power are ... The courts are the independent branch of government and the legislature and executive are, directly and indirectly respectively, the elected branches of government. Independence makes the courts more suited to deciding some kinds of questions and being elected makes the legislature or executive more suited to deciding others.[78]

Related considerations have been implicit in various leading judicial statements on deference.[79] The formalistic application of the separation of powers to explain or justify deference, its relevance to deference in principle and practice, has been, however, a continuing source of controversy.[80] Nonetheless, in the case above and in other cases, the separation of powers, although unclear in meaning and application, was assumed and not derived from any authoritative declaration, let alone one comparable to the French Constituent Assembly's sweeping Law of 16–24 August 1790.

Thirdly, the English separation of powers did not approximate to a declared constitutional principle because it has been classifiable as a convention. In regard to judicial review of a draft Order in Council that still required parliamentary approval, Sir John Donaldson MR commented as follows:

I think that I should say a word about the respective roles of Parliament and the courts. Although the United Kingdom has no written constitution, *it is a constitutional convention of the highest importance* that the legislature and the judicature are separate and independent of one

---

[78] Note 74 above, at [75]–[76] (my emphasis). See generally ch. 8 below, pp. 225ff.

[79] See, e.g., Lord Hope's speech in *R* v. *Director of Public Prosecutions ex parte Kebilene* [2000] 2 AC 326 at 380–1; the dissenting judgment of Sir John Laws in *International Transport Roth GmbH* v. *Secretary of State for the Home Department* [2003] QB 728 at [83]–[87]; [2002] EWCA Civ. 158; Lord Bingham's speech in *A* v. *Secretary of State for the Home Department* [2005] 2 AC 68 at [29]; [2004] UKHL 56.

[80] Cf. e.g., M. Hunt, 'Sovereignty's blight: why contemporary public law needs the concept of "due deference"' in N. Bamforth and P. Leyland (eds.), *Public Law in a Multi-Layered Constitution* (Oxford: Hart Publishing, 2003), pp. 337–70, especially at p. 370, n. 97; J. Jowell, 'Judicial deference: servility, civility or institutional capacity?' [2003] *PL* 592; Lord Steyn, 'Deference: a tangled story' [2005] *PL* 346, especially at 350ff; T. R. S. Allan, 'Human rights and judicial review: a critique of "due deference"' [2006] *CLJ* 671.

another, subject to certain ultimate rights of Parliament over the judicature which are immaterial for present purposes. It therefore behoves the courts to be ever sensitive to the paramount need to refrain from trespassing on the province of Parliament or, so far as this can be avoided, even appearing to do so. Although it is not a matter for me, *I would hope and expect that Parliament would be similarly sensitive to the need to refrain from trespassing on the province of the courts.*[81]

That the convention is not the equivalent of a constitutional principle that has been authoritatively declared is evident in the judicial expression of only hope and expectation of sensitivity to the need for compliance.

In orthodox constitutional analysis, expounded in Dicey's *Law of the Constitution*, conventions have been classified with 'understandings, habits, or practices' and contrasted with rules of law, enforced by courts.[82] Whether 'they may usefully be distinguished from other political practices, facts, or precepts' has remained questionable, and they can nonetheless still 'be perceived as an expression and ex post facto legitimation of practices rather than principles'.[83] Even in unorthodox constitutional theory, they have still been identified principally with practice rather than with evaluations of principle. Jennings, for example, denied a substantive distinction between law and convention but adopted a test for recognising conventions that emphasises precedent, in other words, past practice. He suggested that one ask, 'first, what are the precedents; secondly, did the actors in the precedents believe that they were bound by a rule; and thirdly, is there a reason for the rule?'[84] Only the third question invites the identification of a relevant principle. In short, Jennings regarded the establishment of conventions 'connected with internal government' as the 'gradual crystallisation of practice into binding rules'.[85]

---

[81] *Smedley* case, n. 73 above, 593BC (my emphasis). See also *British Coal Corporation* v. *The King* [1935] AC 500 at 511, where the independence of the Judicial Committee of the Privy Council was described as dependent on constitutional convention; Allan, *Law, Liberty, and Justice*, n. 48 above, pp. 52, 72–3.

[82] Note 39 above, p. 24. See *Madzimbamuto* v. *Lardner-Burke* [1969] 1 AC 645; O. Hood Phillips and P. Jackson, *Constitutional and Administrative Law* (London: Sweet & Maxwell, 7th edn, 1987), pp. 113–16.

[83] C. R. Munro, 'Laws and conventions distinguished' (1975) 91 *LQR* 218, especially at 234; D. Feldman, 'None, one or several? Perspectives on the UK's constitution(s)' [2005] *CLJ* 329, especially at 334. See generally G. Marshall, 'The constitution: its theory and interpretation' in V. Bogdanor (ed.), *The British Constitution in the Twentieth Century* (Oxford, Oxford University Press, 2003), pp. 29–68 at pp. 37–42.

[84] *Law of the Constitution*, n. 43 above, ch. 3, especially at p. 136.     [85] *Ibid.* p. 134.

The distinction between law and convention has again been challenged by Trevor Allan, who has sought to elaborate on the principles implicit or reflected in both.[86] He too, however, seems to endorse the test of Jennings and describes convention as 'a reflection of accepted principle', not as constitutional principle in itself.[87] Furthermore, although he presents a separation of governmental powers or functions, at least a minimal separation, as intrinsic to the rule of law and assumed by it,[88] he accepts that its degree and precise nature must reflect tradition and experience. In his discussion of the separation, he comments on the limits posed by the prohibition of legislative adjudication: 'The difficulty of ascertaining the ambit of limits to parliamentary sovereignty on analogous grounds [i.e., in cases of legislative adjudication] is compounded by constitutional history. Parliament's gradual evolution from court to legislature makes it hard to assess the relevance of tradition in determining the nature of the modern separation of powers'.[89] Elsewhere, he emphasises 'the special symbolic importance of the common law's adherence to its own conception of judicial independence'.[90] In these passages, Allan does suggest or emphasise the significance of history, tradition, and symbolic adherence, of practice that did not evolve to become consistent, in accordance with some abstract theory, analytical doctrine or declared constitutional principle.

## The recent constitutional reforms

On 12 June 2003, in the context of a cabinet reshuffle and in the name of modernisation, the government announced 'a substantial package of reform measures'.[91] These included the creation of the Department for Constitutional Affairs, the abolition of the office of Lord Chancellor and

---

[86] *Law, Liberty, and Justice*, n. 48 above, ch. 10; Allan, *Constitutional Justice*, n. 48 above, pp. 179–87.

[87] *Law, Liberty, and Justice*, n. 48 above, p. 244 and especially at p. 254.

[88] See, e.g, *ibid.*, especially ch. 3; Allan, *Constitutional Justice*, n. 48 above, especially chs. 1, 2, pp. 244ff. Also, in arguing against a doctrine of deference, centred on the separation of powers, Allan rejects a rigid separation and the separation's practical applicability beyond the extent to which it is already implicit in the mechanisms of judicial review, 'Human rights and judicial review', n. 80 above, 677ff.

[89] *Law, Liberty, and Justice*, n. 48 above, p. 71.

[90] *Constitutional Justice*, n. 48 above, p. 9.

[91] 'Modernising government – Lord Falconer appointed Secretary of State for Constitutional Affairs', Downing Street press release, 12 June 2003. See generally Lord Windlesham, 'The Constitutional Reform Act 2005: ministers, judges and constitutional change' [2005] *PL* 806, especially at 808–10; Lord Windlesham, 'The Constitutional Reform Act 2005: the politics of constitutional reform' [2006] *PL* 35,

the creation of a new Supreme Court to replace the system whereby Law Lords act as the judicial committee of the House of Lords in exercising their appellate jurisdiction. The government also announced that Lord Falconer, the first Secretary of State for Constitutional Affairs and charged with exercising all the functions of the Lord Chancellor as necessary for the period of transition, did not intend to sit as a judge in the House of Lords before the new Supreme Court had been established. The reform measures, particularly to abolish the Lord Chancellor's office and establish a Supreme Court, were initially promoted in the media and later in Parliament[92] by invoking the separation of powers and judicial independence. They culminated in the extensive provisions of the Constitutional Reform Act 2005, which include a specific 'Guarantee of continued judicial independence'.[93] How significant they were in effecting the declaration and institutionalisation of a principle of the separation of powers is relative to earlier pressures and an outcome of later developments.

Although little, if any, consultation occurred before the announcements of 12 June 2003,[94] the reform measures did further the government's general modernisation programme in responding to increased criticism of the Lord Chancellor's office and to prominent recent advocacy of a Supreme Court. Already in the late 1980s, Sir Nicolas Browne-Wilkinson had observed incidentally that the Lord Chancellor's dual role as both a government minister and head of the judiciary was 'inconsistent with any doctrine of the separation of powers' and described stresses resulting, *inter alia*, from 'a very substantial shift [from the early 1970s] in the control of the administration of the courts from the judges to civil servants in the Lord Chancellor's Department'.[95] In her influential book, *The Office of Lord Chancellor*, Diana Woodhouse elaborated upon basic changes that increased tension between the Lord Chancellor's roles as both a government minister and the head of the judiciary.[96] One basic change was an expansion in the policy role of the

---

especially at 36–7; R. Stevens, 'Reform in haste and repent at leisure: Iolanthe, the Lord High Executioner and *Brave New World*' (2004) 24 *Legal Studies* 1.

[92] See, e.g., *Hansard*, HL Vol. 657, cols. 927–9 (9 February 2004). See generally Windlesham, 'Politics of constitutional reform', n. 91 above, 35–40.

[93] Section 3.

[94] Windlesham, 'Ministers, judges and constitutional change', n. 91 above, especially at 808–10.

[95] 'The independence of the judiciary in the 1980s' [1988] *PL* 44, especially at 45, 46.

[96] Note 32 above. See also D. Woodhouse, 'The office of Lord Chancellor' [1998] *PL* 617; D. Woodhouse, 'The office of Lord Chancellor: time to abandon the judicial role – the rest will follow' (2002) 22 *Legal Studies* 128.

Lord Chancellor: initially in securing efficiency and limiting public expenditure in legal aid and the administration of the civil courts; later, in effecting the many constitutional reforms of the Labour Government since 1997.[97] The result was that the Lord Chancellor had become 'at the beginning of the twenty-first century . . . above all else a government minister, and, as such, . . . likely to hold different views from the judges on the administration of justice'.[98] Another basic change was the incorporation of the European Convention on Human Rights in the Human Rights Act 1998. In particular, the incorporation of the right to a determination by an independent and impartial tribunal under Art. 6 of the Convention rendered the Lord Chancellor's increasingly rare exercise of his role as a judge, in addition to his role as a government minister, objectionable, especially in any cases involving government.[99] Furthermore, when the Lord Chancellor's role as a judge therefore completely fell away on Lord Falconer's appointment, the Lord Chancellor's related roles as head of the judiciary in judicial deployment, making judicial appointments, taking disciplinary action etc. also became incongruous and questionable in being exercised by an executive rather than a high judicial officer.[100]

In view of the changes, Woodhouse concluded that it was time to 'consign the office of Lord Chancellor to history' and confer its responsibilities upon other institutions.[101] Lord Steyn cited her book with approval and invoked the separation of powers in arguing that the Lord Chancellor should cease to be head of the judiciary and that a Supreme Court should be established.[102] Whereas Lord Bingham also called for the creation of a Supreme Court,[103] Lord Irvine as Lord Chancellor defended his office's dual roles, as had his predecessors and a few senior judges.[104]

---

[97] See Woodhouse, *Office of Lord Chancellor*, n. 32 above, ch. 3, especially at pp. 47ff, ch. 4, especially at pp. 80ff.

[98] *Ibid.* p. 36. See also *ibid.* pp. 207ff.

[99] See generally *ibid.* ch. 5, especially at pp. 126ff. See also J. Steyn, 'The case for a Supreme Court', Neill Lecture, All Souls College, Oxford, 1 March 2002, published in (2002) 118 *LQR* 382 at 385f.

[100] Lord Bingham, 'The old order changeth' (2006) 122 *LQR* 211, especially at 220f.

[101] *Office of Lord Chancellor*, n. 32 above, especially at p. 212; Woodhouse, 'Office of Lord Chancellor' (2002), n. 96 above, especially at 128.

[102] 'The case for a Supreme Court', n. 99 above, especially at 385–6.

[103] Gustave Tuck Lecture, Constitution Unit, University College London, 1 May 2002.

[104] See, e.g., Lord Woolf, 'Judicial review – the tensions', n. 72 above, 582ff. See generally Bingham, 'Old order changeth', n. 100 above, 215ff.

The controversy preceding the announcements of 12 June 2003 was slight in comparison to that which followed. Apart from severely negative reactions to the way in which the reform measures had been taken,[105] the subsequent consultation papers of the Department for Constitutional Affairs[106] provoked substantial and widely-reported judicial opposition in the House of Lords[107] and in the formal responses of the Judges' Council and of the Law Lords.[108] Central to the opposition was traditional scepticism towards the domestic applicability of the separation of powers doctrine and concern about losing the Lord Chancellor as an advocate of judicial interests and as a guarantor of judicial independence within government. The English separation of powers was being seen to be threatened at the same time as the government was claiming to act as its champion. The initial positive outcome of the controversy was *the concordat* agreed between Lord Woolf as Lord Chief Justice and Lord Falconer as Lord Chancellor and lodged in the libraries of both Houses of Parliament on 26 January 2004.[109] In recognition that the Lord Chancellor's office would be abolished, *the concordat* provided an outline of new arrangements to be incorporated in legislation, specifically designed to 'reinforce the independence of the judiciary'[110] and generally involving a transfer of judicial

---

[105] See, e.g., S. Cretney, 'Abolishing the office of Lord Chancellor: the question of departmental responsibility and some other consequential issues', Conference on 'Judicial reform: function, appointment and structure', Centre for Public Law, University of Cambridge, 4 October 2003; 'On the back of an envelope . . .: constitutional reform or constitutional vandalism?', Seminar on the British Constitution, Lincoln's Inn, London, 15 September 2004. See generally Windlesham, 'Ministers, judges and constitutional change', n. 91 above, 818f; Stevens, 'Reform in haste', n. 91 above; ch. 1 above, pp. 3f.

[106] *Constitutional Reform: a new way of appointing judges* (CP 10/03, July 2003); *Constitutional Reform: A Supreme Court of the United Kingdom* (CP 11/03, July 2003); *Constitutional Reform: reforming the office of the Lord Chancellor* (CP 13/03, September 2003).

[107] See, e.g., *Hansard*, HL Vol. 652, cols. 119, 123, 127–8 (8 September 2003).

[108] Department for Constitutional Affairs, *Judges' Council Response to the Consultation Papers on Constitutional Reform* (6 November 2003); Department for Constitutional Affairs, *The Law Lords Response to the Government's Consultation Paper: A Supreme Court for the United Kingdom* (7 November 2003). See generally Windlesham, 'Ministers, judges and constitutional change', n. 91 above, 812ff.

[109] Department for Constitutional Affairs, *Constitutional Reform, The Lord Chancellor's judiciary-related functions: Proposals ('the concordat')*, January 2004. See generally Lord Woolf, 'The rule of law and a change in the constitution', The Squire Centenary Lecture, Faculty of Law, University of Cambridge, 3 March 2004, published in [2004] *CLJ* 317 at 323ff; Windlesham, 'Ministers, judges and constitutional change', n. 91 above, 819ff.

[110] Paragraph 5.

functions to the Lord Chief Justice, a specific statutory duty upon the Secretary of State for Constitutional Affairs to uphold judicial independence and a sharing of responsibilities between the Secretary and the Lord Chief Justice. The consequent Constitutional Reform Bill was introduced in the Lords, referred to a Special Select Committee in the face of opposition, extensively debated by members of both Houses and subject to amendments the cumulative effect of which was that the Lord Chancellor's office was retained in a modified form for the exercise of the functions originally envisaged for the Secretary of State for Constitutional Affairs.[111]

The Constitutional Reform Act 2005 has enacted important changes – an authoritative written declaration of the principle of judicial independence, provision for the Supreme Court and the Judicial Appointments Commission etc. – but its provisions and the process by which they were determined have also illustrated numerous continuities amidst the many changes. First, the office of Lord Chancellor has not been abolished but has been retained although substantially modified. Secondly, as in the case of *the concordat*, judicial independence – the traditional preoccupation of the English separation of powers – has remained central. It has been specifically guaranteed, reinforced with statutory duties upon the Lord Chancellor and other Ministers of the Crown[112] and further institutionalised mainly through the provisions for an independent Judicial Appointments Commission,[113] the Supreme Court[114] and for the Lord Chief Justice to be President of the Courts of England and Wales and the Head of the Judiciary of England and Wales.[115] Thirdly, the Lord Chancellor's duties in relation to judicial independence and support for the judiciary, on the one hand, and the Lord Chief Justice's power to make written representations on judicial matters to Parliament, on the other,[116] have been enacted to serve as functional equivalents of the duties and powers implicit in the Lord Chancellor's former role.

Fourthly, a separation of powers has been, as in the past, both confirmed and compromised or negated by the reforms or in the reform process. Introducing a Secretary of State for Constitutional Affairs, as announced together with the other reform measures on 12 June 2003, shortly thereafter was likened to conferring upon one team captain the

---

[111] On the passage of the Bill through Parliament, see Windlesham, 'Politics of constitutional reform', n. 91 above.
[112] Section 3. See also the amendment to the Lord Chancellor's oath, s 17.
[113] Part 4.    [114] Part 3.    [115] Section 7.    [116] Section 5.

power to set the rules of the game.[117] The separation of powers – in this instance between executive power and constitutional law-making power – thus appeared to be negated at the very moment it became prominent. Furthermore, although prominent in the initial promotion of the reforms, the separation of powers as such, insofar as it requires more than judicial independence, lost prominence presumably to avoid the objection that the doctrine of the separation is alien to domestic constitutional arrangements.[118] The separation of powers was still invoked in the overview of *the concordat*[119] but was barely mentioned in the Explanatory Notes to the Constitutional Reform Act 2005, where the aim of making 'a distinct constitutional separation between the legislature and judiciary' was simply presented as background to the provisions for the Supreme Court.[120] The guarantee in the Act is of judicial independence, not the separation of powers. Whatever separation is implicitly institutionalised by the Act, it is far from rigid. The Lord Chancellor is 'to be qualified by experience'[121] and therefore need not necessarily be a lawyer, but has retained significant responsibilities and powers in relation to the judiciary. These include upholding judicial independence, providing guidance and rejecting selections made by the Commission and selection panels in judicial appointments and exercising disciplinary powers or agreeing to their exercise by the Lord Chief Justice.[122] For his part, the Lord Chief Justice may lay before Parliament written representations relating to the judiciary.[123] The 2005 Act does contain an authoritative affirmation of the principle of judicial independence but also reflects and perpetuates the uneven English separation of powers in practice.

Fifthly and finally, the dramatic reform measures of 12 June 2003 provoked a reaction, particularly in the House of Lords, that resulted in development charactersitic of the historical constitution. Lord Windlesham has good reason to conclude as follows:

> The legislative sequence was broadly characteristic of a process of evolutionary gradualism. After an uncertain start, all three branches of the

---

[117] 'The British constitution – can we learn from history?', Panel discussion, British Academy, London, 18 June 2003.

[118] See generally Windlesham, 'Ministers, judges and constitutional change', n. 91 above, 812ff; Windlesham, 'Politics of constitutional reform', n. 91 above, 35ff.

[119] Note 109 above, para. 2.      [120] Paragraph 61.

[121] Constitutional Reform Act 2005, s 2.

[122] See, e.g., ss 3, 29, 30, 65, 66, 73, 74, 82, 83, 90, 91, 108ff.      [123] Section 5.

constitution, Parliament, the executive, and the judiciary, were engaged in a process that could reasonably be described as being pragmatic reform. Party politics played a relatively minor part, at least until the final parliamentary exchanges. Both Houses of Parliament gave much time, on and off the floor of their respective chambers, to reshaping and defining the proposed changes.[124]

Doubts about the outcome persist and may be dispelled in due course[125] but the mode of reformation has been typical. The Lord Chancellor's office was to be 'consigned to history'.[126] By the Constitutional Reform Act 2005, the Lord Chancellor's office and the uneven English separation of powers it represents have been consigned to a history that lives on in the historical constitution.

## The English paradox

In England the separation of powers has long been both assumed and denied in important ways, arguably present and arguably absent. Before the recent constitutional reforms, its ambiguous 'presence or absence' was cited as evidence of a 'radical confusion' in the history of thinking about the constitution.[127] Indeed, continuing confusion about the separation of powers was illustrated in an exchange between Sir Stephen Sedley and John Griffith. Sedley had observed that 'one of the great silences in our constitution ... exists in the space between the

---

[124] 'Politics of constitutional reform', n. 91 above, 57. At the outset, the consultation papers were described as seemingly 'dangerously radical' to Conservatives and 'in so many other ways ... immensely conservative and unimaginative', Stevens, 'Reform in haste', n. 91 above, 35.

[125] 'There can be no doubt that since June 2003 the mountains have laboured mightily: it remains to be seen whether they have brought forth a mouse, or a valuable measure of overdue reform, or a monster', Bingham, 'Old order changeth', n. 100 above, 223.

[126] Woodhouse, 'Office of Lord Chancellor' (2002), n. 96 above, 128. See also Woodhouse, *Office of Lord Chancellor*, n. 32 above, p. 212. Cf. generally also the continuing implications for the separation of powers of the position of the Attorney General, a Law Officer of the Crown and as such still required 'to serve two masters, the government and the law, and thus to combine the role of a politician with that of a lawyer', D. Woodhouse, 'The Attorney General' (1997) 50 *Parliamentary Affairs* 97 at 97. See generally N. Walker, 'The antinomies of the Law Officers' in M. Sunkin and S. Payne (eds.), *The Nature of the Crown: A Legal and Political Analysis* (Oxford: Oxford University Press, 1999), pp. 135–9.

[127] P. Allott, 'The theory of the British Constitution' in H. Gross and R. Harrison (eds.), *Jurisprudence: Cambridge Essays* (Oxford: Oxford University Press, 1992), pp. 173–205 at p. 187.

nominal unity of state power in the Crown and the factual and necessary division of that power between discrete and sometimes conflicting bodies of the state'.[128] He later argued that 'there are within the separate powers of the modern British State two [not three] sovereignties, those of Parliament and the courts'.[129] Griffith criticised Sedley's argument for confusing separate powers, functions and institutions and for relegating government beneath a sovereign parliament and sovereign courts.[130] Despite his analytical criticism of Sedley's treatment of the separation of powers, elsewhere he also stated that the separation of powers in the United Kingdom had never been such that it was possible to argue that the further extension of judicial review of executive decision making was 'something unconstitutional or unhistorical or logically perverse' as opposed to 'politically unwise or undesirable'.[131] Sedley's and Griffith's various observations afford strong evidence for Martin Loughlin's recent claim that the 'copying' of Montesquieu's mistake by Blackstone 'has ever since been a source of confusion about the nature of the office of government within the British system'.[132] Loughlin nonetheless recognises the 'great imaginative sway' that 'the appeal to impartiality holds ... over us' to be the reason for the special power of 'the aspiration to establish a law-governed state' as a 'state-building technique'.[133]

Amidst the continuing confusion, the Lord Chancellor's office has been reformed and provision has been made for the Supreme Court to replace the House of Lords in its function as a judicial committee. The separation of powers has continued to evolve and is consequently now more clearly present but still absent in important ways: present particularly in the initial promotion of the reforms; absent in the many compromises that have been made in response to the reaction that the proposals for reform provoked.

---

[128] 'The sound of silence: constitutional law without a constitution' (1994) 110 *LQR* 270 at 272.

[129] 'The Crown in its own courts' in C. F. Forsyth and I. Hare (eds.), *The Golden Metwand and the Crooked Cord: Essays on Public Law in Honour of Sir William Wade QC* (Oxford: Oxford University Press, 1998), pp. 253–66, especially at p. 254.

[130] J. A. G. Griffith, 'The common law and the political constitution' (2001) 117 *LQR* 42 at 54–5.

[131] J. A. G. Griffith, 'The brave new world of Sir John Laws' (2000) 63 *MLR* 159 at 174–5, especially at 175.

[132] *The Idea of Public Law* (Oxford: Oxford University Press, 2003), p. 24.

[133] *Ibid.* p. 52.

The continuing paradox of a separation of powers both present and absent is explicable. In the English historical constitution, the separation of powers has evolved and is perpetuated both in judicial and legislative practice through a general customary mode of formation. To the extent it is more than a general requirement of judicial independence, it is still only present as an uneven customary practice, absent as a constitutional principle authoritatively declared and, as such, to be consistently observed. Limited clarity or consistency, which may be troubling from analytical and normative perspectives or in comparison with the clarity or consistency achieved or expected through a written constitutional enactment of principle, accords with the historical constitution. As evident in the English separation of powers, it allows for flexibility – both continuity and change – in the relationship formed between its institutions of government and is thus a potential source of appeal to both conservatives and advocates of progress. Furthermore, the far-reaching recent reform measures to abolish the office of Lord Chancellor, which were modified in response to the reaction they provoked with the effect that greater continuity was secured in their implementation, illustrate the historical constitution's continuing significance.

The peculiarity of the English historical constitution, although traditionally exaggerated, I will argue in relation to its doctrines of parliamentary sovereignty and the rule of law,[134] is still manifest in the English separation of powers when compared with that of the French. The separation of powers, common to English and French constitutional development, evolved and continues to evolve as an English customary practice different in form and substance[135] from the long-declared constitutional principle in France. The playwright, George Bernard Shaw, is supposed to have spoken of England and America as 'two countries divided by a common language'. In view of modern English and French constitutional development, we can similarly speak of two constitutions divided by a common concept.

---

[134] See chs. 5–8 above.     [135] See the references in n. 6 above.

# 5

# Parliamentary sovereignty and the European Community: the economy of the common law

The orthodox English legal view of parliamentary sovereignty has been insular in comparison with that of the separation of powers, the subject of the previous chapter, in which European interactions and English constitutional peculiarities have long been manifest. Dicey claimed that the 'historical reason why Parliament has never succeeded in passing immutable laws ... lies deep in the history of the English people and in the peculiar development of the English constitution'.[1] Dicey's insular historical claim is quoted with approval by Jeffrey Goldsworthy in his influential and important work on the doctrine of parliamentary sovereignty.[2] From a Commonwealth perspective on the English common law rather than its European context, Goldsworthy contributes to debates on the doctrine's current status by way of a historical study that understandably attaches little significance to European influences, ends with the start of the twentieth century and only touches, in passing, on the impact of Britain's joining of the European Community.[3]

Dicey's view of the history of parliamentary sovereignty in particular and that of the English constitution in general is unacceptably insular. Prominent medieval examples of Continental European influence are evident in the provisions of Magna Carta[4] and the work of Bracton.

---

This chapter was developed from 'Parliamentary sovereignty, Europe and the economy of the common law' in M. Andenas (ed.), *Liber Amicorum in Honour of Lord Slynn of Hadley: Judicial Review in International Perspective* (The Hague: Kluwer Law International, 2000), pp. 177–94. I am grateful to the late Professor Sir William Wade for kindly allowing me access to his correspondence with H. L. A. Hart.

[1] A. V. Dicey, *An Introduction to the Study of the Law of the Constitution* (London: Macmillan, 10th edn, 1959), p. 69, n. 1.

[2] J. Goldsworthy, *The Sovereignty of Parliament: History and Philosophy* (Oxford: Oxford University Press, 1999), p. 7.

[3] See *ibid.* pp. 8, 244–5. Cf. generally H. W. Arndt's perspective on Dicey's rule of law, 'The origins of Dicey's concept of the "rule of law"' (1957) 31 *Australian Law Journal* 117.

[4] R. H. Helmholz, 'Continental law and common law: historical strangers or companions?' [1990] *Duke Law Journal* 1207. See also generally C. Donahue, '*Ius commune*, Canon law, and common law in England' (1992) 66 *Tulane Law Review* 1745, especially at 1754, 1760ff.

Goldsworthy begins his historical survey of the evolution of Parliament's sovereignty from that of the medieval English King by discussing Bracton's notion of kingship.[5] He quotes the claim of Gaines Post that Bracton 'comes close to seeing in the public rights of king and crown the same kind of sovereignty as that defined by Jean Bodin some three centuries later'.[6] In a later section of the same sentence, however, Post explains Bracton's view as the outcome of 'the influence of the Roman law on the powers of the emperor'.[7] Elsewhere, in an influential article, Post also shows how Bracton used the Romano-Canonical maxim that requires the consent of those affected by particular measures, *Quod omnes tangit ab omnibus comprobetur*.[8] In royal writs that summoned community representatives to Parliament, this maxim proved useful, and for its use, Post suggests Bracton's work may have been partly responsible. Continental European thinking influenced Bracton and the very practice of representation by which Parliament's sovereignty acquired legitimacy.

In this chapter, as in previous chapters, I will attempt to do justice to both European influence and the peculiarity of the common law. I will elaborate on two prominent modern interactions since Dicey wrote *Law of the Constitution*. One is the response of the English courts, in their interpretation of the European Communities Act (ECA) 1972, to the European Court of Justice's (ECJ's) claim[9] to the supremacy of Community law. The other is the influence of the Continental understandings of a legal system and its fundamentals on leading English analytical approaches to parliamentary sovereignty. I will consider the extent to which both these analytical approaches and the liberal normativist alternative appreciate the character and, in particular, what I will

---

[5] *Sovereignty of Parliament*, n. 2 above, pp. 22ff.
[6] G. Post, Review of *The Problem of Sovereignty in the Later Middle Ages* by M. J. Wilks (1964) 39 *Speculum* 365 at 368.
[7] *Ibid.*
[8] 'That which affects all must be approved by all' from C. 5. 59. 5. 2; G. Post, 'A Romano-canonical maxim, "Quod omnes tangit" in Bracton' (1946) 4 *Traditio* 197. See also G. Post, *Studies in Medieval Legal Thought: Public Law and the State, 1100–1322* (Princeton: Princeton University Press, 1964), pp. 163–238; B. Tierney, *Religion, Law, and the Growth of Constitutional Thought, 1150–1650* (Cambridge: Cambridge University Press, 1982), pp. 19–25; J. Martínez-Torrón, *Anglo-American Law and Canon Law: Canonical Roots of the Common Law Tradition* (Berlin: Duncker & Humblot, 1998), pp. 151ff.
[9] Decisively stated in *Costa* v. *ENEL* (Case-6/64) [1964] ECR 585.

suggest is the economy of the common law demonstrated[10] in the judicial interpretation of the 1972 Act. I will argue that various prominent approaches, particularly those under the influence of Continental theory, have mistaken or inadequately described the response of the English courts to Community law. Finally, I will elaborate on the economy of the common law exemplified in that response as characteristic in the historical constitution. I will suggest that it continues to affect the realism of expectations and requires recognition, at least, as a complement to an analytical approach or the liberal normativist alternative.

## Dicey's orthodoxy

For Dicey, parliamentary sovereignty or the legislative supremacy of Parliament was 'the very keystone of the law of the constitution'.[11] In his analysis, he famously described it in both positive and negative terms, as Parliament's 'right to make or unmake any law whatever' and the absence of any body with 'a right to override or set aside the legislation of Parliament'.[12] He also endorsed the maxim that Parliament cannot so bind its successors with statutory terms so as to limit the legislative authority of future Parliaments.[13] He asserted categorically that 'one law, whatever its importance, can be passed and changed by exactly the same method as every other law'.[14]

As an exposition of a common-law doctrine or constitutional principle, recognised or developed by the courts in conformity with his own notion of the rule of law,[15] Dicey's account was vulnerable to criticism. He did not recognise a judicial discretion or an interpretive judicial role

---

[10] In purely domestic law, the Appellate Committee of the House of Lords also recently adopted various similar approaches to deal with the issue of the legal validity of the Hunting Act 2004, passed without the consent of the House of Lords, and thus with the issue of the legal validity of the Parliament Act 1949, which laid down the procedure that was followed in the passing of the 2004 Act and which was itself passed without the consent of the House of Lords in the exercise of a power conferred by the Parliament Act 1911. In *Jackson* v. *Attorney General* [2006] 1 AC 262; [2005] UKHL 56, the Law Lords endorsed or echoed the various approaches in their speeches, and more than one approach in at least one of them. See also below, pp. 109f. and nn. 40, 41, 42, 44, 52, 99, 108. See generally M. Plaxton, 'The concept of legislation: *Jackson* v. *Her Majesty's Attorney General*' (2006) 69 MLR 249.

[11] *Law of the Constitution*, n. 1 above, p. 70.

[12] *Ibid.* pp. 39–40.    [13] *Ibid.* pp. 64ff.    [14] *Ibid.* p. 90.

[15] See the third meaning Dicey attributes to the rule of law, *ibid.* pp. 195ff.

in identifying Parliament's sovereignty. The maxim, 'Parliament cannot bind its successors', omits the role of the courts. Dicey was therefore criticised by Sir William Wade for not properly realising that 'the seat of sovereign power' is to be discovered by looking at the practice of the courts, rather than at Acts of Parliament.[16] Furthermore, he did not describe or anticipate the evolutionary change that one would expect of other common-law doctrines. For Dicey, parliamentary sovereignty was 'an undoubted legal fact', 'fully recognised by the law of England', a matter of plain truth.[17]

What was plain to Dicey was not what was plain to the English courts after Britain's joining of the European Community. In the second *Factortame* case, the House of Lords decided that provisions of the Merchant Shipping Act 1988 be disapplied in the light of the ECA 1972. Lord Bridge held that 'whatever limitation of its sovereignty Parliament accepted when it enacted the European Communities Act 1972 was entirely voluntary'.[18] In numerous ways, Dicey's account is ill-suited to explain what happened. By deciding that the provisions of the 1988 Act be disapplied, the House of Lords affirmed or ensured that the Parliament which enacted the 1972 Act had so bound its successors as to limit the discretion of later Parliaments to repeal its provisions by implication. It therefore allowed a contradiction of the maxim central to Dicey's discussion. Dicey did not anticipate a departure from the maxim or indeed deal adequately with constitutional change in general. So as to focus on the existing English constitution, as discussed in Chapter Two, he expressly relegated historical approaches that were sensitive to change in the evolving English constitution.[19] Furthermore, in Dicey's analysis, any voluntary partial surrender of sovereignty – 'whatever limitation ... Parliament accepted'[20] – was logically impossible. Dicey recognised only the complete surrender of sovereignty, through transfer or abdication.[21] Whilst remaining true to his own analysis, he could not have countenanced English judicial acquiescence in a gradual shift to a federal Europe. He expressly used federalism in the USA as an opposite with which to illustrate and emphasise unitarianism in English

---

[16] H. W. R. Wade, 'The basis of legal sovereignty' [1955] *CLJ* 172 at 196.

[17] *Law of the Constitution*, n. 1 above, pp. 68, 39, 70.

[18] *R. v. Secretary of State for Transport ex parte Factortame Ltd (No. 2)* [1991] 1 AC 603 at 659A.

[19] Dicey, *Law of the Constitution*, n. 1 above, pp. v–vii, 15ff.

[20] Lord Bridge in the second *Factortame* case, n. 18 above, 659A.

[21] *Law of the Constitution*, n. 1 above, pp. 68–9, n. 1.

constitutional law, 'the habitual exercise of supreme legislative authority by one central power, which in the particular case is the British Parliament'.[22] Here and elsewhere, he presented other jurisdictions, not as actual or potential sources of influence, but as anti-models with which to demonstrate the peculiarity or the peculiar genius of the existing English constitution.[23] In short, Dicey's analytical legal method,[24] both insular and insufficiently sensitive to change, could not do justice[25] to evolution in the historical constitution whether through internal development or external influence.

## Rules of manner and form

Jennings and Heuston used an analytical legal approach to reach an unorthodox conclusion. From the orthodox analytical starting point that Parliament can enact any law, they argued that Parliament can bind its successors with formal restrictions by changing the rules of manner and form by which courts identify parliamentary statutes.[26] Their New View of parliamentary sovereignty was severely criticised by Wade[27] but did show a greater fidelity to the common law than did Dicey's doctrine. It provided for constitutional evolution through amendments to rules of manner and form and recognised a judicial role in responding to those amendments.[28] Jennings was therefore dismissive of Dicey's statutory precedents of Parliamentary failure to bind its successors: 'they show what Parliament thought of its own powers, and not what the courts thought those powers were'.[29] Jennings and Heuston specifically advocated their New View as faithful to the common law: 'The great advantage of the new doctrine is that

---

[22] *Ibid.* ch. 3, especially at pp. 139–40.

[23] See, e.g., *ibid.* pp. 122ff, chs. 3, 12; J. W. F. Allison, *A Continental Distinction in the Common Law: A Historical and Comparative Perspective on English Public Law* (Oxford: Oxford University Press, rev. pbk edn, 2000), pp. 18–23.

[24] See ch. 2 above, pp. 7ff.

[25] For the argument from a critical external perspective that a Diceyan positivist ideology and formalist methodology 'have served the unwritten constitution well, helping the judges . . . "to keep their heads below the parapet"', see C. Harlow, 'Disposing of Dicey: from legal autonomy to constitutional discourse' (2000) 48 *Political Studies* 356, especially at 365. Cf. generally below, pp. 169f.

[26] W. I. Jennings, *The Law and the Constitution* (London: University of London Press, 5th edn, 1959), ch. 4; R. F. V. Heuston, *Essays in Constitutional Law* (London: Stevens & Sons, 2nd edn, 1964), ch. 1.

[27] 'Basis of legal sovereignty', n. 16 above.

[28] See, e.g., Jennings, *Law and the Constitution*, n. 26 above, pp. 160–2.

[29] *Ibid.* p. 169.

it enables these tremendous issues [of sovereignty] to be decided according to the ordinary law in the ordinary courts. By redefining the doctrine of sovereignty from within its own four corners the common law has shown its instinctive wisdom.'[30] Heuston described the new doctrine as 'couched in the calm, hard, tightly knit style of the common lawyer rather than in the vague and emotional language of the political scientist' and he dismissed the orthodox doctrine as the product of Oxford academia.[31]

The judicial response to the ECA 1972 has provided limited support for the New View. In his minority judgment in *Macarthys*, Lord Denning recognised the EEC Treaty as an 'overriding force' in statutory construction but made a telling observation:

> If the time should come when our Parliament deliberately passes an Act with the intention of repudiating the Treaty or any provision in it or intentionally of acting inconsistently with it and says so in express terms then I should have thought that it would be the duty of our courts to follow the statute of our Parliament.[32]

By implication, Lord Denning recognised that the 1972 Act had introduced[33] a procedural rule that repeal of the Act or of applicable provisions of European Community law be express – a rule that was analogous to the rules of manner and form central to the New View. Furthermore, in the second *Factortame* case, Lord Bridge's emphasis on Parliament's acceptance of Community law and its supremacy in the 1972 Act is comparable to the New View's emphasis on Parliament's initiation of change to rules of manner and form.[34] Craig suggests the likely reason: 'The courts do not wish to be seen as making a "political choice" at the "boundary of the legal system". They would prefer to express the matter as one in which the essential choice has been made by the legislature, in this instance the legislature of the early 1970s.'[35] The New View responded to the judicial need to play a minimal role in two ways. First, it portrayed Parliament, rather than the court, as the initiator of change. Secondly, it envisaged

---

[30] Heuston, *Essays in Constitutional Law*, n. 26 above, p. 31. See also, e.g., Jennings, *Law and the Constitution*, n. 26 above, pp. 167–8.

[31] *Essays in Constitutional Law*, n. 26 above, pp. 1ff., especially at p. 6.

[32] *Macarthys Ltd* v. *Smith* [1981] 1 QB 180 at 329CD.

[33] Cf. the Court of Appeal's interpretation of the effect of the Acquisition of Land (Assessment of Compensation) Act 1919 in *Ellen Street Estates* v. *Minister of Health* [1934] 1 KB 590, especially at 597.

[34] Note 18 above, 658G–659B.

[35] P. P. Craig, 'Sovereignty of the United Kingdom Parliament after *Factortame*' (1991) 11 *Yearbook of European Law* 221 at 252.

judicial control of procedure, not substance, a control that in other contexts[36] the courts have readily developed. The New View of parliamentary sovereignty in the common law allowed for an economy of judicial response[37] to fundamental constitutional issues.

Jennings and Heuston tried to be true to the common law but still expected further reaching controls than the English courts have proved willing to provide. To avoid encroaching on the province of Parliament, the courts have been wary even of procedural control in relation to Acts of Parliament.[38] Authoritative precedents for the Westminster Parliament's being generally bound by rules of manner and form have not been forthcoming either before[39] of after the passing of the ECA 1972. In the *obiter dictum* in *Macarthys* quoted above, Lord Denning implicitly recognised the single formal requirement that repeal of the 1972 Act or any provision of European Community law be express. He did not endorse or mention the applicability of general rules of manner and form. His requirement that courts follow a statute of the Westminster Parliament that is deliberately inconsistent with the 1972 Act is therefore readily interpreted as introducing, not a rule of manner and form, but a presumption of statutory construction that future legislation is intended to be applied consistently with Community law unless express provision is made to the contrary. In the recent *Jackson* case, two Law Lords conceived of binding rules of manner and form that could be altered by Parliament,[40] but others were unreceptive,[41] and the majority of the Appellate Committee of the House decided the case on a narrower, more economical,[42] basis. The New View suggested a

---

[36] Note the judicial elaboration of the rules of natural justice and the duty to act fairly. Cf. generally N. Bamforth, 'Parliamentary sovereignty and the Human Rights Act 1998' [1998] *PL* 572 at 578ff.

[37] See below, pp. 123ff.     [38] See, e.g., *Pickin* v. *British Railways Board* [1974] AC 765.

[39] See Wade, 'Basis of legal sovereignty', n. 16 above, 182ff. Cf. the Commonwealth cases involving legislatures, conceived as subordinate or treated comparably: *A–G for New South Wales* v. *Trethowan* [1932] AC 526; *Harris* v. *Minister of the Interior* 1952 (2) SA 428.

[40] Note 10 above: Lord Steyn at [81]–[86]; Baroness Hale at [159]–[164]. See also Laws LJ in *Thoburn* v. *Sunderland City Council* [2003] QB 151, especially at [59], [63]; [2002] 1 CMLR 50; [2002] EWHC 195.

[41] Lord Hope at [113]; Lord Carswell at [174]; Lord Brown at [187]. See generally A. L. Young, 'Hunting sovereignty: *Jackson v Her Majesty's Attorney General* [2006] *PL* 187.

[42] Their economical approaches included emphasis upon construing the Parliament Act 1911, concessions to the political reality that Parliament had long accorded validity to the Parliament Act 1949 by the procedure of which the Hunting Act 2004 had been passed, and declining to decide upon general issues, i.e., those beyond the particular

common law approach to Parliament's sovereignty but has remained
vulnerable to Wade's criticism for its lack of accepted authority.

## Judicial revolution

Apart from the issue of authority, Sir William Wade rejected the New
View for failing to appreciate the peculiar character of the common-law
rule requiring judicial obedience to statutes: '[it] is ... a rule which is
unique in being unchangeable by Parliament – it is changed by revolution, not by legislation; it lies in the keeping of the courts, and no Act of
Parliament can take it away from them'.[43] In his leading analysis, Wade
described that rule variously as the 'ultimate *political* fact', 'one of the
fundamental rules upon which the legal system depends' and '[w]hat
Salmond calls the "ultimate legal principle" '.[44] Like Dicey, he conceived
of parliamentary sovereignty as a matter of fact, but, unlike Dicey and
Jennings, he clearly located it within the common law in the keeping of
the courts and open to change – revolutionary change, exemplified in
the judicial response to the ECA 1972.[45] Whether the first two
*Factortame* cases or *Macarthys* before them, landmarks in the judicial
interpretation of the ECA 1972, are adequately analysed as revolutionary
deserves careful attention.[46]

In *Macarthys*, the Court of Appeal held that directly-effective provisions of Community law prevail when inconsistent with a subsequent
Act of the Westminster Parliament: 'It is important now to declare – and
it must be made plain – that the provisions of article 119 of the E.E.C.
Treaty take priority over anything in our English statute on equal pay
which is inconsistent with article 119. That priority is given by our law. It

---

issues before the House. See, e.g., Lord Bingham at [24], [32], [36]; Lord Nicholls at
[61]–[64], [67]–[69]; Lord Hope at [124]–[127]; Lord Rodger at [132], [136], [138];
Lord Walker at [141]; Lord Carswell at [168]–[171], [176]–[178]; Lord Brown at [194].
See generally R. Cooke, 'A constitutional retreat' (2006) 122 *LQR* 224.

[43] 'Basis of legal sovereignty', n. 16 above, at 189.

[44] *Ibid.* 188, 187, 189. For a recent illustration of a similar analysis in a purely domestic
context, see the speech of Lord Hope in the *Jackson* case, n. 10 above, at [119], [120],
[124]–[128]. In that case, Lord Steyn also made a passing reference to the possibility of
'a new *Grundnorm*', at [99].

[45] W. H. R. Wade, 'Sovereignty – revolution or evolution?' (1996) 112 *LQR* 568, especially
at 573. Cf. generally J. D. B. Mitchell, 'What happened to the constitution on 1st January
1973?' (1980) 11 *Cambrian Law Review* 69.

[46] For a detailed discussion of the case law beyond the scope of this chapter, see M. Hunt,
*Using Human Rights in English Courts* (Oxford: Hart Publishing, 1997), pp. 63ff.

is given by the European Community Act 1972 itself.'[47] Lord Denning specifically attributed the priority of Community law to the 1972 Act, and Lawton LJ, in his earlier majority judgment, observed that he could 'see nothing in this case which infringes the sovereignty of Parliament'.[48] If a revolution was initiated, it went apparently unnoticed by its judicial agents.

In the first *Factortame* case, the facts of which are well known, the House of Lords held that, as a matter of English law, the courts had no jurisdiction to grant interim relief in a form that would entail disapplication of provisions of the Merchant Shipping Act 1988. As did the judgments in the Court of Appeal,[49] Lord Bridge's speech contained an orthodox affirmation of Parliament's sovereignty:

> If the applicants fail to establish the rights they claim before the E.C.J., the effect of the interim relief granted would be to have conferred upon them rights directly contrary to Parliament's sovereign will . . . I am clearly of the opinion that, as a matter of English law, the court has no power to make an order which has these consequences.[50]

In the second *Factortame* case, after the ECJ had affirmed that, as a matter of Community law, the courts had jurisdiction notwithstanding the sole obstacle of any rule of national law, the House of Lords concluded that interim relief be granted in the terms of the Divisional Court's original order that provisions of the Merchant Shipping Act 1988 be disapplied. Only Lord Bridge spoke of implications for the doctrine of parliamentary sovereignty:

> Some public comments on the decision of the European Court of Justice . . . have suggested that this was a novel and dangerous invasion by a Community institution of the sovereignty of the United Kingdom Parliament. But such comments are based on a misconception . . . Under the terms of the Act of 1972 it has always been clear that it was the duty of a United Kingdom court . . . to override any rule of national law found to be in conflict with any directly enforceable rule of Community law. Similarly when decisions of the European Court of Justice have exposed areas of United Kingdom statute law which failed to implement Council directives, Parliament has always loyally accepted the obligation to make appropriate and prompt amendments. Thus

---

[47] Lord Denning in his majority judgment, n. 32 above, 200EF.    [48] *Ibid.* 334E.

[49] *R.* v. *Secretary of State for Transport ex parte Factortame Ltd* [1989] 2 *CMLR* 353 at [19], [30], [43].

[50] *R.* v. *Secretary of State for Transport ex parte Factortame Ltd* [1990] 2 AC 85 at 143AB.

> there is nothing in any way novel in according supremacy to rules of
> Community law in those areas to which they apply.[51]

Judicial reliance on the terms of the 1972 Act, the failure expressly to
modify the doctrine of implied repeal to exclude its application, Lord
Bridge's earlier orthodox affirmation of Parliament's sovereignty as a
matter of English law and his later denial of anything novel or dangerous
in the supremacy of Community law are all acts and omissions, not of
judicial revolution, at least in any ordinary sense, but of judicial self-
restraint, if not self-abnegation.

At various points in his writings on parliamentary sovereignty, Wade
suggested that courts merely recognise political facts. He described how
they follow 'the movement of political events', 'turn a blind eye to
constitutional theory' and so illustrate the constitution's 'bending
before the winds of change'.[52] He appreciated a certain self-restraint,[53]
which is misrepresented with a notion of judicial revolution.

Two lines of defence are discernible in Wade's writings. First, Wade
described the revolution in the second *Factortame* case as a 'constitutional revolution', 'at least in a technical sense'.[54] For the concept of
revolution to be appropriate, however, it must refer to something more
than important change, for example, to 'a fresh start',[55] an overturning
of the existing order or a break in continuity of fundamental significance. It could be used to describe a departure from the fundamental
rule upon which a legal system depends, but whether whatever change
has occurred could rightly be characterised as such is in issue. In the
common law, if parliamentary sovereignty is in the keeping of the

---

[51] Note 18 above, at 658G–659B. See also the quotation for which n. 18 above provides the
citation.

[52] 'Basis of legal sovereignty', n. 16 above, 191; 'Revolution or evolution?', n. 45 above,
575. For recent judicial responses to political reality in a different context, see the
emphasis upon, or the numerous concessions to, the political reality that Parliament
had long accorded validity to the Parliament Act 1949, *Jackson* case, n. 10 above: Lord
Bingham at [36]; Lord Nicholls at [68], [69]; Lord Hope at [119], [120], [124]–[128];
Lord Carswell at [171].

[53] Cf. generally the activism of a constitutional court expected by Mitchell, 'What happened to the constitution?', n. 45 above, especially at 77–81, 83.

[54] 'Revolution or evolution?', n. 45 above, 568. See also *ibid*. 574.

[55] Wade expressly used the concept of revolution in this sense in a letter (dated April 1956)
to H. L. A. Hart. See also, e.g., Dicey's orthodox notion of revolution in the following
passage: 'where . . . the right to individual freedom is part of the constitution because it
is inherent in the ordinary law of the land, the right is one which can hardly be destroyed
without a thorough revolution in the institutions and manners of the nation', *Law of the
Constitution*, n. 1 above, p. 201.

courts, judicial denial of, or failure to identify, any change throws into doubt its occurrence or, if change is evident nonetheless, the very idea of a fundamental rule and the systemic coherence of the case law system it is supposed to support.

Secondly, Wade dismissed legal argument to the contrary as camouflage in peaceful revolutions: '[w]hen sovereignty is relinquished in an atmosphere of harmony, the naked fact of revolution is not so easy to discern beneath its elaborate legal dress'.[56] At times of actual or potential crisis, however, legal argumentation is more than mere camouflage. Facilitating orderly constitutional adaptation through the legitimacy it confers, it is intrinsic to the judicial response. John Eekelaar rightly suggests that 'there are good reasons for courts to sustain legal continuity' based on assumptions about its value 'in permitting constitutional development to proceed in an orderly fashion within the discipline of established legal methodology and argumentation rather than to depend on the shifting sands of political convenience'.[57] In the second *Factortame* case, Lord Bridge expressly responded with legal argument to public claims that the ECJ's decision was a new and dangerous violation of the sovereignty of the Westminster Parliament.[58] To the common law court, 'the boundaries of the law' are blurred, and the judicial conscience is uneasy if the court fails to find legal answers to whatever questions, be they legal or political, it is required to decide at times of crisis or significant change.[59] At least from an internal point of view, from the perspective of the court, revolution, even a technical revolution, is not effected but assiduously avoided.

### Hart's rule of recognition

Sir William Wade described the change in the second *Factortame* case in terms of, *inter alia*, a 'new "rule of recognition"' and cited *The Concept of*

---

[56] 'Basis of legal sovereignty', n. 16 above, 191. See also *ibid.* 196; Wade, 'Revolution or evolution?', n. 45 above, 575.

[57] 'The death of parliamentary sovereignty – a comment' (1997) 113 *LQR* 185 at 187.

[58] Note 18 above, at 658G–659C. For a South African example, see the *Harris* case, n. 39 above, which Wade admits was argued throughout 'as if there was a right or wrong legal answer', 'Basis of legal sovereignty', n. 16 above, 192.

[59] *Contra* 'to a lawyer the boundaries of the law need not be obscure, and his conscience may be easy if, by observing them, he avoids attempting to give legal answers to political questions': Wade 'Basis of legal sovereignty', n. 16 above, 197.

*Law*.[60] Hart's approach to constitutional fundamentals was similar to Wade's, but, in private correspondence, Hart criticised Wade for introducing a 'tender use of the concept of a "legal revolution"' and called for a 'careful description of what it is for a *Grundnorm* to change' including criteria to distinguish 'non-revolutionary changes from "revolutions"'.[61] In *The Concept of Law*, Hart did not adopt a notion of legal or judicial revolution. One reason why he might not have can be extrapolated from his famous passage on the judicial authority to decide on fundamental constitutional issues:

> The truth may be that, when courts settle previously unenvisaged questions concerning the most fundamental constitutional rules, they *get* their authority to decide them after the questions have arisen and the decision has been given. *Here all that succeeds is success* ... [W]hat makes possible these striking developments by courts of the most fundamental rules is, in great measure, the prestige gathered by courts from their unquestionably rule-governed operations over the vast, central areas of the law.[62]

So as not to put success at risk or place an intolerable burden on judicial prestige for its realisation, judges can be expected to avoid any suggestion of judicial revolution when deciding on constitutional fundamentals. Wade's use of the concept of revolution did not reflect their point of view.

In the postscript to the second edition of *The Concept of Law*, published posthumously, Hart described, in passing, the rule of recognition as 'in effect a form of judicial customary rule existing only if it is accepted and practised in the law-identifying and law-applying operations of the courts'.[63] By implication, it changes as practice or custom changes. It evolves with practice in the absence, presumably, of real revolutionary circumstances.

Hart's description in his postscript of the rule of recognition as a form of judicial customary rule, through its narrow focus upon judicial practice, misrepresents his original analysis in *The Concept of Law*.[64] In his original

---

[60] 'Revolution or evolution?', n. 45 above, 574; H. L. A. Hart, *The Concept of Law* (Oxford: Oxford University Press, 1961).

[61] Letter (dated 15 December 1955) addressed to Wade in which Hart commented on an offprint of Wade's article, 'Basis of legal sovereignty', n. 16 above. The second quotation is from a postcard (dated 10 April 1956) to Wade.

[62] H. L. A. Hart, *The Concept of Law* (Oxford, 2nd edn, 1994), pp. 153, 154 (the emphasis on the sentence is mine).

[63] *Ibid.* p. 256. See generally J. Coleman (ed.), *Hart's Postscript: Essays on the Postscript to the Concept of Law* (Oxford: Oxford University Press, 2001).

[64] Goldsworthy, *Sovereignty of Parliament*, n. 2 above, p. 241, n. 18.

analysis, the rule of recognition is not merely in the keeping of the courts but exists as a 'practice of the courts, officials, and private persons in identifying the law'.[65] Evidence of a new rule in that complex practice has been partial and difficult to identify. The speeches of their Lordships in the second *Factortame* case did not acknowledge a change and Lord Bridge's denial left its extent, if not its actual occurrence, uncertain.[66] Evidence of a new rule of recognition effected through the Human Rights Act 1998, discussed in Chapter Eight below,[67] has been similarly obscure. In the White Paper, *Rights Brought Home: The Human Rights Bill*, the Government did not acknowledge any change. It sought to give effective protection to the European Convention for the Protection of Human Rights and Fundamental Freedoms, but defined parliamentary sovereignty in an orthodox way and gave it as the reason for not conferring on courts the power to set aside Acts of Parliament.[68] Parliament's intention to maintain parliamentary sovereignty as traditionally understood is evident in the limited scope of ss 3 and 4 of the Human Rights Act 1998. Whereas s 3 only requires that a court interpret legislation to achieve compatibility with Convention rights, s 4 only provides for a judicial declaration where incompatibility is found to exist. However strained judicial interpretation under s 3 has become,[69] the Government and Parliament sought[70] to avoid contradicting Parliament's sovereignty even more assiduously than did the English courts in interpreting the ECA 1972. Talk of a new rule of recognition overstates and oversimplifies[71] whatever change of official practice has in fact occurred.

---

[65] *Concept of Law*, n. 62 above, p. 110.

[66] Wade admitted that 'it is hazardous to draw conclusions' and that to 'predict just what that change may entail can only be guesswork': 'Revolution or evolution?', n. 45 above, 575.

[67] Pages 221ff.

[68] Cm 3782 (1997), para. 2.13. Elsewhere, the former Lord Chancellor, similarly emphasised parliamentary sovereignty but also recognised the profound impact of the ECA 1972, and the likely impact of the Human Rights Act 1998, on the general process of deciding cases: Lord Irvine, 'The development of human rights in Britain under an incorporated Convention on Human Rights' [1998] PL 221, especially at 225, 229–32.

[69] Cf., e.g., *R v. A (No. 2)* [2002] 1 AC 45; [2001] UKHL 25; *R (Anderson) v. Secretary of State for the Home Department* [2003] 1 AC 837; [2002] UKHL 46; *Ghaidan v. Godin-Mendoza* [2004] 2 AC 557; [2004] UKHL 30.

[70] See generally Bamforth, 'Parliamentary sovereignty and the Human Rights Act 1998', n. 36 above.

[71] For a response to complexity through an elaboration on inconsistent rules of recognition in a pluralist model of a legal system, see N. W. Barber, 'Legal pluralism and the European Union' (2006) 12 *European Law Journal* 306.

## The analytical preoccupation with legal system

Why Sir William Wade should have analysed common law practice, traditionally preoccupied[72] with procedures, precedents and the *minutiae* of statutory construction, in terms of fundamental facts, ultimate legal principles and judicial revolutions requires explanation. The formative influences on Wade's analysis are not entirely clear. On occasion, Wade used Kelsen's term, the *Grundnorm*,[73] but made only a passing reference to Kelsen in his 1955 article. There, he quoted John Salmond's exposition of an 'ultimate legal principle' with approval and merely noted the similarity between it and Kelsen's exposition of the *Grundnorm*.[74]

In his book on jurisprudence, Salmond did not acknowledge the sources of influence on his own exposition. According to Glanville Williams, the editor of the tenth edition,

> The reader who seeks a connected exposition of the views of Kelsen, Duguit, the American 'realists', or any other shade of jurisprudential thought differing from Salmond's, will look here in vain. Salmond's method in writing the book was to give a smooth and lucid presentation of his own point of view, mostly as though it were the only opinion in the world.[75]

In content and style, however, Salmond's book exemplifies the genre of English textbooks on general jurisprudence that were published in the nineteenth and early twentieth centuries to provide a systematic treatment of law for teaching purposes in the proliferating new law schools and that were based on Continental, often Pandectist, systematic

---

[72] See generally Allison, *Continental Distinction in the Common Law*, n. 23 above, pp. 122–35.

[73] E.g., in a letter (dated April 1956) to H. L. A. Hart and in discussion at 'The Foundations of Judicial Review', Conference, Centre for Public Law, University of Cambridge, 22 May 1999. Cf. generally Wade's notion of judicial revolution with Kelsen's shift of *Grundnorm*: H. Kelsen, *Pure Theory of Law*, M. Knight (tr.) (Berkeley: University of California Press, 1967), especially at pp. 208–11; J. W. Harris, 'When and why does the Grundnorm change?' [1971] *CLJ* 103.

[74] Note 16 above, 187 and n. 43. J. W. Salmond, *Jurisprudence* (London: Sweet and Maxwell, 10th edn, 1947), pp. 155–6. In private discussion on 17 January 2000, nearly 50 years later, Wade suggested to me that his analysis was essentially the product of his own thinking, that at the time he thought he was stating the obvious and that he was only influenced by Salmond when he found the passage he cited.

[75] *Jurisprudence*, n. 74 above, p. ix.

models.[76] Considerable Continental European influence at least on Salmond's systematic enterprise is highly probable.

Salmond's concern to present for the student a system of law and the logic of a legal system is overriding in the passage cited by Wade:

> All rules of law have historical sources. As a matter of fact and history they have their origin somewhere, though we may not know what it is. But not all of them have legal sources. Were this so, it would be necessary for the law to proceed *ad infinitum* in tracing the descent of its principles. It is requisite that the law should postulate one or more first causes, whose operation is ultimate and whose authority is underived ... The rule that a man may not ride a bicycle on the footpath may have its source in the by-laws of a municipal council; the rule that these by-laws have the force of law has its source in an Act of Parliament. But whence comes the rule that Acts of Parliament have the force of law? This is legally ultimate; its source is historical only, not legal ... It is the law because it is the law, and for no other reason that it is possible for the law itself to take notice of. No statute can confer this power upon Parliament, for this would be to assume and act on the very power that is to be conferred.[77]

Salmond presented the ultimate legal principle of a legal system as a postulate with which to avoid an infinite regress into legal sources and illustrated it by invoking parliamentary sovereignty.

Wade shared Salmond's concern with legal system. He was particularly attracted by Salmond's logic in the passage above:

> Once this truth is grasped, the dilemma is solved. For if no statute can establish the rule that the courts obey Acts of Parliament, similarly no statute can alter or abolish that rule. The rule is above and beyond the reach of statute, as Salmond so well explains, because it is itself the source of the authority of statute. This puts it into a class by itself among rules of common law, and the apparent paradox that it is unalterable by Parliament turns out to be a truism. The rule of judicial obedience is in one sense a rule of common law, but in another sense – which applies to

---

[76] See P. G. Stein, 'Continental influences on English legal thought, 1600–1900' in P. G. Stein, *The Character and Influence of the Roman Civil Law: Historical Essays* (London: The Hambledon Press, 1988), pp. 209–29, especially at pp. 223ff. See, e.g., J. Austin, *Lectures on Jurisprudence* or *The Philosophy of Positive Law* (London: J. Murray, 5th edn, 1885); W. Markby, *Elements of Law Considered with Reference to Principles of General Jurisprudence* (Oxford: Oxford University Press, 6th edn, 1905); T. E. Holland, *The Elements of Jurisprudence* (Oxford: Oxford University Press, 13th edn, 1924); F. Pollock, *A First Book of Jurisprudence for Students of the Common Law* (London: Macmillan, 6th edn, 1929).
[77] Salmond, *Jurisprudence*, n. 74 above, p. 155.

> no other rule of common law – it is the ultimate *political* fact upon which
> the whole system of legislation hangs.[78]

Wade's notion of judicial revolution was the outcome of deduction, as was the political factual character of the fundamental rule. If a system's first cause or fundamental rule were to be changed, the change would be revolutionary *a priori*. Wade's analytical exposition of fundamental rule and judicial revolution was in service of his notion of legal system, the systemic coherence of which required a first cause.

Hart, whose views generally converged with Wade's, was similarly pre-occupied with system. He noted that his ultimate rule of recognition resembled Salmond's 'insufficiently elaborated conception of "ultimate legal principles"' and acknowledged his general indebtedness to Kelsen on various occasions.[79] Through his linguistic empiricism, however, Hart domesticated Kelsen. Whereas Kelsen elaborated on pure normative legal cognition on the presupposition of his *Grundnorm*, Hart produced an 'essay in descriptive sociology' by way of an enquiry into the meanings we give to words such as rule, obligation etc.[80] According to Hart's analytical thesis, the ultimate rule of recognition is not merely presupposed but actually enjoys official acceptance in the operation of a system of law.[81]

In applying his analytical thesis by identifying or illustrating the rule of recognition in English legal practice,[82] Hart made empirical claims comparable to Salmond's assertion that the sources of parliamentary sovereignty as the ultimate legal principle are historical and that of Wade in describing that principle as ultimate political fact. Their empirical claims are peculiarly problematic in the context of the common law.[83] Kelsen wrote in the Continental systematic tradition, which has produced 'in modern times constitutions and basic laws which are, as it were, the legally uncaused cause of all legal effects'.[84] In contrast, Salmond, Wade and Hart laid claim to something similarly simplistic in the common law's seamless

---

[78] 'Basis of legal sovereignty', n. 16 above, 187–8.

[79] *Concept of Law*, n. 62 above, pp. 292ff.; N. MacCormick, *H. L. A. Hart* (London: Edward Arnold, 1981), especially at pp. 25–6, 165–6.

[80] Hart, *Concept of Law*, n. 62 above, p. v. See generally Hart's defence of his descriptive enterprise in his postscript, *ibid*. pp. 239–44. See generally R. Cotterrell, *The Politics of Jurisprudence: A Critical Introduction to Legal Philosophy* (London: LexisNexis, 2nd edn, 2003), pp. 83–7.

[81] See *Concept of Law*, n. 62 above, pp. 108ff.     [82] See, e.g., *ibid*. pp. 107f.

[83] Cf. generally Goldsworthy's use of pre-twentieth century history to support his philosophical argument about the modern doctrine of parliamentary sovereignty, *Sovereignty of Parliament*, n. 2 above, especially at p. 8, chs. 9, 10.

[84] MacCormick, *H. L. A. Hart*, n. 79 above, p. 4.

web of judicial decisions, to which those on the supremacy of Community law are recent additions. To describe that web in terms of evolving custom[85] or an array of precedents would have been less ambitious than, in a relentless analytical embrace, to elaborate on an implicit system of rules with defined interrelations or identifiable lineage.

Hart's descriptive sociology, in general, and his notion of the rule of recognition, in particular, as operative in an actual legal system of law, have been criticised for 'sociological drift', for lacking a thorough investigation of actual practices and attitudes.[86] His description, however, of the rule of recognition as a form of judicial customary rule in his postscript, suitably modified to transcend judicial practice, changing by implication as custom changes, is less vulnerable to sociological criticism than is Wade's analysis of a fundamental rule changed only by judicial revolution. To view Parliament's sovereignty as an ultimate rule of recognition in the common law and a judicial revolution when it changes is somehow to imagine the omnipotence of a *deus ex machina* at work in the quicksand of English case law. Sir William Wade located parliamentary sovereignty in the common law, in the keeping of the courts, but, under the influence of Salmond and the European notions of legal system reflected in Salmond, he neglected the common law's evolutionary case law character and thus a central feature of the English historical constitution viewed from an analytical legal perspective.

## Principles of legal and political morality

A prominent theoretical approach to parliamentary sovereignty offered as an alternative to the systematic analytical approach of authors such as Dicey and Wade is the interpretive approach of the liberal normativist, as discussed in Chapter Two.[87] By this approach, influenced by Ronald Dworkin's writings on legal principle, Parliament's sovereignty is conceived, not as a legal system's fundamental rule, but as a typical common-law doctrine interpreted in accordance with principles of legal and political morality. Trevor Allan's interpretive constitutional theory in *Law*,

---

[85] See generally A. W. B. Simpson, 'The common law and legal theory' in A. W. B. Simpson (ed.), *Oxford Essays in Jurisprudence (Second Series)* (Oxford: Oxford University Press, 1973), pp. 77–99.

[86] R. Cotterrell, *Politics of Jurisprudence*, n. 80 above, pp. 90–2, 95–6.

[87] See above, pp. 29ff.

*Liberty, and Justice* is exemplary.[88] He asserts that '[l]egal questions which challenge the nature of our constitutional order can only be answered in terms of the political morality on which that order is based'.[89] He does not identify a revolution in the judicial interpretation of the ECA 1972: 'There is no real need to resort to notions of "revolution" or "shifts of *Grundnorm*" to explain the result of the *Factortame* litigation. It is simply the legitimate consequence of the interpretation of sovereignty which best reflects new conceptions of the political community.'[90] In Allan's constitutional theory, the ECA 1972 is interpreted, as are all statutes, in view of whatever constitutional or legal political principles are at stake.

In *Law, Liberty, and Justice*, the main text of which was written before[91] the second *Factortame* case, Allan's approach to parliamentary sovereignty hinges on the role of principles. For his conception of principles, as discussed in Chapter Two,[92] Allan draws on Dworkin and emphasises that it 'is not possible for *principles* to be enacted, rather than rules, because a principle has no real existence apart from its weight' and that a 'principle is applied to particular facts because – and only to the extent that – it is *understood* to be appropriate'.[93] Allan accentuates the role of such principles in the judicial interpretation of ECA 1972. In relation to *Macarthys*, he concludes that the precedence of Community law 'has been achieved, for all practical purposes, by adoption of a principle of construction of unusual force, reflecting the courts' perception of the contemporary demands of political morality'.[94] After discussing *Pickstone*, his formulation is similar: 'The strength and force of the principle of statutory construction (the presumption that Parliament intended to conform with obligations under the Treaty of Rome) reflects changing judicial perception of the political community which the constitutional order exists to serve'.[95] In the passages above and elsewhere,[96] Allan claims, not that principles of political morality were articulated, but merely that they are reflected or

---

[88] T.R.S. Allan, *Law, Liberty, and Justice: The Legal Foundations of British Constitutionalism* (Oxford: Oxford University Press, 1993), ch. 11. Cf. generally Craig, 'Sovereignty of the United Kingdom Parliament', n. 35 above, and Goldsworthy, *Sovereignty of Parliament*, n. 2 above, pp. 246ff.

[89] *Law, Liberty, and Justice*, n. 88 above, p. 266.

[90] *Ibid.* p. 280.   [91] See *ibid.* p. 277, n. 58, p. 280, n. 69.   [92] See above, pp. 29f.

[93] *Ibid.* p. 93; R. Dworkin, *Taking Rights Seriously* (London: Duckworth, 1977), pp. 22ff., 71ff.

[94] *Law, Liberty, and Justice*, n. 88 above, p. 276; *Macarthys*, n. 32 above.

[95] *Ibid.* p. 279; *Pickstone* v. *Freemans Plc.* [1989] 1 AC 66.

[96] See also, e.g., *Law, Liberty and Justice*, n. 88 above, pp. 280, 282.

mirrored in the judicial application of principles or presumptions of construction. Allan's limited claim is judicious. Apart from their general references to sovereignty, the courts in *Macarthys* and *Pickstone* did not articulate the principles of political morality at stake. Allan too does not specify exactly which principles are evident, nor does he suggest a principle comparable to Dworkin's famous example, 'no man may profit from his own wrong'.[97] In short, he does not elaborate on whatever principle of political community be implicit in judicial understandings so as to be able to specify whether, or in what respects, that community be England, Britain or the European Union.

The weight of a principle may well not be amenable to enactment but, if principles of political morality are not specified or even articulated, they cannot be identified or debated as requirements of 'justice or fairness or some other dimension of morality'.[98] They are indistinguishable from private sentiments, cultural predispositions and the political preferences or prejudices according to which principles or presumptions of construction may potentially be manipulated. Their content, if not also their character as principles, is in doubt, as is the weight they do or should carry in rational decision making. In the absence of principles of political morality actually articulated by the courts or specified and elaborated by Allan through an interpretation of case law, his theoretical account of their centrality is not an exposition of existing judicial practice.

In the second *Factortame* case, the House of Lords again[99] did not offer principles of legal and political morality in justification, apart from a vague contractarian principle implicit in Lord Bridge's argument that the United Kingdom voluntarily accepted the supremacy of Community law because that supremacy was well established when the United Kingdom joined the Community and the European Communities Act 1972 was passed.[100] In response, Allan seems to have accepted that his

---

[97] *Taking Rights Seriously*, n. 93 above, p. 25.

[98] The definition of principle is Dworkin's, *ibid.* p. 22.

[99] See also the recent *Jackson* case, n. 10 above, in which Lord Steyn did emphasise questions of legal and political principle but did not regard them as critical to the outcome of the case, at [71], [73], [101], [102]. A few of the other Law Lords talked of constraints upon parliamentary sovereignty but also did not regard them as critical or treated them as political rather than legal or constitutional: see, e.g., Lord Hope at [104], [126], [127]; Lord Walker at [141]; Baroness Hale at [159]; Lord Brown at [194]. See generally J. Jowell, 'Parliamentary sovereignty under the new constitutional hypothesis' [2006] PL 562.

[100] Note 18 above, at 658H–659A; Craig, 'Sovereignty of the United Kingdom Parliament', n. 35 above, 249; P. P. Craig, 'The European Community, the Crown and the state' in

theoretical account is mainly prescriptive rather than expository. In his comment on the case, he recognises the 'absence of relevant discussion in the *Factortame* judgments' and that the decision of the House of Lords 'is presented in largely technical terms, with little serious attempt to articulate the constitutional considerations at stake'.[101] He argues in general that when 'constitutional debate is opened up to ordinary legal reasoning, based on fundamental principles, we shall discover that the notion of unlimited parliamentary sovereignty no longer makes any legal or constitutional sense'.[102] Allan is here advocating his principled approach as an alternative to that of the courts.

If constitutional judicial debate were opened up as Allan recommends, how might principles of legal and political morality conceivably influence a decision on the relationship between English and Community law? In his comment on the second *Factortame* case, Allan suggests the relevance of two principles – legal certainty and the democratic principle that the choice of people and Parliament, expressed in a referendum and the ECA 1972, to join a supra-national entity be respected.[103] Both these principles, however, each simultaneously pull in two opposite directions. The principle of legal certainty might be interpreted to require, on the one hand, consistency with the decisions of the ECJ, and, on the other, that a British statute's clear and ascertainable provisions prevail over the myriad of directives and activist judicial decisions of Community law. Similarly, the principle of democracy might be interpreted to require fidelity, on the one hand, to the ECA 1972, and, on the other, to a more recent British statute passed by a Parliament not suffering from the democratic deficit for which the institutions of the European Union are criticised. To democracy and legal certainty, one might add the principle of legal equality. This too can be variously interpreted to require, on the one hand, the equal application of Community law throughout the European Union, and, on the other, that the Merchant Shipping Act be applied as any other British statute. How any or all of these versatile and unruly principles can decisively influence or justify a decision is unclear, as is their weight relative to that of the vague contractarian principle implicit[104] in Lord Bridge's argument.

---

M. Sunkin and S. Payne (eds.), *The Nature of the Crown: A Legal and Political Analysis* (Oxford: Oxford University Press, 1999), pp. 315–36 at pp. 330ff.

[101] T. R. S. Allan, 'Parliamentary sovereignty: law, politics, and revolution' (1997) 113 LQR 443 at 448.

[102] *Ibid.* 449.     [103] *Ibid.* 445.

[104] The second *Factortame* case, n. 18 above, at 658H–659A.

Goldsworthy's description of principles of political morality suggests reasons why the English courts have traditionally been wary of invoking them:

> As well as being abstract and imprecise, these fundamental moral principles [such as justice, democracy, and the rule of law] are inherently defeasible: situations can be envisaged in which each one is outweighed or overridden by one or more of the others. Even the most basic human rights, to life, liberty, and property, can be overridden in unusual circumstances. Opinions can differ as to whether it is better to entrust elected legislators, or judges, with ultimate authority to weigh up competing moral principles, and decide which of them ought to prevail. But in either case, their decisions will depend on controversial judgments of political morality.[105]

Were courts to invoke such principles at times of actual or potential constitutional crisis, they would risk political controversy, disagreement with and amongst executive and legislative officials and a further loss of stability in the legal and political system. In his discussion of the second *Factortame* case, Allan explains the absence of such principles with reference to 'the judges' understandable reluctance to risk political controversy' but dismisses the explanation for not reflecting 'any credit on what is our highest constitutional court'.[106] To serve as a realistic alternative, however, the approach recommended by Allan must recognise the reality of that judicial reluctance and a principle underlying it. The judicial interpretation of the ECA 1972 has been characterised, not by principles of political morality, but, if any be evident, by a certain principle of political economy, enjoining an economy of political principle.

## The economy of the common law

Allan's comment on *Macarthys* lacks the emphasis of his later work on principles of legal and political morality. He applauds Lord Denning's deftness, 'dexterity' and 'cautious wisdom' in developing a principle of construction stronger than the *prima facie* presumption that Parliament intended to comply with international obligation: 'Lord Denning's interpretation of section 2(4) of the European Communities Act results in an even stronger principle of interpretation: Parliament must state expressly that inconsistent Community law is not to prevail if the

---

[105] *Sovereignty of Parliament*, n. 2 above, p. 258.
[106] 'Parliamentary sovereignty', n. 101 above, 448.

presumption against conflict between Community law and national legislation is to be rebutted.'[107] Lord Denning's interpretation was dexterous because of its economy. Free of tendentious statements of political principle, it affirmed the tradition of Parliament's sovereignty, was expressly preoccupied with statutory construction and suggested minimal change to its rules and presumptions.

The *Factortame* litigation produced further examples[108] of the common law's economy. In the first *Factortame* case, Mr David Vaughan QC, counsel for the applicants, advocated a simple exercise in statutory construction: 'Where there is an apparent inconsistency between . . . two Acts [a later and an earlier Act] it is simply an exercise of construction to determine whether the later Act is intended to take effect subject to the provisions of the earlier Act or whether it impliedly repeals (or supersedes) those earlier provisions.'[109] When interpreting the ECA 1972 in the first *Factortame* case, Lord Bridge performed just such an exercise:

> By virtue of section 2(4) of the Act of 1972 Part II of the Act of 1988 is to be construed and take effect subject to directly enforceable Community rights and those rights are, by section 2(1) of the Act of 1972, to be 'recognised and available in law, and . . . enforced, allowed and followed accordingly; . . .' *This has precisely the same effect as if a section were incorporated in Part II of the Act of 1988* which in terms enacted that the provisions with respect to registration of British fishing vessels were to be without prejudice to the directly enforceable Community rights of nationals of any member state of the E.E.C.[110]

As suggested by Sir John Laws, the implicit rule that the constructive exercise should not occur when precluded by Parliament with express words is not unprecedented. It is comparable to the existing rule that statutes should not be construed to exact taxes or impose criminal liability unless express words so provide.[111]

---

[107] T. R. S. Allan, 'Parliamentary sovereignty: Lord Denning's dexterous revolution' (1983) 3 *OJLS* 22, especially at 33, 31.

[108] For a famous earlier example, see *Anisminic Ltd* v. *Foreign Compensation Commission* [1969] 2 AC 147. For recent economical judicial emphasis upon statutory construction in the *Jackson* case, n. 10 above, see the speeches of Lord Bingham, Lord Nicholls, Lord Rodger, especially at [132], [136], [138], and Lord Carswell, especially at [169].

[109] The first *Factortame* case, n. 50 above, at 96F.    [110] *Ibid.* 140BC (my emphasis).

[111] 'Law and Democracy' [1995] PL 72 at 89, n. 48. Cf. generally the extrajudicial reference of Lord Woolf to fairy tales and Sir Stephen Sedley's strong extrajudicial advocacy of 'bi-polar sovereignty of the Crown in Parliament and the Crown in its courts', which are unconstrained by the economy of approach exemplified by the courts: Woolf,

In the second *Factortame* case, Lord Bridge performed another such exercise through his tacit or unknowing abandonment of the doctrine of implied repeal in his argument that 'whatever limitation of its sovereignty Parliament accepted when it enacted the European Communities Act 1972 was entirely voluntary'.[112] Carol Harlow rightly stresses the formalism of Lord Bridge's speech:

> This passage [where he addresses the issue of sovereignty] neutralises the decision, bringing it within the bounds of the classic constitution and rendering it apparently uncontroversial. Divesting the courts of all responsibility for an outcome presented as inevitable, the speech formally allocates responsibility to Parliament, which should have perceived the implications of the legislation it was passing on accession ... [T]he metaphor of legal autonomy, the ideology of positivism and the methodology of formalism, have served the unwritten constitution well, helping the judges in a famous metaphor 'to keep their heads below the parapet' and facilitating dispute resolution in highly charged political cases.[113]

Analytical formalism is a Diceyan legacy but one still serving the unwritten or historical constitution characterised by its economy, particularly in cases of political controversy.

The forms of economy available in the common law are various. At least five are brought into issue by the different approaches discussed in this chapter. One form is exemplified in judicial review on the ground of procedural irregularity. The court imposes procedural controls – rules of manner and form – and so leaves the authority free to decide on substance. A second form is minimal revision or piecemeal development of the law. The court minimises change, and, where change is necessary, the appearance of change, certainly any semblance of radical or revolutionary change. Conversely, it maximises continuity or the appearance of continuity. A third form involves avoiding the contentious abstraction of principle or reducing the significance of versatile, imprecise and contested principles of legal and political morality with their unpredictable weight in future cases. A fourth form is statutory construction through the formalistic coupling of a judicial decision to the intention

---

'Droit public – English style' [1995] *PL* 57, especially at 67; Sedley 'Human rights: a twenty-first century agenda' [1995] *PL* 386 at 389. See also Sedley, 'The sound of silence: constitutional law without a constitution' (1994) 110 *LQR* 270 at 289–91; ch. 8 below, pp. 216ff.

[112] Note 18 above, 659A.    [113] 'Disposing of Dicey', n. 25 above, at 363, 365.

of Parliament. The court defers or appears to defer to the will of Parliament, and its decision is restricted to the application of a particular statute, which Parliament is free to amend, although in the case of the ECA 1972, not by implication. Finally, a fifth form is general obfuscation[114] through a failure to explain or acknowledge all the issues at stake and thus not clearly or specifically to address them.

The various forms of economy are the outcome of judicial pragmatism, a reluctance to risk political controversy, understandings of the rough English separation of powers[115] and the sparing deployment or engagement of judicial resources. In the common law, they are traditional. They are manifest in the restrictions on the judicial role in adversarial procedure[116] and the many historic uses of legal fiction, by which the courts avoided the controversy and unpredictability of openly changing the law. They are also evident in the judicial interpretation of the ECA 1972. In their effect upon parliamentary sovereignty, one of Dicey's two fundamental principles, they illustrate the historical constitution's economical legal mode of formation.

## Resilience through change and continuity

European influences and English peculiarities have been manifest in the modern legal development of the doctrine of parliamentary sovereignty. The English courts have accommodated the ECJ's claim to the supremacy of Community law, and influential English doctrinal writers – particularly Salmond, Wade and Hart – in their analytical writings on parliamentary sovereignty, have been affected by the Continental preoccupation with legal system. The common law courts have responded to fundamental and controversial legal and political issues in traditional ways. As the ground has been moving beneath the nation state in an era of globalisation, interdependence and transnationalism,[117] they have demonstrated a characteristic economy. They have secured the

---

[114] I am grateful to Jeffrey Goldsworthy for drawing my attention to this fifth form.

[115] See generally ch. 4 above.

[116] See generally Allison, *Continental Distinction in the Common Law*, n. 23 above, pp. 216ff.

[117] See generally N. MacCormick, 'Beyond the sovereign state' (1993) 56 *MLR* 1; N. MacCormick, *Questioning Sovereignty: Law, State, and Nation in the European Commonwealth* (Oxford: Oxford University Press, 1999); N. Walker (ed.), *Relocating Sovereignty* (Dartmouth: Ashgate, 2006), The International Library of Essays in Law & Legal Theory, Second Series, Part III; Hunt, *Using Human Rights Law*, n. 46 above, pp. 1–7.

supremacy of Community law and adapted to it by means of minimal change to their practices or rules of statutory construction. They have secured change and simultaneously demonstrated continuity in the historical constitution, both apparent and substantial.

To be readily applicable and realistic in expectation, theories of parliamentary sovereignty must take account of the various forms of economy, long demonstrated in the common law.[118] If Parliament's sovereignty be exercised according to legal rules of manner and form, how they might be imposed economically by courts is in issue. If an ultimate rule of recognition be indispensable for an English legal system, it would need somehow to be formulated to allow for its own minimal and gradual revision. If parliamentary sovereignty be weighed with other constitutional principles, principles of minimal revision and political economy would require recognition alongside principles of legal and political morality. Whether advocating (or opposing) an analytical or an interpretive approach, participants in the ongoing debate about parliamentary sovereignty have reason to recognise a continuing source of resilience for the historical constitution – the common law's traditional economy of judicial response, particularly to legal issues that are the subject of political controversy.

---

[118] Cf. generally Goldworthy's distrust of piecemeal judicial development in *Sovereignty of Parliament*, n. 2 above, pp. 270–1, and Hunt's advocacy of a general principle of statutory construction to achieve compatibility with international obligation precisely because of what were potentially far-reaching implications for human rights, *Using Human Rights Law*, n. 46 above, especially at p. 83.

# 6

## The brief rule of a controlling common law

From a historical constitutional perspective on the Crown's evolution and the key doctrinal developments that have already been discussed, the constitution is lacking in systemic elaboration and limited in express normativity. The Crown, the constitution's institutional centrepiece, remains analytically obscure – the ambivalent outcome of institutional change and conservation.[1] The rough English separation of powers was not established through authoritative declarations of principle but has evolved and continues to evolve as an uneven customary practice in doctrine, case law and legislation.[2] In accommodating the supremacy of Community law, the judicial adaptations to the doctrine on parliamentary sovereignty, Dicey's one pillar of the constitution, discussed in Chapter Five, illustrate, not the articulation of principles of legal and political morality, but the traditional economy of principle in the common law. Amidst the elusive principles, half-submerged in common-law practice, the rule of law, Dicey's other pillar – its formation, clarity and capacity to serve as the normative linchpin in the historical constitution, or as itself a form[3] of constitution – requires consideration.

The rule of law, for example, was invoked to justify and applaud the judicial recognition of the availability of an injunction and contempt jurisdiction against officers of the Crown, discussed in Chapter Three.[4] It may also be interpreted to curtail residual Crown immunities[5] or to embrace a Republican principle of equality that precludes the very

---

[1] See ch. 3 above.  [2] See ch. 4 above.

[3] T. R. S. Allan, *Law, Liberty, and Justice: The Legal Foundations of British Constitutionalism* (Oxford: Oxford University Press, 1993), pp. 4ff. See ch. 2 above, pp. 31ff.

[4] See pp. 67ff above. See, e.g., *M* v. *Home Office* [1993] 3 WLR 433 at 466F; H. W. R. Wade, 'The Crown – old platitudes and new heresies' (1992) 142 *New Law Journal* 1275, 1315.

[5] See, e.g., M. Gould, '*M* v. *Home Office*: government and the judges' [1993] *PL* 568 at 577–8; Sir Stephen Sedley, 'The sound of silence: constitutional law without a constitution' (1994) 110 *LQR* 270 at 288ff; T. Cornford, 'Legal Remedies against the Crown and its officers before and after *M*' in M. Sunkin and S. Payne (eds.), *The Nature of the Crown: A Legal and Political Analysis* (Oxford: Oxford University Press, 1999), pp. 233–65.

concept of the Crown and the centrality of the monarch it connotes. It deserves detailed consideration as a fundamental constitutional principle with which to assess appeals to history or continuity, for example, to the historical compromise represented by the 'immunity of the Crown and the non-immunity of its servants',[6] the call for change,[7] and the concrete effects of whatever be the contended balance between change and continuity on remedies, institutions[8] and private persons. If the historical constitution is necessarily to be more than a vehicle for the formation of rules, principles and practices relating to government through various pragmatic modes of change – evolutionary, customary and economical – a principle, or set of principles, is required with which to assess the balance between change and continuity, the counterpoise of old to new, the success or efficiency of constitutional innovation and the continuing necessity of apparent anachronism. Through this and the next two chapters, I will suggest that, although the rule of law be put to work as such a principle, while it has evolved and continues to evolve in scope and function, it is itself in need of assessment, at issue in a debate that is itself illustrative of an overarching feature of the historical constitution – a continuing preoccupation with change and continuity and with providing pragmatically for both.

In this and the next two chapters, I will use the historical constitutional approach explained in Chapter Two to focus on formative legal contributions and the debates they have provoked in the evolution of the rule of law. I will elaborate in this chapter on the work of Sir Edward Coke, described by Maitland as 'the great dividing line' between the medieval and the modern.[9] Chapter Seven deals with Dicey's *Law of the Constitution*, the foundational work in which he coined[10] or

---

[6] H. W. R. Wade, 'Crown, ministers and officials: legal status and liability' in Sunkin and Payne (eds.), *Nature of the Crown*, n. 5 above, pp. 23–32 at p. 32 (for the full quotation, see pp. 71f above). Cf. Paul Craig's appeal to 'our historical heritage', 'Ultra vires and the foundations of judicial review' [1998] *CLJ* 63, especially at 89.

[7] See, e.g., C. Vincenzi, *Crown Powers, Subjects and Citizens* (London: Pinter, 1998), especially at p. 316; A. Tomkins, *Our Republican Constitution* (Oxford: Hart Publishing, 2005), pp. 118ff, 139f.

[8] See generally the approach of T. Daintith and A. C. Page, *The Executive in the Constitution: Structure, Autonomy, and Internal Control* (Oxford: Oxford University Press, 1999), especially at p. 394.

[9] C. Hill, 'Sir Edward Coke – myth-maker' in C. Hill, *Intellectual Origins of the English Revolution* (London: Panther, 1972), pp. 225–65 at p. 227.

[10] F. H. Lawson, *The Oxford Law School, 1850–1965* (Oxford: Oxford University Press, 1968), p. 72.

popularised[11] the phrase 'the rule of law' to describe what he regarded as a peculiar feature of the constitution. If Coke stands between the medieval and the modern, Dicey divides the analytical approaches to the constitution that he pioneered from the historical approaches that preceded him and that he tried to distinguish and relegated in significance. Finally, in Chapter Eight, I will elaborate on the attempts, in recent decades, to develop or transcend Dicey's thinking about the rule of law and its relationship to the sovereignty of Parliament.

In these chapters on the development of the rule of law, I will again attempt to do justice to both Continental European influence and the peculiarity of the common law. I will argue that, despite Dicey's suggestions to the contrary and the obvious conceptual differences between the English rule of law and the Continental equivalent, the *Rechtsstaat*, centred on the concept of the state,[12] interactions between English and Continental European developments profoundly affected both of the legal contributions under consideration and thus the historical constitution through their formative influence. I will suggest that even Coke's famous invocation of Bracton's notion of a King under God and the law and Dicey's celebration in the peculiarity of the English constitution's rule of law in a Europe of ascendant nations states were influenced, inspired or motivated by events across the Channel. I will argue in this chapter that recognition of both Continental European influence and the common law's peculiarity facilitates our understanding of Coke's paradoxical and much-debated elaboration of a controlling common law alongside a transcendent Parliament. Coke's enduring contribution remains a resource, I will suggest, of historical constitutional significance.

---

[11] The phrase 'the general rule of law' was already used in *Mersey Docks Trustees* v. *Gibbs* (1866) 11 HLC 686, at 710 (see p. 154 below). Furthermore, Dicey wrote of 'the rule *or* supremacy of law', *An Introduction to the Study of the Law of the Constitution* (London: Macmillan, 10th edn, 1959), p. 184 (my emphasis). 'The supremacy of the law' is the title to para. 7, ch. 3 in W. E. Hearn, *The Government of England: Its Structure and Development* (London: Longmans, Green, Reader, and Dyer, 1867), p. iii. The rule of law is certainly a phrase 'which has come to be most closely connected with his name', H. G. Hanbury, *The Vinerian Chair and Legal Education* (Oxford: Basil Blackwell, 1958), ch. 8, especially at p. 135.

[12] See generally R. C. van Caenegem, 'The "Rechtsstaat" in historical perspective' in R. C. van Caenegem, *Legal History: A European Perspective* (London: The Hambledon Press, 1991), pp. 185–99; N. W. Barber, 'The *Rechtsstaat* and the rule of law' (2003) 53 *University of Toronto Law Journal* 443.

## Coke's common law of reason

An equivalent of Dicey's two pillars – the rule of law and parliamentary sovereignty – and the issue of their relative stability can be identified in the writings and reports of Sir Edward Coke, Chief Justice of the King's Bench from 1613 to 1616.

On the one hand, Coke emphasised the common law's controlling power. He claimed 'that the surest construction of a statute, is by the rule and reason of the common law'.[13] In *Bonham's Case*, according to his published reports, Coke, as Lord Chief Justice of Common Pleas, held that the Royal College of Physicians did not have certain powers that would involve imposing a fine in which it would have a pecuniary interest although they were conferred by patent and confirmed by statute.[14] His argument, which was to become famous, was presented with various other arguments that Coke also regarded as decisive. It was that such powers would have encroached upon *Nemo debet esse iudex in propria causa*, which has become known, alongside *audi alteram partem*, as one of the two principles of natural justice in developed English administrative law. His published report records a resounding and oft-quoted assertion of the controlling power of the common law:

> And it appears in our law books, that in many cases, the common law will controul acts of parliament, and sometimes adjudge them to be utterly void: for when an act of parliament is against common right and reason, or repugnant, or impossible to be performed, the common law will controul it, and adjudge such act to be void.[15]

Coke himself attached considerable importance to these words and twice copied them out in manuscript.[16]

On the other hand, apart from the common law's controlling power, Coke emphasised, particularly in his *Institutes of the Laws of England*, the pre-eminence of Parliament:

> Of the power and jurisdiction of the Parliament, for making of laws in proceedings by bill, it is so transcendent and absolute, as it cannot be confined either for causes or persons within any bounds. Of this court

---

[13] Co. Inst. I, 272b.    [14] (1610) 8 Co. Rep. 107.    [15] *Ibid.* 118a.

[16] Sir John Baker, 'Human rights in English legal history', Inaugural Lecture, Center for Law and History, Washington & Lee University School of Law, 12 September 2003, p. 23. Cf. C. M. Gray, 'Bonham's Case reviewed' (1972) 116 *Proceedings of the American Philosophical Society* 35, especially at 46, 49–50 (see n. 108 below).

it is truly said: *Si antiquitatem spectes, est vetustissima, si dignitatem, est honoratissima, si jurisdictionem, est capacissima.*[17]

Elsewhere in his *Institutes*, Coke described Parliament as 'the highest and most honourable and absolute court of justice in England, consisting of the king, the lords of parliament, and the commons' with a jurisdiction 'so transcendent, that it maketh, inlargeth, diminisheth, abrogateth, repealeth, and riviveth lawes, statutes, acts, and ordinances, containing matters ecclesiasticall, capitall, criminall, common, civill, martiall, maritime, and the rest'.[18] Furthermore, according to Coke, '[e]very statute ought to be expounded according to the intent of them that made it, *where the words thereof are doubtfull and uncertain*, and according to the rehearsall of the statute; and there a *generall* statute is construed particularly upon consideration had of the cause of making of the act, and of the rehearsall of all the parts of the act'.[19] By implication, Coke recognised the straightforward application of statutory words that are not doubtful and uncertain and of statutes that he did not regard as general, whether because of their 'speciall words' or some expressed 'limitation or saving'.[20]

In *Rowles v. Mason*, Coke admired both pillars – a controlling common law and the statutes of a transcendent Parliament. He said that all agreed that 'Statute Law ... corrects, abridges, and explains the common law ... But the common law Corrects, Allows, and Disallows ... Statute Law ...', for if there be repugnancy in Statute ... the Common Law Disallows and rejects it, as it appears by Doctor *Bonham's* case'.[21] Both common law and statute law stand proudly, side by side, as first among equals.

## Contrasting interpretations

Coke's contradictory[22] or paradoxical descriptions of a controlling common law alongside a transcendent Parliament are troubling from

---

[17] Co. Inst. IV, 36. His statement on Parliament's pre-eminence considerably exceeded Sir John Fortescue's emphasis upon its necessary prudence and wisdom, *De Laudibus Legum Anglie*, S. B. Chrimes (ed.) (Cambridge: Cambridge University Press, 1942), ch. 18.

[18] Co. Inst. I, 109b, 110a.     [19] Co. Inst. IV, 330 (my emphasis).     [20] *Ibid.*

[21] (1612) 2 Brownl 192, 198. Cf. generally Dicey, *Law of the Constitution*, n. 11 above, ch. 13.

[22] See generally C. Hill, 'Sir Edward Coke' in Hill, *Intellectual Origins of the English Revolution*, n. 9 above, pp. 225–65.

an analytical or theoretical perspective. They have been variously inter-preted. Prominent writers on Coke's common law have inclined in varying degrees to either of two contrasting interpretations: one of a European emanation, the other of an indigenous English development. Both, I will suggest, are difficult to sustain.

One group of writers[23] have identified Coke's invocation of the rule and reason of the common law with the European natural law tradition, which developed, particularly in canonist doctrine, from the law of nature in Greek and Roman thought and became influential in both England and on the Continent in the late Middle Ages. These writers have often been concerned to identify the historical background to the judicial review of legislation under the higher law of the US constitution. In an early article[24] on judicial review, based on two lectures, Mauro Cappelletti explicitly presented Coke as the champion of the common law as a higher law in the era of natural justice. In Cappelletti's dialectical analysis, *natural justice* was the thesis to which *legal justice* or *positive justice*, characterised by the primacy of parliamentary statute, was the

---

[23] See, e.g., F. Pollock, *The Expansion of the Common Law* (London: Stevens and Sons, 1904), especially at pp. 121–2; E. S. Corwin, 'The "higher law" background of American constitutional law' (1928) 42 *Harvard Law Review* 149, 365, especially at 368–73. See also J. P. Sommerville's account, *Politics and Ideology in England, 1603–1640* (London: Longman, 1986), ch. 3, especially at pp. 105–8, and C. H. McIlwain's description of the fundamental law 'often identified with the law of nature' but the inviolability of which 'was due in the first place to its universality as a custom', *The High Court of Parliament and Its Supremacy: An Historical Essay on the Boundaries between Legislation and Adjudication in England* (New Haven, Yale University Press, 1910), ch. 2, especially at p. 99. Cf. A. Cromartie, *Sir Matthew Hale, 1609–1676: Law, Religion and Natural Philosophy* (Cambridge: Cambridge University Press, 1995), ch. 1, and Cromartie's suggestion that the common law 'could be seen as nature's law for England', *The Constitutionalist Revolution: An Essay on the History of England, 1450–1642* (Cambridge: Cambridge University Press, 2006), pp. 209–10, and came to be seen 'as natural law applied to English life', 'The constitutionalist revolution: the transformation of political culture in early Stuart England' (1999) 163 *Past and Present* 76 at 82. In a lecture a few years ago, Sir John Baker recognised the significance of natural law in theory but identified a greater judicial reliance on flexible principles of interpretation in practice, 'Human rights in English legal history', n. 16 above. On the principle that general statutes would not be taken to derogate from particular local customs, he commented that 'it is easy to see how the same principle of interpretation could be extended in the hands of a Coke to include provisions which conflicted with natural justice', *ibid.* p. 23.

[24] M. Cappelletti, 'The significance of judicial review of legislation in the contemporary world' in E. von Caemmerer, S. Mentschikoff and K. Zweigert (eds.), *Ius Privatum Gentium: Festschrift für Max Rheinstein*, 2 vols. (Tübingen: J. C. B. Mohr, 1969), Vol. I, pp. 147–64, especially at p. 156.

antithesis. The Hegelian synthesis was *constitutional justice*, as initiated by the US Supreme Court when it assumed the power to review the constitutionality of legislation.

The simple identification of Coke with the European natural law tradition is problematic for two main reasons – the one semantic or formal, the other substantive. The first and more obvious is that Coke elaborated on the general character of the common law as a law of reason rather than as itself natural law. Coke spoke famously of the 'artificial reason' of the common law with which he contrasted 'natural reason'.[25] In *Bonham's Case*, Coke emphasised 'common right and reason'[26] and made no mention of natural law. In *Calvin's Case*, where he did refer expressly to the law of nature, he did not equate it with the common law but presented it as 'the moral law ... written with the finger of God in the heart of man' and as a 'part of the law of England' that 'was before any judicial or municipal law' in the world.[27] While emphasising the influence of natural law in England, Pollock explained, with the help of St German, the longstanding reluctance of common lawyers to invoke the law of nature as such.[28] In St German's famous dialogue between Doctor and Student, the first edition of which was published in 1528, the law of reason is given as the 'fyrst grounde of the lawe of Englande'.[29] The Student of the Common Law then explains to the Doctor of Divinity that it 'is not used amonge them that be lernyd in the lawes of Englande to reason what thynge is commaundyd or prohybyt by the lawe of nature and what not' but that if it 'be prohybyt by the lawe of nature', they 'say it is agaynst reason, or that reason wyll not suffre that it be don'.[30] Pollock attributed the reluctance to invoke the law of nature as such to a longstanding English suspicion of ecclesiastical authority:

> [A]t no time after, at latest, the Papal interference in the English politics of the first half of the thirteenth century, was the citation of Roman canonical authority acceptable in our country, save so far as it was necessary

---

[25] *Prohibitions del Roy* (1608) 12 Co. Rep. 63 at 65.     [26] Note 14 above, at 118a.

[27] (1609) 7 Co. Rep. 1, 12b.

[28] Pollock, *Expansion of the Common Law*, n. 23 above, pp. 109ff.

[29] St German, *Doctor and Student*, Dialogue, 1, ch. 5, as translated into English, *St German's Doctor and Student*, T. F. T. Plucknett and J. L. Barton (eds.) (London: Selden Society, Vol. 91, 1974), pp. 31, 33. See generally Introduction, *ibid.*; J. A. Guy, Introduction, *Christopher St German on Chancery and Statute* (London: Selden Society, Supplementary Series 6, 1985); M. D. Walters, 'St German on reason and parliamentary sovereignty' [2003] *CLJ* 335.

[30] *Doctor and Student*, n. 29 above, Dialogue 1, ch. 5.

for strictly technical purposes. Besides, as such citation might have been construed as a renunciation of independence, or a submission of questions of general policy to the judgment of the Church.[31]

Whatever the sufficiency of Pollock's explanation, the semantic reluctance of English lawyers to invoke the law of nature as such is one reason for not simply viewing Coke's common law as an emanation of European natural law.

A second reason is substantive and many have contributed to the semantic reluctance. Coke's common law of reason differed in substance from the abstract natural law of canonist doctrine. It lacked the Thomist contrast between natural law and positive law, the one deriving its force from whatever be the very nature of things, the other, from human agreement or statute.[32] Instead of such a contrast was Coke's identification of the common law of reason in the concrete precedents of England's powerful central courts, in the feudal compact of Magna Carta – 'a restitution and declaration of the ancient common law'[33] – and in relation to the specific statutes of a transcendent Parliament. Coke's common law reflected the English institutions by which it had been given substance and the particular practices through which it had evolved.

A second group of writers, often imbued with a sense of the distinctness of English law and its heritage, have presented Coke's approach to the common law as indigenous.[34] In reacting to Pollock's view, Samuel Thorne suggested that 'to some extent at least, later doctrines of natural law have been reflected backward upon Coke's statement' in *Bonham's*

---

[31] *Expansion of the Common Law*, n. 23 above, p. 113, cited with approval by M. Cappelletti, *Judicial Review in the Contemporary World* (New York: The Bobbs-Merrill Company Inc., 1971), p. 36; M. Cappelletti, *The Judicial Process in Comparative Perspective* (Oxford: Oxford University Press, 1989), pp. 126–7. Cf. Corwin, 'The "higher law" background', n. 23 above, 368–9, n. 11.

[32] See *Summa Theologica* II–II, q. 60, Art. 5. See also *ibid.* I–II, q. 95, Art. 2.

[33] Co. Inst. II, 8. See also Co. Inst. I, 81a: 'This statute of *Magna Charta* is but a confirmation or restitution of the common law'.

[34] S. E. Thorne, 'Dr Bonham's Case' (1938) 54 *LQR* 542. See also Gray, 'Bonham's Case reviewed', n. 16 above, especially at 41–2. Cf. J. W. Gough, *Fundamental Law in English Legal History* (Oxford: Oxford University Press, 1955), ch 3, p. 48; J. G. A. Pocock, *The Ancient Constitution and the Feudal Law, A Study of English Historical Thought in the Seventeenth Century: A Reissue with a Retrospect* (Cambridge: Cambridge University Press, 1987), Pt. 1, chs. 2, 3, Pt. 2, ch. 1. For an account of the diverse literature on *Bonham's Case*, see J. Goldsworthy, *The Sovereignty of Parliament: History and Philosophy* (Oxford: Oxford University Press, 1999), pp. 110ff.

*Case*.[35] According to Thorne, Coke was, in that argument, interpreting a statute, as he was in the other four arguments he put forward in that case. Thorne argued that Coke was merely applying rules of statutory construction with reference to common law precedents on impossibility and repugnancy or contradiction in statutes, which were therefore against common right and reason. Coke, was, according to Thorne, applying those rules to avoid the absurdity of a statutory construction that would have given the Royal College of Physicians a pecuniary interest in the fines it imposed. Thorne agreed with Plucknett[36] that the various cases cited by Coke do not support a constitutional theory of a higher law by which statutes that contravene it are void. Rather, he presented them as cases either of strict interpretation or of the court's quietly ignoring an unambiguous statute without raising any constitutional issue.[37] Thorne's overall view was that, although Coke's argument is 'phrased in very wide terms, it visualizes no statute void because of a conflict between it and common law, natural law, or higher law, but simply a refusal to follow a statute absurd on its face'.[38] As further evidence of a mere exercise in statutory construction, Thorne cited *Rowles* v. *Mason*, in which Coke gave *Bonham's Case* as authority for the proposition that 'if there is repugnancy in statute or unreasonableness in custom, the common law disallows and rejects it'.[39]

Thorne's argument was cited in Cappelletti's later writings, but not in his initial article on the significance of judicial review. In response to Thorne in those later writings, Cappelletti conceded that Coke's position in *Bonham's Case* 'reflected a belief that statutes could not contradict fundamental law, even if this belief stemmed more from English legal rules than from natural law ideas current on the Continent'.[40] In his concession, Cappelletti assumed a questionable contrast between English legal rules and Continental natural law as sources of greater and lesser significance. He did not clarify the extent of the relative insignificance of Continental natural law to Coke's belief. He retained, furthermore, his dialectical account of a synthesis in the *constitutional*

---

[35] 'Dr Bonham's Case', n. 34 above, 545.

[36] See T. F. T. Plucknett, 'Bonham's Case and judicial review' (1926) 40 *Harvard Law Review* 30.

[37] Thorne, 'Dr Bonham's Case', n. 34 above, 550.     [38] *Ibid.* 548.

[39] *Ibid.* 550. See *Rowles* v. *Mason*, n. 21 above, 198.

[40] *Judicial Review in the Contemporary World*, n. 31 above, p. 37, n. 45. See also Cappelletti, *Judicial Process in Comparative Perspective*, n. 31 above, p. 128, n. 33. Cf. Cappelletti, 'Significance of judicial review', n. 24 above, pp. 156–7.

*justice* initiated by the US Supreme Court to which *natural justice* and *positive* or *legal justice* were the thesis and antithesis.[41] From Cappelletti's concession, however, one can infer the conflation in Coke of features of Cappelletti's thesis, antithesis and synthesis – the thesis of a higher law, the statutes of a transcendent Parliament in antithesis, and a synthesis through the judicial application of established English legal rules of statutory construction. In Cappelletti's later writings, the significance of Continental ideas of natural law and the tenability of his Hegelian dialectic in the English context were left unclear.

However untenable or irrelevant Cappelletti's dialectical analysis may be, the view of Coke's common law of reason as indigenous, resting, for instance, merely on statutory construction in *Bonham's Case*, is not without its own difficulties. As in the case of identification of Coke with the European natural law tradition, it is problematic for both formal and substantive reasons.

In *Bonham's Case*, as reported in his published reports, Coke phrased his argument 'in very wide terms', recognised by Thorne.[42] Coke suggested that the common law will control an Act of Parliament and adjudge it to be void not only when it is 'repugnant, or impossible to be performed' but also when it is 'against common right and reason'.[43] If Coke regarded a statutory provision that violates *Nemo debet esse iudex in propria causa* as a legal impossibility or a repugnancy, whether direct or indirect, as Thorne argued, Coke's additional reference to what is against common right and reason would be superfluous. Furthermore, the cases upon which Coke relied did not contain resounding references to a controlling common law or grand adjudgments of statutes against law and right and of statutes utterly void. In *Tregor's Case*, Judge Herle's reference to 'some statutes made which even the maker would not wish put into effect'[44] was amplified by Coke to read 'some *statutes . . . made against law and right*, which those who made them perceiving, would not put them in execution'.[45] Coke's strongest precedent, *Cessavit 42*, was an example of a decision in which the court 'quietly ignored an

---

[41] *Judicial Process in Comparative Perspective*, n. 31 above, pp. 131–2.

[42] 'Dr Bonham's Case', n. 34 above, 548. Cf. Gray, 'Bonham's Case reviewed', n. 16 above, especially at 46, 49–50.

[43] Note 14 above, at 118a.

[44] T. F. T. Plucknett, *Statutes & Their Interpretation in the First Half of the Fourteenth Century* (Cambridge: Cambridge University Press, 1922), pp. 68–70, especially at p. 69; Plucknett, 'Bonham's Case', n. 36 above, 35.

[45] Note 14 above, at 118a (my emphasis).

unambiguous statute', in other words, an illustration of the common law's economy.[46] It was decided in an earlier period when the judges' preoccupation has been described as simply 'to apply the best law they knew as courageously as they could'.[47] In contrast, Coke's famous argument, couched in strong, uneconomical, language, added to other arguments that Coke regarded as themselves decisive was important to Coke but, in the context of the case, not strictly necessary and unduly contentious. His language suggested wider judicial powers of interpretation in the face of express statutory words than was sustainable. It fuelled Lord Chancellor Ellesmere's criticism, which contributed to Coke's eventual removal from the bench. In his speech when Sir Henry Montagu was sworn in as Chief Justice of the King's Bench in place of Coke, Ellesmere officially reproved Coke, *inter alia*, with the following reference to *Bonham's Case*:

> He [Ellesmere] challenged not power for the Judges of this Court to correct all misdemeanors as well extrajudicial as judicial, nor to have power to judge Statutes and Acts of Parliament to be void, if they conceived them to be against common right and reason: *but left the King and the Parliament to judge what was common right and reason.* I speak not of impossibilities or direct repugnancies.[48]

Why Coke should have unnecessarily provoked or exposed himself and his court to the criticism that they were encroaching upon the King and Parliament's determination of common right and reason requires explanation. Coke's combative character, exemplified in his various clashes[49] with Ellesmere, doubtlessly, played a role, as did his rigorous rhetorical method aimed at producing copious arguments.[50] But the question of substantial natural law influence upon Coke's thinking, with which to complement the explanation and make it compelling, is difficult to avoid.

*Calvin's Case*[51] was decided shortly before *Bonham's Case*. There, Coke presented the law of nature as part of the law of England and as

---

[46] Thorne, 'Dr Bonham's Case', n. 34 above, 550. See generally ch. 5 above.

[47] Plucknett, *Statutes & Their Interpretation*, n. 44 above, p. 71.

[48] Francis Moore's Reports, 828. See also Gough, *Fundamental Law*, n. 34 above, pp. 37–8.

[49] For other examples, see C. Holmes, 'Statutory interpretation in the early seventeenth century: the courts, the Council, and the Commissioners of Sewers' in J. A. Guy and H. G. Beale (eds.), *Law and Social Change in British History* (London: Royal Historical Society, 1984), pp. 107–17.

[50] See pp. 147f below.    [51] Note 27 above.

the foundation of government, recognised its immutability and cited St German as authority.[52] By the end of the sixteenth century, St German's *Doctor and Student* had become a profoundly influential legal textbook, a classic text with an authority that has been likened to Bracton's.[53] His identification of the law of reason as the common law's equivalent of the law of nature in the words of the Student of the Laws of England was well known, and his presentation of the law of reason and the law of nature as synonymous was recognised by Coke.[54] The Doctor of Divinity also asserts *iura naturalia immutabilia sunt*, and both he and the Student proceed to envisage the voidness of statutes contrary to the law of God and contrary to what they identify as the law of primary reason.[55] St German regarded that voidness as legally important although its remedial implications and general practical relevance are unclear in his various writings.[56]

In *Calvin's Case*, Coke commented as follows upon St German's immutable natural law:

> Seeing then that faith, obedience, and ligeance are due by the law of nature, it followeth that the same cannot be changed or taken away; for albeit judicial and municipal laws have inflicted and imposed in several places, or at several times, divers and several punishments and penalties, for breach or not observance of the law of nature, (for that law only consisted in commanding or prohibiting, without any certain punishment or penalty), yet the very law of nature itself never was nor could be altered or changed. And therefore it is certainly true, that *jura naturalia sunt immutabilia*. And herewith agreeth Bracton, lib. 1. cap. 5. and Doctor and Student, cap. 5 and 6.[57]

Coke thus emphasised that the law of nature is immutable and recognised that, for breach of that law, judicial and municipal laws might impose actual sanctions, not determined by it. He did not mention voidness but proceeded to give examples of parliamentary enactments limited in scope under the law of nature.[58]

---

[52] *Ibid.* 12b–14a.
[53] Guy, Introduction, *St German on Chancery and Statute*, n. 29 above, especially at p. 94.; Walters, 'St German', n. 29 above, especially at 359.
[54] *Modus Decimandi Case* (1608) 13 Co. Rep. 12, 16.
[55] *Doctor and Student*, n. 29 above, Dialogue 1, chs. 4–8, 11, especially chs. 2, 5. See Walters, 'St German', n. 29 above, especially at 343–4.
[56] Walters, 'St German', n. 29 above, 355–8.
[57] Note 27 above, at 13b.   [58] *Ibid.* 14a.

In *Bonham's Case*, Coke did not cite St German's reference to the immutability of natural law, quite possibly for the reason it was commonly known. A few years later, however, in *Day* v. *Savadge*, Chief Justice Hobart identified the substance of Coke's famous argument in *Bonham's Case* with the immutability of natural law upon which Coke had elaborated in *Calvin's Case*: 'Even an Act of Parliament, made against natural equity, as to make a man judge in his own case, is void in itself, for, *Jura naturae sunt immutabilia*'.[59] Hobart did not cite *Bonham's Case* presumably because it was well known and an object of Lord Chancellor Ellesmere's disapproval. Hobart had good reason, however, to relate Coke's famous argument to the immutability of natural law. In *Calvin's Case*, with reference to that immutability, Coke elaborated upon the limited reach of Parliamentary authority. In *Bonham's Case*, he did likewise although in the strong terms of a controlling common law, utterly void statutes and judicial adjudgments of common right and reason rather than with express reference to the law of nature.

In the early seventeenth century, Coke and Hobart were far from the only jurists to be sympathetic or receptive to natural law thought. Sir Henry Finch and Sir John Davies were, for example, eloquent in their appreciation of natural law and its closeness to the common law. Sir Henry Finch, Serjeant at Law, wrote of the 'Law of nature and of reason, or the Law of reason primary and secondary, with the rules framed and collected thereupon. Which three are as the Sun and the Moon, and the seven Stars, to give light to all the positive laws of the world. *Positive are laws framed by their light*, and from thence come the grounds and maxims of all Common Law ... Therefore Laws positive, which are directly contrary to the former, lose their force, and are no Laws at all.'[60] In contrast, Sir John Davies, Attorney General for Ireland, described the English common law as 'coming neerest to the lawe of Nature' but recognised that Parliament could alter its 'fundamentall points', albeit at considerable inconvenience to the Commonwealth.[61]

---

[59] (1614) Hobart 85 at 87.

[60] *Law, or a Discourse thereof, in Four Books* (London: H. Twyford *et al.*, 1678), pp. 74, 75.

[61] *Le Primer Report des Cases et Matters en Ley Resolues & Adiudges en les Courts del Roy en Ireland* (London: Company of Stationers, 1628), p. 4 of Preface.

## *Rex . . . sub Deo et lege*

The role of natural law thought as expressed in *Calvin's Case* and as identified by Hobart CJ with the substance of Coke's famous argument in *Bonham's Case* is not the most telling manifestation of Continental European influence upon Coke's controlling common law. Continental European influence is clearest in the conclusion to the famous exchange between King James I and the Judges of England assembled at Hampton Court, as reported by Chief Justice Coke.[62] Archbishop Bancroft had instilled in the King the notion that the King had the authority to decide cases in his own person because the judges were his delegates. According to Coke, the judges informed the King 'that no King after the Conquest assumed to himself to give any judgment in any cause whatsoever, which concerned the administration of justice within this realm, but these were solely determined in the Courts of Justice'.[63] To the King's reply that 'he thought the law was founded upon reason, and that he and others had reason, as well as the Judges', Coke answered as follows:

> [T]rue it was, that God had endowed His Majesty with excellent science, and great endowments of nature; but His Majesty was not learned in the laws of his realm of England, and causes which concern the life, or inheritance, or goods, or fortunes of his subjects, are not to be decided by natural reason but by the artificial reason and judgment of law, which law is an act which requires long study and experience, before that a man can attain the cognizance of it.[64]

According to Coke, the 'King was greatly offended, and said, that then he should be under the law, which was treason to affirm, as he said; to which I said, that Bracton saith, *quod Rex non debet esse sub homine, sed sub Deo et lege*'.[65]

Bracton's argument that the King is under God and the law because the law makes the King, which has been echoed by generation upon generation of common lawyers, was stated by Bracton immediately after the dictum recited by Coke to the King: '*Ipse autem rex non debet esse sub homine sed sub deo et sub lege, quia lex facit regem. Attribuat igitur rex legi, quod lex attribuit ei, videlicet dominationem et potestatem*'.[66] The

---

[62] *Prohibitions del Roy*, n. 25 above.    [63] *Ibid*. 64.    [64] *Ibid*. 64–5.    [65] *Ibid*. 65.
[66] *De Legibus* 5b: 'The king must not be under man but under God and under the law, because the law makes the king. Let him therefore bestow upon the law what the law bestows upon him, namely, rule and power', S. E. Thorne (ed. and tr.), *Bracton on the Laws and Customs of England*, 2 vols. (Cambridge, Mass.: Belknapp Press and Selden Society, 1968), Vol. II, p. 33.

argument was repeated elsewhere in *De Legibus*: '*Item nihil tam proprium est imperii quam legibus vivere, et maius imperia est legibus submittere principatum, et merito debet retribuere legi quod lex tribuit ei, facit enim lex quod ipse sit rex*'.[67] Amidst the many arguments of Bracton taken from a variety of English, civilian and canonist writings, this argument was derived from a gloss by Azo.[68] Azo had explained a slightly obscure declaration by the emperors that they were resolved to be bound by the law in that[69] their own authority was dependent upon the law's with the words '*quia de lege scilicet regia pendet auctoritas principalis quia per eam populus transtulit omne imperium in principem[,] merito et ipse hoc retribuat legi ut servet eam*'.[70] Bracton repeated the substance of Azo's explanation but transformed it 'into a short proverbial *dictum* . . . by introducing both the antithesis *tribuere-retribuere* and the rhyme'.[71]

The tranformation of Azo's explanation contributed to the appeal and enduring significance of Bracton's dictum. Although not influenced by feudal law, Bracton's dictum must have resonated with residual feudal notions[72] of reciprocity and mutuality, however questionable their relevance to the relationship between the King and the law. It was reinforced by Coke's famous invocation. The idea of reciprocity or of a return present by the King to the law may be unconvincing in the modern era[73] but that of an authority bound by the law but not by its

---

[67] *De Legibus*, f107b: 'Nothing is more fitting for a sovereign than to live by the laws, nor is there any greater sovereignty than to govern according to law, and he ought properly to yield to the law what the law has bestowed upon him, for the law makes the king', Thorne (ed. and tr.), *Bracton on the Laws and Customs of England*, n. 66 above, p. 306. Cf. generally John of Salisbury's ecclesiastical view of a prince, who as a prince and unlike a tyrant, rules in accordance with the law as the gift of God: *The Stateman's Book of John of Salisbury: Policratus*, J. Dickinson (tr.) (New York: Alfred A. Knopf, 1927), ch. XVII. See generally F. Schulz, 'Bracton on kingship' (1945) 60 *English Historical Review* 136, 164–5.

[68] Thorne, *Bracton on the Laws and Customs of England*, n. 66 above, p. 33, n. 7, p. 306, n. 4; Schulz 'Bracton on kingship', n. 67 above, 168–9. See also B. Tierney, *Church Law and Constitutional Thought in the Middle Ages* (London: Variorum, 1979), pp. 299–305.

[69] Cod. 1. 14. 4 ('*adeo de auctoritate iuris nostra pendet auctoritas*').

[70] Summa cod. 1. 14: 'For the reason that the prince's royal authority does, for sure, depend on the law, because through it the people confer all sovereign power upon the prince, he rightly gives back to the law so as to protect it'.

[71] Schulz, 'Bracton on kingship', n. 67 above, 169.

[72] See generally W. Ullman, *The Individual and Society in the Middle Ages* (Baltimore: The John Hopkins Press, 1966).

[73] Schulz, 'Bracton on kingship', n. 67 above, 169. See Dicey, *Law of the Constitution*, n. 11 above, p. 18.

sanctions[74] or bound by the statutory instrument through which it is created is less so. Bracton's argument may not be amenable to the rigours of modern analysis,[75] but acquired a lasting symbolic significance.[76] William Blackstone proudly presented it as a maxim of English law and a point of contrast with the civil law.[77] In respect of origin, however, the converse would be correct if the contrast were to be drawn. Bracton's resounding argument for his assertion that the King is under God and under the law,[78] with which Coke answered the King, was civilian, not English, in origin.

### The European and the English in reason and rhetoric

An alternative to the contrasting and problematic interpretations to which the two groups of writers described above have inclined – one of Coke's common law as a European emanation, the other of it as an indigenous development – it to avoid the contrast. It is neither to assimilate Coke's common law to European natural law in view of the later notion of a higher law in the USA, nor to exaggerate its peculiarity though a preoccupation with the distinctness of the English legal heritage. It is to be receptive to both the generally European and the peculiarly English in Coke's common law in a context that was both European and English.[79] Therefore, on the one hand, the European in

---

[74] See Tierney, *Church Law and Constitutional Thought in the Middle Ages*, n. 68 above, pp. 299–305.

[75] M. Loughlin, *The Idea of Public Law* (Oxford: Oxford University Press, 2003), p. 134f.

[76] In the nineteenth century, Bracton's dictum was, e.g., prominently used by Earl John Russell as the epigraph for his fifteenth chapter to encapsulate the contribution of lawyers to the furtherance of liberties in England, *An Essay on the History of the English Government and Constitution from the Reign of Henry VII to the Present Time* (London: Longman, Green, Longman, Roberts, & Green, new edn, 1865), p. 134. In recent decades, it has also, e.g., been invoked by Sir Stephen Sedley in recent debates about bi-polar sovereignty, 'Sound of silence', n. 5 above, 290.

[77] *Commentaries on the Laws of England*, 4 vols. (Chicago: The University of Chicago Press, Facsimile of 1st edn of 1765–1769, 1979), Vol. I, p. 232. Henry Hallam presented the very perversions of Bracton's gloss as 'proof that no other doctrine could be admitted in the law of England', *View of the State of Europe during the Middle Ages*, 3 vols. (London: John Murray, 2nd edn, 1819), Vol. II, p. 459f, especially at p. 460.

[78] Cf. generally the other great rule of law dictum presented by Harrington as 'the Empire of Laws, and not of Men' and attributed by him to Aristotle and Livy, *The Oceana of James Harrington, Esq; and his Other Works*, J. Toland (ed.) (Dublin: J. Smith and W. Bruce, 1737), p. 37.

[79] For a balanced approach, see generally Van Caenegem, *Legal History: A European Perspective*, n. 12 above, pp. 192ff.

Coke's common law is to be sought below, not in natural law doctrine assimilated as such, but in the centrality of reason and in the heritage of classical rhetoric. On the other hand, the English in Coke's common law is to be sought in the elaboration upon reason and its rhetorical exercise in English legal practice. In short, what is suggested below is an English spin on reason and classical rhetoric.

Reason or *ratio* was variable in meaning and generally lacking in precision however it was meant. The reason in which Coke celebrated is dimly illuminated by that with which it was contrasted. It was not the universal human reason of the Stoics in which all men participated through their humanity or human nature. As explained by Coke in his exchange with King James I, it was not a natural reason[80] or native intelligence. Rather, Coke invoked as against rival notions[81] 'the artificial reason . . . of the law' necessitating 'long study and experience'[82] and thus refined from the natural reason of generations of learned men as distinct from the natural reason of all.

Coke elaborated upon the artificial reason of the law in his *Commentary upon Littleton*:

> [R]eason is the life of the law, nay the common law itselfe, is nothing else but reason; which is to be understood of an artificiall perfection of reason, gotten by long study, observation, and experience, and not of every man's naturall reason; for *Nemo nascitur artifex*. This legall reason *est summa ratio*. And therefore if all the reason that is dispersed into so many severall heads, were united into one, yet could he not make such a law as the law in *England* is; because by many successions of ages it hath beene fined and refined by an infinite number of grave and learned men, and by long experience growne to such a perfection, for the government of this realme, as the old rule may be justly verified by it, *Neminem oportet esse sapientiorum legibus*: no man out of his own private reason ought to be wiser than the law, which is the perfection of reason.[83]

---

[80] *Prohibitions del Roy*, n. 25 above, 65. According to Cromartie, 'Coke's enemy was always "natural" reason, reason unguided by professionals, personified, he may have thought, by the presumptuous layman who was his lawful king', *Sir Matthew Hale*, n. 23 above, ch. 1, especially at p. 21.

[81] Apart from the reason which the King claimed to have in common with others, consider 'the supreme Reason above all reasons' invoked to justify the Privy Council's instruction that the common law courts not entertain further actions against the Commissioners of Sewers and that complaints henceforth be by petition to the Privy Council, Francis Moore's Reports, 824ff, especially at 825–6. See generally Holmes, 'Courts, Council and Commissioners of Sewers', n. 49 above.

[82] *Prohibitions del Roy*, n. 25 above, 65.  [83] Co. Inst. 1, 97b.

Coke's *summa ratio*, as an artificial reason, was fashioned and perfected by generations of learned jurists and, in particular, practised judges through their incremental refinements. In *Calvin's Case*, Coke claimed that '*judex est lex loquens*'.[84] His selective emphasis on Cicero's notion[85] of the judge as the law speaking expressed a main point of distinction between the artificial reason of the common law and the universal human reason of the Stoics.

Coke's identification of artificial reason with collective judicial experience and refinement was similar to Sir Henry Finch's description of 'common reason' as 'refined reason' with its rules 'confirmed by judgement, learning, and much experience'.[86] It also accorded with Sir Matthew Hale's celebration in the 'various Experiences of wise and knowing men ... better suited to the Convenience of Laws, than the best Invention of the most pregnant witts not ayded by Such a Series and tract of Experience'.[87] In his exposition of artificial reason, Coke articulated what was becoming the self-understanding of common lawyers.

Judicial appreciation of increasing legislative activity in the Tudor period may have helped make of reason the chord to be struck by Coke in the common law.[88] His celebration of reason elevated the common law at a time when the clearly made law of proliferating statutes and the common lawyers' own declared law of ancient origin were increasingly juxtaposed. It subsumed notions of 'common right and reason' and 'natural equity', which were recurring or becoming more prominent in attempts to reconcile the construction of various new statutes with local customs and ancient common law.[89] Coke identified the common law with a *summa ratio* by which statutory change might be embraced without negating or appearing to negate continuity.[90] In comparison

---

[84] Note 27 above, at 4a. See also *ibid.* 27a.    [85] Cicero *De Legibus* III, I, 2–3.
[86] Note 60 above, pp. 75, 5.
[87] 'Reflections by the Lrd. Cheife Justice Hale on Mr. Hobbes his Dialogue of the Lawe', as published in W. S. Holdsworth, *A History of English Law*, Vol. V (London: Methuen, 1924), pp. 500–13, p. 504, a passage twice quoted by Holdsworth in *Some Lessons from our Legal History* (New York: Macmillan 1928), p. 8, n. 4, pp. 158–9. See generally Cromartie, *Sir Matthew Hale*, n. 23 above, especially at pp. 100ff.
[88] See A. von Mehren, 'The judicial conception of legislation in Tudor England' in P. Sayre (ed.), *Interpretation of Modern Legal Philosophies, Essays in Honor of Roscoe Pound* (New York: Oxford University Press, 1947), pp. 751–66.
[89] *Bonham's Case*, n. 14 above, at 118a; *Day v. Savadge*, n. 59 above, at 87.
[90] Von Mehren describes Augustus' use in the Principate of formal continuity with the Roman Republic as comparable, and he writes of the English legal development in terms of change and continuity: 'The English genius for preserving continuity was at work adapting medieval institutions, with a minimum of change, to serve the needs of the

with the revolutionary crisis of legitimacy, to which the 'great moments' of European natural law have on occasion been attributed,[91] substantial change was in the semblance of reasoned continuity within the common law.

The requirements of Coke's artificial reason – refined through collective judicial experience – were not the speculative or philosophical product of sudden ideological crisis. They were not inferred from a Thomist notion of natural right distinct from positive right[92] or incorporated as natural rights distinct from positive law.[93] They were not abstracted into a separate fundamental or higher law with which uneconomically to override positive law and of uncertain relevance to concrete cases. Rather, they were exemplified in judicial precedents and were enshrined in Magna Carta.[94] They were upheld though the remedies of powerful central courts and were manifest in practices of statutory construction, which avoided contrast, and minimised contradiction, between statutory rights and common law. One such practice was strictly to construe statutes in derogation of common law rights. Another was to presume, despite the apparent meaning of the words of a statute, that Parliament did not intend what would be contrary to reason, whether that be, for example, an absurdity, repugnancy or the legal impossibility of statutory violation of a rule of natural equity. Artificial reason, as 'the life of the law' in Coke's definition,[95] animated the common law itself, which was practical in orientation and concrete in character.

Coke's artificial reason seems to have been roughly fashioned from, or related to, the notion of artificial logic in rhetoric, the other European manifestation crucial to Coke's common law.[96] About twenty years

---

emerging national state', 'Judicial conception of legislation in Tudor England', n. 88 above, p. 762.

[91] See, e.g., E. Levy, 'Natural law in Roman thought' (1949) 15 *Studia et Documenta Historiae et Iuris* 1, especially at 21–3; M. Weber, *Law in Economy and Society*, M. Rheinstein (ed. and tr.) (Cambridge, Mass.: Harvard University Press, 1954), pp. 287f. Cf. generally ch. 3 above.

[92] Cf. generally St Thomas Aquinas, *Summa Theologica* II–II, q. 60, Art. 5.

[93] Cf. generally R. Tuck, *Natural Rights Theories: Their Origin and Development* (Cambridge: Cambridge University Press, 1979). See also B. Tierney, 'Tuck on rights: some medieval problems' (1983) 4 *History of Political Thought* 429.

[94] See Co. Inst. I, 81a; Co. Inst. II, 8 (quoted on p. 135 above).

[95] Co. Inst. I, 97b.

[96] A. D. Boyer, *Sir Edward Coke and the Elizabethan Age* (Stanford: Stanford University Press, 2003), pp. 88ff. See also A. D. Boyer, 'Sir Edward Coke, Ciceronianus: classical rhetoric and the common law tradition' (1997) 10 *International Journal for the Semiotics*

before Coke's reference to artificial reason in his exchange with King James I, Abraham Fraunce, inspired by Ramus, elaborated on artificial logic as an art of reasoning:

> It is therefore said here, that Logike is an Art, to distinguish artificiall Logike from naturall reason. Artificiall Logike is gathered out of divers examples of naturall reason, which is not any Art of Logike, but that ingraven gift and facultie of wit and reason shining in the particuler discourses of severall men, whereby they both invent, and orderly dispose, thereby to judge of that they have invented.[97]

Artificial reason bears a striking resemblance to Fraunce's artificial logic. As in the case of artificial logic, it was derived from diverse examples of natural reason and was perfected through long training and in practice. Tudor lawyers were drilled in classical rhetoric. Coke, in particular, was drilled in the rhetoric of Cicero, *inter alia*, at the Norwich grammar school, in his curriculum at Trinity College Cambridge and in moots at the Inns of Courts.[98] In significant ways, Coke and other Tudor lawyers practised professionally the rhetorical methods in which they were drilled. In practice, lawyers aimed to produce numerous proofs and copious arguments,[99] such as Coke's five arguments in *Bonham's Case*. In their arguments, they would cite cases, such as the 'examples' or precedents that following the famous passage in *Bonham*,[100] which epitomised the relevant law and that resembled rhetorical *exempla* – the telling instances in various forms, such as the maxim, the judgment,[101] the proverb or the parable, at the disposal of the rhetorician. Lawyers, such as Coke, would also record useful cases in personal notebooks comparable to the Commonplace Books in which the rhetorician or student of rhetoric collected useful *exempla*.[102] Their technical legal skill would be demonstrated, not in abstract reasoning or speculation, but in telling arguments that drew upon comparable cases in view of

---

*of Law* 3, 31ff. For a general account of forensic rhetoric with reference to classical or Renaissance sources, see I. Maclean, *Interpretation and Meaning in the Renaissance: The Case of Law* (Cambridge: Cambridge University Press, 1992), pp. 75–82.

[97] *The Lawiers Logike, Exemplifying the Præcepts of Logike by the Practise of the Common Lawe* (London: Thomas Gubbin and T. Newman, 1588), Bk. 1, ch. 1, p. 2 (sig. B. ii).

[98] Boyer, *Sir Edward Coke*, n. 96 above, pp. 12ff, 28ff.

[99] See generally *ibid.* pp. 94–7.    [100] *Bonham's Case*, n. 14 above, at 118a.

[101] *Judicia* constituted one category of *exempla*, Boyer, 'Sir Edward Coke, Ciceronianus', n. 96 above, 25–6. See *ibid.* 27–31.

[102] Boyer, *Sir Edward Coke*, n. 96 above, pp. 31–3.

their various facts and the details of a concrete case.[103] The law's artificial reason was refined through collective judicial experience in the practice of a professional legal rhetoric.

## A controlling common law and a transcendent Parliament

Reason and rhetoric are the entwined chords, both English and European, with which to unravel and try to resolve Coke's paradoxical descriptions cited above.[104] Coke's assertion in his famous argument in *Bonham's Case* that the common law will control Acts of Parliament by adjudging them 'utterly void' when 'against common right and reason' ('or repugnant, or impossible to be performed'),[105] should be viewed as a judicial refinement of artificial reason in a rhetorical context.[106] As the law speaking, as the oracle of the law, in one and the same breath as he did common law rules of statutory construction, Coke voiced a requirement of reason that approximated to an immutable principle of natural law, and made it effective. The resounding phrases, however, with which he invoked reason and used or abused rules of statutory construction were limited in force when seen in their professional rhetorical context. In a leading judicial address, he was using them with purpose and characteristic vigour to reinforce *Nemo debet esse iudex in propria causa*, a principle of peculiar professional concern.[107] In effect, Coke was asserting and emphasising a common professional priority of independent judgment and its remedial implication that a remedy be granted by a judge and not by a party or by a judge who is also a party or shares a party's interest. Furthermore, in its rhetorical context, Coke's famous argument is but one of his five arguments, the fourth in his published report. Listed with other arguments that he regarded as also decisive of *Bonham's Case* and not used to decide the case by other members of the court,[108] it was important in principle but did not carry the rhetorical weight that later commentators have placed upon it.

---

[103] *Ibid.* pp. 97ff.     [104] See pp. 131ff.     [105] Note 14 above, at 118a.
[106] Cf. generally the arguments in a Grey's Inn Moot in the 1520s that, with respect to certain entitlements relating to land, Parliament could not enact what was repugnant, absurd or contrary to law and reason, Sir John Baker, *The Oxford History of the Laws of England, Volume VI, 1483–1558* (Oxford: Oxford University Press, 2003), p. 80.
[107] See also *Day* v. *Savadge*, n. 59 above, at 87; *City of London* v. *Wood* (1701) 12 Mod. 669 at 687. But see *ibid.* 678.
[108] Gray, 'Bonham's case reviewed', n. 16 above, 38–41, 50. On the basis of a manuscript report that lacks Coke's famous passage about the voidness of an Act of Parliament

Coke compiled his *Institutes* after his judicial career had ended, thus in a context far removed from that of his rhetoric in *Bonham's Case*. In his *Institutes*, Coke presented an abstract or detached historical overview of Parliament, in all its antiquity, as a High Court with transcendent and absolute jurisdiction.[109] Coke's description of Parliament was similar to Sir Thomas Smith's,[110] published posthumously in 1583 but written more than half a century before Coke compiled his *Institutes*. In later centuries, Coke's detached description of Parliament lived on in the approving citations of both Blackstone and Dicey.[111] His description and its lasting influence demonstrated the continuing effect of a historical view of Parliament as a court[112] after much of its judicial business had been lost (that is, from hearing petitions for the redress of wrongs not cognisable elsewhere) or appropriated to the Lords, and before judicial and legislative functions were being expressly or consistently distinguished.[113]

Where Coke described the historical High Court of Parliament in the abstract and in retrospect, its supreme remedial jurisdiction over some or other wrong of which the ordinary courts did not take cognisance, did not contradict or negate a controlling common law of which it too was the authoritative voice. Within the realm of the common law itself, however, Coke's description did not preclude an institutional contradiction between high courts or highest courts – King's Bench, Common

against common right and reason, Gray entertains the possibility that Coke only added it after the event, *ibid.* 49. That Coke conceivably did not speak the resounding words would further suggest their lack of rhetorical significance in resolving the case.

[109] See pp. 131f above.

[110] 'The most high and absolute power of the realme of Englande, consisteth in the Parliament ... The Parliament abrogateth olde lawes, maketh newe, giveth orders for thinges past, and for thinges hereafter to be followed, changeth rightes, and possessions of private men ... appointeth subsidies, tailes, taxes, and impositions, giveth most free pardons and absolutions, restoreth in bloud and name *as the highest court*, condemneth or absoluteth them whom the Prince will put to that triall', *De Republica Anglorum: A Discourse on the Commonwealth of England*, L. Alston (ed.) (Cambridge: Cambridge University Press, 1906), Bk. 2, ch. 1, pp. 48, 49 (my emphasis).

[111] Blackstone, *Commentaries*, n. 77 above, Vol. I, p. 156; Dicey, *Law of the Constitution*, n. 11 above, p. 41.

[112] See McIlwain, *High Court of Parliament*, n. 23 above, ch. 3, especially at pp. 130ff, 139ff; Corwin, 'The "higher law" background', n. 23 above, 378ff; Gough, *Fundamental Law*, n. 34 above, pp. 3ff, 48f; M. J. C. Vile, *Constitutionalism and the Separation of Powers* (Indianapolis: Liberty Fund, 2nd edn, 1998), pp. 26ff.

[113] See, e.g., Sir Matthew Hale, *The Jurisdiction of the Lords House, or Parliament*, F. Hargrave (ed.) (London: T. Cadell and W. Davies, 1796), especially at pp. 80–5, 205–8. See J. H. Baker, *An Introduction to English Legal History* (London: Butterworths LexisNexis, 4th edn, 2002), pp. 207–8.

Pleas, the House of Lords and the High Court of Parliament – exercising contested or controversial[114] jurisdiction and voicing variable determinations of common right and reason. Furthermore, at an abstract level, the issue of contradiction or compatibility between the functions of a controlling common law and of a transcendent Parliament came to the fore insofar Parliament as such – acting through both Houses – began to be usually identified with only its legislative functions and not its judicial functions, which had been generally appropriated to the House of Lords. To the extent Parliament's decline as a court was appreciated and its legislative functions began to be expressly if not consistently distinguished from the judicial functions of the ordinary courts, that issue of functional contradiction between legislative and judicial supremacy, became difficult to avoid. Its legal effects, however, were long ameliorated in restrictive statutory construction by pragmatic common lawyers generally inclined to see continuity, harmony and organic unity in the English legal and political body politic whatever the abstract contradiction. Despite the odd contradiction occasionally manifest in controversy or serious conflict, Coke's common law was generally coherent in practice if not in abstract analysis or theory. His contradiction between a transcendent Parliament and a controlling common law, although troubling in theory or analysis, is not incongruous when viewed from a historical constitutional perspective upon evident domestic peculiarity and European influence.

## The eclipse of Coke's controlling common law

More than 250 years separate Coke's common law and Dicey's rule of law, the formative legal contributions with which this and Chapter Seven are concerned. The complex developments of these years are beyond the scope of these chapters. Whatever the extent to which Parliament's sovereign authority had long been assumed[115] and its earlier decline as a court appreciated, Parliament did, in this period, continue to develop conspicuously as a legislature, despite periods of conflict and inactivity. In the seventeenth century constitutional struggles, after more than a decade during which Parliament had not been summoned, the Long

---

[114] See generally, e.g., Hale, *Jurisdiction of the Lords House*, n. 113 above.
[115] See generally Goldsworth, *Sovereignty of Parliament*, n. 34 above; M. D. Walters, 'Common law, reason, and sovereign will' (2003) 53 *University of Toronto Law Journal* 65.

Parliament introduced numerous legislative reforms. It passed wide-ranging and radical legislation, much of which was either not actually implemented or did not survive the Restoration. Early in the *Interregnum*, however, it abolished the various prerogative courts, notably the Star Chamber, which were closely associated with the ministerial exercise of the royal prerogative. Unlike most of the radical reforms during the *Interregnum*, their abolition was lasting and left the common law courts without serious judicial rivals to their legal authority. In effect, the Long Parliament established a unitary central jurisdiction. Apart from securing the role of the common law courts in the revolutionary settlement, Parliament ultimately triumphed as the representative institution through which the monarch was required to rule. Early in the eighteenth century, the monarch became bound by convention to give the Royal Assent to bills passed by both Houses of Parliament. Thereafter, in the generally moderated exercise of its legislative function, Parliament repeatedly confirmed its own controlling and reforming power. In the nineteenth century, Parliament's legislative reformation of itself as a representative institution, particularly through the various extensions of the franchise, enhanced its representative status and the democratic force of its enactments.

Parliament's development as a legislature affected the significance of parliamentary legislation relative to that of common law principle. The response to Coke's famous dictum in *Bonham's Case*[116] through this period is considered below briefly to suggest how they evolved in relative significance and as such formed the historical backdrop to Dicey's *Law of the Constitution*.[117] Judicial and doctrinal treatment of Coke's dictum is presented to reflect what became of Coke's contradiction between a controlling common law and a transcendent Parliament.

Lord Chancellor Ellesmere's reproof when Sir Henry Montagu was sworn in as Chief Justice of the King's Bench in place of Coke officially marked the beginning of a gradual eclipse of Coke's dictum in *Bonham's Case*.[118] A couple of years earlier, in *Day* v. *Savadge*, Hobart CJ repeated the substance of Coke's argument and identified it with the immutability of natural law but did not cite *Bonham's Case*[119] of which the Lord Chancellor was already, presumably, known to disapprove. A reference to *Bonham's Case* is also notable for its absence in *Godden* v. *Hales*, the judicial culmination of the controversy concerning the use of the

---

[116] Note 14 above, at 118a.      [117] Note 11 above.
[118] Note 48 above, 828. See p. 138 above.      [119] Note 59 above, 81. See p. 140 above.

dispensing power by James II.[120] Through an exercise of his royal
prerogative, the King had dispensed with an oath that the defendant
was required to make by statute. Herbert CJ did not cite *Bonham's Case*
in support of his assertion 'that the king had a power to dispense with
any of the laws of the government [contrasted by counsel with the laws
of property]' and 'that no act of parliament could take away that
power'.[121] A power under the common law to disregard an Act of
Parliament affected, not only the judicial protection of common law
principle, but also the competing claims of both Parliament and
the King.

Shortly after the revolutionary struggles between Parliament and the
King had culminated in a settlement, Holt CJ cited *Bonham's Case* with
approval in *City of London* v. *Wood*:

> [I]t is against all laws that the same person should be party and judge in
> the same cause, for it is a manifest contradiction ... And what my Lord
> Coke says in Dr. *Bonham's Case* in his 8. Co. is far from any extravagancy,
> for it is a very reasonable and true saying, That if an act of parliament
> should ordain that the same person should be party and judge, or, which
> is the same thing, judge in his own cause, it would be a void act of
> parliament; for it is impossible that one should be judge and party, for
> the judge is to determine between party and party, or between the
> government and the party; and an act of parliament can do no wrong,
> though it may do several things that look pretty odd ... An act of
> parliament may not make adultery lawful, that is, it cannot make it lawful
> for A. to lie with the wife of B. but it may make the wife of A. to be the wife
> of B. and dissolve her marriage with A.[122]

Holt CJ thus narrowed the scope of Coke's dictum by clearly attributing
the voidness of an Act of Parliament to impossibility and manifest
contradiction, and not also to contravention of common right and
reason. His subsequent assertion that an Act of Parliament cannot
make adultery lawful is, however, difficult to understand as a deduction
from analogous impossibility or manifest contradiction. Furthermore,
his discussion of Acts of Parliament void for impossibility followed an
earlier passage in which he asserted 'that a by-law is liable to have its
validity brought in question, but an act of parliament is not'.[123] In *City
of London* v. *Wood*, the unquestionable validity of all Acts of Parliament

---

[120] (1686) 2 Shower 475.  [121] *Ibid.* 478.
[122] See n. 107 above, at 687–8.  [123] *Ibid.* 678.

was recognised alongside their voidness, according to Coke's dictum, in cases of impossibility or manifest contradiction.

Ambivalence towards Coke's dictum was still evident in Blackstone. On the one hand, Blackstone simply repeated much of the substance of Coke's dictum in *Bonham's Case*: 'acts of parliament that are impossible to be performed are of no validity; and if there arise out of them collaterally any absurd consequences, manifestly contradictory to common reason, they are, with regard to those collateral consequences, void.'[124] He also explained that general legislative words are to be construed to avoid what is unreasonable, such as a person's judging in his own cause.[125] On the other hand, he qualified the substance of Coke's dictum in deference to the legislative power of Parliament:

> I lay down the rule with these restrictions; though I know it is generally laid down more largely, that acts of parliament contrary to reason are void. But if the parliament will positively enact a thing to be done which is unreasonable, I know of no power that can control it: and the examples usually alleged in support of this sense of the rule do none of them prove, that where the main object of a statute is unreasonable the judges are at liberty to reject it; for that were to set the judicial power above that of the legislature, which would be subversive of all government ... But if we should conceive it possible for the parliament to enact, that he [a person] should try as well his own causes as those of other persons, there is no court that has power to defeat the intent of the legislature, when couched in such evident and express words, as leave no doubt whether it was the intent of the legislature or no.[126]

Elsewhere in his *Commentaries*, Blackstone quoted Coke's description of the transcendent and absolute power and jurisdiction of Parliament and attributed to Parliament 'sovereign and uncontrolable authority in making, confirming, enlarging, restraining, abrogating, repealing, reviving, and expounding of law, concerning matters of all possible denominations, ecclesiastical, or temporal, civil, military, maritime, or criminal'.[127] In short, Blackstone embraced both Coke's dictum in *Bonham's Case* and the transcendence of Parliament but, through his 'restrictions' or qualifications ultimately relegated the dictum beneath Parliament's 'sovereign and uncontrollable authority'.[128]

In the early nineteenth century, much of the substance of Coke's dictum (without reference to *Bonham's Case*) was, for what must have

---

[124] *Commentaries*, n. 77 above, Vol. I, p. 91.
[125] *Ibid.*   [126] *Ibid.*   [127] *Ibid.* p. 156.   [128] *Ibid.* pp. 91, 156.

been one of the last times, unequivocally endorsed in George Custance's *Concise View of the Constitution of England*.[129] In discussing statutory construction, Custance observed, both that statutes derogating from the power of subsequent Parliaments are not binding and that those 'which are impossible to be performed, are of no validity'.[130] He added that 'if there arise out of them collaterally any absurd consequences, manifestly contradictory to reason, they are, with regard to those consequences, void'.[131] Through the course of the nineteenth century, the position was, however, clarified to the contrary in case law. In *Stewart* v. *Lawton*,[132] counsel for the plaintiffs cited *Bonham's Case* to show cause why the plaintiffs did not need to be examined under oath as to the amount of premium paid under an indenture of apprenticeship although required to do so by statute. Counsel for the defendants argued that the 'doctrine in *Dr Bonham's* case applies only where a statute requires something impossible to be done; but here the oath of the party is the chief security for ensuring to the revenue the duty upon the exact premium paid'.[133] In his judgment, Park J simply asserted that if 'an act of parliament requires it, a Plaintiff may undoubtedly be examined'.[134] The court confirmed, in brief, Parliament's overriding power.

Further judicial citations of *Bonham's Case* in the nineteenth century are few and far between. In *Mersey Docks Trustees* v. *Gibbs*,[135] reference was made to the principle of *Nemo debet esse iudex in propria causa* (the *nemo iudex* principle). The case was decided when extension of the franchise was again at the centre of political debate, that is, shortly before the first Reform Act[136] was broadened significantly through the provisions of the second Reform Act.[137] Mr Justice Blackburn declared as follows:

> It is contrary to the general rule of law, not only in this country but in every other, to make a person judge in his own cause; and though the Legislature can, and no doubt in a proper case would, depart from that general rule, an intention to do so is not to be inferred except from much clearer enactments than any to be found in these statutes.[138]

Mr Justice Blackburn thus identified the *nemo iudex* principle under 'the general rule of law' but accepted the overriding legislative power to

---

[129] London: the Author, 1808.     [130] *Ibid.* p. 41.     [131] *Ibid.*     [132] (1823) 1 Bingham 374.
[133] *Ibid.* 376.     [134] *Ibid.*     [135] Note 11 above.     [136] Reform Act 1832.
[137] Representation of the People Act 1867.     [138] Note 11 above, at 710–11.

'depart from that general rule'.[139] In the same year, William Hearn cited Coke's dictum in *Bonham's Case* as well as St German, Lord Chief Justice Hobart in *Day* v. *Savadge* and Blackstone, *inter alia*.[140] He concluded, however, that it 'is *now* universally conceded that the authority of Parliament in matters of legislation is unlimited' and that 'when the meaning is clear, it is the duty of the Court not to question the wisdom of the statute but to obey its commands'.[141]

A few years after the Representation of the People Act 1867, and 14 years before the first edition of Dicey's *Law of the Constitution* was published, *Lee* v. *Bude and Torrington Junction Railway Co.* was decided.[142] Willis J referred to the *nemo iudex* principle but emphatically rejected authority for disregarding an Act of Parliament that violates it. In resounding rhetoric, he unequivocally expressed judicial subservience to the Queen and Parliament:

> I would observe, as to these Acts of Parliament, that they are the law of this land; and we do not sit here as a court of appeal from parliament. It was once said – I think in Hobart – that, if an Act of Parliament were to create a man judge in his own cause, the Court might disregard it. That dictum, however, stands as a warning, rather than an authority to be followed. We sit here as servants of the Queen and the legislature. Are we to act as regents over what is done by parliament with the consent of the Queen, lords and commons? I deny that any such authority exists. If an Act of Parliament has been obtained improperly, it is for the legislature to correct it by repealing it: but so long as it exists as law, the Courts are bound to obey it. The proceedings here are judicial, not autocratic, which they would be if we could make laws instead of administering them.[143]

The eclipse of Coke's dictum was complete. Hobart CJ in *Day* v. *Savadge*, and not Coke in *Bonham's Case*, was cited, and its authority was denied. Parliament could enact that a person be judge and party in the same cause and thus override the *nemo iudex* principle of the common law. In the general context of Parliament's long history and recent and continuing[144] reform as a representative legislature, the contradiction between a transcendent Parliament and Coke's

---

[139] *Ibid.* See also H. Cox, *The Institutions of the English Government; Being an Account of the Constitution, Powers, and Procedure, of its Legislative, Judicial, and Administrative Departments with Copious References to Ancient and Modern Authorities* (London: H. Sweet, 1863), pp. xliii–xliv, 8–9.

[140] *Government of England*, n. 11 above, pp. 47–50.

[141] Ibid. p. 50.     [142] (1871) LR 6 CP 576.     [143] *Ibid.* 582.

[144] Ballot Act 1872; Representation of the People Act 1884.

controlling common law was negated,[145] in effect, with an eloquent simplicity – unequivocal recognition of the overriding legislative authority of Parliament.

## The historical constitutional significance of Coke's common law

Despite the brevity of its rule and its contradictory character at least at an abstract level, Coke's controlling common law has been and remains profoundly significant to the historical constitution in various ways. First, his formative legal contribution between the medieval and the modern was both English and European in the centrality accorded to artificial reason, in the role of classical rhetoric and even in his famous invocation of Bracton's dictum about the King's being under God and the law. Secondly, its contradictory character has itself contributed to the depth of the historical constitution's resources. Coke's contradictory assertions of a transcendent Parliament and a controlling common law have been theoretically and analytically problematic but they have also been sources of the constitution's reformation, whether in negating or resolving the contradiction or expressly accentuating one of its sides.[146] Contradictory assertions have a potential significance comparable to that of conceptual vagueness and ambivalence, which contributed to the Crown's evolutionary accommodation of representative institutions of government described in Chapter Three. For any particular proposed constitutional development, one side of a lasting contradiction may be a source of continuity, the other, a source of change, and either or both, a source of appeal to conservatives, modernisers and moderates. Thirdly, Coke's controlling common law and its eclipse by the unequivocal judicial recognition of the overriding legislative authority of Parliament both form the historical backdrop to Dicey's pioneering analysis of the rule of law, the subject of the next chapter.

---

[145] Cf. generally the influence of Coke in the American colonies: Plucknett, 'Bonham's Case', n. 36 above, 68ff; Corwin, 'The "higher law" background', n. 23 above, 394ff.; Gough, *Fundamental Law*, n. 34 above, ch. 12.

[146] Cf. generally, e.g., T. R. S. Allan, *Law, Liberty, and Justice*, n. 3 above, pp. 267ff; T. R. S. Allan, *Constitutional Justice: A Liberal Theory of the Rule of Law* (Oxford: Oxford University Press, 2001), Epigraph, p. v, pp. 204–6; Goldswothy, *Sovereignty of Parliament*, n. 34 above, especially at pp. 109ff, 231f; J. Goldsworthy, 'The myth of the common law constitution' in D. Edlin (ed.), *Common Law Theory* (New York: Cambridge University Press, forthcoming in 2007).

# 7

# Dicey's progressive and reactionary rule of law

Since Dicey coined[1] or popularised[2] the phrase 'the rule of law' to describe a main and peculiar[3] feature of the English constitution, questions about its character and relationship to parliamentary sovereignty have been crucial in orthodox English constitutional analysis. They are related to further fundamental questions about the rule of law's appeal and the basis for fidelity to the law of the constitution. Dicey's own leading analysis of the rule of law, I will suggest, is not properly understood and these questions are not adequately answered in purely Diceyan analytical terms and without appreciating, in particular, Dicey's own historical view and that of the whig historians upon which he relied but nonetheless formally relegated in his *Law of the Constitution*.[4] In this chapter, as in previous chapters, I will attempt fully to recognise the European effects upon Dicey's peculiar rule of law, commonly contrasted, for example, with the Continental European notion of the *Rechtsstaat*.[5] My concern is again the extent to which Dicey's rule of law illustrates both the history in the English historical constitution and interaction with developments in the legal and political communities of Continental Europe.

---

[1] F. H. Lawson, *The Oxford School of Law, 1850–1965* (Oxford: Oxford University Press, 1968), p. 72.

[2] The phrase 'the general rule of law' was already used in *Mersey Docks Trustees* v. *Gibbs* (1866) 11 HLC 686, at 710 (see pp. 154f above). 'The supremacy of the law', is the title to para. 7, ch. 3 in W. E. Hearn, *The Government of England: Its Structure and Development* (London: Longmans, Green, Reader, and Dyer, 1867), p. iii, and is treated by Dicey as synonymous with the rule of law, *An Introduction to the Study of the Law of the Constitution* (London: Macmillan, 10th edn, 1959), p. 184. See ch. 6 above, n. 11.

[3] *Ibid.* chs. 4, 12, especially at p. 184.

[4] *Ibid.* pp. vii, 15ff. See ch. 2 above, pp. 7ff.

[5] See, e.g., R. C. van Caenegem, 'The "*Rechtsstaat*" in historical perspective' in R. C. van Caenegem, *Legal History: A European Perspective* (London: The Hambledon Press, 1991), pp. 185–99. See generally N. W. Barber, 'The *Rechtsstaat* and the rule of law' (2003) 53 *University of Toronto Law Journal* 443.

Dicey's analysis of the constitution was not one-sided in its emphasis on parliamentary sovereignty. It reflected both Coke's controlling common law and Parliament's overriding legislative authority, which had received unequivocal judicial recognition in *Lee* v. *Bude and Torrington Junction Railway Co.* fourteen years before the publication of Dicey's first edition of *Law of the Constitution*.[6] Dicey presented both the sovereignty of parliament and the 'rule or supremacy of law' as ancient and fundamental features of the English constitution.[7] In what became chapter 13 of *Law of the Constitution*, he suggested that the 'sovereignty of Parliament ... favours the supremacy of the law' and that the 'Rule of Law favours Parliamentary sovereignty'.[8] His paradoxical suggestion echoed or resembled Coke's assertion in *Rowles* v. *Mason* that 'Statute Law ... corrects, abridges, and explains the common law ... But the common law Corrects, Allows, and Disallows ... Statute Law'.[9] Whether Dicey avoided, resolved, or reinstated the contradiction in Coke between a controlling common law and a transcendent Parliament depends upon the three meanings and relative significance he attributed to the rule of law. Pervasive in influence,[10] still the object of both apology and diatribe and variously interpreted in defence of opposing or differing views,[11] his analysis requires careful reconsideration.

### The formality of Dicey's three meanings

By the rule of law, Dicey meant, in the first place, 'the absolute supremacy or predominance of regular law as opposed to the influence of arbitrary power', and, as such, regarded it as excluding 'the existence of arbitrariness, of prerogative, or even of wide discretionary authority on the part of the government'.[12] Accordingly, 'no man is punishable or can be lawfully made to suffer in body or goods except for a distinct breach of law established in the ordinary legal manner before the ordinary

---

[6] (1871) LR 6 CP 576, especially at 582. See ch. 6 above, pp. 155f.

[7] *Law of the Constitution*, n. 2 above, pp. 183ff, especially at p. 184.

[8] *Ibid.* pp. 406, 411.    [9] (1612) 2 Brownl 192 at 198.    [10] See ch. 8 below, pp. 188ff.

[11] See, e.g., G. Marshall, *Constitutional Theory* (Oxford: Oxford University Press, 1971), pp. 137–9; J. Jowell, 'The rule of law today' in J. Jowell and D. Oliver (eds.), *The Changing Constitution* (Oxford: Oxford University Press, 5th edn, 2004), pp. 5–25; P. P. Craig, 'Formal and substantive conceptions of the rule of law: an analytical framework' [1997] *PL* 467 at 470–4; T. R. S. Allan *Constitutional Justice: A Liberal Theory of the Rule of Law* (Oxford: Oxford University Press, 2001), pp. 13–21, 214–15; Lord Bingham, 'Dicey revisited' [2002] *PL* 39.

[12] *Law of the Constitution*, n. 2 above, p. 202.

courts of the land'.[13] Starkly contrasting arbitrary power with punishment for distinct breach of the law, Dicey articulates no substantive principle or criterion with which to determine arbitrariness.[14] He does not here define the rule of law to require that the law have any particular substantive content. The rule of law would be respected provided a person were only punished where the ordinary law, however deplorable in content, were distinctly broken. As meant by Dicey in the first place, it imposes only a formal constraint upon the arbitrary exercise of power.

By the rule of law, Dicey meant, in the second place, 'that here every man, whatever be his rank or condition, is subject to the ordinary law of the realm and amenable to the jurisdiction of the ordinary tribunals'.[15] He explains that the rule of law in this sense 'excludes the idea of any exemption of officials or others from the duty of obedience to the law which governs other citizens or from the jurisdiction of the ordinary tribunals'.[16] In analysing his second definition, Dicey does not proffer substantive principles with which to justify what should be generally provided in law or where special treatment or consideration would be warranted. Rather, Dicey simply equates 'the idea of legal equality' and 'the universal subjection of all classes to one law administered by the ordinary courts', which, he presents, at one point, as alternative formulations of the same notion.[17] He envisages a jurisdictional equality – the subjection of all to the same jurisdiction – and does not provide substantive principles with which to evaluate the jurisdiction. His concept of equality is unrefined and limited in application.[18]

By the rule of law, Dicey meant, in the third place, 'that the general principles of the constitution (as for example, the right to personal liberty...) are with us the result of judicial decisions determining the rights of private

---

[13] *Ibid.* p. 188.

[14] Craig, 'Formal and substantive conceptions of the rule of law', n. 11 above, 470–2. See also Marshall, *Constitutional Theory*, n. 11 above, pp. 137–9. Cf. Allan, *Constitutional Justice*, n. 11 above, p. 18 (see pp. 166f, 210ff below).

[15] *Law of the Constitution*, n. 2 above, p. 193.    [16] *Ibid.* pp. 202–3.    [17] *Ibid.* p. 193.

[18] See Marshall, *Constitutional Theory*, n. 11 above, pp. 137–9; Jowell, 'Rule of law today', n. 11 above, pp. 23–4; Craig, 'Formal and substantive conceptions of the rule of law', n. 11 above, pp. 472–3. Cf. T. R. S. Allan, 'The rule of law as the rule of reason: consent and constitutionalism' (1999) 115 *LQR* 221 at 242–3; Allan, *Constitutional Justice*, n. 11 above, pp. 17–20 (see pp. 211f below); R. Dworkin, 'Hart's postscript and the character of political philosophy' (2004) 24 *OJLS* 1 at 30. Dworkin does not elaborate upon his passing suggestion that Dicey exemplifies one who has 'in mind substantial and not merely formal equality before the law' where he offers his second meaning of the rule of law, *ibid.*

persons in particular cases brought before the courts'.[19] In analysing this third meaning, Dicey celebrates in two features of the English rule of law – the availability of real remedies and the absence of rights declared or defined in the abstract. On the one hand, he emphasises the remedies of the ordinary English courts and, in particular, *habeas corpus*, a remedy expressed with phrase that epitomises both the personal[20] and remedial character of his rule of law: 'The Habeas Corpus Acts declare no principle and define no rights, but they are for practical purposes worth a hundred constitutional articles guaranteeing individual liberty ... [T]hese Acts are of really more importance not only than the general proclamations of the Rights of Man which have often been put forward in foreign countries, but even than such very lawyer-like documents as the Petition of Right or the Bill of Rights.'[21] Elsewhere in *Law of the Constitution*, Dicey describes the right to personal freedom: '*A*'s right to personal freedom is ... only the right of *A* not to be assaulted, or imprisoned, by *X*, or (to look at the same thing from another point of view) is nothing else than the right of *A*, if assaulted by *X*, to bring an action against *X*, or to have *X* punished as a criminal for the assault'.[22] Here Dicey simply equates right and remedy. On the other hand, in analysing his third meaning, he emphasises that there 'is in the English constitution an absence of those declarations or definitions of rights so dear to foreign constitutionalists'.[23] He refers to the 'so-called principles of the constitution' as 'mere generalizations', as 'inductions ... based upon particular decisions pronounced by the courts as to the rights of given individuals'.[24] The constitution is therefore to Dicey 'the result of the ordinary law of the land'.[25] Averse to abstract formulations, Dicey does not articulate substantive principles with which to explain the methodological superiority of the English judge-made constitution[26] or to assess the adequacy of its remedies or their absence in what might be a remedial black hole.

The formality of Dicey's rule of law is manifest in his discussion of *Wolfe Tone's Case*.[27] According to Dicey, Wolfe Tone, 'an Irish rebel', participated

---

[19] *Law of the Constitution*, n. 2 above, p. 195.
[20] Cf. the *Rechtsstaat* in Continental thought. See J. W. F. Allison, *A Continental Distinction in the Common Law: A Historical and Comparative Perspective on English Public Law* (Oxford: Oxford University Press, rev. pbk edn, 2000), pp. 78–9.
[21] *Law of the Constitution*, n. 2 above, pp. 199, 221.
[22] *Ibid.* p. 284.   [23] *Ibid.* p. 197.   [24] *Ibid.* pp. 197, 197–8.   [25] *Ibid.* p. 203.
[26] Craig, 'Formal and substantive conceptions of the rule of law', n. 11 above, 473–4.
[27] (1798) 27 St. Tr. 614. The facts in this report, which Dicey cites, and Dicey's own brief account of them (*Law of the Constitution*, n. 2 above, pp. 293–4) are substantially confirmed in Marianne Elliott's biography, *Wolfe Tone: Prophet of Irish Independence* (New Haven: Yale University Press, 1989), ch. 29, especially at pp. 392–400.

in a French invasion of Ireland, was captured and court-martialed by the English army in Dublin although he was commissioned, not as an English officer, but as an officer in the army of the French Republic. On the morning of his execution, the Irish King's Bench granted a writ of *habeas corpus*. Dicey presents the case as a triumph for the rule of law: 'When it is remembered that Wolfe Tone's substantial guilt was admitted, that the court was made up of judges who detested the rebels, and that in 1798 Ireland was in the midst of a revolutionary crisis, it will be admitted that no more splendid assertion of the supremacy of the law can be found than the protection of Wolfe Tone by the Irish Bench'.[28] Dicey's account is highly selective to say the least. According to the case report[29] cited by Dicey (and substantially confirmed in Marianne Elliott's biography),[30] Wolfe Tone had already slit his own throat so as to prevent, as some supposed, his being paraded through the streets prior to execution by public hanging (and not by firing squad as he had requested). On order of the Lord Chief Justice, the sheriff proceeded to the army barracks so as to prevent Tone's execution while a writ was still being prepared. The sheriff faced a barrage of refusals, claims from various high-ranking military officers to be acting under superior orders and, from the Brigadier-Major of the Dublin garrison, a reference to the ultimate authority of the Lord Lieutenant of Ireland. After the sheriff had received further orders from the Lord Chief Justice to take Tone's body as well as two of the high-ranking officers into custody, he was again refused admittance at the barracks, but returned with a surgeon sent to court by the Dublin district commander. Although Tone's body could not be brought to court because it was in no condition to be moved, the court did finally order that a rule suspending the execution be made and served. Wolfe Tone was not executed but, in the words of the case reporter, 'having endured . . . the most excruciating pain', died a week later. The court's protection of Tone through its 'splendid assertion of the supremacy of the law'[31] was, at its best, precarious, at its worst, purely formal. Celebrating the rule of law in all its skeletal formality, Dicey discounted much of what lay beyond it.

### The sway of a sovereign Parliament

Between his formal rule of law and the sovereignty of Parliament, Dicey identified a relationship of mutual support.[32] On the one hand, he

---

[28] *Law of the Constitution*, n. 2 above, p. 294.
[29] *Wolfe Tone's Case*, n. 27 above, at 621–6.    [30] Note 27 above.
[31] Dicey, *Law of the Constitution*, n. 2 above, p. 294.    [32] *Ibid.* ch. 13.

argued that the sovereignty of Parliament favours the supremacy of the law in that its enactments are subject to judicial interpretation. On the other hand, he argued that the supremacy of the law favours parliamentary sovereignty through the judicial interpretation of the words of an enactment and through the exceptional parliamentary legislation needed to avoid the executive's constantly being hampered by the rigidity of the law as interpreted by the courts. That Dicey's rule of law was, nonetheless, under the sway of parliamentary sovereignty is evident in various ways.

First, Dicey presents statutory interpretation as narrowly focused upon the words of a statute. He explains the narrow focus as a result of the refusal of English judges 'in principle at least, to interpret an Act of Parliament otherwise than by reference to the words of the enactment'.[33] Extraordinary executive powers are therefore *confined by the words* of the Act itself, and ... by the interpretation put upon the statute by the judges'.[34] Secondly, Dicey presents exceptional legislation as the answer to the rigidity of the law resulting from judicial interpretation.[35]

Thirdly, throughout *Law of the Constitution*, Dicey repeatedly presents exceptional legislation as overriding, even conclusive, in its effect. His chapter on martial law contains at least two examples. In one paragraph, he stresses that the Secretary of State is under the ordinary law of the land and cannot, therefore, 'for reasons of state, arrest, imprison, or punish any man' but adds 'except, *of course*, where special powers are conferred upon him by statute, as by an Aliens Act or by an Extradition Act'.[36] In another paragraph, Dicey describes the Riot Act 1714: 'That statute provides, in substance that if twelve rioters continue together for an hour after a magistrate has made a proclamation to them in terms of the Act ... ordering them to disperse, he may command the troops to fire upon the rioters or charge them sword in hand'.[37] Although Dicey stresses that necessity would still need to be proved, he writes simply of this as 'the effect of the enactment'.[38]

Dicey's chapter on personal freedom contains another telling example of the effect of exceptional legislation. Dicey acknowledges that a Habeas Corpus Suspension Act, 'coupled with the prospect of an Indemnity Act ['the legalisation of illegality'], does in truth arm the executive with arbitrary powers'.[39] Dicey reassures his reader that the

---

[33] *Ibid.* p. 407.   [34] *Ibid.* p. 413 (my emphasis).   [35] *Ibid.* p. 411.
[36] *Ibid.* p. 285 (my emphasis).   [37] *Ibid.* p. 290.   [38] *Ibid.*
[39] *Ibid.* p. 236. The insertion is taken from *ibid.* p. 237.

Suspension Act 'is not, in reality, more than a suspension of one particular remedy' and that an Indemnity Act might not be forthcoming where gross abuse of power is suspected and that 'everything depends on the terms of the Act of Indemnity', that is, on whether they be 'narrow or wide'.[40] Dicey's apparent unease and each of his reassurances are, however, themselves further evidence that he regarded exceptional legislation[41] as overriding and assumed substantial judicial acquiescence.

In summary, Dicey's two pillars of the constitution – the rule of law and parliamentary sovereignty – were unequal in height.[42] His analysis reflected both the rule of law's formal constraints in famous cases, such as *Entick* v. *Carrington*[43] and *Wilkes* v. *Woods*,[44] and Parliament's overriding or supreme legislative authority[45] as emphasised in Blackstone and famously exercised, for example, in the Act of Settlement 1701 and confirmed in various other cases.[46] Whatever was required by Dicey's formal rule of law – be it the exclusion of arbitrary power or the availability of remedies like *habeas corpus* – was subject to a legislative override – that arbitrary power be not conferred, or remedies removed, by exceptional parliamentary enactment.

---

[40] *Ibid.* pp. 202, 236.

[41] The effect of the converse – not passing exceptional legislation – is similarly treated by Dicey: e.g., 'the refusal of the English Parliament in 1695 to renew the Licensing Act did permanently establish the freedom of the press in England', *ibid.* p. 263. For further examples of the legislative effect Dicey assumed, see his assertion that 'the whole existence and discipline of the standing army' in time of peace depends on the Mutiny Act, *ibid.* p. 309, and his description of the consequences of '[a]ny deviation ... from the exact terms' of the Merchant Shipping Acts for the detention of unseaworthy ships, *ibid.* p. 397.

[42] See also Marshall, *Constitutional Theory*, n. 11 above, p. 138; P. P. Craig, 'Dicey: unitary, self-correcting democracy and public law' (1990) 106 *LQR* 105 at 106ff; Bingham 'Dicey revisited', n. 11 above, especially at 43ff. Cf. Allan *Constitutional Justice*, n. 11 above, pp. 13–21. The plight of Dicey's rule of law under the Apartheid regime in South Africa is not surprising in view of the then racially constructed electorate and the priority accorded by Dicey to parliamentary sovereignty. John Dugard contrasts the governmental 'accolades bestowed upon his [Dicey's] affirmation of parliamentary supremacy' with 'the absence of any reference to his views on the Rule of Law', *Human Rights and the South African Legal Order* (Princeton: Princeton University Press, 1978), p. 33. For an example from Apartheid South Africa of a rule of law constraint minimal in its formality, see *Loza* v. *Police Station Commander, Durbanville* 1964 (2) SA 545.

[43] (1765) 19 St. Tr. 1029.    [44] (1769) 19 St. Tr. 1406.

[45] Dicey, *Law of the Constitution*, n. 2 above, pp. 41ff.

[46] See, e.g., *Stewart* v. *Lawton* (1823) 1 Bingham 374; *Mersey Docks Trustees* v. *Gibbs* (1866) 11 *HLC* 686. See ch. 6 above, pp. 154ff.

## A constitutional conundrum

Dicey's constitutional analysis has been the object of continuing and comprehensive criticism.[47] Apart from exposing contradictions or other inadequacies in the text of *Law of the Constitution*, critics have focused on Dicey the author – his character and his methods – and on the context in which he wrote. Dicey has been described as an'erratic thinker'[48] and as a 'man of passion and of passions'.[49] His passionate willfulness has been demonstrated, if not clearly in his embrace of both referenda and parliamentary sovereignty,[50] then in his obstinate adherence to his thesis on *droit administratif*. In chapter 12 of edition after edition of *Law of the Constitution*, he described the development of *droit adminstratif* as utterly incompatible with the English rule of law although he appreciated inadequacies in the French authorities upon which he relied and knew of mounting evidence to the contrary. Apart from criticism of his historical and comparative methods[51] evident in his treatment of *droit administratif*, Dicey has also been criticised for misunderstanding his own political context. With reference to Dicey's *Lectures on the Relation between Law and Public Opinion in England during the Nineteenth Century*,[52] Paul Craig considers Dicey's overall view of the self-correcting English democracy that he presupposed in *Law of the Constitutution*. Craig argues, in broad outline, that Dicey believed that the threat of majoritarian tyranny would be averted through the working of representative democracy in Parliament, through the influence of cross-currents of public opinion beyond it and through occasional protection of individuals by the ordinary courts under the rule of law as understood by Dicey. Craig explains, however, that Dicey's political premises were crucially mistaken. In brief, Dicey underestimated the growth of executive power in the late nineteenth

---

[47] Cf. the more generous responses of F. H. Lawson, 'Dicey revisited' (1959) 7 *Political Studies* 109, 207; Allan, *Constitutional Justice*, n. 11 above, pp. 13–21; Bingham, 'Dicey revisited', n. 11 above.

[48] Sir Stephen Sedley, Annual Meeting of the European Group of Public Law, Cape Sounion, Greece, September 1999.

[49] R. Errera, 'Dicey and French administrative law: a missed encounter?' [1985] *PL* 695 at 706.

[50] See R. Weill, 'Dicey was not Diceyan' [2003] *CLJ* 474.

[51] See, e.g., R. A. Cosgrove, *The Rule of Law: Albert Venn Dicey, Victorian Jurist* (London: Macmillan, 1980), pp. 93–4, 102; Allison, *Continental Distinction in the Common Law*, n. 20 above, pp. 18–23.

[52] London: Macmillan, 2nd edn, 1914.

century and overestimated the capacity of the representative Parliament to control it.[53]

The continuing and wide-ranging criticism of Dicey's constitutional analysis has been proportionate to Dicey's undeniable influence.[54] The comprehensive criticism of *Law of the Constitution* has, however, been such as to create a conundrum. Constitutionalists have reason to explain how Dicey's text – enshrining a formal rule of law beneath a sovereign Parliament – of an erratic thinker, obstinate comparativist and poor historian, prone to a passionate willfulness, in mistaken response to his political context, could have appealed to successive generations of politicians and constitutional lawyers and thereby affected even those to whom it did not, or does not, appeal. The answer, I would suggest, lies in Dicey's use of history and comparison.

## Progressive whig history

As elaborated upon in Chapter Two, Dicey professed to be an 'expounder' of the constitution with the duty 'simply to explain its laws' and thus adopted an analytical legal view.[55] He expressly distinguished the legal view from the historical view and relegated the historical view in legal study so that lawyers might properly study 'the law as it now stands' and not 'think so much of the way in which an institution has come to be what it is, that they cease to consider with sufficient care what it is that an institution has become'.[56] Dicey's expository purpose and analytical legal view were not such as to preclude abundant historical references. Four illustrate their scope and prominence. First, Dicey presents the rule of law and the 'royal supremacy [that] has now passed into the sovereignty of Parliament' as two features that 'have at all times since the Norman conquest characterised the political institutions of England'.[57] Secondly, he presents the personal liability of Crown officers for wrongful arrest as a 'legal dogma, as old at least as the time of Edward the Fourth'.[58]

---

[53] Craig, 'Unitary, self-correcting democracy', n. 42 above.

[54] See ch. 8 below, pp. 188ff.

[55] *Law of the Constitution*, n. 2 above, p. 4.

[56] *Ibid.* pp. 12ff, especially, pp. vii, 15. See generally ch. 2 above, pp. 7ff. For other late nineteenth-century approaches to the relationship between historical and current legal or political views of the constitution, see *ibid.* pp. 12ff.

[57] *Law of the Constitution*, n. 2 above, p. 183.    [58] *Ibid.* p. 287.

Thirdly, Dicey reinforces his analysis of the incompatibility of administrative law with the English rule of law by invoking the constitutional struggles of the seventeenth century. In his chapter on administrative law, Dicey observes 'how nearly it came to pass that something very like administrative law at one time grew up in England' through the development of the King's prerogative jurisdiction by the Privy Council and Star Chamber in the sixteenth and early seventeenth centuries.[59] While recognising that the Privy Council and Star Chamber did then 'confer some benefits on the public', he emphasises their arbitrary authority and identifies them principally with the tyranny of the Stuart monarchs.[60] In the constitutional struggles of the seventeenth century, Dicey identifies the resistance of the 'fanatics for the common law' against the 'tyranny of the Stuarts' and the eventual triumph of the 'friends of freedom' in the abolition of the Star Chamber and the disappearance of the Privy Council's 'arbitrary authority'.[61] Dicey explains that, thereafter, Parliament 'did not suffer any system of administrative courts or of administrative law to be revived or developed in England'.[62] Fourthly, according to Dicey, the triumphant abolition of the Star Chamber, which had regulated all English presses, *inter alia*, was followed under the Restoration by the Licensing Act 1662. Parliament's refusal in 1695 to renew the 1662 Act, which provided for continued censorship but subjected it to statutory regulation – itself 'a triumph of legality' (although not of toleration) – founded freedom of the press in England.[63]

Dicey's invocations of history are normative and highly selective. In certain passages, Dicey presents sheer antiquity or lasting continuity as a virtue. In others, he celebrates in fundamental change as a triumph. His invocations of history are not analytical appeals under a doctrine of precedent. For Dicey, 'the appeal to precedent is in the law courts merely a useful fiction by which judicial decision conceals its transformation into judicial legislation'.[64] Dicey endorses, for example, the rule established by Coke CJ in *Prohibitions del Roy* regardless of the complete lack of analytical rigour with which it was established:

> Nothing can be more pedantic, nothing more artificial, nothing more unhistorical, than the reasoning by which Coke induced or compelled James to forego the attempt to withdraw cases from the courts for his

[59] *Ibid.* p. 379.   [60] *Ibid.*   [61] *Ibid.* pp. 379–80.
[62] *Ibid.* p. 380.   [63] *Ibid.* pp. 259ff, especially at p. 268.   [64] *Ibid.* p. 19.

Majesty's personal determination. But no achievement of sound argument, or stroke of enlightened statesmanship, ever established a rule more essential to the very existence of the constitution than the principle enforced by the obstinacy and the fallacies of the great Chief Justice.[65]

Another general example of Dicey's non-analytical use of history is suggested by Paul Craig. In the role of the ordinary courts in Dicey's rule of law, Craig suggests a non-sequitur elevation of their success in their battles against rival jurisdictions 'to the level of grand constitutional principle'.[66] Dicey's celebration of past triumphs was independent of the analytical rigour with which they were achieved and has remained exposed to analytical objection.

In the writing of *Law of the Constitution*, Dicey relied heavily on various whig historians. In the preface to his first edition, he describes Gardiner, Hallam and Freeman as historians 'whose books are in the hands of every student' and without constant reference to which not 'a page of my lectures could have been written'.[67] He describes Gardiner as 'the historian who most nearly meets the wants of lawyers' as they consider the seventeenth century struggles, Coke's confrontation with King James etc., all of which Dicey presents as 'matters which touch not remotely upon the problems of actual law'.[68] Dicey's second paragraph of *Law of the Constitution* is an extended quotation from Hallam. In the quoted passage, Henry Hallam[69] describes 'the long and uninterruptedly increasing prosperity of England' as 'the most beautiful phænomenon in the history of mankind' and attributes the English reconciliation of 'the discordant elements of wealth, order, and liberty' to the spirit of English laws.[70] While Dicey recognises that 'we cannot *exactly* echo the fervent self-complacency of Hallam', he describes him and Freeman as 'distinguished guides' to the history of the constitution.[71] Hallam's history was a history of progress to the present with reference to key developments

---

[65] *Ibid.* p. 18. On *Prohibitions del Roy* (1608) 12 Co. Rep. 63, see ch. 6 above, pp. 141ff.

[66] 'Unitary, self-correcting democracy', n. 42 above, 117–18, especially at 117.

[67] *Law of the Constitution*, n. 2 above, p. vi.    [68] *Ibid.* p. 17.

[69] Hallam was a whig historian despite his opposition to the bill that became the Reform Act 1832, H. Butterfield, *The Whig Interpretation of History* (London: W. W. Norton, 1965), p. 4.

[70] *View of the State of Europe during the Middle Ages*, 3 vols. (London: John Murray, 2nd edn, 1819), Vol. II, ch. 8, pp. 374–5, cited by Dicey, *Law of the Constitution*, n. 2 above, pp. 1–2. Cf. Montesquieu, *The Spirit of the Laws*, A. M. Cohler, B. C. Miller and H. S. Stone (ed. and tr.) (Cambridge: Cambridge University Press, 1989), Bk. 1, ch. 3, pp. 8–9.

[71] *Law of the Constitution*, n. 2 above, pp. 3, 7 (my emphasis).

such as the creation of Magna Carta or Bracton's assertion that the King is subject to God and the law.[72] Immediately after the passage quoted by Dicey, Hallam states that the object of his chapter is to trace the gradual formation of the English system of government of his own day.[73] Hallam's history was also openly abridged – the concise outcome of a 'severe retrenchment of superfluous matter'.[74] Although Hallam recognised that historians attentive to the particular 'may justly deem such general sketches imperfect and superficial', he was content that his 'labours will not have proved fruitless, if they still conduce to stimulate the reflection, to guide the researches, to correct the prejudices, or to animate the liberal and virtuous sentiments of inquisitive youth'.[75] To Hallam, his educative liberal purpose justified his history despite its lack of detail and resulting imperfections.

Dicey used Edward Freeman's *Growth of the English Constitution* as a 'first-rate specimen' with which to illustrate the antiquarianism of the historian's view of the constitution.[76] According to Dicey, 'vigorous statements' by Freeman forced upon his attention 'the essential difference between the historical and the legal way of regarding our institutions'.[77] Dicey was responding to Freeman's claim in the preface to his first edition that 'constitutional history has been perverted at the hands of lawyers' through their complete inattention to original sources.[78] Dicey nonetheless recognised Freeman's book, like the books of Gardiner and Hallam, as indispensable to the writing of *Law of the Constitution* and as to him 'a model (far easier to admire than to imitate) of the mode in which dry and even abstruse topics may be made the subject of effective and popular exposition'.[79] Freeman asserted that even our 'ancient history is the possession of the Liberal' and aimed 'to show that the earliest institutions of England ... are not mere matters of curious speculation, but matters closely connected with our present political being'.[80] The histories of Freeman, Gardiner and Hallam all illustrate the form and content of whig history.

---

[72] See, e.g., Hallam, *State of Europe during the Middle Ages*, n. 70 above, Vol. II, pp. 459–60, 471–2.

[73] *Ibid.* p. 375.    [74] *Ibid.* Vol. I, p. xii.    [75] *Ibid.* p. xiii.

[76] *Law of the Constitution*, n. 2 above, pp. 12f.    [77] *Ibid.* p. vii.

[78] E. A. Freeman, *The Growth of the English Constitution from the Earliest Times* (London: Macmillan, 3rd edn, 1876), pp. x–xii, especially at p. x.

[79] *Law of the Constitution*, n. 2 above, pp. vi–vii, especially at p. vii.

[80] Freeman, *Growth of the English Constitution*, n. 78 above, pp. x, ix.

As mentioned in Chapter Two, Herbert Butterfield exposed the deficiencies of whig history in historical study. In *The Whig Interpretation of History*, he describes it as abridged, broad in scale, and, as such, oversimplified. He repeatedly stresses its schematic or formulaic quality that suggests belief in an 'unfolding logic in history': 'The total result of this method [of whig history] is to impose a certain form upon the whole historical story, and to produce a scheme of general history which is bound to converge beautifully upon the present – all demonstrating through the ages the workings of an obvious principle of progress.'[81] The whig history Butterfield criticises 'is divided by great watersheds', such as the Reformation[82] (or the seventeenth century conflict between Crown and Parliament), beyond which the whig historian does not enquire. It is a story of progress to the present that assumes 'a false continuity in events' and endorses or promulgates judgments of value.[83] Butterfield describes its 'exaltation' or 'over-dramatisation' as a battle between the advocates and opponents of progress with a simple emphasis on the actors or agents in history.[84] Most importantly, it is orientated to the present – its origins, how the past anticipates or turns into the present – to which 'direct and perpetual reference' is made.[85] As a result, the 'fervour of the whig historian very often comes from what is really the transference into the past of an enthusiasm for something in the present, an enthusiasm for democracy or freedom of thought or the liberal tradition'.[86] Whig history is a vehicle for expressing a fervour for something in the present and demonstrating the developing appreciation of its value in the past.

From Butterfield's perspective, whig history detracts from the concrete study of the past for its own sake and in all its detailed or nuanced complexity. For the same reason, however, and other reasons elaborated on in Chapter Two, it suited the historical constitution encapsulated in Dicey's analytical account. Abridgment, oversimplification and the imposition of form were sources of constitutional accessibility, unity and apparent rationality. The dramatisation of the story of progress and its enactment of values were sources of general appeal. Most fundamentally, a past understood in terms of the present served present needs and was a vehicle of fervour for the present. In the absence of Founding Fathers, a break with the past and consequent written constitution

---

[81] Note 69 above, pp. 41–2, 12.    [82] *Ibid.* pp. 51–2, especially at p. 51.
[83] *Ibid.* chs. 4, 6, especially at pp. 87f.    [84] *Ibid.* pp. 49ff, especially at pp. 113, 128.
[85] *Ibid.* p. 11.    [86] *Ibid.* p. 96.

understood as 'the legally uncaused cause of all legal effects',[87] actors or agents divided by the great watersheds of history enacted a story of constitutional progress to the present understood in terms of the past. Looking in the past for what had already been found in the present might have been a circular historical enquiry[88] but the history it produced was, for constitutional purposes, intelligible, accessible, foundational, the focus of fervour and a source of fidelity. Each of the main features of whig history, even its circularity, exposed by Butterfield, thus enhanced the historical constitution.

Whig history began to be written well before the nineteenth century. It was, for example, evident in the celebration of Magna Carta by Coke, presented by Butterfield as the most influential early whig historian – 'almost the extreme example of the whig interpretation of history'.[89] It has also been echoed on occasion in court. In *Entick v. Carrington*, for example, counsel for the plaintiff deplored the ministerial practice of granting warrants of search and seizure and called upon the court 'which has ever been the protector of liberty and property of the subject, to demolish this monster of oppression, and to tear into rags this remnant of Star-chamber tyranny'.[90] By the mid-to-late-nineteenth century, the comprehensive histories of whig historians, such as Hallam, Freeman and Gardiner, were influencing generations of students, and a progressive understanding of English constitutional history had become central to political thought.[91] If Coke was the most influential early whig historian, Dicey was its most consistent proponent in constitutional legal doctrine. Upon his skeletal analysis, he grafted a whig skin for a receptive English audience much of which had come to share a whig historical understanding of the progressive English nation in an era of assertive nation states.

Butterfield briefly explains the prevalence of whig history in his influential book. He writes of 'a tendency for all history to veer over

---

[87] N. MacCormick, *H.L.A. Hart* (London: Edward Arnold, 1981), p. 4.

[88] See Butterfield, *Whig Interpretation of History*, n. 69 above, pp. 62–3.

[89] H. Butterfield, *The Englishman and His History* (Cambridge: Cambridge Universtiy Press, 1944), pp. 40, 47–68, especially at p. 49. See generally ch. 6 above.

[90] Note 43 above, at 1039.

[91] See, e.g., Earl John Russell, *An Essay on the History of the English Government and Constitution from the Reign of Henry VII to the Present Time* (London: Longman, Green, Longman, Roberts, & Green, new edn, 1865), ch. 1. Note especially Russell's reliance on Hallam, although Hallam had strongly opposed the bill that became the Reform Act 1832, Butterfield, *Whig Interpretation of History*, n. 69 above, p. 4.

into whig history', and to do so in proportion to its abridgment.[92] He refers also to the extent 'the historian has been Protestant, progressive, and whig, and the very model of the 19th century gentleman'.[93] By implication, whig history reflected whig views that prevailed in the present. Different views might, however, have prevailed, or may in future prevail, to be reflected in other histories, different in content but similarly objectionable in method. One criticism of Butterfield is that his objections to whig history would be applicable to whatever the history produced in the service of present needs. He describes the object of his criticism with a name, 'whig history', that is misleading in its substantive focus. What Butterfield calls whig history would rightly be characterised by its method and not its content.

A second criticism of Butterfield in *The Whig Interpretation of History*,[94] is that, in his wide-ranging criticism of the method of the whig historian, he neglects its comparative dimension. As in previous chapters, that comparative dimension is elaborated upon below as a corrective not only to Butterfield's account but also to Dicey's own insular view of his rule of law. Dicey had a strong sense of the peculiarity of the English constitution and its key doctrines, as discussed above. For Dicey, the 'historical reason why Parliament ... has always retained its character of a supreme legislature, lies deep in the history of the English people', and the rule of law is, similarly, a 'peculiarity of our polity'.[95] The English rule of law has commonly been distinguished in legal theory from the developed Continental notion of the *Rechtsstaat*, centred on

---

[92] *Whig Interpretation of History*, n. 69 above, pp. 6–7, especially at p. 6.

[93] *Ibid.* pp. 3–4. See also Butterfield, *Englishman and his History*, n. 89 above.

[94] Cf. the greater comparative dimension to Butterfield's later work, published towards the end of the Second World War, *Englishman and his History*, n. 89 above, expecially pp. v–vii, 1–11, 103–17, and his emphasis on the influence of the nineteenth century German historical school in England, *Man on His Past: The Study of the History of Historical Scholarship* (Cambridge: Cambridge University Press, 1955), especially at p. 22. Cf. generally Pocock's emphasis on comparison, the relevance of a basis for comparison and French humanist influences upon modern historiography, *The Ancient Constitution and the Feudal Law, A Study of English Historical Thought in the Seventeenth Century: A Reissue with a Retrospect* (Cambridge: Cambridge University Press, 1987), Pt. 1, chs. 1, 3, 4, Pt. 2, ch. 1. See also J. P. Sommerville, 'The ancient constitution reassessed: the common law, the court and the languages of politics in early modern England' in R. M. Smuts (ed.), *The Stuart Court and Europe: Essays in Politics and Political Culture* (Cambridge: Cambridge University Press, 1996), pp. 39–64; J. P. Sommerville, 'English and European political ideas in the early seventeenth century: revisionism and the case of absolutism' (1996) 35 *Journal of British Studies* 168.

[95] *Law of the Constitution*, n. 2 above, pp. 68–9, n. 1, p. 184.

the concept of the state.[96] Dicey's own analysis of it has previously been dismissed as an 'unfortunate outburst of Anglo-Saxon parochialism'.[97] His insular view of the rule of law has been shared by both critical and sympathetic commentators[98] and requires a comparative complement.

### English reactions and Continental comparisons

Relatively little of Dicey's rule of law, with its emphasis on the personal liability of individuals and officials alike under the ordinary law of the ordinary courts, was evident in domestic writings on the constitution before the last decades of the eighteenth century or in later writings under their influence, particularly that of Blackstone.[99] Rather, notions later subsumed under Dicey's rule of law developed significantly thereafter in relation to Continental European developments. Their relational development, it will be argued, occurred in two main ways – first, in reaction to Continental developments, and secondly, in reliance on the approving accounts of the English constitution by Continental commentators who articulated a liberal national self-criticism through critical comparison.

[96] See, e.g., Van Caenegem, 'The Rechtsstaat', n. 5 above.

[97] J. N. Shklar, 'Political theory and the rule of law' in A. C. Hutchinson and P. Monahan (eds.), *The Rule of Law: Ideal or Ideology* (Toronto: Carswell, 1987), pp. 1–16 at p. 5. See also R. Cotterrell, 'The rule of law in transition: revisiting Franz Neumann's sociology of legality' (1996) 5 *Social & Legal Studies* 451 at 452–3.

[98] See also, e.g., Craig's domestic focus in 'Unitary, self-correcting democracy', n. 42 above, especially at 133ff, and Allan's focus on the common law in the 'Rule of law as the rule of reason', n. 18 above, especially at 242–3, and in *Constitutional Justice*, n. 11 above, especially at pp. 18–19.

[99] See, e.g., J. Locke, *Two Treatises of Government* P. Laslett (ed.) (Cambridge: Cambridge University Press, 1988); G. Jacob, *Lex Constitutionis* or *The Gentleman's Law: Being, a Compleat Treatise of all the Laws and Statutes* (London: B. Lintot, 1719); R. Acherley, *The Britannic Constitution* or *The Fundamental Form of Government in Britain* (London: A. Bettesworth et al. 1727); J. T. Philipps, *The Fundamental Laws and Constitutions of Seven Potent Kingdoms and States in Europe: viz. Denmark, Sweden, Germany, Poland, England, Holland and Swisserland* (London: W. Meadows, 1752); W. Blackstone, *Commentaries on the Laws of England*, 4 vols. (Chicago: The University of Chicago Press, Facsimile of 1st edn of 1765–1769, 1979); F. S. Sullivan, *Lectures on the Constitution and Laws of England, with a Commentary on Magna Charta, and Illustrations of Many of the English Statutes* (London: Edward and Charles Dilly and Joseph Johnson, 2nd edn, 1776); G. Bowyer, *Commentaries on the Constitutional Law of England* (London: Owen Richards, 2nd edn, 1846), especially at pp. 1, 58ff, 231–4 (but cf. his contrast between the British 'law of the land' and a written code on p. 2f). See generally H. W. Arndt, 'The origins of Dicey's concept of the "rule of law"' (1957) 31 *Australian Law Journal* 117 at 118f.

The reaction was, in particular, to the Spanish Inquisition, the *Ancien Régime*, the French Revolution, the Terror and Napoleon Bonaparte, all of which were, or became in some degree, pejorative and laden with normative significance. In the mid-eighteenth century, the reaction was still absent, for example from *The Fundamental Laws and Constitutions of Seven Potent Kingdoms and States in Europe* by Philipps.[100] Philipps examined the fundamental laws of other powerful nations in Europe but stressed that they 'have been always held in great Esteem, as they must be supposed to give a true and just Idea of the Genius and particular Inclination of the respective People that constitute Empires, Kingdoms and Commonwealths'.[101] In the late eighteenth century, however, a reaction became increasingly prominent. In *Entick* v. *Carrington*, for example, counsel for the plaintiff described the granting of warrants of search and seizure by Secretaries of State as 'worse than the Spanish inquisition; for ransacking a man's secret drawers and boxes, to come at evidence against him, is like racking his body to come at his secret thoughts'.[102] More pervasive in its general effects upon the English historical constitution than the reaction to the Spanish Inquisition in criminal procedure was the reaction to the French Revolution of 1789. It was encapsulated in Burke's *Reflections on the Revolution in France*[103] and as such was to be invoked repeatedly in England for more than a century.

Reaction to the French Revolution did not preclude a continuing reaction also to absolute monarchy under the *Ancien Régime*. That lasting reaction is evident in James Ferris's book with the revealing full title *A Standard of the English Constitution, with a Retrospective View of Historical Occurrences before and after the [English] Revolution Illustrated with Critical Remarks on the Nature and Effects of Despotism, Compared with the Nature and Effects of Free Government*.[104] Ferris elaborated on free mixed English government by way of comparison with despotism, which Ferris equated with absolute monarchy.[105] Exclaiming 'Happy island, whose laws have no respect of persons!', he gave pride of place in the constitution to English laws – 'equally and universally binding' and 'published, read, and know of all men' – and to judicial power and

---

[100]  Note 99 above.    [101]  *Ibid*. p. iii.    [102]  Note 43 above, at 1038.

[103]  C. C. O'Brien (ed.) (London: Penguin, 1968). See, e.g., Burke's criticism of the exemption of administrative bodies from the ordinary law under the emergent radical French separation of powers, *ibid*. p. 329f, and, in the words of Dicey, his 'just hatred' of the perpetrators of the Terror, *Law of the Constitution*, n. 2 above, p. 3.

[104]  London: the Author, 1805.    [105]  *Ibid*. p. 2.

proceedings (not to parliamentary sovereignty).[106] He concluded his treatment of English laws by citing Blackstone's attribution to them of successful resistance to the civil law under which political liberties had been lost on the Continent.[107]

Within two decades of the French Revolution, the English reaction to Continental developments had been fuelled by the military threat of Napoleon, that is, when 'all the horrors of sanguinary revolution' had passed 'under the iron yoke of military despotism'.[108] An extreme form of that reaction is expressed in George Custance's *Concise View of the Constitution of England*, published in 1808. His purpose was 'simply to instruct the rising generation in the fundamental principles of that admirable constitution which equalises the rights of all, from the king to the peasant; which is venerable for its antiquity, because it was founded upon freedom, in the earliest ages; which many of our forefathers defended by their swords; and which every Briton should be ready to seal with his blood'.[109] Custance emphasised that the 'beauties of our constitution should be engraven, rather than painted, upon the minds of our youth', as such, much like Roman youth 'taught to commit to memory the *twelve tables*'.[110] Military motives and metaphors[111] are abundant in his account of the constitution. Even a *rex sub lege* is a reason for the monarch 'to be loved, obeyed, and *defended* by his brave and loyal subjects'.[112] For Custance, cultivation of knowledge of the constitution in all was to ensure that 'England would not be disappointed in *"expecting every man to do his duty."*'[113] Knowledge of equal rights under the constitution and thus, by assumed implication, equal duties was a means to an effective military response to the Napoleonic threat from the Continent.

In the nineteenth century, reaction to the French Revolution had become central to English political thought, whether of conservatives

---

[106] *Ibid.* pp. 4–61, especially at pp. 9, 4. See also *ibid.* pp. vi, 60.

[107] *Ibid.* p. 61, where he cites Blackstone, *Commentaries*, n. 99 above, Vol. I, pp. 66–7. See also *ibid.* pp. 73–4; Hearn, *Government of England*, n. 2 above, ch. 2, para. 1, pp. 35–6, where resistance to the civil law is similarly explained.

[108] Custance, *A Concise View of the Constitution of England* (London: the Author, 1808), p. 65.

[109] *Ibid.* p. 8.     [110] *Ibid.* pp. xiv, xv.     [111] See, e.g., *ibid.* pp. xvi–xvii.

[112] *Ibid.* p. xxiii (my emphasis). See ch. 6 above, pp. 141ff. Cf. generally Walter Bagehot's notion of the 'dignified parts' of a constitution that 'raise an army' but, in contrast to the 'efficient parts', do not 'win the battle', *The English Constitution*, M. Taylor (ed.) (Oxford: Oxford University Press, 2001), p. 7.

[113] *Constitution of England*, n. 108 above, p. xxiii.

intent on resisting change or liberals intent on incremental reform. Earl John Russell described how 'the French Revolution is ascribed to everything, and everything is ascribed to the French Revolution'.[114] Russell himself used the comparison with Revolutionary France to explain the very incrementalism of English constitutional reform. In his *English Government and Constitution*, first published in 1821, he wrote 'let Englishmen bear in mind that the old monarchies of the continent were so vicious in structure, and so decayed in substance, as to require complete renovation, while the abuses of our constitution are capable of amendments strictly conformable to its spirit, and eminently conducive to its preservation'.[115] Forty years later, Russell was so struck by the significance of his own comparison in this passage that he opened his New Edition of *English Government and Constitution* by quoting his own passage and adding 'events have justified my belief'.[116] Elsewhere, by way of comparison with the reign of terror in France after the Revolution, Russell elaborated similarly upon civil liberty under Magna Carta and as secured by *habeas corpus*.[117]

The nineteenth-century whig historians, such as Hallam and Gardiner, similarly expressed the reaction to Continental developments in their writings. Hallam, for example, in a passage cited with approval by Russell, first contrasted the equality of civil rights in England with the French divisions under the *Ancien Régime* and then explained the historical causes why English 'law has never taken notice of gentlemen'.[118] Hallam's 'self-complacency' was for Dicey 'natural . . . to an Englishman who saw the institutions of England standing and flourishing, at a time when the attempts of foreign reformers to combine freedom with order had ended in ruin'.[119] The *Ancien Régime*, the French Revolution, the Terror and Napoleon Bonaparte had become laden with the normative significance of that which England had successfully avoided and were, as such, a stimulant of national pride and a source of English self-satisfaction. Through their writings, whig historians perpetuated the reaction to

---

[114] *English Government and Constitution*, n. 91 above, p. 324.
[115] *An Essay on the History of the English Government and Constitution, from the Reign of Henry VII to the Present Time* (London: Longman, Hurst, Rees, Orme, and Brown, 2nd edn, 1823), pp. xv–xvi.
[116] Note 91 above, p. xiii.    [117] *Ibid.* pp. 96ff.
[118] *State of Europe during the Middle Ages*, n. 70 above, Vol. II, pp. 476ff, especially at p. 476, cited by Russell, *English Government and the Constitution*, n. 91 above, pp. 9–10. See also *ibid.* p. 117.
[119] *Law of the Constitution*, n. 2 above, p. 3.

Continental developments for the benefit of Russell, Dicey and generations of English students.

Samuel Gardiner provided another example of a reaction in whig
history, which was to prove lasting. In a chapter on Coke's dismissal
from the King's Bench, he discussed Bacon's writ *De non procendo Rege
inconsulto*, by which a case that affected the interests of the English
Crown might be removed from the jurisdiction of the common law
courts. Gardiner compared its effect with that of the French constitutional prohibition of the ordinary French tribunals from summoning
government agents to appear before them.[120] Gardiner, who, in some
degree, appreciated the danger of 'over-eagerness to make practical
application' of recent history,[121] only footnoted his comparison.
Gardiner's footnote, however, was Dicey's inspiration. Dicey explained
in the preface of the first edition of *Law of the Constitution* how 'Mr.
Gardiner's *History of England* has suggested to me the conclusion on
which ... stress is frequently laid in the course of the following pages,
that the views of the prerogative maintained by Crown lawyers under the
Tudors and Stuarts bear a marked resemblance to the legal and administrative ideas which at the present day under the Third Republic still
support the *droit administratif* of France'.[122] Gardiner's brief comparison was elevated to Dicey's main text and, in chapter 12 of the later
editions of *Law of the Constitution*, transformed into a four-page
description of the likeness of French administrative law and old
English ideas, long rejected, still negatively associated with the abuses
of the Tudor and Stuart monarchs and contrary to the equal subjection
of individuals and officials under the English rule of law.[123] In reacting
to *droit administratif*, Dicey complemented his whig history with normative comparison, which together enhanced the appeal of his rule of
law to his readers versed in the same comparative history.

Dicey's rule of law developed not only in reaction to developments on
the Continent but also in reliance on Continental commentators. The
English reaction was confirmed and maintained by reliance on their
approving accounts of the English constitution. Dicey devoted about
one-third of his fourth chapter of *Law of the Constitution* to analytical

---

[120] S. R. Gardiner, *History of England from the Accession of James I to the Outbreak of the
Civil War, 1603–1642*, 10 vols. (London: Longmans, Green, and Co., 1883), Vol. III,
pp. 7–8, n. 2.

[121] *Ibid.* Vol. X, p. vii.

[122] *Law of the Constitution*, n. 2 above, pp. vi–vii.     [123] *Ibid.* pp. 369–73.

exposition of the rule of law's three meanings and the remaining two-thirds to historical and comparative references. In those references, Dicey invokes '[f]oreign observers', such as Voltaire and De Lolme, and stresses that they 'have been far more struck than have Englishmen themselves with the fact that England is a country governed, as is scarcely any other part of Europe, under the rule of law'.[124] Dicey treats the comparison of Voltaire and De Lolme as if of current relevance although the *Ancien Régime* was in their comparative view. Dicey opens his chapter on the rule of law with a one-page analytical exposition of the two main features – parliamentary sovereignty and the rule of law – of the English constitution. He then demonstrates 'supremacy of the law as the distinguishing characteristic of English institutions' with three pages in which he mainly quotes De Tocqueville's critical comparison of England with Switzerland.[125] His reliance on De Tocqueville's comparison was unaffected by its applicability only to the period before the creation in 1848 of the Swiss Federal Constitution.[126]

Dicey's chapter on the rule of law continues as it began. Dicey's first meaning of the rule of law is expounded in eight lines and reinforced by nearly five pages of normative historical comparison.[127] He refers, in particular, to Voltaire's visit to England and emphasises that Voltaire's 'predominant sentiment . . . was that he had passed out of the realm of despotism to a land where the laws might be harsh, but where men were ruled by law and not by caprice'.[128] Dicey adds that Voltaire, who had been sent to the Bastille for a poem he had not written, 'had good reason to know the difference'.[129] For Dicey, despotism was worse, although less noticed, in other parts of Continental Europe, where the fall of the Bastille was felt 'to herald in for the rest of Europe that rule of law which already existed in England'.[130] Voltaire's admiration for England was genuine, but Dicey does not mention that Voltaire's idealised account neglected the defects of English government and society[131] and was variously motivated. The preface to Voltaire's *Letters Concerning the*

---

[124]  *Ibid.* p. 184.
[125]  *Ibid.* pp. 183–7, especially at p. 187; De Tocqueville, *Oevres Complètes*, Vol. VIII (Paris: Michel Lévy Frères, 1865), pp. 455–7.
[126]  *Law of the Constitution*, n. 2 above, p. 184, n. 2.    [127]  *Ibid.* pp. 188–93.
[128]  *Ibid.* pp. 189–90. See also Dicey's description of what redress Votaire would have had under the ordinary English law of Dicey's day, *ibid.* pp. 209–13.
[129]  *Ibid.* p. 190.    [130]  *Ibid.* pp. 192–3.
[131]  See, e.g., De Voltaire, *Letters Concerning the English Nation* (London: C. Davis and A. Lyon, 1733), pp. 67–8; D. Fletcher, *Voltaire: Lettres Philosophiques* (London: Grant & Cutler, 1986), pp. 27ff.

*English Nation* describes the 'high Esteem which Mr. *de Voltaire* has discover'd for the *English*' as 'a Proof how ambitious he is of their Approbation'.[132] Apart from Votaire's concern to flatter his English hosts and promote his work to an English audience, Voltaire was expressing explicit and implicit patriotic criticism of France:

> Voltaire's compatriots are being invited to learn from England's example. The accuracy of Voltaire's picture is open to question from the outset. His patriotism (never of the 'my country, right or wrong' variety) finds expression in criticisms, both implicit and overt, of his native land which often appears benighted in comparison with its neighbour'.[133]

Voltaire's preface also expresses doubts about his account of the English constitution:

> Some of his [Voltaire's] *English* Readers may perhaps be dissatisfied at his not expatiating farther on their Constitution and their Laws, which most of them revere almost to Idolatry; but this Reservedness is an Effect of Mr. *de Voltaire*'s Judgment. He contented himself with giving his Opinion of them in general *Reflexions* . . . Besides, how was it possible for a Foreigner to pierce thro' their Politicks, that gloomy Labyrinth, in which such of the *English* themselves as are best acquainted with it, confess daily that they are bewilder'd and lost.[134]

Dicey was not deterred from relying on Voltaire by the avowed superficiality of his general and idealised observations.

In similar fashion, Dicey elaborates upon his rule of law's second and third meanings and then illustrates their application. His second meaning is expounded in one-and-a-half pages and then amplified through a critical comparison with *droit administratif* in support of his rhetorical conclusion that the idea of administrative law 'is utterly unknown to the law of England, and . . . is fundamentally inconsistent with our traditions and customs'.[135] Dicey devotes the whole of his chapter 12 to that critical comparison. In that chapter, he relies extensively on Tocqueville's criticism of the *Conseil d'Etat* to demonstrate the protection afforded to official wrongdoers both under the *Ancien Régime* and *droit administratif.*[136] Dicey invokes Tocqueville although he recognises

---

[132] Note 131 above, p. A2.
[133] Fletcher, *Voltaire: Lettres Philosophiques*, n. 131 above, p. 14.
[134] *Letters Concerning the English Nation*, n. 131 above, p. A4.
[135] *Law of the Constitution*, n. 2 above, pp. 193–5, especially at p. 203.
[136] *Ibid.* pp. 355–8.

that Tocqueville 'by his own admission knew little or nothing of the actual working of *droit administratif* in his own day', that he had failed to recognise the changed character of *droit administratif* and that he had distorted French history by exaggerating the continuity of France before and after the Revolution.[137] In the manner of the Doctrinaire liberals before him, Tocqueville was criticising the centralised administrative state[138] epitomised by the pre-Revolutionary *Conseil du Roi* and the post-Revolutionary *Conseil d'Etat*. As in the case of his reliance on Voltaire's comparison critical of the French *Ancien Régime*, Dicey is invoking a French critic of French public law regardless of his reliability and domestic political agenda.

Dicey's third meaning is expounded in one-and-a-half pages and reinforced in five-and-a-half pages of comparison with the written constitutional provisions of mainly Belgium and France.[139] Through his comparison, Dicey contrasts the real remedies of the ordinary English courts with 'those declarations or definitions of rights so dear to foreign constitutionalists'.[140] After concluding his discussion of the rule of law's third meaning and summarising its three meanings, Dicey outlines his method of approach in subsequent chapters. He explains that comparison would be used frequently to illustrate topics and, because 'comparison is essential to recognition', to suggest the extent to which relevant principles are recognised in English law.[141] In the remaining chapters in his Part Two on the rule of law, Dicey uses his comparative method to highlight the relative liberality of English laws, including various Acts of Parliament passed or not renewed, in contrast to those on the Continent.[142]

---

[137] *Ibid.* pp. 358, 392–3, especially at p. 392.
[138] Allison, *Continental Distinction in the Common Law*, n. 20 above, pp. 53–9. See also *ibid.* pp. 142–6.
[139] *Law of the Constitution*, n. 2 above, pp. 195–202.     [140] *Ibid.* p. 197.     [141] *Ibid.* p. 205.
[142] See, e.g., his comparative explanation for the non-renewal of the Licensing Act 1662 by which, he argues, freedom of the press was established in England, *ibid.* pp. 252–69. See also, e.g., his comparison between England and France in ch. 8 on martial law, *ibid.* pp. 287–8, 291–3, and his description of the political common sense of educated Englishmen, one or two centuries in advance of their French and German counterparts, in imposing special legislative obligations, but not exemptions, upon soldiers, *ibid.* ch. 9, especially at pp. 298f. Cf. generally Allan's argument that the reference to ordinary law in Dicey's analytical exposition refers to the common law through which Dicey is said to provide criteria to determine arbitrariness and thus a substantive rule of law, *Constitutional Justice*, n. 11 above, p. 18.

Dicey was far from the first constitutionalist to rely heavily on Continental commentators in elaborating upon the English constitution. Dicey's *Law of the Constitution* was a continuation, in supposedly analytical form, of literature going back at least 120 years. A new period in the literature of constitutional law seems to have begun in about 1745. The English revolutionary settlement had been consolidated and, as such, began to attract the attention of foreign writers, and English writers became increasingly interested in foreign institutions.[143] Montesquieu's general comparative approach and, in particular, his chapter on the English constitution in *Spirit of the Laws* attracted considerable attention in England.[144] The author of *British Liberties*, published in 1766, repeatedly invoked the 'inestimable work' of the 'great Montesquieu' and his approval of the constitution of England as '[o]ne nation ... in the world, that has for the direct end of its constitution POLITICAL LIBERTY'.[145] The author relied explicitly and heavily on Montesquieu: 'we shall borrow from *Montesquieu* every thing we think necessary, to give the reader what is here proposed, *viz. a concise view of the* British *constitution as it presently exists*, adding a few observations which we have intermixed, with *Montesquieu*'s system, and some quotations from our own great countryman *Locke*.'[146] Montesquieu had, however, stressed that it 'is not for me to examine whether at present the English enjoy this liberty or not. It suffices for me to say that it is established by their laws, and I seek no further.'[147] The author of *British Liberties* invoked Montesquieu, although Montesquieu was more concerned to elaborated upon his own political theory rather than accurately describe the English constitution and its actual effect.[148] Dicey was to invoke other Continental commentators, but the practice of invoking

---

[143] W. S. Holdsworth, *A History of English Law*, Vol. XII (Boston: Little, Brown, 1938), pp. 341–2.

[144] Note 70 above, Bk. 11, ch. 6.

[145] Anon., *British Liberties or The Free-born Subject's Inheritance; Containing the Laws that Form the Basis of those Liberties; with Observations thereon* (London: Edward and Charles Dilly, 1766), pp. i–ii. The quotation of Montesquieu is from *Spirit of the Laws*, Bk. 11, ch. 5.

[146] *British Liberties*, n. 145 above, pp. i–ii. See also the reliance on Montesquieu by Ferris, *English Constitution*, n. 104 above, pp. 1–2.

[147] *Spirit of the Laws*, n. 70 above, Bk 11, ch. 6, p. 166.

[148] See generally the extensive criticism of Montesquieu's theory or of its applicability in England: Lord Brougham, *Political Philosophy* (London: Society for the Diffusion of Useful Knowledge, 1842), p. 32; Dicey, *Law of the Constitution*, n. 2 above, pp. 337–8; W. S. Holdsworth, *A History of English Law*, Vol. X (London: Methuen, 1938), pp. 713–24; R. Shackleton, *Montesquieu: A Critical Biography* (Oxford: Oxford

them and the readiness to accept their reliability is already evident in *British Liberties*.

Whereas Montesquieu's chapter six on the English constitution came to be treated with increasing scepticism, De Lolme's *Constitution of England*, first published in English in 1775, enjoyed a different reception. J. L. de Lolme was born in Geneva but came to England in 1767. As a foreigner, he laid claim to disengaged or objective enquiry comparable to that of a mathematician and, with the help of further metaphors, to 'a degree of advantage' over the English themselves, who 'having their eyes open ... upon their liberty, from their first entrance into life, are perhaps too much familiarised with its enjoyment, to inquire, with real concern, into its causes'.[149] For De Lolme, the English were 'like the recluse inhabitant of a Palace' who has 'never experienced the striking effect of its external structure and elevation' or like 'a Man who, having always had a beautiful and extensive scene before his eyes, continues for ever to view it with indifference'.[150] Confident in his external perspective, De Lolme elaborated upon the constitution of England at the 'summit of liberty', with which he compared France, 'sunk under the most absolute monarchy'.[151] While he recognised parliamentary sovereignty – that 'the Legislative power can change the Constitution, as God created the light',[152] he also recognised much of what was later subsumed under Dicey's rule of law as a distinguishing feature of the English constitution. In particular, he emphasised the equal application of the laws and the equal availability of redress, for instance through *habeas corpus*, [153]to all, including servants of the Crown, such as to pose limitations on executive power with which he could 'find nothing comparable in any other free States, ancient or modern'. In strong rhetoric, De Lolme praised judicial impartiality in England:

University Press, 1961), especially pp. 300–1; M. J. C. Vile, *Constitutionalism and the Separation of Powers* (Indianapolis: Liberty Fund, 2nd edn, 1998), ch. 4; Allison, *Continental Distinction in the Common Law*, n. 20 above, pp. 16ff; ch. 4 above, pp. 83f.

[149] *The Constitution of England or An Account of the English Government; in which it is Compared with the Republican Form of Government, and Occasionally with the other Monarchies in Europe* (Dublin: W. Wilson, 1775), pp. 2–3.

[150] *Ibid.* p. 3.    [151] *Ibid.* p. 9.

[152] *Ibid.* p. 112. But according to Holdsworth, *History of English Law*, Vol. XII, n.143 above, p. 344, n. 5, Dicey seems to have mistakenly attributed to De Lolme the principle 'that Parliament can do everything but make a "woman a man, and a man a woman"', Dicey, *Law of the Constitution*, n. 2 above, p. 43 (see also *ibid.* p. 87).

[153] *Constitution of England*, n. 149 above, pp. 202ff, especially at p. 206.

> Indeed, to such a degree of impartiality has the administration of public Justice been brought in England, that it is saying nothing beyond the exact truth, to affirm that any violation of the laws, though perpetuated by men of the most extensive influence, nay, though committed by the special direction of the very first Servants of the Crown, will be publickly and completely redressed. And the very lowest of subjects will obtain such redress, if he has but spirit enough to stand forth, and appeal to the laws of his Country. – Most extraordinary circumstances these![154]

De Lolme's eulogy was to appeal to various English writers on the constitution.

De Lolme's disengaged foreign view may well have contributed to his ability to abstract and articulate constitutional principles from what was taken for granted in England. Its degree of real and apparent objectivity at least rendered it attractive. His book was widely read in England and on the Continent, and his eulogy must have appealed to English national pride.[155] Thomas Western described the 'excellent Treatise of M. de Lolme' as 'the best written work' upon the English constitution and claimed that the fourth edition, published in 1784, 'met with universal approbation, even from men of opposite parties'.[156] Western claimed that De Lolme's 'arguments upon the superior excellence of the English Constitution over that of every other nation, shewing that it is the only Constitution fit for a great state and a free people, remain as vivid and as applicable as at the time they were written'.[157] Indeed, so impressed was Western that he incorporated an updated version of much of De Lolme's text in his own text which was designed to serve as a supplement to Blackstone's *Commentaries*. Reliance on De Lolme furthered Western's overall purpose of investigating the English constitution so that it might be better understood and thus more valued.[158]

Homersham Cox's use of De Lolme in his *Institutions of English Government* was more measured and more analytical than Western's. He elaborated upon the 'legal responsibility and immunities of various persons and classes' and 'the *methods* by which the supremacy of the law is secured' (particularly the writs of *habeas corpus*, *mandamus* and

---

[154] *Ibid.* p. 212.
[155] Holdsworth, *History of English Law*, Vol. XII, n. 143 above, p. 344; Arndt, 'Origins of Dicey's rule of law', n. 99 above, 120.
[156] *Commentaries on the Constitution and Laws of England, Incorporated with the Political Text of the Late J. L. De Lolme, LL.D. Advocate: Embracing the Alterations to the Present Time* (London: Lucas Houghton, 1838), p. v.
[157] *Ibid.* p. vi.    [158] *Ibid.* pp. vi–ix.

prohibition) in a single chapter entitled 'The Supreme Power of the Law'.[159] His purpose presented at the start of the chapter was 'to give a general statement of the extent to which, and the means by which, every class of persons in England is subject to the laws'.[160] He adds that the 'supreme power of the law is in our constitution more effectually secured than in any other with which we are acquainted'.[161] In his preface, he states that, for 'the sake of brevity, it has been generally deemed expedient to omit statements of authority in the text, and to confine them to the notes'.[162] His chapter on the supremacy of the law generally illustrates the omission of such statements. It nonetheless ends with De Lolme's eulogy of the thorough and unparalleled disregard of wealth and influence in the execution of English laws against powerful persons, which is quoted at length in the body of Cox's text.[163]

A few years later, the first edition of William Hearn's *Government of England* was published.[164] Hearn, a Burkean Tory with a strong sense of his British heritage, became the first Dean of the Faculty of Law at the University of Melbourne.[165] To Hearn, Dicey acknowledged considerable indebtedness. Apart from using Hearn (and Bagehot) to illustrate the political theoretical view of the constitution as distinct from the lawyers' view, Dicey claimed that 'Hearn's *Government of England* has taught me more than any other single work of the way in which the labours of lawyers established in early times the elementary principles which form the basis of the constitution'.[166] Much of what Dicey brought together in a single chapter on the rule of law is in various paragraphs of Hearn's book. In a paragraph entitled 'The Supremacy of the Law' in a chapter entitled 'The Legal Expression of the Royal Will in Judicature', Hearn presents the equal subjection of all to the law as 'an

---

[159] *The Institutions of the English Government; Being an Account of the Constitution, Powers, and Procedure, of its Legislative, Judicial, and Administrative Departments with Copious References to Ancient and Modern Authorities* (London: H. Sweet, 1863), Bk. 2, ch. 5, pp. 407–63, especially at p. 407.

[160] *Ibid.* p. 407.    [161] *Ibid.*    [162] *Ibid.* p. ix.

[163] *Ibid.* pp. 462–3. See also Cox's lengthy invocation of De Lolme and general expression of national superiority, particularly evident in his endorsements of Erskine's description of England as 'the Morning Star which has enlightened Europe', *The British Commonwealth* or *A Commentary on the Institutions and Principles of British Government* (London: Longman, Brown, Green, and Longmans, 1854), pp. 320–2, 566ff, especially at p. xxiv.

[164] Note 2 above.

[165] Arndt, 'Origins of Dicey's rule of law', n. 99 above. Burke's influence is manifest in Hearn's Introduction, *Government of England*, n. 2 above, especially at pp. 3–6.

[166] *Law of the Constitution*, n. 2 above, p. vi. See also *ibid.* pp. 6–7, 19ff.

ancient maxim of the Common Law'.[167] He describes '[o]ur noble insomnia' and 'the equal rights which are the birthright of every subject of our Queen' as 'the theme of just and frequent eulogy' and refers to De Lolme's admiration.[168] In another chapter entitled 'The Legal Expression of the Royal Will in Administration', Hearn articulates the personal liability of Crown officers before the ordinary courts as a principle 'of the highest importance in Constitutional law'.[169] He even cites Gardiner's *History of England* on Bacon's writ *De non procedendo Rege inconsulto* and makes a comparative reference to Tocqueville on the position in France, as did Dicey.[170]

Whig history and comparisons, whether in reaction to Continental developments or in reliance on Continental commentators, were evident in constitutional writings well before Dicey's *Law of the Constitution*. They were particularly prominent in Hearn's various paragraphs on equal subjection to the law and the liability of officials before the ordinary tribunals.[171] In Dicey's unified and supposedly analytical account of the rule of law, they were encapsulated in a simple, elegant and accessible form for consumption by generations of students.

## Dicey's appeal

Dicey's rule of law stood at the juncture of English self-satisfaction and the national self-criticism of Continental liberals, such as Tocqueville, Voltaire and De Lolme. It was significantly effected in reaction to Continental developments and in reliance on the approving accounts of the English constitution by Continental commentators. It was an analytical variant upon whig comparative history, in other words, of Butterfield's whig history but with its comparative complement. Its context was English and European. In a Europe of ascendant nation states, Dicey's rule of law was not insular. It was significantly motivated or inspired by developments in legal and political communities across the Channel with which English developments continued to be

---

[167] *Government of England*, n. 2 above, ch. 3, para. 7, especially at p. 87.
[168] *Ibid.* especially pp. 87–8.
[169] *Ibid.* ch. 4, paras. 5–8, especially at p. 100. See also *ibid.* pp. 9–10.
[170] *Ibid.* ch. 4, para. 8, pp. 106–8.
[171] Cf. generally Arndt's presentation of Hearn's *Government of England* as an Australian contribution to Dicey's rule of law and Arndt's relative neglect of European influences or effects, 'Origins of Dicey's rule of law', n. 99 above. European influences or effects are manifest in both Hearn and Dicey.

compared. It derived much of its appeal from a whig historical and comparative understanding common to Dicey, the whig historians who influenced him and many of the English constitutionalists and constitutional lawyers before and after him.

By recognising the historical and the European in Dicey's *Law of the Constitution*, the constitutional conundrum described above[172] can be resolved. Dicey's formal rule of law under the sway of a sovereign Parliament was not simply a mistaken response to the growth of executive power. Apart from responding to his domestic political reality as he saw it, Dicey was confirming English constitutional triumphs, reacting to past and present threats from Continental Europe and invigorating his relatively brief analysis with both. In the process, he relied on various Continental comparisons, and was inclined to ignore even those limits to their relevance and reliability of which he was aware. Dicey used history and comparison at best selectively and at worst indiscriminately to expound the doctrines of the English historical constitution in a way that would, and did, appeal to common English understandings of its superiority. What Dicey lacked in analytical rigour and what his rule of law lacked in substance and appeal, he made up for in normative history and comparison for an English audience versed in whig comparative history.

Dicey's historical and comparative references cannot be dismissed as mere rhetoric. They suggested a dramatised whig comparative history and, as such, constituted the 'theatrical elements' or the 'dignified parts'[173] of the historical constitution that Dicey subjected to legal analysis. In the English legal and political community, they were a source of unity, appeal and historic legitimacy. To the sympathetic reader from that community, they expressed the reality of English constitutional achievement – a triumph of incrementalism – in relation to the failures of constitutional transformation in Continental Europe. Dicey's account of the rule of law, supposedly but only partly analytical, was attractive and enormously influential because of the normative comparative history with which he eloquently demonstrated the superior development and operation of the English historical constitution that his account repeatedly evoked. However scant in analysis, it amply illustrates a whig version of the history in that constitution.

[172] See pp. 164f.    [173] Bagehot, *The English Constitution*, n. 112 above, pp. 9, 7.

# 8

## Beyond Dicey

Dicey's historical and comparative analytical account of the rule of law, described in Chapter Seven, was central to English constitutional doctrine for much of the twentieth century. Whether as a starting point for reform or point of reference for reaction, it remained central to the constitution's further evolution even for those to whom it had lost much of its appeal. What had evolved from Coke's controlling common law, described in Chapter Six, and what had been made an accessible and appealing object of constitutional analysis was Dicey's rule of law beneath the sway of a sovereign Parliament. It was taken for granted during a period of considerable 'constitutional quiescence'[1] between the liberal legal reforms of the first part of the twentieth century and the renewed focus upon constitutional law reform in recent decades. Its appeal began to wane with that of the whig comparative history[2] from which its historical and comparative references derived their force. On the one hand, whig assumptions of historical progress were undermined, in law,[3] by the administrative legal problems that accompanied

---

[1] V. Bogdanor, 'Introduction' in V. Bogdanor (ed.), *The British Constitution in the Twentieth Century* (Oxford: Oxford University Press, 2003), pp. 1–28, especially at p. 5. See also Sir Stephen Sedley's description of the 'long sleep' of public law, 'The sound of silence: constitutional law without a constitution' (1994) 110 *LQR* 270, especially at 282. Keith Ewing describes the twentieth century as 'a century of radical constitutional change, a reality obscured by the emphasis given to the current crop of reforms', 'The politics of the British constitution' [2000] *PL* 405 at 405. Undeniably, substantial change in government and governance did occur, particularly after the Second World War and then again as a result of privatisation initiatives after 1979. Much of the change, however, was institutional and not presented or realised in constitutional legal terms.

[2] See generally ch. 7 above, pp. 165ff.

[3] See, e.g., A. V. Dicey, 'The development of administrative law in England' (1915) 31 *LQR* 148; reprinted in A. V. Dicey, *An Introduction to the Study of the Law of the Constitution* (London: Macmillan, 10th edn, 1959), pp. 493–9; Lord Hewart, *The New Despotism* (London: Ernest Benn, 1929); A. T. Denning, *Freedom under the Law* (London: Stevens & Sons, 1949); Lord Scarman, *English Law – The New Dimension* (London: Stevens & Sons,

a developing and increasingly complex administration and, in general,[4] by the decline of Empire, belated recognition of its fundamental failures, the devastations of two world wars and, beginning in the 1960s and increasing in the 1970s, a sense that Britain was failing economically to keep up with her Continental and other competitors. On the other hand, the normative comparisons central to whig history were undermined in the later decades of the twentieth century by English appreciation, not only of the relative economic success of Continental competitors, but of the successful development of public law[5] across Continental Europe and beyond. Dicey's rule of law attracted criticism and doctrinal debate roughly proportionate to recognition of its continuing influence. As constitutional quiescence gave way to a renewal of interest in constitutional law reform, they were pressures for the rule of law's continued evolution in an English historical constitution increasingly detached from the assumptions of whig history. Attempts in recent decades to develop or transcend Dicey's thinking are the subject of this chapter.

Doctrinal debate has centred on Dicey's twin pillars of the rule of law and parliamentary sovereignty, both of which have been criticised and reinterpreted or reconceived. This chapter will consider, in relation to Dicey's continued influence, approximations to a substantive rule of law, endorsements of bi-polar sovereignty and the significance of the Human Rights Act 1998. In respect of each, I will, as in previous chapters, attempt to do justice to both Continental European influences and the peculiarity of the common law. Also at issue is the normativity of an evolving rule of law, its constitutional centrality, the coherence and normative direction it affords the historical constitution and that constitutution's continued significance now that much of the common conviction that whig history formerly carried has dissipated. I will argue that the recent and current evolution of the rule of law beyond Dicey's formal conception is a contemporary manifestation of characteristic doctrinal development. As such, it continues to illustrate the rough workings of the English historical constitution, centred on the

---

1974); Lord Hailsham, *The Dilemma of Democracy: Diagnosis and Prescription* (London: Collins, 1978).

[4] For expression of a sense of crisis in the 1970s, see, e.g., Hailsham, *Dilemma of Democracy*, n. 3 above, ch. 3, entitled 'The eclipse of Britain'. See also *ibid.* chs. 2, 35, 37. See generally A. W. B. Simpson, *Human Rights and the End of Empire: Britain and the Genesis of the European Convention* (Oxford: Oxford University Press, 2001), ch. 6.

[5] See, e.g., C. J. Hamson, *Executive Discretion and Judicial Control: An Aspect of the French Conseil d'État* (London: Stevens & Sons, 1954); Scarman, *The New Dimension*, n. 3 above, especially Pt. 2.

mode of change, ready to react and adapt to Continental European developments and pragmatic in its preoccupation with necessary change and reassuring continuity.

## Dicey's continuing influence

In and beyond the period of constitutional legal inactivity that lasted for several decades of the twentieth century, Dicey's influence was manifest[6] in ongoing opposition to an administrative jurisdiction and a preoccupation with a remedial, jurisdictional or formal equality subject to Parliament's overriding authority. Lord Chief Justice Hewart invoked Dicey's rule of law famously to denounce the proliferating administrative tribunals and the statutory provisions by which their jurisdiction was conferred. Relying heavily on Dicey and using history and comparison as did Dicey, he warned of a new despotism. For Hewart, Dicey's parliamentary sovereignty and the rule of law were the constitution's main features but the one was being used 'to defeat the other, and to establish a despotism on the ruins of both'.[7] Hewart's solution centred on statutory repeal and amendment and the prevention of further objectionable enactments.[8] Although he emphasised that 'to re-assert, in grim earnest, the Sovereignty of Parliament and the Rule of Law' was necessary,[9] parliamentary statute was assumed to be the principal means of reassertion. Through the exercise of its overriding power, Parliament was expected to resolve[10] what was assumed to be a problem of its own making. Hewart's account of the new despotism was Diceyan in both form and content.

In the mid-1950s, Dicey's rule of law and the 'obsessive proportions' assumed by the legal doctrine of parliamentary sovereignty were still the distinct backdrop to an account of the historical origins of judicial review.[11] In the decades thereafter, three famous or notorious cases involving the recognition, denial and extension of basic remedies – *Burmah*

---

[6]  See generally W. I. Jennings, 'In praise of Dicey, 1885–1935' (1935) 13 *Public Administration* 123; R. W. Blackburn, 'Dicey and the teaching of public law' [1985] *PL* 679; N. Johnson and P. McAuslan, 'Dicey and his influence on public law' [1985] *PL* 717.

[7]  *The New Despotism*, n. 3 above, p. 17.    [8]  *Ibid.* pp. 147ff.    [9]  *Ibid.* p. 151.

[10]  For the statutory subordination of administrative tribunals to the ordinary courts, see the Tribunals and Inquiries Act 1958. See generally J. W. F. Allison, *A Continental Distinction in the Common Law: A Historical and Comparative Perspective on English Public Law* (Oxford: Oxford University Press, rev. pbk edn, 2000), pp. 158–63.

[11]  L. L. Jaffe and E. G. Henderson, 'Judicial review and the rule of law: historical origins' (1956) 72 *LQR* 345, especially at 345.

*Oil, Malone* and *M* v. *Home Office* – were reminders of their enduring significance.[12]

In regard to the first case, *Burmah Oil Co. Ltd* v. *Lord Advocate*, the entitlement to compensation for the wartime destruction of installations through the exercise of prerogative power, which had been recognised by the House of Lords in an innovative ruling, was successfully overridden with retroactive effect in the War Damage Act 1965. Parliament demonstrated its capacity decisively to override remedial equality in Dicey's rule of law. In the second case, *Malone* v. *Metropolitan Police Commissioner*, Sir Robert Megarry V-C declined to develop legal authority so as to provide remedial safeguards against the tapping of telephones, although he recognised the requirements of privacy and confidentiality under the European Convention on Human Rights and that 'in any civilised system of law the claims of liberty and justice would require that telephone users should have effective and independent safeguards against possible abuses'.[13] For the court, telephone tapping by officials and smoking by individuals were equally lawful in the absence of express prohibition.[14] Telephone tapping was not made an occasion for judicial recourse to the rule of law but was recognised as plainly 'a subject which cries out for legislation'.[15] A recognised problem beyond the perceived formality of the English rule of law necessitated correction through the exercise of Parliament's overriding authority.

In the third and most recent case, *M* v. *Home Office*, the House of Lords reinterpreted s 21 of the Crown Proceedings Act 1947 to bar an injunction against officers of the Crown only in the rare situation where they exercise powers conferred upon the Crown as such and not in the usual situation where they exercise powers conferred upon them in their own official capacities. The rule of law was seen to be at stake and ultimately to have been vindicated.[16] Individuals and officials were rendered equally subject to an ordinary remedy of the ordinary courts, but under parliamentary statute as reinterpreted and therefore not where an injunction is still barred by s 21, thus not where officers

---

[12] *Burmah Oil Co. Ltd* v. *Lord Advocate* [1965] AC 75; *Malone* v. *Metropolitan Police Commissioner* [1979] Ch. 344; *M* v. *Home Office* [1993] 3 WLR 433.

[13] Note 12 above, at 381A.   [14] *Ibid.* 366E–367A.   [15] *Ibid.* 380G.

[16] *M* v. *Home Office*, n. 12 above, at 449A–E; H. W. R. Wade, 'The Crown – old platitudes and new heresies' (1992) 142 *NLJ* 1275, 1315.

exercise powers conferred upon the Crown itself.[17] What was vindicated was Dicey's rule of law beneath the sway of a sovereign Parliament.

During the period of constitutional legal inactivity in the last century, manifestations of Dicey's continuing influence did provoke criticism or countervailing proposals. A prominent example was William Robson's response to the Diceyan rejection of proliferating administrative tribunals as the institutional means to an English administrative law. In contrast to Lord Chief Justice Hewart, Robson praised their development and proposed their refinement into a system headed by an Administrative Appeal Tribunal.[18] Apart from *M* v. *Home Office* (which was broadly welcomed insofar as it did extend the availability of an injunction under s 21 of the Crown Proceedings Act 1947), the cases cited above – *Burmah Oil* and *Malone* – afford further well-known examples. The *Burmah Oil* case culminated in the War Damage Bill, which was condemned by JUSTICE for violating the rule of law but was nonetheless enacted in 1965 to become a *locus classicus* for debating the rule of law's meaning and compatibility with the sovereignty of Parliament.[19] More definitively, the *Malone* case resulted in a ruling that the European Convention on Human Rights had been violated and thereafter in corrective legislation.[20]

In recent decades, the renewal of interest in constitutional law reform has also been directed at the rule of law and has been accompanied by continuing debate. In view of the debate about Dicey's rule of law and its lasting influence, leading judges have recognised, judicially and

---

[17] See, e.g., the criticism of M. Gould, '*M* v. *Home Office*: government and the judges' [1993] *PL* 568 at 577–8; T. Cornford, 'Legal remedies against the Crown and its officers before and after *M*' in M. Sunkin and S. Payne (eds.), *The Nature of the Crown: A Legal and Political Analysis* (Oxford: Oxford University Press, 1999), pp. 233–65, especially at p. 265. See generally Sir Stephen Sedley, 'The Crown in its own courts' in C. F. Forsyth and I. Hare (eds.), *The Golden Metwand and the Crooked Cord: Essays on Public Law in Honour of Sir William Wade QC* (Oxford: Oxford University Press, 1998), pp. 253–66; ch. 3 above, pp. 66ff.

[18] *Justice and Administrative Law: A Study of the British Constitution* (London: Macmillan, 1928). See generally W. A. Robson, 'The Report of the Committee of Ministers' Powers' (1932) 3 *Political Quarterly* 346; W. A. Robson, 'Administrative justice and injustice: a commentary on the Franks Report' [1958] *PL* 12.

[19] See, e.g., C. Turpin, *British Government and the Constitution; Text, Cases and Materials* (London: Butterworths LexisNexis, 5th edn, 2002), pp. 85–8; C. Harlow and R. Rawlings, *Law and Administration* (London: Butterworths, 2nd edn, 1997), pp. 47–52.

[20] *Malone* v. *United Kingdom* (1984) 7 EHRR 14; Interception of Communications Act 1985.

extra-judicially, both its shortcomings and its essential value.[21] Beneath Dicey's twin pillars of the constitution, participants in that debate have invoked substantive values and the notion of bi-polar sovereignty.

## A substantive rule of law

The recourse to substantive values or a substantive rule of law became evident in the decades before the passing of the Human Rights Act 1998 and was both judicial and jurisprudential. The judicial recourse was principally through the development of modern principles of public law in the judicial review or control of administrative action. It was made possible or facilitated by the landmark cases of the 1960s, such as *Padfield* and *Anisminic*,[22] in the development or recognition of principles of public law. In his oft-quoted speech in the *GCHQ* case, Lord Diplock emphasised that, case by case, English public law had been 'virtually transformed ... over the last three decades'.[23] He heralded the arrival of a stage of development at which the grounds of review could be classified under the three heads of illegality, irrationality and procedural impropriety and entertained the possibility of adopting the Continental principle of proportionality in future.[24] Before the advent of the Human Rights Act 1998, the courts did not accept proportionality as part of the common law independently of the *Wednesbury* ground of review and were reluctant thus to consider the substantive considerations relevant to its independent application.[25] Apart from proportionality, however, the courts are commonly known to have accorded substantive content and, in certain circumstances, substantive protection to legitimate expectations.[26]

In the fifth edition of *The Changing Constitution*, as in previous editions, Jeffrey Jowell's chapter on the rule of law reflects the change in judicial practice. In the development of judicial review by the courts, Jowell identifies the realisation of a rule of law reconceived as a

---

[21] See, e.g., Lord Steyn in *R* v. *Secretary of State for the Home Department ex parte Pierson* [1998] AC 539 at 591A–F; Lord Bingham, 'Dicey revisited' [2002] *PL* 39, especially at 50–1.

[22] *Padfield* v. *Minister of Agriculture, Fisheries and Food* [1968] AC 997; *Anisminic Ltd* v. *Foreign Compensation Commission* [1969] 2 AC 147.

[23] *Council of Civil Service Unions* v. *Minister for Civil Service* [1985] AC 374 at 407H.

[24] *Ibid.* 410D–E.

[25] *R* v. *Secretary of State for the Home Department ex parte Brind* [1991] 1 AC 696 at 766H–767G.

[26] See *R* v. *North and East Devon Health Authority ex parte Coughlan* [2001] QB 213.

'principle of institutional morality' that guides official decision making and constrains the abuse of government power, particularly with procedural protections and the principle of legal certainty.[27] For Jowell, judicial review of administrative action is the primary means by which it is practically implemented and its content elaborated by judges – '[p]erhaps the most enduring contribution of our common law'.[28] With reference to Lord Diplock's classification of the grounds of review and cases on the substantive protection of legitimate expectations, *inter alia*, he concludes that the rule of law 'contains both procedural and substantive content, the scope of which exceeds by far Dicey's principal attributes of certainly and formal rationality'.[29] While recognising the rule of law's substantive content, he does not endorse a fully substantive rule of law. He acknowledges that the judges have been cautious in the area of substantive administrative policy, that the rule of law is primarily concerned with the enforcement and application, not the content, of law and that it is insufficiently elastic to encompass various requirements of democracy, including, to some extent, the human rights protected nationally or internationally. Furthermore, as in Dicey's analysis, the principle of equality is formal, not substantive, and the rule of law can be expressly overridden by Parliament.[30]

Jowell's view of the rule of law in *The Changing Constitution* is focused on the development of judicial practice and is therefore open to change with that practice or with interpretations of it or according to suggestions that it be further changed.[31] Elsewhere, in an influential article authored with Anthony Lester, Jowell suggested that judicial review be developed further. With references to cases such as *Wheeler* and *Malone*, Jowell and Lester suggested that a range of substantive principles of administrative law, including proportionality, legal certainty and fundamental human rights, be developed for the review of administrative discretion beyond the rubric of *Wednesbury* unreasonableness.[32]

---

[27] 'The rule of law today' in J. Jowell and D. Oliver (eds.), *The Changing Constitution* (Oxford: Oxford University Press, 5th edn, 2004), pp. 5–25, especially at p. 19.

[28] *Ibid.* p. 24.    [29] *Ibid.* p. 25.

[30] *Ibid.* pp. 18–24. On the formality of Dicey's rule of law, see ch. 7 above, pp. 158ff.

[31] See Craig's criticism of the middle way between a formal and a substantive conception of the rule of law, P. P. Craig, 'Formal and substantive conceptions of the rule of law: an analytical framework' [1997] *PL* 467 at 484–6.

[32] 'Beyond *Wednesbury*: substantive principles of administrative law' [1987] *PL* 368; *Malone*, n. 12 above; *Wheeler* v. *Leicester City Council* [1985] AC 1054.

On various occasions before the implementation of the Human Rights Act 1998, leading judges, judicially or extra-judicially, attributed substantive content to the rule of law. In *Pierson*, Lord Steyn cited both Dicey's and Jowell's accounts of the rule of law with approval in support of his decision that the Home Secretary had no general power retrospectively to increase a period of sentence fixed and communicated to a prisoner.[33] On the rule of law, his Lordship concluded that, in the absence of express statutory provision to the contrary, it 'enforces minimum standards of fairness, both substantive and procedural'.[34] Lord Steyn found both substance in Dicey's rule of law and recognised Parliament's overriding authority.

Speaking or writing extra-judicially, Sir Stephen Sedley on one side and Sir John Laws on another, judges of similar prominence but divergent in approach and general outlook, went further in endorsing a substantive rule of law or in emphasising its substantive content. On the one hand, in view of public law's awakening from its long sleep, Sir Stephen Sedley called for the development of a principled constitutional order.[35] Elsewhere, he presented substantive equality before the law as a principle requiring rigorous treatment in a culture where the content of rights needs to be freed from subordination to the 'Diceyan monolith'.[36] On the other hand, Sir John Laws advocated the use of the European Convention on Human Rights as 'a text to inform the common law' although he opposed its incorporation through a presumption of their applicability.[37] He advocated use of the Convention not only in cases of linguistic ambiguity but as an aid to the development of the common law's substantive principles by way of the incremental method of the common law. He presented proportionality as central to the shift in judicial practice away from *Wednesbury* unreasonableness. In a later article, he expressly endorsed a substantive conception of the rule of law, one that 'colours the substance of what the law should be' with notions of 'freedom, certainty, and fairness', implying requirements of 'universality and equality'.[38]

---

[33] Note 21 above, at 591A–F.   [34] *Ibid.*

[35] 'Sound of silence', n. 1 above. See generally, e.g., Sir Stephen Sedley's judgment in *R* v. *Minister of Agriculture, Fisheries and Food ex parte Hamble Fisheries Ltd* [1995] 2 All ER 714.

[36] 'Human rights: a twenty-first century agenda' [1995] *PL* 386 at 397–8, especially at 398.

[37] 'Is the High Court the guardian of fundamental constitutional rights?' [1993] *PL* 59, especially at 63.

[38] 'The constitution: morals and rights' [1996] *PL* 622 at 630–1. Cf. generally his judgment in *R* v. *Secretary of State for Transport ex parte Richmond-upon-Thames London Borough Council* [1994] 1 WLR 74, especially at 92A–94F.

Coinciding with the judicial recourse to substantive values has been a jurisprudential recourse under the influence, in particular, of Ronald Dworkin's[39] emphasis on the underlying body of legal principles by reference to which the interpretation of legal rules is justified. In constitutional theory, it is exemplified in the recent work of Trevor Allan. Allan focuses on the fundamental principle of equality in Dicey's rule of law and, in his developed work,[40] likens it to Dworkin's ideal of integrity that obliges government to show equal concern and respect through the principled extension of substantive standards of justice to all citizens. As interpreted by Allan, the principle of equality is substantive. It requires that the legal distinctions and classifications by which government confers benefits and imposes burdens should be justified by reference to the common good. Allan explains that the 'principle of equality imposes a fundamental requirement of justification: legislative and administrative distinctions or classifications must be reasonably related to genuine public purposes, reflecting an intelligible and defensible view of the common good, consistent with accepted principles of the legal and constitutional order.'[41] So that their justification be open to public scrutiny, it also requires that legal distinctions and classifications respect the individual rights and freedoms of speech, conscience and so forth, presented by Allan as intrinsic to the rule of law in a liberal democracy. In elaborating upon implications in administrative law, Allan endorses the substantive protection of legitimate expectations and the necessarily moral judgments in the application of proportionality.[42]

For Allan, the rule of law is complemented rather than contradicted by the sovereignty of Parliament. By way of an abstract jurisprudential contrast between the particularity of judicial decision and the generality of legislation,[43] each is accorded its own realm. Supposing, in a

---

[39] Dworkin presents a comprehensive theory of law and adjudication and does not elaborate upon the rule of law as such. See Craig, 'Formal & substantive conceptions of the rule of law', n. 31 above, 477–9.

[40] T. R. S. Allan, *Constitutional Justice: A Liberal Theory of the Rule of Law* (Oxford: Oxford University Press, 2001), pp. 17–20, 40–1. See also, T. R. S. Allan, *Law, Liberty, and Justice: The Legal Foundations of British Constitutionalism* (Oxford: Oxford University Press, 1993), pp. 21, 44ff, 163ff; T. R. S. Allan, 'The rule of law as the rule of reason: consent and constitutionalism' (1999) 115 *LQR* 221 at 232–3. Cf. Allan's passing reference to Dworkin and reliance upon Hayek in his earlier article 'Legislative supremacy and the rule of law: democracy and constitutionalism' [1985] *CLJ* 111 at 111, n. 1.

[41] *Constitutional Justice*, n. 40 above, p. 122.

[42] *Ibid.* pp. 125–32; Allan, 'The rule of law as the rule of reason', n. 40 above, 233–4.

[43] In Allan's analysis, acts of attainder do not qualify as 'law', *Constitutional Justice*, n. 40 above, p. 202. See generally *ibid.* pp. 148ff.

particular case, the absence of actual legislative intention (as distinct from general legislative objectives) and emphasising its judicial construction, Allan suggests that courts 'almost always' have ample resources with which to avoid conflict with the sovereignty of Parliament.[44] In judicial interpretation, Parliament's formal enactments are respected but do not override Allan's substantive rule of law.

Expansive conceptions of the rule of law have long been the subject of jurisprudential debate. In his influential early work 'The rule of law and its virtue', Joseph Raz responded to substantive conceptions with an avowedly formal conception so that the rule of law might perform a discrete but useful function, rather than embrace a complete social philosophy.[45] Raz elaborated upon a literal sense of the rule of law – that people be ruled by law and that they should obey it – as therefore requiring that the law be such as to be capable of being obeyed or of guiding the behaviour of people. From that requirement, he derived various principles – that laws should be general, prospective, relatively stable etc. In this early analysis of Raz, the rule of law does not require that laws have a particular substantive content or source, for example, that they are democratically made or that they conform with fundamental rights, but has value[46] in the respect it accords human dignity and the autonomy of people in determining their own conduct under the law. To Raz's formal conception of the rule of law, Allan's substantive conception was, in part, a response. In Allan's account, the generality of law is also to be respected, but in the promotion of equality and subject to departures from generality specifically justified in terms of the common good.[47]

### English and European sources or resources

The judicial recourse to modern principles of public law and a more substantive rule of law was a domestic English development in the judicial review or control of administrative action. It followed a decline in wartime judicial attitudes[48] to the executive and a slow or belated

---

[44] *Ibid.* ch. 7, especially at p. 210.   [45] (1977) 93 *LQR* 195.

[46] Cf. Raz's later analysis of the rule of law's 'political significance and moral justification' specifically in the common law tradition and in British political culture, *Ethics in the Public Domain: Essays in the Morality of Law and Politics* (Oxford: Oxford University Press, rev. pbk edn, 1995), ch. 17, especially p. 370.

[47] *Constitutional Justice*, n. 40 above, pp. 37ff. See also Allan, *Law, Liberty, and Justice*, n. 40 above, pp. 23ff.

[48] See, e.g., *Liversidge* v. *Anderson* [1942] AC 206; *Carltona Ltd* v. *Commissioner of Works* [1943] 2 All ER 560.

awakening to the further administrative problems resulting from the rapid post-War expansion of the administration and the need for effective democratic control.[49] English judges responded to domestic needs but were also influenced to some extent by the principles developed in the Continental systems of public law and in European Community law, the success or utility of which helped further undermine Diceyan normative comparative assumptions of English legal superiority. The extent of influence is not readily apparent. The concept of legitimate expectation and the principle of proportionality are illustrative. For his concept of legitimate expectation, Lord Denning did not cite authority in *Schmidt* v. *Secretary of State for Home Affairs*[50] and later claimed that he felt sure that 'it came out of my own head and not from any continental or other source'.[51] Furthermore, although Lord Diplock in the *GCHQ* case suggested for possible adoption the principle of proportionality recognised in the administrative law of members of the European Community on the Continent, his suggestion provoked a lasting debate on whether proportionality is within or beyond the existing English doctrine of *Wednesbury* unreasonableness.[52]

Whereas the development of judicial review by judges was an essentially English development under Continental European influence, often unacknowledged and of uncertain depth, the theoretical reconstruction of the rule of law to reflect or understand that judicial development has made express use of both English and Continental European sources or resources. For example, in the fifth edition of *The Changing Constitution*, as in previous editions, Jeffrey Jowell claims that the rule of law has substantive content and cites, *inter alia*, the article he authored with Anthony Lester on *Wednesbury* unreasonableness and articles by Sir John Laws and Sir Stephen Sedley, all published before the Human Rights Act 1998.[53] With specific reference to leading English cases, European principles of proportionality, certainty and consistency and the fundamental human rights of the European Convention, Jowell

---

[49] See generally Denning, *Freedom under the Law*, n. 3 above; Sedley, 'Sound of silence', n. 1 above, especially at 282ff.

[50] [1967] 2 Ch. 149.

[51] Letter to Christopher Forsyth, 19 January 1987, C. F. Forsyth, 'The provenance and protection of legitimate expectations' [1988] *CLJ* 238, especially at 241.

[52] Note 23 above, at 410E. See generally J. Jowell and A. Lester, 'Proportionality: neither novel nor dangerous' in J. Jowell and D. Oliver (eds.), *New Directions in Judicial Review* (London: Stevens & Sons, 1988), pp. 51–72; S. Boyron, 'Proportionality in English administrative law: a faulty translation?' (1992) 12 *OJLS* 236. See pp. 230ff below.

[53] 'Rule of law today', n. 27 above, p. 23, n. 81.

and Lester argued for the further development of substantive principles of administrative law by way of the incremental method of the common law.[54] Similarly, in one of the cited articles, 'Is the High Court the guardian of fundamental constitutional rights?', European standards permeated Sir John Laws' advocacy of the development of substantive principles by way of the incremental method of the common law (in preference to legislative incorporation of Convention rights).[55] The European Convention as interpreted in the case law accompanying it was the principle source or point of reference of his question (Is the High Court the guardian of fundamental constitutional rights?), his motive (equivalent respect for fundamental rights), his main means (proportionality) and his measure for assessing the answer to be provided through the incremental development of the common law. His use of English and European resources – the European Convention as a model and the common law as a method – in accordance with what he presented elsewhere as the democratic imperative of higher order law[56] may be compared with that of Sir Stephen Sedley in his contribution to debate from a historical point of view. Sedley was responding to a domestic history marked by Dicey's legacy and what Sedley described[57] as the long sleep of public law. Sedley therefore promoted a human rights agenda for the twenty-first century not only with reference to very old and new English authorities but also by looking beyond the English context at a range of international authorities and developments, whether in Europe, the USA or Commonwealth countries.[58]

The jurisprudential debate about a substantive rule of law, conducted at a high level of theoretical abstraction, has not been preoccupied with or drawn narrowly upon sources or resources, whether English, European or of other common law jurisdictions. On the one side, Joseph Raz, in his influential early article 'The rule of law and its virtue', derived discrete principles by elaborating upon an abstract meaning of the rule of law. In a mere footnote, he dismissed Dicey with the words 'English writers have been mesmerised by Dicey's unfortunate doctrine for too long'.[59] On the other side of the debate, Trevor Allan has elaborated on the rule of law and its ideal of equality with reference to

---

[54] 'Beyond *Wednesbury*', n. 32 above, especially at 374ff.
[55] Note 37 above.  [56] See 'Law and democracy' [1995] *PL* 72, especially at 84ff.
[57] 'Sound of silence', n. 1 above.
[58] 'Human Rights: a twenty-first century agenda', n. 36 above.
[59] Note 45 above, 202, n. 7.

various theorists including Dworkin, Hayek, Fuller and Raz.[60] So as to consider the extent to which both Raz and Allan have used English and European resources, detailed attention will be given to their writings in general and to their use of F. A. Hayek in particular.

In the concluding chapter of his later work, *Ethics in the Public Domain*, Raz focuses on the political significance and moral justification of the rule of law in Britain and restricts the applicability of his conclusions to other countries in proportion to the degree their political culture resembles the British.[61] He transcends a formal conception of the rule of law by drawing on domestic resources in two ways, one methodological and the other substantive. First, he draws on the tradition-oriented approach of the common law to require principled and faithful application of the law – principled in setting limits to majoritarian democracy but also faithful to the legislation of a democratic legislature.[62] Secondly, partly by presupposition and partly by implication of what is required methodologically, he draws upon 'legal tradition enshrined in doctrine' and upon British legal culture with a 'backbone' of civil rights to supply the substance of principled and faithful application of the law.[63] In Raz's account of the rule of law in Britain, the courts are required to 'tame the democratic legislature' through principled application that integrates legislation with the liberties of the individual in traditional doctrine.[64]

Whereas Raz in his later work relies on assumed aspects of British legal culture in general, Allan frequently invokes leading English authorities (as well as those from various common law jurisdictions) in elaborating on his comprehensive constitutional theory. Coke's famous dictum in *Bonham's Case* is in the epigraph to *Constitutional Justice* and is cited with approval in various places.[65] Furthermore, Allan is concerned to identify his own substantive theory of the rule of law with Dicey's theory as best understood. He refutes a common understanding that parliamentary sovereignty overrides the rule of law in Dicey's account 'by insisting on a more plausible reading of Dicey, that takes

---

[60] See, e.g., *Constitutional Justice*, n. 40 above, chs. 1, 2.

[61] Note 46 above, ch. 17, especially at p. 370.

[62] *Ibid.* especially at pp. 373ff.    [63] *Ibid.* especially at p. 376.

[64] *Ibid.* especially at p. 375. Raz does not mention the long-standing scepticism about basic rights that is also swirling in the great grey soup of British legal culture.

[65] Note 40 above, pp. v, 204–6; Allan, *Law, Liberty, and Justice*, n. 40 above, pp. 267ff. See also the dicta from other old English cases that make up the epigraph to his earlier article, 'Legislative supremacy and the rule of law', n. 40 above.

proper account of both limbs of his theory of constitutional authority'.[66] He also refutes the claim that Dicey's rule of law is purely formal in that it provides no substantive criterion for determining arbitrariness or the specific content of law required by the principle of equality.[67] He does so by invoking the common law itself – its precedents and substantive principles. Into Dicey's references to the 'ordinary courts', he reads an assumption that the content of the common law itself would provide the substantive criteria, an appeal 'to principles that he assumed the common law embodied and expressed', and an adherence to a doctrine of precedent to ensure their systematic application.[68]

Participants in the jurisprudential debate have focused on the common law but have not been confined to its resources. A complex interacting of English and Continental European thought is manifest in Friedrich von Hayek and his lasting[69] significance in contributing a concept of the rule of law that is better able to withstand criticism than Dicey's. Formulated with greater clarity, rigour and succinctness than the three ambiguous or imprecise meanings attributed to it by Dicey, Hayek's rule of law has been used critically by contributors on both sides of the jurisprudential debate.

On the one side of the debate, in his early work on the rule of law, Raz was as approving of Hayek's formulation as he was dismissive of Dicey's doctrine. Raz's influential article begins with a quotation:

> F. A. Hayek has provided one of the clearest and most powerful formulations of the ideal of the rule of law: 'stripped of all technicalities this means that government in all its actions is bound by rules fixed and announced beforehand – rules which make it possible to foresee with fair certainty how the authority will use its coercive powers in given circumstances, and to plan one's individual affairs on the basis of this knowledge'.[70]

---

[66] *Constitutional Justice*, n. 40 above, pp. 13–21, especially at p. 13.

[67] See Craig, 'Formal & substantive conceptions of the rule of law', n. 31 above, 470–4; G. Marshall, *Constitutional Theory* (Oxford: Oxford University Press, 1971), pp. 137–9; ch. 7 above, pp. 158ff.

[68] *Constitutional Justice*, n. 40 above, especially at p. 18. See also Allan, 'The rule of law as the rule of reason', n. 40 above, pp. 242–3.

[69] See, e.g., A. W. Bradley and K. D. Ewing, *Constitutional and Administrative Law* (Harlow, England: Pearson Education, 14th edn, 2007), p. 104, n. 70. See generally Jowell, 'Rule of law today', n. 27 above, pp. 6–10; M. Loughlin, *Public Law and Political Theory* (Oxford: Oxford University Press, 1992), pp. 84ff.

[70] 'Rule of law and its virtue', n. 45 above, 195; quoting F. A. Hayek, *The Road to Serfdom* (London: Routledge, 1944), p. 54.

For Hayek, the rule of law's requirements of generality and predictability protect individual freedom under the law and preclude necessarily ad hoc governmental interference in the economy. He was criticised by Raz for his 'exaggerated expectations' of the rule of law, for failing to recognise that the rule of law was not by itself sufficient to guarantee freedom and was always to be balanced with other values.[71] Raz was reacting to the substantive economic or political conclusions drawn by Hayek from the rule of law. He was, however, nonetheless analysing it expressly in the spirit of Hayek's conception and 'following in the footsteps of Hayek' by sharing his understanding of its meaning.[72]

On the other side of the debate, Allan drew extensively from Hayek at an early stage in the development of his own substantive conception of the rule of law. Allan's considerable initial indebtedness to Hayek (not Dworkin) is manifest in his early article 'Legislative supremacy and the rule of law'.[73] Allan quotes Hayek to express the idea of the rule of law in terms of a relationship between general rules and individual freedom from the arbitrary rule of another.[74] At one point, he asserts that the 'greater the extent of government involvement in social and economic management, the great correspondingly is the need for discrimination between individuals and groups by means of more particular rules'.[75] Here, Allan expresses a Hayekian view of the rule of law in opposition to governmental interference in economic planning. As Allan proceeds to apply the Hayekian idea of the rule of law to Dicey's constitutional theory, he echoes Hayek in distinguishing the merely formal principle of legality with which wide discretionary, even dictatorial, powers are rendered compatible if conferred by law.[76] He then criticises English judicial treatment of the rule of law and attributes blame to Dicey:

> In striking contrast to the doctrine of parliamentary sovereignty, it has been the fate of the rule of law to operate *sub silentio*. Its implications are recognised in a variety of contexts, but there has been little attempt at systematic exposition. Judicial references to the rule of law tend to be rather acknowledgments of the importance of constitutionalism, as a form of government, than conscientious attempts to articulate the specific requirements of the legal principle. The failure of the courts to develop a clear and coherent doctrine, and the relative infrequency of references to such a doctrine in the majority of cases in which public

[71] Raz, 'Rule of law and its virtue', n. 45 above, 209.
[72] *Ibid.* 196.    [73] See n. 40 above.    [74] *Ibid.* 113.    [75] *Ibid.*
[76] *Ibid.* 113–14; Hayek, *Road to Serfdom*, n. 70 above, pp. 61f.

authority is challenged, are equally the consequence of Dicey's own failure to present his theory in clear juristic terms. Although it was his intention to seek the 'guidance of first principles' in expounding the law of the constitution, Dicey's account of the rule of law fluctuates between statement of legal principle and description of relevant constitutional characteristics.[77]

The significance of Hayek is apparent. For Allan, Hayek served to correct incoherence or lack of clarity in Dicey and thus to reinforce Dicey's one pillar of the constitution.[78]

In his more recent work, Allan has recognised force in Raz's criticism that Hayek's conception of the rule of law, the general rules of which preclude the necessarily ad hoc governmental interference in the economy, 'is too much dependent on a controversial theory of justice'.[79] Embracing a Dworkinian concept of equal citizenship, Allan also criticises Hayek's conception of equality as generality for exaggerating the merits of general rules and for ignoring the role of general legal principles through respect for which executive discretion is fairly exercised.[80] He has distanced himself from Hayek but nonetheless confirmed Hayek's identification of the core of the rule of law in government according to general rules formulated in advance and thus protective of the freedom of the individual to whom they are subsequently applicable.[81]

Hayek's importance as a Continental European influence upon the English rule of law lies in his personal background, his political preoccupation and the sources of his concept of the rule of law. Hayek was an economist and political theorist who came to London from Vienna in the early 1930s.[82] He held a chair in the University of London until 1950, when he moved to a chair in the University of Chicago. In his preface to *The Constitution of Liberty*, he commented on the significance of his personal background:

[77] 'Legislative supremacy and the rule of law', n. 40 above, 114–15.

[78] Allan asserts that study of 'Hayek's work in political theory enables us to perceive the underlying strengths, as well as weaknesses and limitations, of Dicey's analysis of the rule of law, in which the constitutional primacy of the "ordinary" private law was also clearly marked', *Constitutional Justice*, n. 40 above, p. 16.

[79] 'The rule of law as the rule of reason', n. 40 above, 221.

[80] *Constitutional Justice*, n. 40 above, pp. 125ff, especially at p. 127. See also *ibid.* pp. 15f, 32ff.

[81] 'The rule of law as the rule of reason', n. 40 above, 225.

[82] See D. Snowman, *The Hitler Émigrés: The Cultural Impact in Britain of Refugees from Nazism* (London: Chatto & Windus, 2002), pp. 147–52, 185–91, 195–8.

> [T]hough I am writing in the United States and have been a resident of this country for nearly ten years, I cannot claim to write as an American. My mind has been shaped by a youth spent in my native Austria and by two decades of middle life in Great Britain, of which country I have become and remain a citizen. To know this fact about myself may be of some help to the reader, for the book is to a great extent the product of this background.[83]

In *The Road to Serfdom*, which he wrote while still in England, Hayek similarly acknowledged, indeed emphasised, the formative intellectual influence upon him of his Austrian background, 'in close touch with German intellectual life'.[84]

Hayek's political preoccupation is most clearly expressed in *The Road to Serfdom*, published towards the end of the Second World War:

> The following pages are the product of an experience as near as possible to twice living through the same period – or at least twice watching a very similar evolution of ideas ... [B]y moving from one country to another, one may sometimes twice watch similar phases of intellectual development. The senses have then become peculiarly acute ... It is necessary now to state the unpalatable truth that it is Germany whose fate we are in some danger of repeating ... [T]here is more than a superficial similarity between the trend of thought in Germany during and after the last war and the present current of ideas in this country.[85]

In short, Hayek laid claim to special insight from his once being an outsider. He saw a parallel between the loss of freedom through the trend of ideas that culminated in the National Socialism of the Nazi period and a loss of freedom in Britain through the development of socialist or collectivist ideas of central planning recently effected, for defense purposes, in the organisation of a nation at war. His rule of law was his answer to collectivist or totalitarian economic planning[86] of socialism and National Socialism.

The source of Hayek's concept of the rule of law was not Dicey. In a footnote of *The Road to Serfdom*, Hayek cited Dicey's first meaning as a 'classical exposition' but added a revealing comment:

> Largely as a result of Dicey's work this term has, however, in England acquired a narrower technical meaning which does not concern us here.

---

[83] London: Routledge & Kegan Paul, 1960, p. viii.
[84] Note 70 above, p. 2.    [85] *Ibid.* pp. 1–2.
[86] Chapter 7 of *The Road to Serfdom*, n. 70 above, is entitled 'Planning and the rule of law'.

The wider and older meaning of the concept of the rule or reign of law, which in England had become an established tradition which was more taken for granted than discussed, has been most fully elaborated, just because it raised what were there new problems, in the early nineteenth-century discussions in Germany about the nature of the *Rechtsstaat*.[87]

What was suggested in this footnote, Hayek later explained in various chapters of *The Constitution of Liberty*. There, Hayek described the early nineteenth-century German discussions of the *Rechtsstaat* to which he accredited the most fully elaborated concept of the rule of law. According to Hayek, the theoretical conception of the *Rechtsstaat* was developed systematically by liberal German theorists in discussions about the problem of an administrative jurisdiction within the state administration and about the issue of independent judicial control of that administration either by the ordinary courts, or by separate administrative courts.[88] Derived from these discussions, Hayek's theory was a theory of the *Rechtsstaat* in the literal sense of a 'law state' or 'state under law', although treated by him as if it were synonymous with the rule of law.[89] Whereas Dicey's rule of law was directed at individuals – officials and private persons – Hayek's was directed at the state administration[90] – central to Continental public law and political theory – and was conceived as prescriptive of the general rules through which it is required to act.[91]

The formative influence of Continental thought upon Hayek is evident both in his focus upon the state and in his refusal to confine the rule of law to a mere formal principle of legality. His argument involved a *reductio ad absurdum*. The absurdity he suggested was the implied dependence of the rule of law upon the legality or constitutionality of the means by which a dictator, whether in Nazi Germany or fascist Italy, obtained absolute or arbitrary power.[92] In *The Constitution of Liberty*, Hayek elaborated on the rise of a merely formal concept of the *Rechtsstaat*.[93] According to Hayek, in the second half of the nineteenth century, the merely formal concept came to predominate within a

---

[87]  *Ibid.* p. 54, n. 1.    [88] Note 83 above, pp. 198ff.
[89]  See, e.g. *ibid.* p. 237; Hayek, *Road to Serfdom*, n. 70 above, p. 58.
[90]  See generally Allison, *Continental Distinction in the Common Law*, n. 10 above, chs. 4, 5, especially at pp. 78–9.
[91]  See, e.g., Hayek's treatment of the state as itself an agent, *Road to Serfdom*, n. 70 above, pp. 56–7.
[92]  *Ibid.* pp. 61–2.    [93] Note 83 above, pp. 234ff.

doctrine of legal positivism in Germany to a degree unknown in other countries but to which it began to spread.

Hayek's own conception of the rule of law, developed in opposition to the ascendant formal conception and, beneath the dark cloud of the Second World War, in view of fascist regimes that achieved power with varying degrees of constitutionality, was not simply the product of a stark reality and theoretical discussions about the *Rechtsstaat* in Continental Europe. In the *Constitution of Liberty*, Hayek also elaborated on what he regarded as the origins of the rule of law in England of the seventeenth and early eighteenth centuries. In particular, he attributed lasting effects to Locke, from whom he derived what Hayek regarded as the crucial insight that there is 'no liberty without law'[94] and that 'whoever has the legislative or supreme power of any commonwealth is bound to govern by established standing laws promulgated and known to the people, and not by extemporary decrees; by indifferent and upright judges, who are to decide controversies by those laws; and to employ the forces of the community at home only in the execution of such laws'.[95] According to Hayek, the formative English contributions to the principles of freedom, although they were preserved in the main[96] beyond the nineteenth century, ended with the rise of Benthamite utilitarianism.[97] For further development of these principles, Hayek directed the reader elsewhere and, in particular, to the nineteenth-century German discussions about the *Rechtsstaat*.[98]

Hayek's rule of law was a Continental European notion of the *Rechtsstaat* principally derived from nineteenth-century discussions about the state administration and from seventeenth-century Lockian ideas about law. It was developed in opposition to a predominantly Continental European notion of the *Rechtsstaat* as involving no more than a formal principle of legality. There is a double intersection of English and Continental European thought in Hayek's conceptual contribution to both sides in the English debate about a substantive

---

[94] *Road to Serfdom*, n. 70 above, p. 62, n. 1. A passage from Locke that expresses this insight is the epigraph to Hayek's chapter on the origins of the rule of law, *Constitution of Liberty*, n. 83 above, ch. 11, p. 162.

[95] Locke, *Second Treatise of Government*, para. 131 (as quoted by Hayek, *Constitution of Liberty*, n. 83 above, p. 170).

[96] With reference to Dicey's later complaints about a marked domestic decline in veneration for the rule of law and Hewart's *The New Despotism*, Hayek also noted developments away from the rule of law in England, *Constitution of Liberty*, n. 83 above, pp. 240ff.

[97] *Ibid*. pp. 174–5.    [98] See *ibid*. ch. 13.

rule of law. His central significance in that debate, as well as the numerous other Continental European influences upon the judicial recourse to
substantive values and consequent theoretical reconstruction of a more
substantive rule of law, illustrate the openness of the English historical
constitution to Continental European influence, the depth of its
resources and the flexibility even of one of its most fundamental principles, posed as a pillar of Dicey's law of the constitution.

## The issue of change and continuity

A changing rule of law – much debated, open to wide-ranging influences
and increasingly taken to subsume substantive values – illustrates the
historical constitution's flexibility. It is also a reason to question the rule
of law's continuing character and the balance between change and
continuity in conceiving of it as a key constitutional principle. A clear
or definite answer, I will suggest, is not readily to be found in judicial
practice, legal culture or normative constitutional theory.

Judicial practice in the decades before the passing of the Human
Rights Act 1998 has been mentioned above.[99] Courts increasingly
invoked substantive values, and leading judges, such as Sir Stephen
Sedley and Sir John Laws, embraced a more substantive rule of law.
Judicial practice, however, and the underlying needs, attitudes and
assumptions in relation to which it developed, are open to further
significant and foreseeable changes. Sedley rightly emphasises the
'reality . . . that standards of justice do change'.[100] In renewal of judicial
activism or in retreat to judicial restraint, or deference towards the
executive and Parliament, whether in reaction to earlier developments
and the consequent demands upon the institutional and procedural
competence of courts, or in response to the new problems of a legal
environment that has been changing rapidly in recent years, courts
might further embrace, but might also retreat from, a substantive rule
of law. In the *Roth* case, the comments of Sir John Laws about the
common law before the passing of the Human Rights Act 1998 were
revealing: 'Not very long ago, the British system was one of
Parliamentary supremacy pure and simple. Then, the very assertion of

---

[99] Pages 191ff.
[100] 'The common law and the constitution' in Lord Nolan and Sir Stephen Sedley, *The
Making and Remaking of the British Constitution* (London: Blackstone Press, 1997),
pp. 15–31 at p. 21.

constitutional rights as such would have been something of a misnomer, for there was in general no hierarchy of rights, no distinction between constitutional and other rights'.[101] With reference to the cases of *Derbyshire County Council* v. *Times Newspapers*,[102] *Leech*[103] and *Pierson*,[104] *inter alia*, he explained that 'the common law has come to recognise and endorse the notion of constitutional, or fundamental rights'.[105] Although emphasising that 'their recognition in the common law is autonomous', he added that the 'Human Rights Act 1998 *now* provides a democratic underpinning to the common law's acceptance of constitutional rights'.[106] By implication, the common law's autonomous acceptance previously lacked a democratic underpinning. Laws was here suggesting, or admitting to, the democratic deficit in the common law's earlier acceptance of fundamental rights. His suggestion or admission contradicted his earlier advocacy of the common law's autonomous democratic potential.[107] Furthermore, Laws had previously claimed that ultimate sovereignty lies, not with Parliament, but in the constitution, 'consisting in a framework of fundamental principles', vindicated in the last resort by the courts.[108] In contrast in *Roth*, he emphasised the deference to be paid to the enactments of a sovereign legislature and retracted from his earlier claim: 'In our intermediate constitution the legislature is not subordinate to a sovereign text, as are the legislatures in "constitutional" systems. Parliament remains the sovereign legislator. It, and not a written constitution, bears the ultimate mantle of democracy in the State.'[109] John Laws contradiction and retraction reflected a significant change in judicial attitude to the common law and its relationship to the sovereignty of Parliament with the advent of the Human Rights Act 1998. As perceived judicial necessities in the protection of fundamental rights, the common law's autonomous democratic potential had given way to due deference to a sovereign Parliament in Sir John Laws' thinking.

---

[101] *International Transport Roth GmbH* v. *Secretary of State for the Home Department* [2003] QB 728 at [70]; [2002] EWCA Civ. 158.

[102] [1993] AC 534.

[103] *R* v. *Secretary of State for the Home Department ex parte Leech (No. 2)* [1994] QB 198.

[104] Note 21 above.     [105] *Roth*, n. 101 above, at [71].     [106] *Ibid.* (my emphasis).

[107] 'Is the High Court the guardian of fundamental constitutional rights?', n. 37 above; Laws, 'Law and democracy', n. 56 above.

[108] 'Law and democracy', n. 56 above, especially at 92.

[109] Note 101 above, at [83]. See also *ibid.* [81], [109].

Ever-changing judicial attitudes and practice have the potential to promote substantive values, or, where possible, to avoid invoking them, or the very concept of the rule of law. Since the Human Rights Act 1998 came into force, courts that have invoked Convention rights in what Jeffrey Jowell calls constitutional judicial review have had less of a need, arguably, to subsume them under a concept of the rule of law evolving from, and encumbered by, Dicey's formal conception.[110] If the rule of law's continuing and changed character – a stable balance between change and continuity in what is conceived as the constitutional principle – is sought in judicial practice, what is found, now or in the near future, might be formal, substantive or beyond the rule of law.

In his more recent contribution to the jurisprudential debate on the rule of law, how Joseph Raz draws substantively on British legal culture and methodologically on the tradition-oriented approach of the common law has already been described.[111] He suggests that the rule of law 'respects those civil rights which are part of the backbone of the legal culture, part of its fundamental traditions'.[112] Invoking legal culture even if only by presupposition or implication, obscures, however, at least as much as it illuminates. Legal culture's multiple and often-undifferentiated referents include practices, collective achievements, the environment of attitudes by which they are sustained, cognitive structures, transcendent values and national identities. How it can have the homogeneity or organic coherence to be ascribed a backbone is unclear, as is whether that backbone is rights or remedies, fundamental principles or the pragmatic scepticism that their express use has provoked. In social and political theory, legal culture is elusive – conceivably most influential when unnoticed and not in issue – and inherently problematic – pretending to explain[113] and itself in need of

---

[110] See J. Jowell, 'Beyond the rule of law: towards constitutional judicial review' [2000] *PL* 671. The readiness to invoke the 'rule of law' has varied in recent years. Cf., e.g., *A* v. *Secretary of State for the Home Department* [2005] 2 AC 68 at [74] (Lord Nicholls), [86] (Lord Hoffmann); [2004] UKHL 56; Dame Mary Arden, 'Human rights in the age of terrorism' (2005) 121 *LQR* 604 at 622–3. After the judicial endorsements of the rule of law in *Jackson* v. *Attorney General* [2006] 1 AC 262; [2005] UKHL 56, especially at [27] (Lord Bingham), [107] (Lord Hope), Jeffrey Jowell has also re-emphasised its significance, 'Parliamentary sovereignty under the new constitutional hypothesis' [2006] *PL* 562.

[111] Page 198.     [112] *Ethics in the Public Domain*, n. 46 above, p. 376.

[113] See generally R. Cotterrell, 'The concept of legal culture' in D. Nelken (ed.), *Comparing Legal Cultures* (Aldershot: Dartmouth, 1997), pp. 13–31. On Raz's notion of culture, see his exposition of liberal multiculturalism, according to which the problem of

explanation. Furthermore, even where legal culture is clear or understood, it too can be expected to change significantly. As in the case of judicial practice, it may seem to embrace the rule of law's substantive values, retract from them or, for instance, in time of war or national emergency or under the real or perceived threat of terrorism, call into question the rule of law's formal requirements in addition to its substantive values. To seek the rule of law's continuing or changed substantive character in legal culture, without a theory of how culture does or does not change and of how the concept of culture might usefully be used, would be to look for a key constitutional principle in little-differentiated legal practices as they evolve in a changing legal environment, thus in what is itself unclear and little known.

Whereas Raz invokes legal culture in his later work, Trevor Allan's constitutional theory encompasses a bold normative interpretation of how the rule of law should be conceived and suggests that the rule of law itself 'serves in Britain as a form of constitution' – 'a common law constitution' in the absence of the higher constitutional law of a written constitution.[114] Allan's interpretation does, however, raise questions about the relationship between his rule of law and the existing common law – its historical sources, its judicial institutions and procedures and, as discussed in Chapter Two,[115] what exactly is constituted in its constitution.

Allan's invocation of both Coke and Dicey illustrates his use of the common law's historical sources. Allan invokes Coke's famous assertion of a controlling common law in *Bonham's* Case in the epigraph to *Constitutional Justice*[116] and confronts the question of compatibility between a controlling common law and the Acts of a transcendent Parliament. On the main premise that there is no genuine legislative intention, only a figurative constructed intention, in respect of particular cases, he concludes that there 'is then, no inconsistency between Coke's assertion that "every statute ought to be expounded according to the intent of them that made it", on the one hand, and on the other his

---

invoking culture would seem to be accentuated, *Ethics in the Public Domain*, n. 46 above, ch. 8.

[114] *Law, Liberty, and Justice*, n. 40 above, p. 4. The rule of law enjoys a comparable centrality in *Constitutional Justice*, n. 40 above, subtitled *A Liberal Theory of the Rule of Law*.

[115] Pages 30ff.

[116] See also *Law, Liberty, and Justice*, n. 40 above, pp. 267ff; Allan, 'The rule of law as the rule of reason', n. 40 above, 241–2.

dictum that "the surest construction of a statute is by the rule and reason of the common law" '.[117] The assertion quoted by Allan is Coke's conclusion to a passage in his *Institutes* dealing with general grants by Act of Parliament, expressed in 'generall words', not 'speciall words', with 'preheminences, prerogatives, franchises, and liberties ... given ... in taile generally without limitation or saving'.[118] Coke's conclusion reads in full as follows:

> Every statute ought to be expounded according to the intent of them that made it, *where the words thereof are doubtfull and uncertain*, and according to the rehearsall of the statute; and there a *generall statute* is construed particularly upon consideration had of the cause of making of the act, and of the rehearsall of all the parts of the act.[119]

Whereas in Allan's normative theory legislation is conceived as general in character[120] and, for that reason, open to interpretation in particular cases by the rule and reason of the common law, in Coke's passage above from which Allan quotes selectively, the common law's rules of construction are specifically presented as applicable to 'doubtfull and uncertain words' and 'a general statute'. By implication, clear and particular statutory provisions, which could conceivably contradict the common law, would not be comparably open to construction by its rule and reason. Coke's passage is not authority for a general interpretive latitude however clear and particular the statute, by which to reconcile his controlling common law and the Acts of a transcendent Parliament, or, in modern terms, the rule of law and parliamentary sovereignty.

Allan is similarly concerned to find support for his constitutional theory in Dicey and generally to identify it with Dicey's pioneering textbook. In answer to the common understanding that parliamentary sovereignty overrides the rule of law in Dicey's account, he insists 'on a more plausible reading of Dicey, that takes proper account of both limbs of his theory of constitutional authority'.[121] With approval, he cites Dicey's argument that parliamentary sovereignty favours the rule of

---

[117] *Constitutional Justice*, n. 40 above, ch. 7, especially at pp. 205–6. Allan is quoting Co. Inst. IV, 330, and Co. Inst. I, 272b. See generally ch. 6 above, pp. 131ff.

[118] Co. Inst. IV, 330.   [119] *Ibid.* (my emphasis).

[120] Through the working of the principles of procedural due process and equality, Acts of Attainder and similarly particularist statutes do not qualify as 'law', *Constitutional Justice*, n. 40 above, p. 202. See generally *ibid.* pp. 148ff.

[121] *Ibid.* p. 13. Cf. generally Allan's earlier more critical stance towards Dicey in 'Legislative supremacy and the rule of law', n. 40 above, 114f (see pp. 200f above).

law and the rule of law favours parliamentary sovereignty through the dependence of parliamentary enactments on the medium of language, which is open to judicial interpretation.[122] Furthermore, Allan addresses Paul Craig's argument that Dicey's account of the rule of law is formal in that it provides no criterion for determining arbitrariness or for determining the content – the scope of the applicable rules – of the ordinary law to which all are equally to have formal access.[123] He does so by reading into Dicey's 'equal subjection of all classes to the ordinary law of the land administered by the ordinary law courts',[124] a reference to the content of the common law – its principles and precedents – as a source of criteria:

> [Dicey] appealed to principles that he assumed the common law embodied and expressed. The monopoly of authoritative legal exegesis enjoyed by the 'ordinary courts' reflected the notion of the common law as a form of governance according to reason, in which the doctrine of precedent ensured the systematic application of general principles to all cases falling within their proper compass . . . Dicey's theory of the rule of law may best be understood as a mode of governance according to a determinate (substantive) conception of the common good, whose concrete requirements in particular cases would be finally settled by judges in accordance with precedent, interpreted as a consistent body of principle.[125]

In short, Allan reads substance into Dicey's rule of law – the principles and precedents of the common law and a substantive conception of constitutional equality like 'Ronald Dworkin's ideal of integrity' – that accords with Allan's own normative constitutional theory.[126]

However normatively attractive Allan's substantive theory of the rule of law may be, its relationship to Dicey's is open to serious question for four reasons. First, to read into Dicey's analytical exposition of the rule of law the entire organic functioning of the common law – its principled reasoning and systematic exegesis by reference to precedent – is contrary to Dicey's expository analytical method, which was 'simply to explain its laws'[127] by expounding a scheme of rules and principles in an arrangement of sets and distinctions. To look beyond Dicey's exposition, or

---

[122] *Constitutional Justice*, n. 40 above, pp. 13–14; Dicey, *Law of the Constitution*, n. 3 above, ch. 13, especially at pp. 413–14.
[123] Craig, 'Formal & substantive conceptions of the rule of law', n. 31 above, 470–4.
[124] *Law of the Constitution*, n. 3 above, p. 202.
[125] *Constitutional Justice*, n. 40 above, pp. 18, 19.    [126] *Ibid.* p. 19.
[127] Dicey, *Law of the Constitution*, n. 3 above, p. 4. See ch. 2 above, pp. 7ff.

between its lines, for explanation of what is crucial is to defeat the purpose of his exposition and, in the process, to demonstrate its formality.

Secondly, if much of what was important to Dicey is rightly sought beyond his analytical exposition or between its lines, to read the doctrine of precedent into his account of the rule of law is incompatible with Dicey's own analysis of precedent. In delineating 'the true nature of constitutional law', Dicey used the doctrine of precedent to illustrate the deficiencies of two misleading views of the constitution – the unreality of the lawyer's view and the antiquarianism of the historian's view:

> [A]ttempts at innovation [English efforts to extend the liberties of the country] have always assumed the form of an appeal to pre-existing rights. But the appeal to precedent is in the law courts merely a useful fiction by which judicial decision conceals its transformation into judicial legislation; and a fiction is none the less a fiction because it has emerged from the courts into the field of politics or of history. Here, then, the astuteness of lawyers has imposed upon the simplicity of historians. Formalism and antiquarianism have, so to speak, joined hands; they have united to mislead students in search of the law of the constitution.[128]

With his reference to the ordinary law of the ordinary courts, Dicey would not have been suggesting or assuming the significance of what he viewed as a misleading doctrine. Dicey did celebrate in the common law, not principally through rational exposition of its principles and precedents, but by way of negative comparison with long-gone periods of English legal history and with their supposed Continental equivalents.[129]

Thirdly, principles and, in particular, the principle of equality are considerably more prominent in Allan's theory than they are in Dicey's *Law of the Constitution*. Whereas principled justification is a requirement of equality in Allan's theory of the rule of law, principles were understood by Dicey in remedial terms.[130] Allan recognises that principles were implicit in Dicey's theory:

> Even if Dicey's theory did not identify particular rights and liberties as constitutive of the rule of law, considered as an abstract principle of legitimate governance, its application to the British context, which was Dicey's main concern, entailed the judicial defence of those rights and

---

[128] *Law of the Constitution*, n. 3 above, pp. 7ff, especially at p. 19.
[129] See, e.g., ch. 7 above, especially pp. 165ff.     [130] See ch. 7 above, pp. 159f.

liberties hallowed by British constitutional tradition. The formal and rationalist elements in his work were balanced, and qualified, by an implicit commitment to values derived from the historical and practical wisdom of the common law.[131]

For Dicey, however, principles were implicit for the reason that his trust in remedies was matched by his scepticism towards the abstract formulation of rights or the principles to which they relate. The tenuous continuity between Dicey and Allan can be appreciated by comparing their conceptions of equality. Dicey expounded only a jurisdictional equality – 'the universal subjection of all classes to one law administered by the ordinary courts'.[132] From this jurisdictional equality in Dicey's exposition (complemented by the principles and precedents read into Dicey's reference to the equal applicability of ordinary law), Allan abstracts the 'equal status of persons, which ... informed Dicey's account of the rule of law' and which is central to his own substantive conception: 'The rule of law is ultimately an ideal of government by consent of the governed, in which the law invokes the assent of the individual conscience by appeal to a morally acceptable view of the common good'.[133] Dicey's limited jurisdictional equality is transformed into a general equality of citizenship.

Fourthly, Dicey's attempted reconciliation of parliamentary sovereignty and the rule of law in chapter 13 of *Law of the Constitution*, cited with approval by Allan,[134] was, at best, partial and, at worst, misleading. It was partial insofar as statutory interpretation that is narrowly focused on statutory words, as it was in Dicey's account, is sufficiently flexible to avoid conflict with the rule of law. It was misleading in that reconciliation was belied in the earlier chapters of *Law of the Constitution* where Dicey frequently presented exceptional legislation as overriding or conclusive in its effect and, in response to which, he assumed substantial judicial acquiescence.[135] As has been argued above, Dicey's rule of law was under the sway of a sovereign Parliament.

In his challenging normative theory, Allan is highly selective and, in that respect, quite Diceyan in his use of authority. He makes of the common law a veritable treasure trove of materials – ideals, principles, practices and a variety of authorities – with which to fashion or aspire

---

[131] *Constitutional Justice*, n. 40 above, p. 20.
[132] *Law of the Constitution*, n. 3 above, p. 193.
[133] *Constitutional Justice*, n. 40 above, pp. 24, 24–5.
[134] *Ibid.* pp. 13–14.    [135] See, e.g., ch. 7 above, pp. 161ff.

towards constitutional justice. The constitution in Allan's normative theory is tenuously linked to constitutional history. Whether Allan is therefore vulnerable to the charge of rewriting or reconceiving the constitution by changing the rule of law with insufficient regard for continuity is debatable. A commentator had reason recently, on the one hand, to defend Allan's theory because of its normativity:

> His work is not intended to be historical, and his view of constitutional history is, therefore, filtered through the lens of his normative theory concerning the foundations of liberal constitutionalism in modern common law jurisdictions. The appeal of his theory, he says, lies in 'normative judgment and evaluation' of 'political morality' and not in the positivist search for 'conclusive evidence' (historical or otherwise) of a morally detached description of the constitution.[136]

On the other hand, in view of the persuasiveness derived from the connections of Allan's theory to the common law tradition, the same commentator also has reason, comparable to that of others,[137] to criticise Allan's marshalling of support in Dicey for his own conception of a sovereign Parliament subject to the legal limits imposed by the common law.[138] As suggested in Chapter Two,[139] Allan would therefore himself have reason to reconsider the potential of the historical constitution (or an expressly historicised common law constitution) as the constitutional umbrella for the express recognition and justification of a selective historical account with which to address such criticism.

Allan's normative reinterpretation of the rule of law places a great weight of expectation upon the judicial institutions and procedures of the common law. Through judicial interpretation, courts are to avoid, where necessary, conflict between a substantive rule of law and the enactments of a sovereign Parliament.[140] By scrutinising the justification for any legal distinction or classification in view of constitutional

---

[136] M. D. Walters, 'Common law, reason, and sovereign will' (2003) 53 *University of Toronto Law Journal* 65 at 74.

[137] See, e.g., M. Loughlin who accuses Allan of 'reinventing Dicey' in *Law, Liberty, and Justice* and disguising the invention as interpretation, 'The pathways of public law scholarship' in G. P. Wilson (ed.), *Frontiers of Legal Scholarship, Twenty Five Years of Warwick Law School* (Chichester: John Wiley & Sons, 1995), pp. 163–88, pp. 179–82, especially at p. 180. See also G. Goldsworthy, *The Sovereignty of Parliament: History and Philosophy* (Oxford: Oxford University Press, 1999), especially at pp. 250–3, 271–2.

[138] Walters, 'Common law, reason, and sovereign will, n. 136 above, 73–4.

[139] Pages 29–33.     [140] See generally *Constitutional Justice*, n. 40 above, ch. 7.

principle and the common good, courts are to ensure adherence to a substantive principle of equality.[141] As the authoritative exponents of the 'common law, which articulates the content of the common good, according to the society's shared values and traditions', they have the tall order of expressing 'the collective understanding, by interpretation of the precedents', and of maintaining the common law 'as a foundation of constitutional government . . . in its inherent commitment to rationality and equality'.[142] Whether judicial institutions inclined to incrementalism or minimal revision of a common law characterised by its economy[143] will accept or successfully[144] bear the weight of expectation is open to doubt.

How judicial procedures in the adversarial tradition of the common law are challenged by what Fuller called significantly polycentric problems is discussed elsewhere.[145] If common law courts were to do what Allan would have them do, their adversarial procedures would be challenged whenever the common good, which is invoked to justify legal distinctions or classifications, is serving or proffered as a suggested solution to a significantly polycentric problem. The common good would be such a solution or a short-hand for it,[146] whenever it involves the allocation of public resources in response to the many, competing, demands usually placed upon the public purse.[147] The dispute before the court would then be significantly polycentric, not bi-polar. For Allan, the 'bi-polar dispute, involving discrete issues for the parties to address

---

[141] See generally *ibid*. ch. 5.

[142] 'The rule of law as the rule of reason', n. 40 above, 39.      [143] See generally ch. 5 above.

[144] See generally J. A. G. Griffith's criticism of the comparable faith in courts evident in the various writing of Sir John Laws, 'The brave new world of Sir John Laws' (2000) 63 *MLR* 159.

[145] J. W. F. Allison, 'Fuller's analysis of polycentric disputes and the limits of adjudication' [1994] *CLJ* 367; J. W. F. Allison, 'The procedural reason for judicial restraint' [1994] *PL* 452; J. W. F. Allison, 'Legal culture in Fuller's analysis of adjudication' in W. J. Witteveen and W. van der Burg (eds.), *Rediscovering Fuller: Essays on Implicit Law and Institutional Design* (Amsterdam: Amsterdam University Press, 1999), pp. 346–63.

[146] If the court simply identifies the common good with the good that the public authority is claiming to further, it would be succumbing to a danger of which Fuller warned when the adjudication of significantly polycentric problems is attempted: 'adjudication, instead of accommodating its forms to a polycentric problem, has accommodated the problem to its forms', L. L. Fuller, 'The forms and limits of adjudication' (1978) 92 *Harvard Law Review* 353, 401ff, especially at 404. See generally also T. Poole, 'Questioning common law constitutionalism' (2005) 25 *Legal Studies* 142 at 155ff.

[147] In Allan's analysis, even the basic common law right to a fair trial in criminal proceedings is 'absolute' but also, unavoidably, only 'in so far as judicial resources can secure it', *Constitutional Justice*, n. 40 above, pp. 271ff, especially at p. 277.

and the court to decide, is sufficiently defined ... by the existence of a claim of legal or constitutional right'.[148] In delineating legal or constitutional right, however, the court would need to consider the justifiability of suggested legal distinctions in terms of the common good. The court would therefore need to consider the scope and seriousness of conceivably complex ramifications for the common good that any proposed decision is alleged to have. The dispute may well prove to be significantly polycentric, and in determining whether it is or is not, the court cannot suppose the sufficiency of its own adversarial adjudicative procedures. By pulling itself up by its own bootstraps, the court cannot establish its own procedural competence.

Furthermore, in Allan's account, legal and constitutional right is itself evolving under judicial scrutiny in the light of the common good:

> Although grounded in conventional morality, in which the wisdom of existing rules is largely taken for granted, adjudication at common law proceeds by recourse to critical morality. Received notions of right and wrong are confronted by considerations of reason and principle based on more detached reflection and inquiry. Settled law must be tested and appraised in the light of explicitly articulated conceptions of the common good: the law is thereby brought into conformity with justice, as currently understood, but within the limits of the requirement of respect for precedent allows.[149]

In aspiring to constitutional justice, however, the more the court invokes, relies upon or lays claim to the common good, the more it draws 'intellectual sustenance' from what Fuller classified as another, basic, form of social ordering – 'organization by common aims' taking the familiar form, not of adjudication, but of elections – to make up for a partial insufficiency of principle and rule in constitutional adjudication.[150] As the court considers the implications of the common good, what exactly is constituted for its guidance and to secure continuity is peculiarly problematic. Precedents change in relevance and authority with the principles by reference to which they are critically interpreted and according to conceptions of the common good by reference to which they are tested and appraised. Those principles themselves, according to Allan, as principles, have 'no real existence' apart from

---

[148] *Ibid.* pp. 188–9.   [149] *Ibid.* pp. 290–1.
[150] See Fuller, 'Forms and limits of adjudication', n. 146 above, 357ff, 372ff, especially at 377.

their weight, which cannot be enacted.[151] How principles existing only in weight and changing with conceptions of the common good can nonetheless be constituted in some sense so as to stand as central constituents in the common law constitution, or be subsumed under a rule of law that is then sufficiently distinct itself to serve as such,[152] is unclear.

The degree of continuity between Allan's rule of law and that which developed in the English common law is in issue, as is that of its congruence with existing judicial institutions and procedures, and its distinctness as itself a form of constitution. The rule of law's continuing and changed character is elusive in judicial practice, amorphous legal culture and normative constitutional theory, such as Allan's, in his outstanding contribution. The rule of law's distinct character may itself be elusive, but implicit or attendant concerns about continuity and change are the traditional preoccupation of the historical constitution.

### Bi-polar sovereignty

A further change to the Diceyan conception of the constitution's fundamental features was also first suggested before the advent of the Human Rights Act 1998. This further change – involving a departure from Dicey more radical than a substantive rule of law – has been expressed with the concept of dual or bi-polar sovereignty. It has been thus to accord actual sovereignty not only to Parliament, as in orthodox doctrine, but to the courts. Lord Bridge's dictum in *X Ltd* v. *Morgan-Grampian (Publishers) Ltd* was a leading statement of this re-conception:

> The maintenance of the rule of law is in every way as important in a free society as the democratic franchise. In our society the rule of law rests upon twin foundations: the sovereignty of the Queen in Parliament in making the law and the sovereignty of the Queen's courts in interpreting and applying the law.[153]

Both Sir Stephen Sedley and Trevor Allan have quoted Lord Bridge's dictum with approval and advocated his reconception. Sedley suggests 'a judicial refashioning, with popular support sufficient to mute political

---

[151] *Law, Liberty, and Justice*, n. 40 above, p. 93.
[152] For Allan, 'the rule of law serves in Britain as a form of constitution', *ibid*. p. 4. See ch. 2 above, pp. 31ff.
[153] [1991] 1 AC 1 at 48EF.

opposition to it, of our organic constitution' and, as a result, 'a new and still emerging constitutional paradigm, no longer of Dicey's supreme parliament to whose will the rule of law must finally bend, but of a bi-polar sovereignty of the Crown in Parliament and the Crown in its courts, to each of which the Crown's ministers are answerable – politically to Parliament, legally to the courts.'[154] Trevor Allan cites Lord Bridge and Sir Stephen Sedley as support for the notion of a dual sovereignty and reinforces it with further theoretical argument. On the main premises that the enactments of Parliament are necessarily general and the judicial authority to apply them is 'necessarily exclusive', he argues that judicial sovereignty is exercised in the application of general law to particular cases.[155]

English authorities, both old and new, are relied upon in the departure from Dicey's conception of legal sovereignty located only in Parliament but juxtaposed with the rule of law. Sedley, in particular, rejects the further refinement of bi-polar sovereignty so as to recognise a third, executive, sovereignty by citing recent cases on the judicial review of the executive's prerogative powers in addition to Bracton's 'Rex . . . sub Deo et lege' dictum and Coke's use of that dictum to answer the King.[156] The occasional endorsement of bi-polar sovereignty is a domestic English development but, as illustrated in the development of other basic doctrines of the English constitution, is not insulated from Continental European influence. Upon the 'distribution and balance of sovereignty between parliament and the courts', Sedley suggests the likely effects of European developments.[157] He does not elaborate but is, presumably, referring to developments likely to affect the judicial application or interpretation of domestic statutes in view of Community law or the European Convention on Human Rights.

The occasional endorsement of bi-polar sovereignty, as in the case of a substantive rule of law, illustrates the flexibility of the English historical constitution but also its recurring problem of achieving a stable, acceptable, balance between change and continuity. Sedley, for example, departs from Diceyan orthodoxy but makes much of the old English authorities of Bracton and Coke and confirms with the attribute of

---

[154] 'Human rights: a twenty-first century agenda', n. 36 above, 389. See also Sedley, 'Sound of silence', n. 1 above, 289–91.

[155] *Constitutional Justice*, n. 40 above, pp. 13–15, 148, 201–2, especially at p. 13.

[156] 'Sound of silence', n. 1 above, 289–91. See *Prohibitions del Roy* (1608) 12 Co. Rep. 63; ch. 6 above, pp. 141ff.

[157] 'Sound of Silence', n. 1 above, 291.

sovereignty the crucial role of the courts, central to the common law tradition. The metaphor of bi-polar sovereignty has an accessible and attractive simplicity with which to challenge polemically the monolithic conception of parliamentary sovereignty. Opponents of the re-conception of a bi-polar sovereignty have, however, various reasons, I would suggest, to reject the conceptual transformation, first, as merely rhetorical, secondly, as abstract and artificial and, thirdly, as overtly contentious from a historical constitutional perspective.

First, courts and Parliament have evolved to differ in function and legitimacy to such an extent that the same concept – sovereignty – is only superficially applicable to both. To call both Parliament and the courts 'sovereign' is a conceptual blur of what Lon Fuller was rightly concerned to distinguish – legislation and adjudication as distinct forms of social ordering.[158] The conceptual transformation might readily be dismissed as mere rhetoric in service of a polemical challenge to the traditional conception of sovereignty.

Secondly, the metaphor of bi-polar sovereignty does connote a relational aspect of the generality of parliamentary enactments in counterpoise with the specificity of judicial applications, but its adequacy would seem to depend upon the sufficiency of a stark normative contrast[159] between general enactment and specific application. Apart from the historic use of Acts of Attainder that the requirement of generality clearly precludes, this abstract theoretical contrast does not register the varying regard that Parliament has, and should have, for particular situations that might arise and the varying degree it should specify them in legislation to secure a more or less specific application. It similarly does not register the varying degree to which courts have regard, and should have regard, not only to the particular facts of a case, but also to the general working of precedent in past and future cases. Extreme instances apart, such as obviously *ad hominem* statutes, the normative applicability of this artificial contrast to varying degrees of both generality and specificity in fact is far from being self-evident. This artificial contrast in support of the simple metaphor of bi-polarity is a limited answer to the problem of the relationship between the power and authority of Parliament and that of the courts.

Thirdly, to entrust the courts with the authoritative exegesis of a substantive rule of law in view of the common good is already to place a great weight of expectation upon them. To take the further step and anoint them

---

[158] See 'Forms and limits of adjudication', n. 146 above.
[159] See generally Allan, *Constitutional Justice*, n. 40 above, pp. 13–15, 148ff, 201ff.

'sovereign' and thus to confer upon them a power and authority comparable to Parliament's, is readily interpreted as a contentious expression of faith in their exercise of what has been in recent decades an expanding judicial role. The exponents of a substantive rule of law and of a judicial sovereignty in addition are vulnerable to Griffith's charge of believing 'that the influence of the judges has increased, is increasing, and ought to be increased still further',[160] if not expressing their belief in so many words.[161] According actual sovereignty to the courts begs the question of the adequacy of their training, experience, procedures and political attitudes to its exercise. In short, the concept of bi-polar sovereignty highlights a superficial likeness and an artificial contrast and, in placing the great weight of sovereignty upon the courts, is overtly contentious. It may well be useful in a polemical challenge to the monolithic conception of parliamentary sovereignty. As itself a key concept, however, with which to effect a stable, acceptable, constitutional balance between change and continuity, it is questionable. A 'judicial sovereignty' will not readily receive widespread recognition in a historical constitution preoccupied with both change and continuity.

The 'familiar common-law mythology that puts the judge (merely by virtue of *being* a judge) in the centre of a notional moral national community, as both its protector and spokesperson' has been said to lie behind Dicey's concept of the rule of law centred on the role of the ordinary common-law courts.[162] Trevor Allan's comprehensive liberal theory of the rule of law is less vulnerable to such criticism. His high expectations of the judge are matched or surpassed by his high expectations of the individual citizen in taking personal responsibility and making moral judgments as the means to the 'citizen's affirmation of the laws on the basis of their contribution to the common good'.[163] For Allan, 'the ideal of personal moral judgment . . . underlies the rule of law itself', which is 'ultimately premised . . . on the "sovereign autonomy" of the individual citizen', rather than the authority of a sovereign

---

[160] J. A. G. Griffith, 'The common law and the political constitution' (2001) 117 *LQR* 42 at 63. See also, e.g., Griffith's criticism of Laws's idea of a sovereign constitution of higher order law guaranteed by the courts for putting 'faith in judges whom I would trust no more than I trust princes', 'The brave new world of Sir John Laws', n. 144 above, 165.

[161] Griffith has attributed to Sedley advocacy of the development of judicial review 'larger in scope and deeper in penetration than anything previously known', 'Common law and the political constitution', n. 160 above, at 64, which Sedley has refuted, 'The common law and the political constitution: a reply' (2001) 117 *LQR* 68 at 70.

[162] R. Cotterrell, 'The rule of law in transition: revisiting Franz Neumann's sociology of legality' (1996) 5 *Social & Legal Studies* 451 at 453.

[163] *Constitutional Justice*, n. 40 above, ch. 9, especially at p. 311.

Parliament.[164] The court, however, is not hereby relieved of the heavy weight of expectation upon it as exponent of the common law by which the content of the common good is authoritatively articulated. That weight of expectation is made heavier by the prospect of intense scrutiny in so far as the affirmation of the individual citizen is sought or expected in individual moral deliberation that does in fact occur.

The problem of balance between the rule of law's continuing and changed character is aggravated by talk of a judicial sovereignty. Whether the suggested reconception of a bi-polar sovereignty is nonetheless generally accepted, perhaps as a necessary corrective to what is widely perceived as a 'long-term dysfunction in the democratic process'[165] or as an outcome of the passing of the Human Rights Act 1998 (considered below), is yet to be seen. In the alternative, it will be, if not explicitly rejected, quietly yet generally avoided as a radical judicial usurpation and, as such, a soft target for Griffith's long-standing criticism[166] of the role of the courts in English law. Official acceptance and public support or confidence, explicit or implicit, whether arising principally from the autonomous affirmation of private citizens or promoted effectively by public officials, are peculiarly important[167] to constitutional development through the common law. Sir John Laws cites the following statement of Sir Gerard Brennan with approval:

> The political legitimacy of judicial review depends, in the ultimate analysis, on the assignment to the Courts of that function by the general consent of the community. The efficacy of judicial review depends, in the ultimate analysis, on the confidence of the general community in the way the Courts perform the function assigned to them. Judicial review has no support other than public confidence.[168]

Although talk of assignment may be 'populist gobbledegook', as Griffith claims,[169] the suggested development of a substantive rule of law and of bi-polar sovereignty in addition, to be effective and constitutional, depends

---

[164] *Ibid.* pp. 311–12, 281.    [165] Sedley, 'Sound of silence', n. 1 above, 282.

[166] J. A. G. Griffith, *The Politics of the Judiciary* (London: Fontana Press, 4th edn, 1991).

[167] Public support and confidence are emphasised by advocates of a substantive rule of law or of bi-polar sovereignty. See, e.g., Sedley, 'Sound of silence', n. 1 above, 282–3; Sedley, 'Human rights: a twenty-first century agenda', n. 36 above, 389; Laws, 'Law and democracy', n. 56 above, 79.

[168] As cited by Laws, 'Law and democracy', n. 56 above, 79, n. 25.

[169] 'The "general community" knows nothing of judicial review, has not assigned its exercise to anyone and has no means of revoking that assignment in the ultimate or any other analysis. The judges exercise this power and, unlike other public bodies, can

upon a high degree of official affirmation and private acceptance (or acquiescence), particularly in the absence of its authoritative expression in a written constitution. That affirmation or acceptance cannot be secured by invoking overarching constitutional principles of sovereignty and the rule of law the character and scope of which are themselves in issue. In the English historical constitution, that affirmation remains significantly dependent, not on abstract theory, although such theory might persuade the constitutional theorist, but on a rough and often implicit appreciation of a stable balance between change and continuity emerging in its evolving doctrines in view of their developing practice.

## The Human Rights Act 1998

The 1998 enactment requires special consideration as a statutory means to a change of practice reflecting affirmation of a more substantive rule of law and a reconception of its relationship with the sovereignty of Parliament. At issue is the 1998 Act's contribution to the emergence of a stable balance between change and continuity in the constitutional conception of the rule of law. I will suggest that, as was evident in the formative developments discussed in the two previous chapters – Coke's exposition of a controlling common law and Dicey's celebration in the rule of law – both the European and the domestic interact in the 1998 enactment. Further, I will argue that, as in the case of recent endorsements of a more substantive rule of law and of a dual or bi-polar sovereignty, it reinstates, rather than resolves by statute, the question of a stable balance between the rule of law's continuing and changed character as it develops in the English historical constitution.

### *The European and the domestic under the 1998 Act*

The Human Rights Act 1998 is described in its Long Title as 'An Act to give further effect to rights and freedoms guaranteed under the European Convention on Human Rights'. Constitutional modernisation and promotion of an awareness of human rights was to occur through an incorporation[170] of Convention rights into domestic law

---

enlarge and diminish its scope at their own wish unless and until Parliament legislates to prevent them', Griffith, 'Brave new world of Sir John Laws', n. 144 above, 174.

[170] After initial reticence and with a degree of ambiguity, Ministers accepted during the passage of the bill though Parliament that an incorporation was involved, although not the full incorporation of the Convention. See J. Cooper and A. Marshall-Williams,

according to the Act's main provisions in ss 3, 4 and 6. Through a statutory incorporation of Convention rights to be interpreted by taking Convention jurisprudence into account,[171] the Human Rights Act is an overt Europeanisation of domestic law. It was heralded as contributing to the development of 'a more overtly principled' and systematic approach to administrative decisions, involving consideration of their merits under the European doctrine of proportionality and in view of substantive as well as recognised procedural values.[172] The Act also reflects, however, its domestic context in three main ways: first, in the very European Convention, the rights of which are the subject of incorporation; secondly, in its own detailed provisions for judicial interpretation or declarations in relation to parliamentary legislation; and thirdly, in the doctrine of deference that has been developed subsequently by the courts as those provisions have been applied.

First, the European Convention is, in general form, one of 'those declarations or definitions of rights so dear to foreign constitutionalists'[173] and unfamiliar in the common law tradition. It has, however, not simply been a European imposition upon it. As one of the major victorious powers in the Second World War, Britain was a key player in the Convention's complicated genesis in its aftermath.[174] Despite a legal tradition of scepticism and an initial unfamiliarity with human rights as such, the Foreign Office played a leading role in negotiating the establishment of the Council of Europe and in drafting the Convention, which Britain was the first to ratify, in March 1951.[175] Although Britain's role was an outcome of post-War British foreign policy rather than an outgrowth of the common law tradition, the English rule of law's

---

*Legislating for Human Rights: The Parliamentary Debates on the Human Rights* Bill (Oxford: Hart Publishing, 2000), pp. 1–18; F. Klug, 'The Human Rights Act 1998, *Pepper v. Hart* and all that' [1999] *PL* 246 at 248–9. See also Lord Irvine, 'The development of human rights in Britain under an incorporated Convention on Human Rights' [1998] *PL* 221; republished in Lord Irvine, *Human Rights, Constitutional Law and the Development of the English Legal System* (Oxford; Hart Publishing, 2003), pp. 17–36.

[171] Human Rights Act 1998, s. 2.

[172] Irvine, 'The development of human rights in Britain', n. 170 above, especially at 229. See generally D. Feldman, 'The Human Rights Act 1998 and constitutional principles' (1999) 19 *Legal Studies* 165.

[173] Dicey, *Law of the Constitution*, n. 3 above, p. 197. See generally ch. 7 above, pp. 159f, 172ff.

[174] See generally Simpson, *Human Rights and the End of Empire*, n. 4 above.

[175] In 1966, Britain submitted to judicial, not merely political, supervision, by recognising the right of individual petition to the European Commission of Human Rights and the compulsory jurisdiction of the European Court of Human Rights.

preoccupation[176] with remedies – requiring that they be equally available against individuals and officials alike – is manifest in the right to an effective remedy, enshrined in Art. 13, for the violation of Convention rights.[177] Traditional scepticism towards abstract generalities contributed, further, to what became a hybrid convention, in which rights are formulated in general terms familiar to the civilian lawyer, but are qualified by a more precise specification of limitations[178] and explicitly reinforced with a remedial right. These limitations reflect public interest considerations to an extent that renders the Convention 'far more closely in tune with the essentially collectivist cultural heritage which forms part of the bedrock on which the constitution of the United Kingdom developed and must build than with American-style liberal individualism'.[179] Shortly after the passing of the 1998 Act, Sydney Kentridge suggested that most of the Convention rights were themselves homegrown: 'Most . . . are to be found in our common law; indeed, most of them may be said to have been derived from the common law of this country'.[180] The principles associated with a number of them were at least implicit in the provisions of Magna Carta and in judicial remedies, such as *habeas corpus*, which evolved within the common law through precedent. For promotional purposes, the Convention's incorporation could be said to be bringing rights home.[181] Its language could, with some justification, be said to echo 'down the corridors of history' and go 'as far back as the Magna Carta'.[182] Accordingly, in the famous *A* case, Lord Hoffmann emphasised the domestic character of the issues at stake:

---

[176] See ch. 7 above, pp. 159ff.

[177] Simpson, *Human Rights and the End of Empire*, n. 4 above, ch. 1. The Human Rights Act 1998 does not incorporate the Convention right in Art. 13 as such, but does expressly provide for judicial remedies in s 8.

[178] Simpson, *Human Rights and the End of Empire*, n. 4 above, especially at pp. 713ff.

[179] Feldman 'The Human Rights Act 1998 and constitutional principles', n. 172 above, especially at 178. See also D. Feldman, 'Content neutrality' in I. Loveland (ed.), *Importing the First Amendment: Freedom of Expression in American, English and European Law* (Oxford: Hart Publishing, 1998), pp. 139–71.

[180] 'The incorporation of the European Convention on Human Rights', Inaugural Conference of the Cambridge Centre for Public Law, Faculty of Law, University of Cambridge, Cambridge, 17–18 January 1998, University of Cambridge Centre for Public Law, *Constitutional Reform in the United Kingdom: Practice and Principles* (Oxford: Hart Publishing, 1998), pp. 69–71 at p. 69.

[181] See the White Paper, *Rights Brought Home: The Human Rights Bill*, Cm 3872 (1997).

[182] Sir Edward Gardner QC, when introducing a Private Members Bill on incorporation in 1987, *Hansard*, HC col. 1224 (6 February 1987). His words were recorded in the White Paper *Rights Brought Home*, n. 181 above, para. 1.5, and later cited by Lord Irvine as

> This is one of the most important cases which the House has had to decide in recent years. It calls into question the very existence of an ancient liberty of which this country has until now been very proud: freedom from arbitrary arrest and detention . . . The technical issue in this appeal is whether such a power can be justified on the ground that there exists a 'war or other public emergency threatening the life of the nation' within the meaning of article 15 of the European Convention on Human Rights. But I would not like anyone to think that we are concerned with some special doctrine of European law. Freedom from arbitrary arrest and detention is a quintessentially British liberty, enjoyed by the inhabitants of this country when most of the population of Europe could be thrown into prison at the whim of their rulers. It was incorporated into the European Convention in order to entrench the same liberty in countries which had recently been under Nazi occupation. The United Kingdom subscribed to the Convention because it set out the rights which British subjects enjoyed under the common law.[183]

Lord Hoffmann overstated the English and understated the European in the Convention but had reason to redress a common perception of the incorporated Convention rights as European, not English.

Secondly, the provisions of the Human Rights Act itself reflect the English common law in various ways. Although a purely home-grown bill of rights may well have looked different,[184] the Act's chief mechanism for achieving compatibility with Convention rights was intended to be judicial interpretation. In view of the interpretative duty under s 3 and the very wide terms in which Conventions rights are formulated, Sir John Laws had good reason to anticipate that 'the Convention will be interwoven in the common law' through the common law's incremental method.[185] For Laws, the proposed incorporation of the Convention rights was cause to claim that 'the rigour of the common law presents the best and only opportunity to enfold the Strasbourg jurisprudence . . . within the traditions of the British state'.[186] Furthermore, the Act was expressly drafted to leave the traditional conception of parliamentary

---

testimony to the 'simple power of the language' of the Convention's articles, 'The development of human rights in Britain', n. 170 above, 223.

[183] *A v. Secretary of State for the Home Department*, n. 110 above, at [86], [88]. See also *ibid.* [89], [91].

[184] See Kentridge, 'The incorporation of the European Convention', n. 180 above, p. 69; Feldman, 'The Human Rights Act and constitutional principles', n. 172 above, 172–3. See generally Bingham, 'Dicey revisited', n. 21 above, 46–8.

[185] 'The limitations of human rights' [1998] *PL* 254, especially at 265.     [186] *Ibid.* 265.

sovereignty intact. As stated in the White Paper and as repeatedly emphasised by Ministers during the passage of the Bill through Parliament, what became ss 3, 4 and 6 were drafted so as not to undermine parliamentary sovereignty.[187] Sections 3 and 4 provide only for interpretation to achieve compatibility with Convention rights in so far as it is possible and, where not possible, only for declarations of incompatibility. Subsection 3(2) specifies that the provisions of s 3 do not affect the validity of any incompatible primary legislation. Under s 6, it is 'unlawful for a public authority to act in a way which is incompatible with a Convention right' but 'public authority' is defined not to include 'either House of Parliament' and an 'act' is defined not to include 'a failure to ... make any primary legislation'.[188] The Human Rights Act has been applauded as ingenious[189] and 'a subtle compromise between the concepts of parliamentary sovereignty and fundamental rights'.[190] It is also a subtle departure from Dicey. In support of Convention rights are two familiar, if not both quite Diceyan, pillars of the constitution – Parliament's sovereignty, on the one side, and, on the other, a rule of law, secured through the interpretation of Parliament's enactments and those of subordinate legislatures by ordinary courts and tribunals and further reinforced with express provision for judicial remedies under s 8 but not the actual Convention right to an effective remedy under Art. 13.

Thirdly, the Human Rights Act has been further domesticated through interpretation and the application of its provisions by the courts. The doctrine by which the European Court of Human Rights accords a margin of appreciation to national authorities in determining the necessity of interference with Convention rights has been an established feature of Convention jurisprudence,[191] which the British courts and tribunals are required to take into account under s 2. The margin of appreciation was emphasised in debate during the passage of the Human Rights Bill through Parliament.[192] At an early stage, however, its

---

[187] *Rights Brought Home*, n. 181 above, para. 2.13. See Cooper and Marshall-Williams, *Legislating for Human Rights*, n. 170 above, Pt. 1; Klug, 'The Human Rights Act 1998, *Pepper v. Hart* and all that', n.170 above.

[188] Subsections 6(1), 6(3)(b), 6(6)(b).

[189] Stephen Sedley, Foreword in S. Grosz, J. Beatson and P. Duffy, *Human Rights: The 1998 Act and the European Convention* (London: Sweet & Maxwell, 2000), p. vii.

[190] Kentridge, 'The incorporation of the European Convention', n. 180 above, p. 69.

[191] See *Handyside* v. *UK* (1976) 1 EHRR 737.

[192] See, e.g., Cooper and Marshall-Williams, *Legislating for Human Rights*, n. 170 above, pp. 248–9; Klug, 'The Human Rights Act, *Pepper v. Hart* and all that', n. 170 above, 251–2.

justification – that a state authority was better placed than a supranational court to determine domestic needs – was recognised as applicable to supranational, not domestic, adjudication.[193] David Pannick therefore called for the recognition of a similar domestic doctrine and listed factors, such as the requisite expertise and the nature and importance of Convention rights, relevant to the degree of deference to be shown by a court to an opinion already formed by a legislature, executive or other authority on compliance with the Human Rights Act.[194] The notion of deference resonated with that of restraint[195] in earlier cases of judicial review of administrative action involving national security and complex economic policy, *inter alia*. These cases were soon cited in discussing the inapplicability to domestic law of the margin of appreciation doctrine of Strasbourg jurisprudence.[196] The courts were quick to develop their own doctrine of deference, suggesting circumstances where deference is due and the limits to deference. In *Kebilene*, Lord Hope confirmed that the doctrine of margin of appreciation was unavailable in the domestic context but recognised an area of judgment, in certain circumstances (such as the relevance of social or economic policy issues), 'within which the judiciary will defer, on democratic grounds, to the considered opinion of the elected body or person whose act or decision is said to be incompatible with the Convention'.[197] In *Roth*, the limits to deference were of decisive significance to the Court of Appeal's determination of incompatibility with Convention rights of a statutory penalty scheme established by parliamentary statute to curb clandestine entry into the United Kingdom.[198] Simon Brown LJ and Parker LJ in their majority judgments and Laws LJ in his dissenting minority judgment all recognised the high degree of deference to be accorded to Parliament but

---

[193] See, e.g., Kentridge, 'The incorporation of the European Convention', n. 180 above, p. 70; Laws, 'Limitations of human rights', n. 185 above, 258.

[194] Comment [1998] *PL* 545.

[195] See generally Allison, 'Procedural reason for judicial restraint', n. 145 above.

[196] See, e.g., Grosz, Beatson and Duffy, *Human Rights: The 1998 Act and the European Convention*, n. 189 above, at 2-05.

[197] *R v. Director of Public Prosecutions ex parte Kebilene* [2000] AC 326, especially at 381B. See generally P. P. Craig, 'The courts, the Human Rights Act and judicial review' (2001) 117 *LQR* 589.

[198] Note 101 above. For another early example of the House of Lords grappling with the relationship between democratic decision making and respect for human rights after the Human Rights Act 1998 had come into force, see *R (Alconbury Developments Ltd)* v. *Secretary of State for the Environment, Transport and the Regions* [2003] 2 AC 295; [2001] UK HL 23, especially Lord Hoffmann's speech at [69], [70].

differed in their emphasis upon it and in demarcating its limits. Laws suggested that 'our judgment as to the deference owed to the democratic powers will reflect the culture and conditions of the British State' and, for that reason, would itself enjoy a margin of appreciation before the European Court of Human Rights.[199] In view of Parliament's sovereignty, Laws presented the principle 'that greater deference is to be paid to an Act of Parliament than to a decision of the executive or subordinate measure' as the first principle of deference.[200] In his judgment, deference was a means by which to maintain a traditional conception of parliamentary sovereignty. Recognised[201] innovation through the Human Rights Act was complemented, most clearly in Laws' judgment, by conservation through the doctrine of deference.

Deference has become a prominent feature of domestic human rights case law[202] and a central issue in academic debate.[203] It has been described as 'understandable' in relation to Parliament, but difficult to justify in relation to the executive:

> In this new climate of judicial statements of deference, reverting to the terms of the old debate: for example, non-interference with 'policy' . . ., or not usurping factual determinations of the decision-maker . . ., or only where those determinations are irrational . . . are both unnecessary and outmoded. In the Human Rights Act era these are the legal equivalent of using a mobile phone to send text messages in Elizabethan English.[204]

Continuity – even Elizabethan English – is nonetheless a feature of the historical constitution. In place of the margin of appreciation of

---

[199] *Roth*, n. 101 above, at [81].   [200] *Ibid.* [83].   [201] See, e.g., *ibid.* [54], [71].

[202] See, e.g., *R (ProLife Alliance)* v. *British Broadcasting Corporation* [2004] 1 AC 185; [2003] UKHL 23 at [74]–[77]; *A* v. *Secretary of State for the Home Department*, n. 110 above, at [29], [42], [44], [107], [176], [226].

[203] See, e.g., M. Hunt, 'Sovereignty's blight: why contemporary public law needs the concept of "due deference"' in N. Bamforth and P. Leyland (eds.), *Public Law in a Multi-Layered Constitution* (Oxford: Hart Publishing, 2003), pp. 337–70; R. A. Edwards, 'Judicial deference under the Human Rights Act' (2002) 65 *MLR* 859; J. Jowell, 'Judicial deference and human rights: a question of competence' in P. P. Craig and R. Rawlings (eds.), *Law and Administration in Europe: Essays in Honour of Carol Harlow* (Oxford: Oxford University Press, 2003), pp. 67–81; J. Jowell, 'Judicial deference: servility, civility or institutional capacity?' [2003] *PL* 592; R. Clayton, 'Judicial deference and "democratic dialogue": the legitimacy of judicial intervention under the Human Rights Act 1998' [2004] *PL* 33; Lord Steyn, 'Deference: a tangled story' [2005] *PL* 346; T. R. S. Allan, 'Human rights and judicial review: a critique of "due deference"' [2006] *CLJ* 671.

[204] I. Leigh, 'Taking rights proportionately: judicial review, the Human Rights Act and Strasbourg' [2002] *PL* 265 at 287, 285.

Strasbourg jurisprudence, the doctrine of deference has flourished in common law soil. Although controversial and variously applied, it has been a source of continuity with the older tradition of restraint in judicial review and the academic debate about its respectability.

The three main ways in which the 1998 Act, as interpreted and applied by the courts, reflects its domestic context render it evolutionary, not revolutionary.[205] Together they still illustrate the English historical constitution. That the Human Rights Act, as interpreted by the courts, is both traditional in these ways and innovative – mandating an explicit human rights jurisprudence and a more substantive rule of law through an incorporation of Convention rights – was central to its promotion[206] and, as will be suggested below, remains central to views on its application and desirability.

As a result of its domestic character, the Act is not simply an outcome of the European or international movement for the protection of human rights through judicial review. It does not represent the eventual triumph here of Cappelletti's *constitutional justice* as a Hegelian synthesis, to which the higher law of *natural justice* and the primacy of parliamentary statute in *positive justice* are the thesis and antithesis in Western countries, and which is typified in the judicial review of the constitutionality of legislation in the USA.[207] A simply internationalist view of a European or international convergence and Cappelletti's more complex dialectical analysis may be applicable elsewhere but do not do justice to the peculiarity of the domestic development of the Human Rights Act 1998 in the common law.

## Questions of change and continuity

In the historical constitution, questions of continuity are the concomitant of change. The Human Rights Act 1998 has spurned a range of such questions,[208] concerning interpretation, doctrine and principle.

---

[205] A traditional contrast rightly emphasised by Feldman, 'The Human Rights Act 1998 and constitutional principles', n. 172 above, especially at 165, 173–4.

[206] See, e.g., Irvine, 'The development of human rights in Britain', n. 170 above.

[207] M. Cappelletti, *The Judicial Process in Comparative Perspective* (Oxford: Oxford University Press, 1989), ch. 3, especially at pp. 131–2. See ch. 6 above, pp. 133f, 136f.

[208] See, e.g., Keith Ewing's critical suggestion that 'despite the incorporation of Convention rights, there is an extraordinary continuity in the approach of the domestic courts in times of crisis', 'The futility of the Human Rights Act' [2004] PL 829, especially at 851, and the reply of Anthony Lester, 'The utility of the Human Rights Act:

The relationship between the interpretive duty under s 3 and the existing common law rules of statutory construction was the subject of early debate. For certain commentators, it involved a drastic alteration, which by introducing the purposive construction of Strasbourg juris-prudence, 'reopens all precedents'.[209] The alteration was a source of criticism from the outset. For Geoffrey Marshall, uncertainty about the meaning of 'possible' and ambiguity in 'compatible' made of s 3 an example, not of ingenuity, but of 'ingenuity gone wrong'.[210] He attrib-uted the confusion and uncertainty – that it is impossible to know what interpretation the courts would place on s 3 – to the 1998 Act's reliance on the judicial distortion or adjustment of meaning rather than a judicial declaration of invalidity under a genuinely incorporated Bill of Rights.[211]

Other, more moderate, early commentators were inclined to iden-tify continuity. For Grosz, Beatson and Duffy, the natural and ordinary meaning of the words of primary legislation would remain the starting point of construction subject to a permissive departure from their clear literal meaning through a purposive construction in cases of potential incompatibility with Convention rights.[212] By way of an analogy with European Community cases, they anticipated the possi-ble adoption of 'strained' construction to achieve compatibility but doubted that an 'unnatural' construction would be permissible.[213] With a similar emphasis on continuity, David Feldman anticipated that the judicial trend strictly to interpret statutes in violation of fundamental rights would be strengthened by s 3 of the 1998 Act.[214] He likened the 1998

---

a reply to Keith Ewing' [2005] *PL* 249. Cf. generally Lord Irvine, 'The importance of the Human Rights Act: Parliament, the courts and the executive' [2003] *PL* 308; repub-lished in Lord Irvine, *Human Rights, Constitutional Law and the Development of the English Legal System*, n. 170 above, pp. 111–32.

[209] F. Bennion, 'What interpretation is "possible" under section 3(1) of the Human Rights Act 1998?' [2000] *PL* 77, especially at 91.

[210] 'Interpreting interpretation in the Human Rights Bill' [1998] *PL* 167, especially at 170; G. Marshall, 'Two kinds of compatibility: more about section 3 of the Human Rights Act 1998' [1999] *PL* 377. Cf. Sedley, Foreword in Grosz, Beatson and Duffy, *Human Rights: The 1998 Act and the European Convention*, n. 189 above, p. vii.; Kentridge, 'The incorporation of the European Convention on Human Rights', n. 180 above, p. 69. See also G. Marshall, 'The lynchpin of parliamentary intention: lost, stolen, or strained?' [2003] *PL* 236.

[211] 'Two kinds of compatibility', n. 210 above, especially at 387.

[212] *Human Rights: The 1998 Act and the European Convention*, n. 189 above, 3–41. Cf. *ibid.* 3–11.

[213] *Ibid.* 3–41.

[214] 'The Human Rights Act 1998 and constitutional principles', n. 172 above, 179.

Act to an Interpretation Act[215] which contributes to an interpretative framework but is also embued with substantive values.

The issue of change and continuity has become central to the developing case law on the scope of the courts' interpretive duty under s 3. In *Ghaidan* v. *Godin-Mendoza*, the majority in the House of Lords embraced change. They ruled that s 3 may require a court to depart from legislative intention, and 'from the unambiguous meaning the legislation would otherwise bear' (i.e. 'to an extent bounded only by what is "possible"' to 'modify the meaning')[216] or to avoid 'an excessive concentration on linguistic features of the particular statute' by adopting 'a broad approach concentrating, amongst other things, in a purposive way on the importance of the fundamental right involved.'[217] In contrast, Lord Millett, in his dissenting opinion, emphasised substantial continuity with existing judicial approaches to statutory construction. In view of the careful crafting of ss 3 and 4 of the 1998 Act to preserve 'the existing constitutional doctrine' of parliamentary sovereignty, he interpreted s 3 to require careful consideration of legislative intent, of 'the essential features of the legislative scheme ... gathered in part at least from the words that Parliament has chosen to use' and of the legislation's 'natural and ordinary meaning', 'construed in accordance with normal principles', from which, if the legislation is then incompatible with the Convention, the interpretative duty arises in the first place.[218] The issue of the extent to which s 3 requires the courts to depart from past practice in statutory construction and of the criteria and principles according to which the departure is to take place is yet to be clearly[219] resolved.

Change and continuity in the relationship between the doctrine of proportionality, which is an established feature of Strasbourg jurisprudence, and the traditional *Wednesbury* ground for the review of the exercise of discretionary power has been another preoccupation, which has been expressed in various judicial statements since the passing of the 1998 Act. As in treatment of the interpretive duty in s 3, the judicial preoccupation with proportionality's relationship to traditional

---

[215] *Ibid.* 180. See also Allan's argument that in 'substance ... the Human Rights Act, and therewith the Convention rights, has been entrenched by a rule of interpetation', *Constitutional Justice*, n. 40 above, pp. 225ff, especially at p. 228.

[216] [2004] 2 AC 557; [2004] UKHL 30 at [30], [32] (Lord Nicholls).

[217] *Ibid.* [41] (Lord Steyn).    [218] *Ibid.* [57], [77], [60].

[219] See also *R* v. *A* (*No. 2*) [2002] 1 AC 45; [2001] UKHL 25; *R (Anderson)* v. *Secretary of State for the Home Department* [2003] 1 AC 837; [2002] UKHL 46.

doctrine illustrates a variable emphasis upon change and/or continuity.[220] On the one hand, Lord Steyn in *Daly* was concerned to distinguish proportionality and the traditional grounds of review although he recognised overlap and that '[m]ost cases would be decided in the same way whichever approach is adopted'.[221] He suggested a 'material difference', that the criteria for determining proportionality are 'more precise and more sophisticated' and that the intensity of review is greater than under the traditional *Wednesbury* ground of review.[222] On the other hand, in *Alconbury*, Lord Slynn stressed continuity in ruling that judicial review of administrative planning decisions was sufficient to secure their compatibility under Art. 6 of the European Convention. He acknowledged a difference between the application of the principle of proportionality and the approach in *Wednesbury* but suggested that 'the difference in practice is not as great as is sometimes supposed', that the time had come to recognise that the principle is a part of English administrative law and that trying 'to keep the *Wednesbury* principle and proportionality in separate compartments seems to me to be unnecessary and confusing'.[223] He was concerned to emphasise that the principle 'does not go so far as to provide for a complete rehearing on the merits of the decision'.[224] Ian Leigh rightly describes the judicial attempt 'to find some common ground or reassuring continuity with the traditional grounds of review': 'The clear strategy has been to calm fears by establishing that the bête noire – merits review – is not in prospect. This tactic is exemplified by Lord Slynn's speech in *Alconbury* in which he sought to allay fears over developing the scope of judicial review by minimising the difference between proportionality and *Wednesbury*.'[225] Further, he describes proportionality's 'chameleon-like appeal', reassuring conservatives that the traditional distinction between appeal and review is retained but also moderates that a more rigorous and structured approach

---

[220] For comparable variations in emphasis and a common preoccupation with change and continuity through the introduction or recognition of privacy, see *Douglas* v. *Hello! Ltd* [2001] QB 967 at [88], [111], [166].

[221] *R (Daly)* v. *Secretary of State for the Home Department* [2001] 2 AC 533; [2001] UKHL 26 at [27].

[222] *Ibid.* [26], [27]. See also *ibid.* [23], [30], [32]; *A* v. *Secretary of State for the Home Department*, n. 110 above, at [40], [44]; Jowell, 'Beyond the rule of law', n. 110 above, 678ff.

[223] Note 198 above, at [51] See also *ibid.* [54].   [224] *Ibid.* [52].

[225] Leigh, 'Taking rights proportionately', n. 204 above, 278.

is introduced.[226] In the historical constitution, proportionality has thus proved useful – a convenient vehicle for expressing both change and continuity in one and the same breath. Its utility is likely to be severely tested in judicial determinations of the proportionality of measures in response to the threats of terrorism and the widespread public fears accompanying it.

The question of what exactly has changed or remained the same in doctrine cannot be answered, it will be argued, simply by invoking the 1998 Act or the principles of parliamentary sovereignty and the rule of law implicit in its provisions. The doctrinal implications of the Strasbourg jurisprudence that the court must take into account under s 2, what interpretations are possible under s 3, or what acts are incompatible under s 6, are sufficiently unclear or imprecise to give the court considerable latitude in interpretation. The orthodox principle of parliamentary sovereignty that the Act was drafted to maintain and the rule of law it was to enhance are themselves in issue and therefore are of uncertain weight in the interpretation of the Act's provisions. In anticipation of Parliament's likely legislative response to any declarations of incompatibility under s 4, the Act, arguably,[227] transferred significant power to the courts in the area of human rights as a matter of constitutional practice, if not legality. Furthermore, the unclear or imprecise interpretive duty in s 3 is open to interpretation suiting the advocacy of an unorthodox conception of bi-polar sovereignty:

> [T]he new arrangements serve to emphasize the dual sovereignty that previously existed. While it is true that no power is conferred on the courts to strike down legislation that cannot be reconciled with the Convention, it is inevitably left to the courts to decide when the statutory language is insufficiently adaptable. It is a reasonable assumption, in accordance with the spirit of the separation of judicial and legislative powers, that what is 'possible' as a manner of reading the statutory text will depend on what is thought *necessary* to preserve the most important requirements of liberty.[228]

---

[226] Ibid. 279. See, e.g., the appreciation of both change and continuity in Jowell, 'Beyond the rule of law', n. 110 above, 678–83.

[227] See K. Ewing, 'The Human Rights Act and parliamentary democracy' (1999) 62 *MLR* 79, especially at 92f.

[228] Allan, *Constitutional Justice*, n. 40 above, p. 226.

Trevor Allan argues that the Act thus highlights a judicial sovereignty exercised through 'an interpretive freedom enjoyed by the courts, whose legitimacy the Human Rights Act affirms'.[229]

The debate about sovereignty is also a debate about the rule of law. If, contrary to Allan's argument and in accordance with the government's intention, an orthodox, Diceyan, conception of parliamentary sovereignty is effectively retained through the statutory restriction of judicial interpretation to what is *possible*, not what is *necessary*, under s 3 and through statutory provision for declarations of incompatibility, not judicial pronouncements on validity, under s 4, whatever the substantive rule of law that is introduced or affirmed by the 1998 Act, it remains under the sway of a sovereign parliament. Through the exercise of its sovereignty, Parliament might amend legislation with prospective effect in response to a judicial interpretation under s 3, conceivably not legislate in response to a declaration of incompatibility under s 4, expressly amend the Act's provisions or even, conceivably, repeal the Act itself.

Apart from the issue of whether or how parliamentary sovereignty has changed, the Act's incorporation of Convention rights was promoted as requiring a shift from form to substance and has been commonly assumed to effect or underpin a fuller, more substantive, rule of law. In the historical constitution, however, common assumptions about change are accompanied by an appreciation of continuity, reflected in assertions that emphasise change, continuity or both change and continuity. For example, shortly after the passing of the Human Rights Act, Jeffrey Jowell anticipated the significant acceleration of a fundamental shift after its implementation. In 'the new constitutional review', he suggested courts would increasingly justify their decisions by reference to constitutional standards that lie beyond the rule of law itself, conceived as limited in character:

> Both the sovereignty of Parliament and the rule of law cover only a limited range of constitutional principles. Elastic as the rule of law is, it cannot comfortably accommodate a number of principles which are enshrined in the written constitutions of other democracies, such as freedom of expression, the right to life, dignity, or even the notion of substantive (as opposed to merely formal) equality.[230]

---

[229] *Ibid.* p. 227.  [230] 'Beyond the rule of law', n. 110 above, 673.

Although his notion of the constitution implicit in his conception of the new constitutional review is a departure, to an extent, from the idea of an evolving constitution in the common law, he nonetheless reassures us that the prohibition of merits review will continue and recognises the rule of law's elasticity. Indeed, the courts have continued[231] to invoke the rule of law and, on occasion, to suggest its substantive content. They can be expected to continue to do so more frequently and to continue varying in their interpretations, particularly now that the rule of law has been enshrined in s 1 of the Constitutional Reform Act 2005 but has been left undefined and thus[232] for the courts to interpret or develop in characteristic ways.

The Human Rights Act 1998 raises, rather than resolves, questions of continuity – both of doctrine and fundamental principle. It does not, by itself, clarify Dicey's twin pillars of the constitution or what has developed in their place. It does not establish a stable relationship between them but reinstates through statute the issue of their character and relative stability. How the various issues of change and continuity – the historical constitution's continuing preoccupation – might endure, subside or be resolved in relation to the 1998 Act is yet to be seen, as is the kind of constitutional formation that may become manifest. Through the evolving and pragmatic appreciation of what has necessarily changed but reassuringly remained the same, the historical constitution develops, and from that rough appreciation, it derives legitimacy. The historical constitution, evolving in principle and practice, is not crystallised in analytical doctrine or constitutional text.

## Formation of doctrine in the historical constitution

European influences and the peculiarities of the English common law are manifest in the Human Rights Act 1998, as they are, to a varying extent, in the judicial and jurisprudential attempts to develop or transcend Dicey by invoking substantive values and the notion of bi-polar sovereignty. They were manifest in Dicey's own doctrine of the rule of law, developed in view of nation states in their ascendancy.[233] During a

---

[231] Cf. generally, e.g, *Pierson*, n. 21 above, at 591A–F; *Alconbury*, n. 198 above, at [69]–[73]. See n. 110 above.

[232] See Lord Bingham, 'The rule of law', Sir David Williams Lecture, Faculty of Law, University of Cambridge, Cambridge, 16 November 2006, published in [2007] *CLJ* 67 at 67–9. See ch. 9 below, pp. 240f.

[233] See ch. 7 above.

formative period before Dicey's, they were evident in Coke's common law of reason with its *Rex ... sub Deo et lege* according to Bracton's proverbial dictum.[234] Even in regard to what it has come to hold most dear, at heart, the English historical constitution has been open, not adamant. Through its openness or flexibility, it can be expected to adapt and react to whatever be the present and future European developments, as it has in formative periods in the past. In adapting and reacting to its European context, the historical English constitution is, furthermore, overtly European and, as such, a readily available model with which to try to conceive an evolving European constitutionalism if a written European constitution proves politically unattainable and, arguably, even if it is attained.[235]

In adapting and reacting the historical constitution demonstrates its flexibility and, at the same time, the ready questionability of its key constituents, which are not fixed or ossified and are accordingly limited in clarity. The doctrine of the rule of law has evolved as a vehicle for normative evaluation with a traditional emphasis on concrete remedies and jurisdictional equality and a more recent invocation of substantive principle. As the debate, however, continues about its substantive scope and relationship to the sovereignty of Parliament, the rule of law itself evolves through pragmatic recognition of necessary innovation and reassuring continuity. In the historical constitution, the relationship between change and continuity cannot be balanced by invoking the rule of law as a constitutional principle with preponderant weight. That relationship is reflected in the rule of law itself. Whatever balance is achieved evolves historically and is drawn pragmatically. Although widely supposed, if not to function as a constitution, to be a central constituent, a principle at the centre of the constitution, the rule of law is itself the object of a debate raising issues of change and continuity and thus illustrating a lasting eclipse of principle by pragmatism in the English historical constitution.

What is constituted at the centre of the historical constitution is not a principle but an overarching mode of change that respects continuity, at least in form, and the reassurance it affords. That mode is not derived from normative theory but has evolved in legal and political practices of conservation and innovation by which the institutions of government are controlled and facilitated as they evolve, and stability is secured or re-established. It is evident and its compromised outcome is to be

---

[234] See ch. 6 above, pp. 141ff.    [235] See ch. 2 above, pp. 44f.

expected, if not in the initial promotion of change, then in responses and attitudes to it and in the course it then follows, whether the change be institutional – the introduction of the Supreme Court or the attempted abolition of the Lord Chancellor's office – or doctrinal. The invocation of substantive values under the rule of law, the tenability of the more contentious bi-polar sovereignty, the enactment and reception of the Human Rights Act 1998 – innovative in substance but 'reassuringly orthodox'[236] in form – all illustrate the rough workings of the English historical constitution.

[236] Allan, *Constitutional Justice*, n. 40 above, p. 228.

# 9

# Conclusions and implications

The historical constitution's modes of formation are variously illustrated in the chapters above. The Crown evolved through institutional change and formal conservation. It accommodated the development of representative institutions through formal continuity, which obscured the scope of the change, was reassuring in appearance and involved the partial and apparent retention of the old while the new was established, tested and refined or further developed in practice. The separation of powers in general and its English variant in particular – the independence of the judicial power – evolved in case law and legislation as an uneven customary practice. Limited in clarity, often developing imperceptibly, observed in varying degrees of consistency, it allowed considerable flexibility in the evolving relationship between the institutions of government. Through the judicial practice of the traditional economy of the common law, the Diceyan doctrine of parliamentary sovereignty was adapted to accommodate the European Court of Justice's claim to the supremacy of Community law. Economical adaptation limited controversy by minimising change, maximising the appearance of continuity and avoiding the contentious abstraction of legal and political principle. Finally, the rule of law – its substantive scope and relationship to parliamentary sovereignty – continues to be the subject of doctrinal debate that illustrates formation or reformation in the historical constitution through its recurring preoccupation – the issue of necessary change and reassuring continuity, yet to subside or clearly be resolved in evolving practice and according to the varying appeal of change and/or continuity.

The principal doubts or objections of the sceptical reader might be twofold. First, from an analytical or normative perspective, the sceptical reader might doubt the rough workings of the historical constitution in comparison with the supposed systematic precision expected from the articulation and enactment of constitutional values and amendment provisions in a written or codified constitution. Secondly, in view of the possible introduction of a written constitution in future and the substantive constitutional significance of statutes such as the European Communities Act 1972, the Human Rights Act 1998 and the Constitutional Reform Act 2005, which have already been enacted, the sceptical reader might doubt the historical constitution's continuing relevance and perhaps suspect this book of a typical response or reaction – an elaboration upon the historical constitution now that it threatens to disappear, an appreciation of continuity at the very moment of change.

Doubts might be dispelled[1] by considering, if a written constitution were introduced, the possible implications of the historical constitutional account of the institutions and doctrines in the chapters above. The Crown – the constitution's institutional centrepiece – as the ambivalent outcome of institutional change and conservation, described in Chapter Three, would be in obvious need of reform or clarification. Its incoherence as a corporation arguably both sole and aggregate,[2] reflecting the historical compromise of a monarchy that has embraced the institutions of a democracy, is the object of continuing criticism that might readily be addressed were it not for a practical political difficulty and the related problem of an alternative. The difficulty would be to confront or circumvent the highly contentious popular issue of retaining the monarchy, the residual formal relevance of which the Crown represents. The extent of that difficulty would be affected, *inter alia*, by the enduring appeal of formal continuity through the Crown and the relative appeal of the alternative to be recognised in law, whether it be the Continental European notion of the state,[3] a concept of government[4] to be developed by the English courts or a statutory tabulation of central authorities. From a historical constitutional perspective, the immense task of introducing a written constitution would seem politically arduous and potentially unsuccessful even in relation to an institution that would be most obviously in need of reform or clarification.

The separation of powers, the subject of Chapter Four, has already recently been the object of legislative ambition and constitutional

---

[1] See also ch. 1 above, pp. 2ff; ch. 2 above, pp. 41ff.
[2] See ch. 3 above, pp. 54–8, pp. 67–8.
[3] See generally J. W. F. Allison, *A Continental Distinction in the Common Law: A Historical and Comparative Perspective on English Public Law* (Oxford: Oxford University Press, rev. pbk edn, 2000), chs. 4 and 5; J. W. F. Allison, 'Theoretical and institutional underpinnings of a separate administrative law' in M. Taggart (ed.), *The Province of Administrative Law* (Oxford: Hart Publishing, 1997), pp. 71–89.
[4] See generally ch. 3 above, pp. 58–64.

enactment.[5] 'The substantial package of ... reform measures' of 12 June 2003, to abolish the Lord Chancellor's Office and to create the Supreme Court, *inter alia*, was announced in the context of a cabinet reshuffle[6] and promoted in the name of constitutional modernisation with particular reference to judicial independence and the separation of powers. In response to the reaction it provoked, it has culminated in the Constitutional Reform Act 2005, much of which is traditional. The 2005 Act contains[7] a confirmation of principle – a 'guarantee of continued judicial independence' – the traditional preoccupation of the English doctrine of the separation of powers, which the courts are left free to interpret in characteristic ways and which is clarified only in respect of what is obvious, that the 'Lord Chancellor and other Ministers of the Crown must not seek to influence particular judicial decisions through any special access to the judiciary'.[8] The Lord Chancellor's office has been retained but substantially reduced in significance. Attendant and other typical compromises of a strict separation of powers have persisted.[9] The reform measures of 12 June 2003 have resulted in significant change but also substantial continuity via a 'legislative sequence ... broadly characteristic of a process of evolutionary gradualism'[10] and thus of the historical constitution. Those who contemplate the far greater task of introducing a written constitution have reason to remember that sequence. If the task were undertaken in haste to meet short-term political objectives, it could be expected to provoke a reaction that would raise the political cost, risk constitutional crisis and, in any event, probably result in failure – a text lacking in legitimacy if not abandonment of the task – or substantial compromise and continuity after protracted political and legal wrangling. The reliable alternative would be long deliberation and painstaking attention both to securing broad consensus through widespread consultation and participation and to relating the detail of the written text to the changing rules, principles and practices of the historical constitution. Whatever the degree of deliberation, the historical constitution's modes of formation would remain relevant to the relationship between the text and the rules, principles and practices it would embrace. They would also

---

[5] See pp. 94ff.

[6] 'Modernising government – Lord Falconer appointed Secretary of State for Constitutional Affairs', Downing Street press release, 12 June 2003.

[7] Section 3.    [8] Subsection 3(5).    [9] See ch. 4 above, pp. 98f.

[10] Lord Windlesham, 'The Constitutional Reform Act 2005: the politics of constitutional reform' [2006] *PL* 35 at 57.

remain relevant both to its later interpretation and amendment in changing circumstances and to the institutions and practices that would be expected to evolve beyond the ambit of its provisions.

If a written constitution were introduced, courts could be expected[11] to interpret its provisions in politically controversial cases with their traditional economy elaborated upon in Chapter Five. That economy was exercised in the accommodation of the European Court of Justice's claim to the supremacy of Community law through judicial interpretation of the European Communities Act 1972.[12] The reasons for its exercise are not specific to the interpretation of the 1972 Act and the problem of the relationship between Community law and the statutes of the Westminster Parliament. As the outcome of judicial pragmatism, a reluctance to risk political controversy, understandings of the rough English separation of powers and the sparing deployment or engagement of judicial resources, the various forms of economy in the common law would be a continuing source of the historical constitution's resilience – with or without a written constitution.

The rule of law, discussed in Chapters Six to Eight, has already been subject, directly and indirectly, to major constitutional enactment – the Constitutional Reform Act 2005 on the one hand and the Human Rights Act 1998 on the other. The 2005 Act contains, apart from a guarantee of continued judicial independence, an articulation[13] of another fundamental principle – that the 'Act does not adversely affect the existing constitutional principle of the rule of law' – which is reflected in the Lord Chancellor's oath amended by the Act to include a promise to 'respect the rule of law' (and 'defend the independence of the judiciary').[14] The 2005 Act does not define or clarify the rule of law, which is therefore for the courts to interpret[15] in characteristic ways. The doctrinal debate[16] about the rule of law's substantive scope and

---

[11] Cf. generally Bickel's description of what he presents as the 'passive virtues' practised by the United States Supreme Court, A. M. Bickel, *The Least Dangerous Branch: The Supreme Court at the Bar of Politics* (New Haven: Yale University Press, 2nd edn, 1986), ch. 4, and Cass Sunstein's emphasis upon the embodiment and promotion of 'incompletely theorized agreements' in a democratic constitution, C. R. Sunstein, *Designing Democracy: What Constitutions Do* (New York: Oxford University Press, 2001), especially at pp. 242–3.

[12] See ch. 5 above, pp. 123ff.   [13] Section 1.   [14] Section 17.

[15] See Lord Bingham, 'The rule of law', Sir David Williams Lecture, Faculty of Law, University of Cambridge, Cambridge, 16 November 2006, published in [2007] *CLJ* 66 at 67–9.

[16] See ch. 8 above, especially at pp. 190ff, pp. 216ff, pp. 228ff.

relationship to parliamentary sovereignty will continue, as will the historical constitutional preoccupation with the attendant issue of change and continuity yet to subside or be resolved in evolving practice. Similarly ill-defined or unclear principles are to be anticipated in a written constitution, particularly if its purpose were to facilitate our 'being sure about and secure in the values that matter: freedom, democracy and fairness'.[17] The more the suggested constitutional principles would be narrowly defined or carefully clarified, the more they would be contentious, difficult to agree upon and likely to date. If unclear and ill-defined, they would be substantiated by courts and thus developed in the ways characteristic of the historical constitution.

The Human Rights Act 1998, by incorporating Convention rights, which have long been the subject of judicial interpretation by the European Court of Human Rights, and by requiring domestic courts to take the European Court's jurisprudence into account, is clearer than the Constitutional Reform Act 2005 in its enactment of principle. The 1998 Act was skilfully drafted to embrace change and respect continuity, to effect an incorporation of the European Convention on Human Rights but through judicial interpretation and according to the sovereignty of Parliament as traditionally understood.[18] However 'ingenuously [it] respects both the Convention and the sovereignty of Parliament',[19] however 'subtle [the] compromise between parliamentary sovereignty and fundamental rights'[20] under ss 3 and 4, it leaves for the courts the difficult problems[21] of determining the scope of interpretations 'possible' and the meanings of 'compatible' and 'incompatible'. The courts are thereby to decide between reliance on interpretation under s 3 or recourse to a declaration of incompatibility

---

[17] Chancellor Gordon Brown, speech to the Labour Party Conference, Manchester, 25 September 2006. For the full quotation, see ch. 2 above, p. 3, n. 11.

[18] See ch. 8 above, pp. 224f.

[19] Sir Stephen Sedley, Foreword in S. Grosz, J. Beatson and P. Duffy, *Human Rights: The 1998 Act and the European Convention* (London: Sweet & Maxwell, 2000), p. vii.

[20] S. Kentridge, 'The incorporation of the European Convention on Human Rights', Inaugural Conference of the Cambridge Centre for Public Law, Faculty of Law, University of Cambridge, Cambridge, 17–18 January 1998, University of Cambridge Centre for Public Law, *Constitutional Reform in the United Kingdom: Practice and Principles* (Oxford: Hart Publishing, 1998), pp. 69–71, especially at p. 69.

[21] See generally, e.g., F. Bennion, 'What interpretation is "possible" under section 3(1) of the Human Rights Act 1998?' [2000] *PL* 77; G. Marshall, 'Interpreting interpretation in the Human Rights Bill' [1998] *PL* 167; G. Marshall, 'Two kinds of compatibility: more about section 3 of the Human Rights Act 1998' [1999] *PL* 377; G. Marshall, 'The lynchpin of parliamentary intent: lost, stolen, or strained?' [2003] *PL* 236; ch. 8 above, pp. 229f.

under s 4. Through the very precision of its wording and the ingenuity of its mechanisms, a written constitution, however carefully it were drafted, could be expected comparably to introduce further complexities in the interpretation of constitutional principle and thus additional interpretive challenges to those that are already familiar in the English historical constitution.

Whether or not the political will to undertake and complete the arduous task of introducing a written constitution will emerge, the historical constitutional approach, by which the historical constitution is conceived beyond the necessarily limited legal provisions of any written constitutional text, will remain relevant despite inconsistencies or shortcomings from an analytical or normative legal perspective. Its continuing relevance lies in three of its main features elaborated upon in Chapter Two – its appreciation of both change and continuity, its accommodation of multiple points of view and its attention to sources of constitutional fidelity.

First, by relating constitutional forms to their formation, the historical constitutional approach focuses upon both continuity and change.[22] It seeks to refuse the legacy of Dicey's relegation of the historical view in constitutional legal analysis and thus to avoid ossifying the changing rules, principles and institutions of the constitution at the relatively arbitrary and fleeting moment of analysis[23] or when they are enacted. The recent interactions between English and European constitutional legal developments are accordingly explained above in relation to earlier interactions. The outcome of these many interactions is a historical constitution that is both peculiarly English and thoroughly European,[24] and, as such, a readily available model with which to consider conceiving constitutionalism in the European Union.[25] The English historical constitution is not a 'fantasy legal constitution' despite its analytical shortcomings but, 'within the integral societies of Europe', a real constitution of formation and reformation.[26]

---

[22] See ch. 2 above, pp. 16ff.     [23] See ch. 2 above, pp. 7–11.

[24] Cf. generally the sensitivity to both domestic peculiarity and European influence in the strictly historical accounts in English private law and Canon law by David Ibbetson and Richard Helmholz: D. J. Ibbetson, *A Historical Introduction to the Law of Obligations* (Oxford: Oxford University Press, 1999); R. H. Helmholz, *The ius commune in England, Four Studies* (Oxford: Oxford University Press, 2001).

[25] See ch. 2 above, pp. 44f.

[26] P. Allott, 'The theory of the British constitution' in H. Gross and R. Harrison (eds.), *Jurisprudence, Cambridge Essays* (Oxford: Oxford University Press, 1992), pp. 173–205, especially at p. 205.

Secondly, from a historical constitutional perspective open to multiple[27] points of view, internal and external, complementary and competing, the historical constitution is not insular, chauvinistic or dogmatic, but open to influence and receptive of difference. Despite past suggestions and appearances to the contrary,[28] the many past and present interactions between English and European constitutional developments illustrate its openness. The historical constitution accommodates difference in approach and outlook. It is available to the exponent of analytical legal doctrine and deserves consideration as a means with which to relate constitutional forms to their formation – whether by legislation, judicial interpretation or written constitutional enactment – and thus to explain their sources of appeal and fidelity and how they are 'legitimated by history'.[29] Its history is readily viewed or interpreted from an expressly normative, pragmatic or political perspective. The historical constitution is therefore also equally available to the liberal normativist, the legal or political pragmatist or the advocate of the management of conflict principally through politics and improved mechanisms of political accountability.[30] In the same way as the historical constitution's history can be expressly reorientated to its European context, as it is in the chapters above, its history can be variously reorientated to the extent it is versatile and the express reorientation is plausible. As the outcome of multiple expressed points of view, the historical constitution is not the preserve of lawyers but of the political community at large, in all its complexity.

Thirdly, the historical constitutional approach illuminates sources of constitutional fidelity or appeal,[31] most clearly exemplified in Dicey's *Law of the Constitution* despite the analytical pretensions of his exposition and relegation of the historical view.[32] Fidelity to the historical constitution is a particular fidelity to the legal values and/or politics that

---

[27] See ch. 2 above, pp. 27ff, pp. 39ff.

[28] See, e.g., Blackstone's references to Bracton's '*rex ... sub ... lege*' maxim, W. Blackstone, *Commentaries on the Laws of England*, 4 vols. (Chicago: The University of Chicago Press, Facsimile of 1st edn of 1765–1769, 1979), Vol. I, p. 232. See generally ch. 6 above, pp. 141–3.

[29] H. W. R. Wade, 'The Crown, ministers and officials: legal status and liability' in M. Sunkin and S. Payne (eds.), *The Nature of the Crown: A Legal and Political Analysis* (Oxford: Oxford University Press, 1999), pp. 23–32, especially at p. 32. See ch. 3 above, pp. 71f; ch. 2 above, pp. 8ff.

[30] See ch. 2 above, pp. 29ff, 33ff.   [31] See ch. 2 above, pp. 19–26.

[32] A. V. Dicey, *An Introduction to the Study of the Law of the Constitution* (London: Macmillan, 10th edn, 1959). See ch. 7 above, especially at pp. 165ff.

it readily accommodates although expressed from multiple points of view. It is also a general or shared fidelity to the true achievements of our historical constitution's history, to debate about what they really are and to the unified pursuit of their determination. From these sources, the historical constitution derives its liberality of aspiration and unity of purpose, which that 'recluse inhabitant of a Palace', referred to by J. L. De Lolme,[33] would still have reason to admire.

---

[33] *The Constitution of England* or *An Account of the English Government; in which it is Compared with the Republican Form of Government, and Occasionally with the Other Monarchies in Europe* (Dublin: W. Wilson, 1775), p. 2. See the Preface above, pp. xi–xii.

# BIBLIOGRAPHY

Acherley, R., *The Britannic Constitution* or *The Fundamental Form of Government in Britain* (London: A. Bettesworth *et al.*, 1727)

Allan, T. R. S., 'Parliamentary sovereignty: Lord Denning's dexterous revolution' (1983) 3 *OJLS* 22

'Legislative supremacy and the rule of law: democracy and constitutionalism' [1985] *CLJ* 111

*Law, Liberty, and Justice: The Legal Foundations of British Constitutionalism* (Oxford: Oxford University Press, 1993)

'Parliament, ministers, courts and prerogative: criminal injuries compensation and the dormant statute' [1995] *CLJ* 481

'Parliamentary sovereignty: law, politics, and revolution' (1997) 113 *LQR* 443

'The rule of law as the rule of reason: consent and constitutionalism' (1999) 115 *LQR* 221

*Constitutional Justice: A Liberal Theory of the Rule of Law* (Oxford: Oxford University Press, 2001)

'The constitutional foundations of judicial review: conceptual conundrum or interpretive enquiry?' [2002] *CLJ* 87

Review of *Our Republican Constitution* by A. Tomkins [2006] *PL* 172

'Human rights and judicial review: a critique of "due deference"' [2006] *CLJ* 671

Allison, J. W. F., 'Fuller's analysis of polycentric disputes and the limits of adjudication' [1994] *CLJ* 367

'The procedural reason for judicial restraint' [1994] *PL* 452

'Cultural divergence, the separation of powers and the public-private divide' (1997) 9 *European Review of Public Law* 305

'Theoretical and institutional underpinnings of a separate administrative law' in M. Taggart (ed.), *The Province of Administrative Law* (Oxford: Hart Publishing, 1997), pp. 71–89

'Legal culture in Fuller's analysis of adjudication' in W. J. Witteveen and W. van der Burg (eds.), *Rediscovering Fuller: Essays on Implicit Law and Institutional Design* (Amsterdam: Amsterdam University Press, 1999), pp. 346–63

*A Continental Distinction in the Common Law: A Historical and Comparative Perspective on English Public Law* (Oxford: Oxford University Press, rev. pbk edn, 2000)

Review of *The Idea of Public Law* by M. Loughlin (2005) 68 *MLR* 344

Allott, P., 'The theory of the British constitution' in H. Gross and R. Harrison (eds.), *Jurisprudence: Cambridge Essays* (Oxford: Oxford University Press, 1992), pp. 173–205

*The Health of Nations: Society and Law beyond the State* (Cambridge: Cambridge University Press, 2002)

Andenas, M. and Fairgrieve, D., 'Reforming Crown immunity – a comparative law perspective' [2003] *PL* 730

Anon., *British Liberties* or *The Free-born Subject's Inheritance; Containing the Laws that Form the Basis of those Liberties; with Observations thereon* (London: Edward and Charles Dilly, 1766)

Arden, Dame Mary, 'Human rights in the age of terrorism' (2005) 121 *LQR* 604

Arendt, H., *On Revolution* (London: Faber & Faber, 1963)

Arndt, H. W., 'The origins of Dicey's concept of the "rule of law"' (1957) 31 *Australian Law Journal* 117

Austin, J., *Lectures on Jurisprudence* or *The Philosophy of Positive Law* (London: J. Murray, 5th edn, 1885)

Azo, P., Summa super Codicem. Instituta Extraordinaria (Augustae Taurinorum: ex Officina Erasmiana, Facsimile of Pavia edn of 1506, 1966)

Bagehot, W., *The English Constitution*, M. Taylor (ed.) (Oxford: Oxford University Press, 2001)

Baker, J. H., 'The conciliar courts' in 'Introduction', *The Reports of Sir John Spelman, Vol. II*, J. H. Baker (ed.) (London: Selden Society, Vol. 94, 1978), pp. 70–4

'Why the history of English law has not been finished', Inaugural Lecture, 14 October 1998 [2000] *CLJ* 62

*An Introduction to English Legal History* (London: Butterworths LexisNexis, 4th edn, 2002)

*The Oxford History of the Laws of England, Volume VI, 1483–1558* (Oxford: Oxford University Press, 2003)

Bamforth, N., 'Parliamentary sovereignty and the Human Rights Act 1998' [1998] *PL* 572

Bamforth, N. and Leyland, P. (eds.), *Public Law in a Multi-Layered Constitution* (Oxford: Hart Publishing, 2003)

Bamforth, N. and Leyland, P., 'Public law in a multi-layered constitution' in N. Bamforth and P. Leyland (eds.), *Public Law in a Multi-Layered Constitution* (Oxford: Hart Publishing, 2003), pp. 1–25

Barber, N. W., 'The *Rechsstaat* and the rule of law' (2003) 53 *University of Toronto Law Journal* 443

'Legal pluralism and the European Union' (2006) 12 *European Law Journal* 306

Barendt, E., 'Constitutional law and the criminal injuries compensation scheme' [1995] *PL* 357

'Separation of powers and constitutional government' [1995] *PL* 599

*An Introduction to Constitutional Law* (Oxford: Oxford University Press, 1998)

Barnes, Sir Thomas, 'The Crown Proceedings Act 1947' (1948) 26 *Canadian Bar Review* 387

Barnes, T. G. 'Star Chamber mythology' (1961) 5 *American Journal of Comparative Law* 1

'Star Chamber litigants and their counsel 1596–1641' in J. H. Baker (ed.), *Legal Records and the Historian* (London: Royal Historical Society, 1978), pp. 7–28

Barrell, J., *Imagining the King's Death: Figurative Treason, Fantasies of Regicide, 1793–1796* (Oxford: Oxford University Press, 2000)

Bell, H. E., *An Introduction to the History and Records of the Court of Wards and Liveries* (Cambridge: Cambridge University Press, 1953)

Bennion, F., 'What interpretation is "possible" under section 3(1) of the Human Rights Act 1998?' [2000] *PL* 77

Bentham, J., *Works*, J. Bowring (ed.), 11 vols. (London: Simpkin, Marshall, & Co., 1843)

Bickel, A. M., *The Least Dangerous Branch: The Supreme Court at the Bar of Politics* (New Haven: Yale University Press, 2nd edn, 1986)

Bingham, Lord, 'Dicey revisited' [2002] *PL* 39

'The old order changeth' (2006) 122 *LQR* 211

'The rule of law' [2007] *CLJ* 67

Blackburn, R. W., 'Dicey and the teaching of public law' [1985] *PL* 679

Blackstone, W., *Commentaries on the Laws of England*, 4 vols. (Chicago: The University of Chicago Press, Facsimile of 1st edn of 1765–1769, 1979)

Bogdanor, V. (ed.), *The British Constitution in the Twentieth Century* (Oxford: Oxford University Press, 2003)

Bogdanor, V., 'Our new constitution' (2004) 120 *LQR* 242

Bowyer, G., *Commentaries on the Constitutional Law of England* (London: Owen Richards, 2nd edn, 1846)

Boyer, A. D., 'Sir Edward Coke, Ciceronianus: classical rhetoric and the common law tradition' (1997) 10 *International Journal for the Semiotics of Law* 3

*Sir Edward Coke and the Elizabethan Age* (Stanford: Stanford University Press, 2003)

Boyron, S., 'Proportionality in English administrative law: a faulty translation?' (1992) 12 *OJLS* 236

Bracton, *Select Passages from the Works of Bracton and Azo*, F. W. Maitland (ed.) (London: Selden Society, Vol. 8, 1895)

*De Legibus et Consuetudinibus Angliae*, G. E. Woodbine (ed.) (New Haven: Yale University Press, 1915–1942)

*Bracton on the Laws and Customs of England*, S. E. Thorne (ed. and tr.), 2 vols (Cambridge, Mass: Belknapp Press and Seldon Society, 1968)

Bradley, A. W., 'Constitutional change and the Lord Chancellor' [1988] *PL* 165

Bradley, A. W. and Ewing, K. D., *Constitutional and Administrative Law* (Harlow, England: Pearson Education, 14th edn, 2007)

Brazier, R., 'A British republic' [2002] *CLJ* 351

    'The Monarchy' in V. Bogdanor (ed.), *The British Constitution in the Twentieth Century* (Oxford: Oxford University Press, 2003), pp. 69–95

Brougham, Lord, *Political Philosophy* (London: Society for the Diffusion of Useful Knowledge, 1842)

Brown, L. N. and Bell, J. S., *French Administrative Law* (Oxford: Oxford University Press, 4th edn, 1993)

Browne-Wilkinson, Sir Nicolas, 'The independence of the judiciary in the 1980s' [1988] *PL* 44

Burke, E., *Reflections on the Revolution in France and on the Proceedings in Certain Societies in London Relative to that Event*, C. C. O'Brien (ed.) (London: Penguin, 1968)

Butterfield, H., *The Whig Interpretation of History* (London: W. W. Norton, 1965)

    *The Englishman and His History* (Cambridge: Cambridge University Press, 1944)

    *Man on His Past: The Study of the History of Historical Scholarship* (Cambridge: Cambridge University Press, 1955)

Caesar, J., *The Ancient State Authoritie, and Proceedings of the Court of Requests*, L. M. Hill (ed.) (Cambridge: Cambridge University Press, 1975)

Cappelletti, M., 'The significance of judicial review of legislation in the contemporary world' in E. von Caemmerer, S. Mentschikoff and K. Zweigert (eds.), *Ius Privatum Gentium: Festschrift für Max Rheinstein*, 2 vols. (Tübingen: J. C. B. Mohr, 1969), Vol. I, pp. 147–64

    *Judicial Review in the Contemporary World* (New York: The Bobbs-Merrill Company Inc., 1971)

    *The Judicial Process in Comparative Perspective* (Oxford: Oxford University Press, 1989)

Chrimes, S. B., 'Introductory essay' in W. S. Holdsworth, *A History of English Law*, Vol. I, A. L. Goodhart and H. G. Hanbury (eds.) (London: Methuen, 7th edn, 1956), pp. 1–77

Cicero, *De Re Publica, De Legibus* (Cambridge, Mass.: Harvard University Press, 1928)

Coke, Sir Edward, *The First Part of the Institutes of the Laws of England* or *A Commentary upon Littleton*, 2 vols. (London: J. & W. T. Clarke, R. Pheney and S. Brooke, 18th edn, 1823)

    *The Second Part of the Institutes of the Laws of England: Containing the Exposition of Many Ancient and Other Statutes*, 2 vols. (London: E. and R. Brooke, 7th edn, 1797)

*The Fourth Part of the Institutes of the Laws of England Concerning the Jurisdiction of the Courts* (London: W. Clarke and Sons, 17th edn, 1817)

Clayton, R., 'Judicial deference and "democratic dialogue": the legitimacy of judicial intervention under the Human Rights Act 1998' [2004] *PL* 33

Coing, H., 'European common law: historical foundations' in M. Cappelletti (ed.), *New Perspectives for a Common Law of Europe* (Leyden: Sijthoff, 1978), pp. 31–44

Coleman, J. (ed.), *Hart's Postscript: Essays on the Postscript to the Concept of Law* (Oxford: Oxford University Press, 2001)

Cooke, R., 'A constitutional retreat' (2006) 122 *LQR* 224

Cooper, J. and Marshall-Williams, A., *Legislating for Human Rights: The Parliamentary Debates on the Human Rights* Bill (Oxford: Hart Publishing, 2000)

Cornford, T., 'Legal remedies against the Crown and its officers before and after *M*' in M. Sunkin and S. Payne (eds.), *The Nature of the Crown: A Legal and Political Analysis* (Oxford: Oxford University Press, 1999), pp. 233–65

Corwin, E. S., 'The "higher law" background of American constitutional law' (1928) 42 *Harvard Law Review* 149, 365

Cosgrove, R. A., *The Rule of Law: Albert Venn Dicey, Victorian Jurist* (London: Macmillan, 1980)

Cotterrell, R., 'Judicial review and legal theory' in G. Richardson and H. Genn (eds.), *Administrative Law and Government Action: The Courts and Alternative Mechanisms of Review* (Oxford: Oxford University Press, 1994), pp. 13–34

'The rule of law in transition: revisiting Franz Neumann's sociology of legality' (1996) 5 *Social & Legal Studies* 451

'The concept of legal culture' in D. Nelken (ed.), *Comparing Legal Cultures* (Aldershot: Dartmouth, 1997), pp. 13–31

*The Politics of Jurisprudence: A Critical Introduction to Legal Philosophy* (London: LexisNexis, 2nd edn, 2003)

Cox, H., *The British Commonwealth* or *A Commentary on the Institutions and Principles of British Government* (London: Longman, Brown, Green, and Longmans, 1854)

*The Institutions of the English Government; Being an Account of the Constitution, Powers, and Procedure, of its Legislative, Judicial, and Administrative Departments with Copious References to Ancient and Modern Authorities* (London: H. Sweet, 1863)

Craig, P. P., 'Dicey: unitary, self-correcting democracy and public law' (1990) 106 *LQR* 105

'Sovereignty of the United Kingdom Parliament after *Factortame*' (1991) 11 *Yearbook of European Law* 221

'Formal and substantive conceptions of the rule of law: an analytical framework' [1997] *PL* 467

'Ultra vires and the foundations of judicial review' [1998] *CLJ* 63

'The European Community, the Crown and the state' in M. Sunkin and S. Payne (eds.), *The Nature of the Crown: A Legal and Political Analysis* (Oxford: Oxford University Press, 1999), pp. 315–36

'The courts, the Human Rights Act and judicial review' (2001) 117 *LQR* 589

'Competence: clarity, containment and consideration' in I. Pernice, and M. P. Maduro (eds.), *A Constitution for the European Union: First Comments on the 2003 Draft of the European Convention* (Baden-Baden: Nomos Verlagsgesellschaft, 2004), pp. 75–93

'Theory, "pure theory" and values in public law' [2005] *PL* 440

Craig, P. P. and Bamforth, N., Review article of *The Constitutional Foundations of Judicial Review* by M. Elliott, 'Constitutional analysis, constitutional principle and judicial review' [2001] *PL* 763

Cromartie, A., *Sir Matthew Hale, 1609–1676: Law, Religion and Natural Philosophy* (Cambridge: Cambridge University Press, 1995)

'The constitutionalist revolution: the transformation of political culture in early Stuart England' (1999) 163 *Past and Present* 76

*The Constitutionalist Revolution: An Essay on the History of England, 1450–1642* (Cambridge: Cambridge University Press, 2006)

Custance, G., *A Concise View of the Constitution of England* (London: the Author, 1808)

Daintith, T. and Page, A. C., *The Executive in the Constitution: Structure, Autonomy, and Internal Control* (Oxford: Oxford University Press, 1999)

Davies, Sir John, *Le Primer Report des Cases et Matters en Ley Resolues & Adiudges en les Courts del Roy en Ireland* (London: Company of Stationers, 1628)

De Lolme, J. L., *The Constitution of England* or *An Account of the English Government; in which it is Compared with the Republican Form of Government, and Occasionally with the other Monarchies in Europe* (Dublin: W. Wilson, 1775)

De Tocqueville, *Oevres Complètes*, Vol. VIII (Paris: Michel Lévy Frères, 1865)

De Voltaire, *Letters Concerning the English Nation* (London: C. Davis and A. Lyon, 1733)

Denning, A. T., *Freedom under the Law* (London: Stevens & Sons, 1949)

Department for Constitutional Affairs, *Constitutional Reform: a new way of appointing judges* (CP 10/03, July 2003)

*Constitutional Reform: A Supreme Court of the United Kingdom* (CP 11/03, July 2003)

*Constitutional Reform: reforming the office of the Lord Chancellor* (CP 13/03, September 2003)

*Judges' Council Response to the Consultation Papers on Constitutional Reform* (6 November 2003)

*The Law Lords Response to the Government's Consultation Paper: A Supreme Court for the United Kingdom* (7 November 2003)

*Constitutional Reform, The Lord Chancellor's judiciary-related functions: Proposals ('the concordat')*, January 2004

Dicey, A. V., *Lectures on the Relation between Law and Public Opinion in England during the Nineteenth Century* (London: Macmillan, 2nd edn, 1914)

'The development of administrative law in England' (1915) 31 *LQR* 148; republished in A. V. Dicey, *An Introduction to the Study of the Law of the Constitution* (London: Macmillan, 10th edn, 1959), pp. 493–9

*An Introduction to the Study of the Law of the Constitution* (London: Macmillan, 10th edn, 1959)

Donahue, C., '*Ius commune*, Canon law, and common law in England' (1992) 66 *Tulane Law Review* 1745

Drago, R., 'La Loi du 24 Mai 1872' (1972) 25 *EDCE* 13

Duff, P. W., *Personality in Roman Private Law* (Cambridge: Cambridge University Press, 1938)

Dugard, J., *Human Rights and the South African Legal Order* (Princeton: Princeton University Press, 1978)

Dworkin, R., *Taking Rights Seriously* (London: Duckworth, 1977)

'Hart's postscript and the character of political philosophy' (2004) 24 *OJLS* 1

Eadmer, *Historia Novorum in Anglia*, M. Rule (ed.) in Rolls Series (London, 1884)

Edwards, R. A., 'Judicial deference under the Human Rights Act' (2002) 65 *MLR* 859

Eekelaar, J., 'The death of parliamentary sovereignty – a comment' (1997) 113 *LQR* 185

Elliott, Marianne, *Wolfe Tone: Prophet of Irish Independence* (New Haven: Yale University Press, 1989)

Elliott, M., *The Constitutional Foundations of Judicial Review* (Oxford: Hart Publishing, 2001)

Elton, G. R., *F. W. Maitland* (London: Weidenfeld and Nicolson, 1985)

Errera, R., 'Dicey and French administrative law: a missed encounter?' [1985] *PL* 695

Ewing, K. D., 'The Human Rights Act and parliamentary democracy' (1999) 62 *MLR* 79

'The politics of the British constitution' [2000] *PL* 405

'The futility of the Human Rights Act' [2004] *PL* 829

Feldman, D., 'Content neutrality' in I. Loveland (ed.), *Importing the First Amendment: Freedom of Expression in American, English and European Law* (Oxford: Hart Publishing, 1998), pp. 139–171

'The Human Rights Act 1998 and constitutional principles' (1999) 19 *Legal Studies* 165

'None, one or several? Perspectives on the UK's constitution(s)' [2005] *CLJ* 329

Fentiman, R., 'Legal reasoning in the conflict of laws: an essay in law and practice' in W. Krawietz, N. MacCormick and G. H. von Wright (eds.), *Prescriptive Formality and Normative Rationality in Modern Legal Systems, Festschrift* for Robert S. Summers (Berlin: Duncker & Humblot, 1994), pp. 443–61

Ferris, J., *A Standard of the English Constitution, with a Retrospective View of Historical Occurrences before and after the [English] Revolution Illustrated with Critical Remarks on the Nature and Effects of Despotism, Compared with the Nature and Effects of Free Government* (London: the Author, 1805)

Finch, Sir Henry, *Law, or a Discourse thereof, in Four Books* (London: H. Twyford et al., 1678)

Fletcher, D., *Voltaire: Lettres Philosophiques* (London: Grant & Cutler, 1986)

Foley, M., *The Silence of Constitutions: Gaps, 'Abeyances' and Political Temperament in the Maintenance of Government* (London: Routledge, 1989)

Forsyth, C. F., 'The provenance and protection of legitimate expectations' [1988] *CLJ* 238

Forsyth, C. F. (ed.), *Judicial Review and the Constitution* (Oxford: Hart Publishing, 2000)

Forsyth, C. F. and Hare, I. (eds.), *The Golden Metwand and the Crooked Cord: Essays on Public Law in Honour of Sir William Wade QC* (Oxford: Oxford University Press, 1998)

Fortescue, Sir John, *De Laudibus Legum Anglie*, S. B. Chrimes (ed.) (Cambridge: Cambridge University Press, 1942)

Fraunce, A., *The Lawiers Logike, Exemplifying the Præcepts of Logike by the Practise of the Common Lawe* (London, Thomas Gubbin and T. Newman, 1588)

Freeman, E. A., *The Growth of the English Constitution from the Earliest Times* (London: Macmillan, 3rd edn, 1876)

Fuller, L. L., 'The forms and limits of adjudication' (1978) 92 *Harvard Law Review* 353

Gardiner, S. R., *History of England from the Accession of James I to the Outbreak of the Civil War, 1603–1642*, 10 vols. (London: Longmans, Green, and Co., 1883)

Garnett, G., 'The origins of the Crown' in J. Hudson (ed.), *The History of English Law: Centenary Essays on 'Pollock and Maitland'* (Oxford: Oxford University Press, 1996), pp. 171–214

Glanvill, *De Legibus et Consuetudinibus Regni Angliae*, G. E. Woodbine (ed.) (New Haven: Yale University Press, 1932)

Goldsworthy, J., *The Sovereignty of Parliament: History and Philosophy* (Oxford: Oxford University Press, 1999)

'The myth of the common law constitution' in D. Edlin (ed.), *Common Law Theory* (New York: Cambridge University Press, forthcoming in 2007)

Gough, J. W., *Fundamental Law in English Legal History* (Oxford: Oxford University Press, 1955)

Gould, M., '*M* v. *Home Office*: government and the judges' [1993] *PL* 568

Gowan, P. and Anderson, P., (eds.), *The Question of Europe* (London: Verso, 1997)

Gray, C. M., 'Bonham's Case reviewed' (1972) 116 *Proceedings of the American Philosophical Society* 35

Griffith, J. A. G., 'The political constitution' (1979) 42 *MLR* 1

   *The Politics of the Judiciary* (London: Fontana Press, 4th edn, 1991)

   'The brave new world of Sir John Laws' (2000) 63 *MLR* 159

   'The common law and the political constitution' (2001) 117 *LQR* 42

Grosz, S., Beatson, J., and Duffy, P. *Human Rights: The 1998 Act and the European Convention* (London: Sweet & Maxwell, 2000)

Guy, J. A., Introduction, *Christopher St German on Chancery and Statute* (London: Selden Society, Supplementary Series 6, 1985)

Hailsham, Lord, *The Dilemma of Democracy: Diagnosis and Prescription* (London: Collins, 1978)

Hale, Sir Matthew, *An Analysis of the Civil Part of the Law* (4th edn, 1779)

   'Reflections by the Lrd. Cheife Justice Hale on Mr. Hobbes his Dialogue of the Lawe', as published in W. S. Holdsworth, *A History of English Law*, Vol. V (London: Methuen, 1924), pp. 500–13

   *The Jurisdiction of the Lords House, or Parliament*, F. Hargrave (ed.) (London: T. Cadell and W. Davies, 1796)

Hallam, H., *View of the State of Europe during the Middle Ages*, 3 vols. (London: John Murray, 2nd edn, 1819)

Hamson, C. J., *Executive Discretion and Judicial Control: An Aspect of the French Conseil d'État* (London: Stevens & Sons, 1954)

Hanbury, H. G., *The Vinerian Chair and Legal Education* (Oxford: Basil Blackwell, 1958)

Hand, G. J., 'A. V. Dicey's unpublished materials on the comparative study of constitutions' in G. J. Hand and J. McBride (eds.), *Droit Sans Frontieres: Essays in Honour of L. Neville Brown* (Birmingham: Holdsworth Club, 1991), pp. 77–93

Harlow, C., 'Disposing of Dicey: from legal autonomy to constitutional discourse' (2000) 48 *Political Studies* 356

Harlow, C. and Rawlings, R. *Law and Administration* (London: Butterworths, 2nd edn, 1997)

Harrington, J., *Oceana*, J. Toland (ed.) (Dublin: J. Smith and W. Bruce, 1737)

Harris, J. W., 'When and why does the Grundnorm change?' [1971] *CLJ* 103

Hart, H. L. A., *The Concept of Law* (Oxford: Oxford University Press, 1961)

   *The Concept of Law* (Oxford, 2nd edn, 1994)

Hayek, F. A. *The Road to Serfdom* (London: Routledge, 1944)

*The Constitution of Liberty* (London: Routledge & Kegan Paul, 1960)

Hearn, W. E., *The Government of England: Its Structure and Its Development* (London: Longmans, Green, Reader, and Dyer, 1867)

Helmholz, R. H., 'Continental law and common law: historical strangers or companions?' [1990] *Duke Law Journal* 1207

*The* ius commune *in England, Four Studies* (Oxford: Oxford University Press, 2001)

Herman, S., '*Utilitas ecclesiae*: the canonical conception of the trust' (1996) 70 *Tulane Law Review* 2239

'Trusts sacred and profane: clerical, secular, and commercial uses of the medieval *commendatio*' (1997) 71 *Tulane Law Review* 869

'*Utilitas ecclesiae* versus *radix malorum*: the moral paradox of ecclesiastical patrimony' (1999) 73 *Tulane Law Review* 1231

Heuston, R. F. V., *Essays in Constitutional Law* (London: Stevens & Sons, 2nd edn, 1964)

Hewart, Lord, *The New Despotism* (London: Ernest Benn, 1929)

Hill, C., 'Sir Edward Coke – myth-maker' in C. Hill, *Intellectual Origins of the English Revolution* (London: Panther, 1972), pp. 225–65

Holdsworth, W. S., *Some Lessons from Our Legal History* (New York: Macmillan, 1928)

*Essays in Law and History*, A. L. Goodhart and H. G. Hanbury (eds.) (Oxford: Oxford University Press, 1946)

*A History of English Law*, Vol. I, A. L. Goodhart and H. G. Hanbury (eds.) (London: Methuen, 7th edn, 1956)

*A History of English Law*, Vol. V (London: Methuen, 1924)

*A History of English Law*, Vol. X (London: Methuen, 1938)

*A History of English Law*, Vol. XII (Boston: Little, Brown, 1938)

Holland, T. E., *The Elements of Jurisprudence* (Oxford: Oxford University Press, 13th edn, 1924)

Holmes, C., 'Statutory interpretation in the early seventeenth century: the courts, the Council, and the Commissioners of Sewers' in J. A. Guy and H. G. Beale (eds.), *Law and Social Change in British History* (London: Royal Historical Society, 1984), pp. 107–17

Hunt, M., *Using Human Rights in English Courts* (Oxford: Hart Publishing, 1997)

'Sovereignty's blight: why contemporary public law needs the concept of "due deference"' in N. Bamforth and P. Leyland (eds.), *Public Law in a Multi-Layered Constitution* (Oxford: Hart Publishing, 2003), pp. 337–70

Ibbetson, D. J., *A Historical Introduction to the Law of Obligations* (Oxford: Oxford University Press, 1999)

'What is legal history a history of?' in A. Lewis and M. Lobban (eds.), *Law and History* (Oxford: Oxford University Press, 2004), pp. 33–40

Irvine, Lord, 'The development of human rights in Britain under an incorporated Convention on Human Rights' [1998] *PL* 221; republished in Lord Irvine, *Human Rights, Constitutional Law and the Development of the English Legal System* (Oxford: Hart Publishing, 2003), pp. 17–36

'The importance of the Human Rights Act: Parliament, the courts and the executive' [2003] *PL* 308; republished in Lord Irvine, *Human Rights, Constitutional Law and the Development of the English Legal System* (Oxford: Hart Publishing, 2003), pp. 111–32

*Human Rights, Constitutional Law and the Development of the English Legal System: Selected Essays* (Oxford: Hart Publishing, 2003)

Jacob, G., *Lex Constitutionis* or *The Gentleman's Law: Being, a Compleat Treatise of all the Laws and Statutes* (London: B. Lintot, 1719)

Jaffe, L. L. and Henderson, E. G., 'Judicial review and the rule of law: historical origins' (1956) 72 *LQR* 345

Jennings, W. I., 'In praise of Dicey, 1885–1935' (1935) 13 *Public Administration* 123

*The Law and the Constitution* (London: University of London Press, 5th edn, 1959)

John of Salisbury, *The Stateman's Book of John of Salisbury: Policratus*, J. Dickinson (tr.) (New York: Alfred A. Knopf, 1927)

Johnson, N. and McAuslan, P., 'Dicey and his influence on public law' [1985] *PL* 717

Jowell, J. 'The rule of law today' in J. Jowell and D. Oliver (eds.), *The Changing Constitution* (Oxford: Oxford University Press, 5th edn, 2004), pp. 5–25

'Beyond the rule of law: towards constitutional judicial review' [2000] *PL* 671

'Judicial deference and human rights: a question of competence' in P. P. Craig and R. Rawlings (eds.), *Law and Administration in Europe: Essays in Honour of Carol Harlow* (Oxford: Oxford University Press, 2003), pp. 67–81

'Judicial deference: servility, civility or institutional capacity?' [2003] *PL* 592

'Parliamentary sovereignty under the new constitutional hypothesis' [2006] *PL* 562

Jowell, J., and Lester, A., 'Beyond *Wednesbury*: substantive principles of administrative law' [1987] *PL* 368

'Proportionality: neither novel nor dangerous' in J. Jowell and D. Oliver (eds.), *New Directions in Judicial Review* (London: Stevens & Sons, 1988), pp. 51–72

Jowell, J. and Oliver, D. *The Changing Constitution* (Oxford: Oxford University Press, 5th edn, 2004)

Kantorowicz, E. H., *The King's Two Bodies: A Study in Medieval Political Theology* (Princeton: Princeton University Press, 1957)

Kelsen, H., *Pure Theory of Law*, M. Knight (tr.) (Berkeley: University of California Press, 1967)

Kentridge, S., 'The incorporation of the European Convention on Human Rights', *Constitutional Reform in the United Kingdom: Practice and Principles* (Oxford: Hart Publishing, 1998), pp. 69–71

King, A., *Does the United Kingdom Still Have Constitution?* (London: Sweet & Maxwell, 2001)

Klug, F., 'The Human Rights Act 1998, *Pepper v. Hart* and all that' [1999] *PL* 246

Krygier, M., 'The traditionality of statutes' (1988) 1 *Ratio Juris* 20

Kunkel, W., *An Introduction to Roman Legal and Constitutional History*, J. M. Kelly (tr.) (Oxford: Oxford University Press, 2nd edn, 1973)

Laws, Sir John, 'Is the High Court the guardian of fundamental constitutional rights?' [1993] *PL* 59

  'Law and democracy' [1995] *PL* 72

  'The constitution: morals and rights' [1996] *PL* 622

  'The limitations of human rights' [1998] *PL* 254

Lawson, F. H., 'Dicey revisited' (1959) 7 *Political Studies* 109, 207

  *The Oxford Law School, 1850–1965* (Oxford: Oxford University Press, 1968)

Le Sueur, A., 'Three strikes and it's out? The UK government's strategy to oust judicial review from immigration and asylum decision-making' [2004] *PL* 225

Leigh, I., 'Taking rights proportionately: judicial review, the Human Rights Act and Strasbourg' [2002] *PL* 265

Lemmings, D., 'The independence of the judiciary in eighteenth-century England' in P. Birks (ed.), *The Life of the Law: Proceedings of the Tenth British Legal History Conference Oxford 1991* (London: Hambledon Press, 1993), pp. 125–49

Lenz, C. O., 'Gemeinsame Grundlagen und Grundwerte des Rechts der Europäischen Gemeinschaften' (1988) 21 *Zeitschrift für Rechtspolitik* 449

Lester, A., 'The utility of the Human Rights Act: a reply to Keith Ewing' [2005] *PL* 249

Levy, E., 'Natural law in Roman thought' (1949) 15 *Studia et Documenta Historiae et Iuris* 1

Lloyd, H. A., 'Constitutionalism' in J. H. Burns (ed.), *The Cambridge History of Political Thought 1450–1700* (Cambridge: Cambridge University Press, 1991), pp. 254–97

Locke, J., *Two Treatises of Government*, P. Laslett (ed.) (Cambridge: Cambridge University Press, 1988)

Loughlin, M., *Public Law and Political Theory* (Oxford: Oxford University Press, 1992)

  'The pathways of public law scholarship' in G. P. Wilson (ed.), *Frontiers of Legal Scholarship, Twenty Five Years of Warwick Law School* (Chichester: John Wiley & Sons, 1995), pp. 163–88

  'The state, the Crown and the law' in M. Sunkin and S. Payne (eds.), *The Nature of the Crown: A Legal and Political Analysis* (Oxford: Oxford University Press, 1999), pp. 33–76

'Constitutional law: the third order of the political' in N. Bamforth and P. Leyland (eds.), *Public Law in a Multi-Layered Constitution* (Oxford: Hart Publishing, 2003), pp. 27–51

*The Idea of Public Law* (Oxford: Oxford University Press, 2003)

'Theory and values in public law' [2005] *PL* 48

MacCormick, N., *H.L.A. Hart* (London: Edward Arnold, 1981)

'Beyond the sovereign state' (1993) 56 *MLR* 1

*Questioning Sovereignty: Law, State, and Nation in the European Commonwealth* (Oxford: Oxford University Press, 1999)

'The health of nations and the health of Europe' (2004–2005) 7 *Cambridge Yearbook of European Legal Studies* 1

Maclean, I., *Interpretation and Meaning in the Renaissance: The Case of Law* (Cambridge: Cambridge University Press, 1992)

Maddox, G., 'Constitution' in T. Ball, J. Farr and R. L. Hanson (eds.), *Political Innovation and Conceptual Change* (Cambridge: Cambridge University Press, 1989), pp. 50–67

Maitland, F. W., 'Why the history of English law is not written', Inaugural Lecture, 13 October 1888, published in H. A. L. Fisher (ed.), *The Collected Papers of Frederic William Maitland, Downing Professor of the Laws of England*, 3 vols. (Cambridge: Cambridge University Press, 1911), Vol. I, pp. 480–97

'Introduction' in O. Gierke, *Political Theories of the Middle Ages*, F. W. Maitland (tr.) (Cambridge: Cambridge University Press, 1900), pp. vii–xlv

'The corporation sole' (1900) 16 *LQR* 335; published in H. A. L. Fisher (ed.), *The Collected Papers of Frederic William Maitland, Downing Professor of the Laws of England*, 3 vols (Cambridge: Cambridge University Press, 1911), Vol. III, pp. 210–43

'The Crown as corporation' (1901) 17 *LQR* 131, published in H. A. L. Fisher (ed.), *The Collected Papers of Frederic William Maitland, Downing Professor of the Laws of England*, 3 vols (Cambridge: Cambridge University Press, 1911), Vol. III, pp. 244–70

Markby, W., *Elements of Law Considered with Reference to Principles of General Jurisprudence* (Oxford: Oxford University Press, 6th edn, 1905)

Marquand, D., 'Pluralism v populism' (1999) *Prospect*, June, p. 27

Marshall, G., *Constitutional Theory* (Oxford: Oxford University Press, 1971)

'Interpreting interpretation in the Human Rights Bill' [1998] *PL* 167

'Two kinds of compatibility: more about section 3 of the Human Rights Act 1998' [1999] *PL* 377

'Metric measures and martyrdom by Henry VIII clause' (2002) 118 *LQR* 493

'The constitution: its theory and interpretation' in V. Bogdanor (ed.), *The British Constitution in the Twentieth Century* (Oxford, Oxford University Press, 2003), pp. 29–68

'The lynchpin of parliamentary intention: lost, stolen, or strained?' [2003] *PL* 236

Martínez-Torrón, J., *Anglo-American Law and Canon Law: Canonical Roots of the Common Law Tradition* (Berlin: Duncker & Humblot, 1998)

McIlwain, C. H., *The High Court of Parliament and its Supremacy: An Historical Essay on the Boundaries between Legislation and Adjudication in England* (New Haven, Yale University Press, 1910)

Mitchell, J. D. B., 'What happened to the constitution on 1st January 1973?' (1980) 11 *Cambrian Law Review* 69

Montesquieu, *The Spirit of the Laws*, A. M. Cohler, B. C. Miller and H. S. Stone (ed. and tr.) (Cambridge: Cambridge University Press, 1989)

Mount, F., *The British Constitution Now* (London: Mandarin, 1993)

Munro, C. R., 'Laws and conventions distinguished' (1975) 91 *LQR* 218
  'The separation of powers: not such a myth' [1981] *PL* 19

Oliver, D., *Constitutional Reform in the UK* (Oxford: Oxford University Press, 2003)

Paine, T., *Rights of Man, Common Sense, and Other Political Writings*, M. Philp (ed.) (Oxford: Oxford University Press, 1995)

Palgrave, F. (ed.), *Parliamentary Writs*, 4 vols. (London, 1827–1834)

Pannick, D., Comment [1998] *PL* 545

Pernice, I. and Maduro, M. P. (eds.), *A Constitution for the European Union: First Comments on the 2003 Draft of the European Convention* (Baden-Baden: Nomos Verlagsgesellschaft, 2004)

Pettit, P., *Republicanism: A Theory of Freedom and Government* (Oxford: Oxford University Press, 1997)

Philipps, J. T., *The Fundamental Laws and Constitutions of Seven Potent Kingdoms and States in Europe: viz. Denmark, Sweden, Germany, Poland, England, Holland and Swisserland* (London: W. Meadows, 1752)

Phillips, O. Hood and Jackson, P., *Constitutional and Administrative Law* (London: Sweet & Maxwell, 7th edn, 1987)

Plaxton, M., 'The concept of legislation: *Jackson* v. *Her Majesty's Attorney General*' (2006) 69 *MLR* 249

Plucknett, T. F. T., *Statutes & Their Interpretation in the First Half of the Fourteenth Century* (Cambridge: Cambridge University Press, 1922)
  'Bonham's Case and judicial review' (1926) 40 *Harvard Law Review* 30

Pocock, J. G. A, *The Ancient Constitution and the Feudal Law, A Study of English Historical Thought in the Seventeenth Century: A Reissue with a Retrospect* (Cambridge: Cambridge University Press, 1987)

Pollock, F., *The Expansion of the Common Law* (London: Stevens and Sons, 1904)
  *A First Book of Jurisprudence for Students of the Common Law* (London: Macmillan, 6th edn, 1929)

Pollock, F. and Maitland, F. W., *The History of English Law before the Time of Edward I* (Cambridge: Cambridge University Press, 1895)
  *The History of English Law before the Time of Edward I* (Cambridge: Cambridge University Press, 2nd edn, 1898)

Poole, T., 'Back to the future? Unearthing the theory of common law constitutionalism' (2003) 23 *OJLS* 435

'Questioning common law constitutionalism' (2005) 25 *Legal Studies* 142

Post, G., 'A Romano-canonical maxim, "quod omnes tangit", in Bracton' (1946) 4 *Traditio* 197

*Studies in Medieval Legal Thought: Public Law and the State, 1100–1322* (Princeton: Princeton University Press, 1964)

Review of *The Problem of Sovereignty in the Later Middle Ages* by M. J. Wilks (1964) 39 *Speculum* 365

Prodi, P., *The Papal Prince, One Body and Two Souls: The Papal Monarchy in Early Modern Europe* (Cambridge: Cambridge University Press, 1987)

Rawlings, R., 'Review, revenge and retreat' (2005) 68 *MLR* 378

Raz, J., 'The rule of law and its virtue' (1977) 93 *LQR* 195

*Ethics in the Public Domain: Essays in the Morality of Law and Politics* (Oxford: Oxford University Press, rev. pbk edn, 1995)

'On the authority and interpretation of constitutions: some preliminaries' in L. Alexander (ed.), *Constitutionalism: Philosophical Foundations* (Cambridge: Cambridge University Press, 1998), pp. 152–93

Reid, Lord, 'The judge as law maker' (1972) 12 *Journal of the Society of Public Teachers of Law* 22

Richardson, H. G., 'The English coronation oath' (1941) 23 *Transactions of the Royal Historical Society* 129

Robson, W. A., *Justice and Administrative Law: A Study of the British Constitution* (London: Macmillan, 1928)

'The Report of the Committee of Ministers' Powers' (1932) 3 *Political Quarterly* 346

*Justice and Administrative Law: A Study of the British Constitution* (London, Greenwood Press, 3rd edn, 1951)

'Administrative justice and injustice: a commentary on the Franks Report' [1958] *PL* 12

Rubini, D. A., 'The precarious independence of the judiciary, 1688–1701' (1967) 83 *LQR* 343

Runciman, D. and Ryan M. (eds.), *State, Trust and Corporation* (Cambridge: Cambridge University Press, 2003)

Russell, Earl John, *An Essay on the History of the English Government and Constitution, from the Reign of Henry VII to the Present Time* (London: Longman, Hurst, Rees, Orme, and Brown, 2nd edn, 1823)

*An Essay on the History of the English Government and Constitution from the Reign of Henry VII to the Present Time* (London: Longman, Green, Longman, Roberts, & Green, new edn, 1865)

*Selections from Speeches of Earl Russell 1817 to 1841 and from Despatches 1859 to 1865*, 2 vols. (London: Longmans, Green, 1870)

Salmond, J. W., *Jurisprudence* (London: Sweet and Maxwell, 10th edn, 1947)

Scarman, Lord, *English Law – The New Dimension* (London: Stevens & Sons, 1974)

Schulz, F., 'Bracton on kingship' (1945) 60 *English Historical Review* 136

Sedley, Sir Stephen, 'The sound of silence: constitutional law without a constitution' (1994) 110 *LQR* 270

'Human rights: a twenty-first century agenda' [1995] *PL* 386

'The common law and the constitution' in Lord Nolan and Sir Stephen Sedley, *The Making and Remaking of the British Constitution* (London: Blackstone Press, 1997), pp. 15–31

'The Crown in its own courts' in C. F. Forsyth and I. Hare (eds.), *The Golden Metwand and the Crooked Cord: Essays on Public Law in Honour of Sir William Wade QC* (Oxford: Oxford University Press, 1998), pp. 253–66

'The common law and the political constitution: a reply' (2001) 117 *LQR* 68

Shackleton, R., *Montesquieu: A Critical Biography* (Oxford: Oxford University Press, 1961)

Shaw, J., 'Europe's constitutional future' [2005] *PL* 132

Shklar, J. N., 'Political theory and the rule of law' in A. C. Hutchinson and P. Monahan (eds.), *The Rule of Law: Ideal or Ideology* (Toronto: Carswell, 1987), pp. 1–16

Simpson, A. W. B., 'The common law and legal theory' in A. W. B. Simpson (ed.), *Oxford Essays in Jurisprudence (Second Series)* (Oxford: Oxford University Press, 1973), pp. 77–99

*Human Rights and the End of Empire: Britain and the Genesis of the European Convention* (Oxford: Oxford University Press, 2001)

Skinner, Q., *Visions of Politics*, 3 vols. (Cambridge: Cambridge University Press, 2002)

'Classical liberty, Renaissance translation and the English civil war' in Q. Skinner, *Visions of Politics*, 3 vols., *Volume II, Renaissance Virtues* (Cambridge: Cambridge University Press, 2002), pp. 308–43

'John Milton and the politics of slavery' in Q. Skinner, *Visions of Politics*, 3 vols., *Volume II, Renaissance Virtues* (Cambridge: Cambridge University Press, 2002), pp. 286–307

Smith, E. (ed.), *Constitutional Justice under Old Constitutions* (The Hague: Kluwer Law International, 1995)

Smith, K. J. M. and McLaren, J. P. S., 'History's living legacy: an outline of "modern" historiography of the common law' (2001) 21 *Legal Studies* 251

Smith, Sir Thomas, *De Republica Anglorum: A Discourse on the Commonwealth of England*, L. Alston (ed.) (Cambridge: Cambridge University Press, 1906)

Snowman, D., *The Hitler Émigrés: The Cultural Impact in Britain of Refugees from Nazism* (London: Chatto & Windus, 2002)

Sommerville, J. P., *Politics and Ideology in England, 1603–1640* (London: Longman, 1986)

'English and European political ideas in the early seventeenth century: revisionism and the case of absolutism' (1996) 35 *Journal of British Studies* 168

'The ancient constitution reassessed: the common law, the court and the languages of politics in early modern England' in R. M. Smuts (ed.), *The Stuart Court and Europe: Essays in Politics and Political Culture* (Cambridge: Cambridge University Press, 1996), pp. 39–64

St German, *Doctor and Student*, T. F. T. Plucknett and J. L. Barton (ed. and tr.) (London: Selden Society, Vol. 91, 1974)

Stein, P. G., 'Continental influences on English legal thought, 1600–1900' in P. G. Stein, *The Character and Influence of the Roman Civil Law: Historical Essays* (London: The Hambledon Press, 1988), pp. 209–29

Stevens, R., 'Reform in haste and repent at leisure: Iolanthe, the Lord High Executioner and *Brave New World*' (2004) 24 *Legal Studies* 1

Steyn, Lord, 'The case for a Supreme Court' (2002) 118 *LQR* 382

'Deference: a tangled story' [2005] *PL* 346

Sullivan, F. S., *Lectures on the Constitution and Laws of England, with a Commentary on Magna Charta, and Illustrations of Many of the English Statutes* (London: Edward and Charles Dilly and Joseph Johnson, 2nd edn, 1776)

Sunkin, M., 'Crown immunity from criminal liability in English law' [2003] *PL* 716

Sunkin, M. and Payne, S., 'The nature of the Crown: an overview' in M. Sunkin and S. Payne (eds.), *The Nature of the Crown: A Legal and Political Analysis* (Oxford: Oxford University Press, 1999), pp. 1–21

Sunkin, M. and Payne, S. (eds.), *The Nature of the Crown: A Legal and Political Analysis* (Oxford: Oxford University Press, 1999)

Sunstein, C. R., *Designing Democracy: What Constitutions Do* (New York: Oxford University Press, 2001)

Thorne, S. E., 'Dr Bonham's Case' (1938) 54 *LQR* 542

Tierney, B., *Church Law and Constitutional Thought in the Middle Ages* (London: Variorum, 1979)

*Religion, Law, and the Growth of Constitutional Thought, 1150–1650* (Cambridge; Cambridge University Press, 1982)

'Tuck on rights: some medieval problems' (1983) 4 *History of Political Thought* 429

Tomkins, A., *Our Republican Constitution* (Oxford: Hart Publishing, 2005)

Tuck, R., *Natural Rights Theories: Their Origin and Development* (Cambridge: Cambridge University Press, 1979)

Turpin, C., *British Government and the Constitution; Text, Cases and Materials* (London: Butterworths LexisNexis, 5th edn, 2002)

Ullman, W., *The Individual and Society in the Middle Ages* (Baltimore: The John Hopkins Press, 1966)

Unger, R. M., *Politics, A Work in Constructive Social Theory*, 3 vols., *Part I, False Necessity: Anti-Necessitarian Social Theory in the Service of Radical Democracy* (Cambridge: Cambridge University Press, 1987)

Van Caenegem, R. C., *Judges, Legislators and Professors* (Cambridge: Cambridge University Press, 1987)

   *The Birth of the English Common Law* (Cambridge: Cambridge University Press, 2nd edn, 1988)

   'The "Rechtsstaat" in historical perspective' in R. C. van Caenegem, *Legal History: A European Perspective* (London: The Hambledon Press, 1991), pp. 185–99

   *An Historical Introduction to Private Law* (Cambridge: Cambridge University Press, 1992)

   *An Historical Introduction to Western Constitutional Law* (Cambridge: Cambridge University Press, 1995)

Van Goethem, H. (ed.), *Gewoonte en Recht* (Brussel; VWK, 2002), Iuris Scripta Historica XVI

Vile, M. J. C., *Constitutionalism and the Separation of Powers* (Indianapolis: Liberty Fund, 2nd edn, 1998)

Vincenzi, C., *Crown Powers, Subjects and Citizens* (London: Pinter, 1998)

Von Gierke, O., *Das Deutsche Genossenschaftsrecht*, 3 vols. (Berlin: Weidmann, 1868–1881)

Von Mehren, A., 'The judicial conception of legislation in Tudor England' in P. Sayre (ed.), *Interpretation of Modern Legal Philosophies, Essays in Honor of Roscoe Pound* (New York: Oxford University Press, 1947), pp. 751–66

Wade, H. W. R., 'The basis of legal sovereignty' [1955] *CLJ* 172

   *Administrative Law* (Oxford: Oxford University Press, 5th edn, 1982)

   'Injunctive relief against the Crown and ministers' (1991) 107 *LQR* 4

   'The Crown – old platitudes and new heresies' (1992) 142 NLJ 1275, 1315

   'Sovereignty – revolution or evolution?' (1996) 112 *LQR* 568

   'The Crown, ministers and officials: legal status and liability' in M. Sunkin and S. Payne (eds.), *The Nature of the Crown: A Legal and Political Analysis* (Oxford: Oxford University Press, 1999), pp. 23–32

Wade, H. W. R. and Forsyth, C. F., *Administrative Law* (Oxford: Oxford University Press, 7th edn, 1994)

   *Administrative Law* (Oxford, Oxford University Press, 9th edn, 2004)

Walker, N., 'The antinomies of the Law Officers' in M. Sunkin and S. Payne (eds.), *The Nature of the Crown: A Legal and Political Analysis* (Oxford: Oxford University Press, 1999), pp. 135–69

   'The idea of constitutional pluralism' (2002) 65 *MLR* 317

   'After the constitutional moment' in I. Pernice and M. P. Maduro (eds.), *A Constitution for the European Union: First Comments on the 2003 Draft of the European Convention* (Baden-Baden: Nomos Verlagsgesselschaft, 2004), pp. 23–43

Walker, N. (ed.), *Relocating Sovereignty* (Dartmouth: Ashgate, 2006), The International Library of Essays in Law & Legal Theory, Second Series

Walters, M. D., 'Common law, reason, and sovereign will' (2003) 53 *University of Toronto Law Journal* 65

'St German on reason and parliamentary sovereignty' [2003] *CLJ* 335

Ward, I., *The English Constitution: Myths and Realities* (Oxford: Hart Publishing, 2004)

Weber, M., *Law in Economy and Society*, M. Rheinstein (ed and tr.) (Cambridge, Mass.: Harvard University Press, 1954)

Weiler, J. H. H., *The Constitution of Europe: "Do the New Clothes Have an Emperor?" and Other Essays on European Integration*' (Cambridge: Cambridge University Press, 1999)

'A constitution for Europe? Some hard choices' (2002) 40 *Journal of Common Market Studies* 563

Weill, R., 'Dicey was not Diceyan' [2003] *CLJ* 474

Western, T., *Commentaries on the Constitution and Laws of England, Incorporated with the Political Text of the Late J. L. De Lolme, LL.D. Advocate: Embracing the Alterations to the Present Time* (London: Lucas Houghton, 1838)

Wieacker, F., 'Foundations of European legal culture' (1990) 38 *American Journal of Comparative Law* 1

Windlesham, Lord, 'The Constitutional Reform Act 2005: ministers, judges and constitutional change' [2005] *PL* 806

'The Constitutional Reform Act 2005: the politics of constitutional reform' [2006] *PL* 35

Winfield, P. H., *Pollock's Principles of Contract* (London: Stevens, 13th edn, 1950)

Woodhouse, D., 'The Attorney General' (1997) 50 *Parliamentary Affairs* 97

'The office of Lord Chancellor' [1998] *PL* 617

*The Office of Lord Chancellor* (Oxford: Hart Publishing, 2001)

'The office of Lord Chancellor: time to abandon the judicial role – the rest will follow' (2002) 22 *Legal Studies* 128

Woolf, Lord, 'Droit public – English style' [1995] *PL* 57

'Judicial review: the tensions between the executive and the judiciary' (1998) 114 *LQR* 579

'The rule of law and a change in the constitution' [2004] *CLJ* 317

Woolf, H. and Jowell, J., *de Smith, Woolf & Jowell, Judicial Review of Administrative Action* (London: Sweet & Maxwell, 5th edn, 1995)

Wright, V., 'La réorganisation du Conseil d'Etat en 1872' (1972) 25 *EDCE* 21

Young, A. L., 'Hunting sovereignty: *Jackson v Her Majesty's Attorney General* [2006] *PL* 187

Zimmermann, R., *Roman Law, Contemporary Law, European Law: The Civilian Tradition Today* (Oxford: Oxford University Press, 2001)

# INDEX